CROSS-BORDER CHILD RELOCATION IN THE EU

CROSS-BORDER CHILD RELOCATION IN THE EU

The Dynamics of Europeanisation

Olga CERAN

INTERSENTIA
Cambridge – Antwerp – Chicago

Intersentia Ltd
8 Wellington Mews
Wellington Street | Cambridge
CB1 1HW | United Kingdom
Tel: +44 1223 736 170
Email: contact@larcier-intersentia.com
www.larcier-intersentia.com

Distribution for the UK and
Rest of the World (incl. Eastern Europe)
NBN International
1 Deltic Avenue, Rooksley
Milton Keynes MK13 8LD
United Kingdom
Tel: +44 1752 202 301 | Fax: +44 1752 202 331
Email: orders@nbninternational.com

Distribution for Europe
Lefebvre Sarrut Belgium NV
Hoogstraat 139/6
1000 Brussels
Belgium
Tel: +32 (0)2 548 07 13
Email: contact@larcier-intersentia.com

Distribution for the USA and Canada
Independent Publishers Group
Order Department
814 North Franklin Street
Chicago, IL 60610
USA
Tel: +1 800 888 4741 (toll free) | Fax: +1 312 337 5985
Email: orders@ipgbook.com

Cross-Border Child Relocation in the EU. The Dynamics of Europeanisation

ISBN 978-1-83970-518-2
D/2024/7849/49
NUR 820

British Library Cataloguing in Publication Data. A catalogue record for this book is available from the British Library.

ACKNOWLEDGMENTS

This book is the result of my PhD research conducted at the European University Institute in Florence. I will be forever grateful for the opportunity to be shaped – as an academic and as a person – by this truly unique and beautiful place. Several people, both within and outside the EUI, made this possible.

First and foremost, I would like to thank my supervisor, Professor Stefan Grundmann, for having believed in me and my research project. His encouraging words and scholarly input were invaluable, allowing me to gain confidence as a scholar.

I would also like to thank the members of my PhD Examining Board – Professor Katharina Boele-Woelki, Professor Martijn Hesselink, and Dr Ruth Lamont – for engaging with my work and providing valuable feedback. Their inspiring ideas have helped to shape my own and it was truly an honour to become a 'doctor' in their presence.

I would also like to acknowledge the financial support of the Polish Ministry of Science and Higher Education that allowed me to experience these exceptional years at the EUI. I extend my gratitude to all the staff of the European University Institute – the sky is truly the limit with such a generous support system.

Last – but definitely not least – I would like to thank my family and friends for their never-ending encouragement and patience during the time of writing my PhD thesis and then turning it into a book. Nothing that I have achieved would have been possible without you.

CONTENTS

LIST OF CASES

EUROPEAN COURT OF JUSTICE

EUROPEAN COURT OF HUMAN RIGHTS

NATIONAL CASE LAW

ENGLAND AND WALES

GERMANY

POLAND

LIST OF LEGISLATION AND OTHER INSTRUMENTS

CONVENTIONS

Council of Europe, European Convention for the Protection of Human Rights and Fundamental Freedoms, as amended by Protocols No. 11 and 14, 4 November 1950, ETS 5
Council of Europe, Protocol No. 4 to the Convention for the Protection of Human Rights and Fundamental Freedoms, securing certain rights and freedoms other than those already included in the Convention and in the first Protocol thereto, 16 September 1963, ETS 46
Hague Conference on Private International Law, Convention of 25 October 1980 on the Civil Aspects of International Child Abduction
Hague Conference on Private International Law, Convention of 19 October 1996 on Jurisdiction, Applicable Law, Recognition, Enforcement and Co-operation in respect of Parental Responsibility and Measures for the Protection of Children
Hague Conference on Private International Law, Protocol of 23 November 2007 on the Law Applicable to Maintenance Obligations

EU LAW

PRIMARY LAW

Charter of Fundamental Rights of the European Union, OJ C 326, 26.10.2012, pp. 391–407
Consolidated Version of the Treaty on the Functioning of the European Union, OJ C 326, 26.10.2012, pp. 47–390
Consolidated Version of the Treaty on European Union, OJ C 202, 7.6.2016, pp. 1–388

SECONDARY LAW

Council Directive 77/486/EEC of 25 July 1977 on the education of the children of migrant workers, OJ L 199, 6.8.1977, pp. 32–33
Directive 98/5/EC of the European Parliament and of the Council of 16 February 1998 to facilitate practice of the profession of lawyer on a permanent basis in a Member State other than that in which the qualification was obtained, OJ L 77, 14.3.1998, pp. 36–43

Council Regulation (EC) No 2201/2003 of 27 November 2003 concerning jurisdiction and the recognition and enforcement of judgments in matrimonial matters and the matters of parental responsibility, repealing Regulation (EC) No 1347/2000, OJ L 338, 23.12.2003, pp. 1–29
Directive 2004/38/EC of the European Parliament and of the Council of 29 April 2004 on the right of citizens of the Union and their family members to move and reside freely within the territory of the Member States amending Regulation (EEC) No 1612/68 and repealing Directives 64/221/EEC, 68/360/EEC, 72/194/EEC, 73/148/EEC, 75/34/EEC, 75/35/EEC, 90/364/EEC, 90/365/EEC and 93/96/EEC 2004, OJ L 158, 30.4.2004, pp. 77–123
Directive 2008/52/EC of the European Parliament and of the Council of 21 May 2008 on certain aspects of mediation in civil and commercial matters, OJ L 136, 24.5.2008, pp. 3–8
Council Regulation (EC) No 4/2009 of 18 December 2008 on jurisdiction, applicable law, recognition and enforcement of decisions and cooperation in matters relating to maintenance obligations, OJ L 7, 10.1.2009, pp. 1–79
Council Regulation (EU) No 1259/2010 of 20 December 2010 implementing enhanced cooperation in the area of the law applicable to divorce and legal separation, OJ L 343, 29.12.2010, pp. 10–16
Regulation (EU) No 492/2011 of the European Parliament and of the Council of 5 April 2011 on freedom of movement for workers within the Union, OJ L 141, 27.5.2011, pp. 1–12
Council Regulation (EU) 2016/1103 of 24 June 2016 implementing enhanced cooperation in the area of jurisdiction, applicable law and the recognition and enforcement of decisions in matters of matrimonial property regimes, OJ L 183, 8.7.2016, pp. 1–29
Council Regulation (EU) 2016/1104 of 24 June 2016 implementing enhanced cooperation in the area of jurisdiction, applicable law and the recognition and enforcement of decisions in matters of the property consequences of registered partnerships, OJ L 183, 8.7.2016, pp. 30–56
Council Regulation (EU) 2019/1111 of 25 June 2019 on jurisdiction, the recognition and enforcement of decisions in matrimonial matters and the matters of parental responsibility, and on international child abduction, OJ L 178, 2.7.2019, pp. 1–115

OTHER INTERNATIONAL AND EU DOCUMENTS

Communication from the Commission to the European Parliament and the Council, 'An area of freedom, security and justice serving the citizen' (COM(2009) 262 final)
Communication from the Commission to the Council, the European Parliament, the European Economic and Social Committee and the Committee of the Regions 'Justice, Freedom and Security in Europe since 2005: An Evaluation of the Hague Programme and Action Plan' (COM(2009) 263 final)
Communication from the Commission to the European Parliament, the Council, the European Economic and Social Committee and the Committee of the Regions, Commission Work Programme 2020, 'A Union That Strives for More' (COM(2020) 37 final)
Council of Europe, 'HUDOC' <https://hudoc.echr.coe.int>
Declarations Annexed to the Final Act of the Intergovernmental Conference which adopted the Treaty of Lisbon, Signed on 13 December 2007, OJ C 326, 26.10.2012, pp. 337–361

European Commission, Directorate-General for Justice and Consumers, 'Study on the assessment of Regulation (EC) No 2201/2003 and the policy options for its amendment – Final report – Analytical annexes' (2015) <https://data.europa.eu/doi/10.2838/53722>

European Parliament resolution of 25 October 2018 on promoting automatic mutual recognition of diplomas, OJ C 345, 16.10.2020, pp. 78–79

European Parliament resolution of 22 November 2023 on proposals of the European Parliament for the amendment of the Treaties (2023) (2022/2051(INL))

HCCH, 'The International Child Abduction Database (INCADAT)' <http://www.incadat.com/en>

Lagarde P., 'HCCH Explanatory Report on the 1996 HCCH Child Protection Convention' (Hague Conference on Private International Law) <https://www.hcch.net/en/publications-and-studies/details4/?pid=2943&dtid=3>

Permanent Bureau of the Hague Conference on Private International Law, 'Conclusions and Recommendations of the Fourth Meeting of the Special Commission to Review the Operation of the Hague Convention of 25 October 1980 on the Civil Aspects of International Child Abduction' (2001) <https://assets.hcch.net/upload/concl28sc4_e.pdf>

Permanent Bureau of the Hague Conference on Private International Law, 'Preliminary Note on International Family Relocation: Preliminary Document No 11 of January 2012 for the Attention of the Special Commission of January 2012 on the Practical Operation of the 1980 Hague Child Abduction Convention and the 1996 Hague Child Protection Convention' (2012) <https://assets.hcch.net/upload/wop/abduct2012pd11e.pdf>

Proposal for a Council Regulation on jurisdiction, applicable law, recognition of decisions and acceptance of authentic instruments in matters of parenthood and on the creation of a European Certificate of Parenthood (COM(2022) 695 final)

Proposal for a Regulation of the European Parliament and of the Council on jurisdiction, applicable law, recognition and enforcement of measures and cooperation in matters relating to the protection of adults (COM(2023) 280 final)

Recommendation CM/Rec(2015)4 adopted by the Committee of Ministers of the Council of Europe on 11 February 2015 at the 1219th meeting of the Ministers' Deputies (2015)

Report from the Commission to the European Parliament, the Council and the European Economic and Social Committee on the Application of Council Regulation (EC) No 2201/2003 Concerning Jurisdiction and the Recognition and Enforcement of Judgements in Matrimonial Matters and the Matters of Parental Responsibility, Repealing Regulation (EC) No 1347/2000 (COM(2014) 0225 final)

UN Committee on the Rights of the Child (CRC), 'General comment No. 12 (2009): The right of the child to be heard', 20.07.2009, CRC/C/GC/12

UN Committee on the Rights of the Child (CRC), 'General comment No. 14 (2013) on the right of the child to have his or her best interests taken as a primary consideration (art. 3, para. 1)', 29.05.2013, CRC/C/GC/14

The Washington Declaration on International Family Relocation, adopted by the Hague Conference on Private International Law & International Centre for Missing and Exploited Children (2010)

NATIONAL LAW AND OTHER DOCUMENTS

GERMANY

Bürgerliches Gesetzbuch (German Civil Code; BGB), BGBl. I S. 42, 2909; 2003 I S. 738, BGBl. I S. 3515

POLAND

Ustawa z dnia 25 lutego 1964 r. – Kodeks rodzinny i opiekuńczy (Polish Family and Guardianship Code, KRO) (Dz.U. 1964 nr 9 poz. 59, t.j. Dz. U. z 2020 r. poz. 1359)
Ustawa z dnia 17 listopada 1964 r. – Kodeks postępowania cywilnego (Polish Civil Procedure Code, KPC) (Dz.U. 1964 nr 43 poz. 296, t.j. Dz. U. z 2020 r. poz. 1575, 1578, 2320, z 2021 r. poz. 11, 1090, 1177)
Konstytucja Rzeczypospolitej Polskiej (Constitution of the Republic of Poland) z dnia 2 kwietnia 1997 r. (Dz.U. 1997 nr 78 poz. 483)
'Interpelacja Nr 6028 w Sprawie Swobodnego Przemieszczania Się Małoletnich Dzieci w Strefie Schengen' (2008) <http://orka2.sejm.gov.pl/IZ6.nsf/INTop/06028?OpenDocument>
'Interpelacja Nr 9442' (2020) <http://www.sejm.gov.pl/sejm9.nsf/interpelacja.xsp?typ=INT&nr=9442&view=null>
'Interpelacja Nr 21013 – Tekst' (2018) <http://www.sejm.gov.pl/Sejm8.nsf/InterpelacjaTresc.xsp?key=57C80A3D>

UK

Children Act 1989, UK Public General Acts 1989, c. 41
European Union (Withdrawal) Act 2018, UK Public General Acts 2018, c. 16

OTHER

Allgemeines Bürgerliches Gesetzbuch (Austrian Civil Code, ABGB), BGBl. I Nr. 175/2021
Australia Family Law Council, 'Relocation: A Report to the Attorney-General' (2006) <https://www.ag.gov.au/FamiliesAndMarriage/FamilyLawCouncil/Documents/Relocation%20report.pdf>
Vorblatt und Erläuterungen zu dem Kindschafts- und Namensrecht-Änderungsgesetz (2013) <https://www.parlament.gv.at/gegenstand/XXIV/I/2004>

CHAPTER 1
INTRODUCTION

1.1. CROSS-BORDER CHILD RELOCATION AND THE EU

This book is about laws on cross-border child relocation, understood as a long-term move to another country by a parent with his or her child.[1] It is also about the European Union (EU), EU law, and what it means 'to live with EU law'.[2] And, bringing these themes together, it is about the influence of European law – both present and prospective – on national child relocation laws. As will be discussed, it is perhaps no longer a novel claim that EU law influences national family laws. EU law does so via legislative provisions on certain aspects of cross-border private relationships and by imposing obligations, as set out by the Luxembourg judges, to adjust national laws of EU Member States to free movement requirements.[3] However, EU legal interventions rarely touch upon the core aspects of substantive family law, consistently considered to constitute a retained competence of EU Member States. While child relocation remains one of these core aspects, nowhere else do cross-border movement and substantive family law come together as clearly, prompting interest in the dynamics and effects of various EU influences in this understudied area of law.[4]

The interest in the intersections of EU law and cross-border child relocation law emerges from three main observations. First, family life – and family law – in the EU have been undergoing significant transformations. Mobility within

1 For a clarification of the concepts used, see Section 1.3.5. below.

2 Editorial Comment, 'EU Law as a Way of Life' (2017) 54 *Common Market Law Review* 357, 359.

3 e.g. K. Carr, 'Deconstructing and Reconstructing Family Law through the European Legal Order' (2014) PhD Thesis, European University Institute <http://cadmus.eui.eu/handle/1814/32811>; S. Ninatti, 'Adjusting Differences and Accommodating Competences: Family Matters in the European Union' (2001) 6 *Jean Monnet Working Papers* (06/10) <https://ideas.repec.org/p/erp/jeanmo/p0282.html>.

4 e.g. K. Boele-Woelki, B. Braat, I. Curry-Sumner, C.J. de Boer, P. Lokin, M. Vonk, N. de Vries and W. Schrama, 'Research Questions in Family Law Derived from a Comparative Synthesis of General Trends and Developments' (2008) 4 *Utrecht Law Review* 279, 281–82. See also Chapter 2.

the EU is increasing along global trends.[5] As EU citizens move, 'they do so as human beings, not as robots; [t]hey fall in love, marry and have families'.[6] These movements also characterise relationship breakdowns and affect an increasing number of children in domestic and cross-border proceedings.[7] With a shift towards joint parental responsibilities, an independent transformation observable in many jurisdictions across Europe and beyond, migrations create additional scope for disputes.[8] In that, child relocation disputes are also likely becoming more frequent, although detailed EU-wide data is lacking.[9] The trans-border and multicultural features of such transformations need to be accommodated by family law, if only as a matter of fact. At the same time, child relocation disputes touch upon the core financial, emotional and autonomy interests of relocating parents.[10] They can also have far-reaching consequences for children's contact with the non-relocating parents and the overall circumstances in which children grow up. While universally resolved in reference to the principle of the best interests of the child, the complexity and high stakes of such disputes lead to a significant differentiation in relocation doctrines and outcomes across the globe.[11] This diversity of approaches and the mobility dimension of

---

5 Eurostat: Statistics Explained, 'Migration and Migrant Population Statistics' <http://ec.europa.eu/eurostat/statistics-explained/index.php/Migration_and_migrant_population_statistics>.

6 Opinion of the Advocate General in Case C-34/09, *Gerardo Ruiz Zambrano v Office national de l'emploi (ONEm)*, ECLI:EU:C:2010:560, para. 128.

7 e.g. European Commission, Directorate-General for Justice and Consumers, 'Study on the assessment of Regulation (EC) No 2201/2003 and the policy options for its amendment – Final report – Analytical annexes' (2015) <https://data.europa.eu/doi/10.2838/53722>.

8 See e.g. P. Parkinson, 'Freedom of Movement in an Era of Shared Parenting: The Differences in Judicial Approaches to Relocation' (2008) *Federal Law Review*, Sydney Law School Research Paper No. 08/87, SSRN Scholarly Paper ID 1181442 <https://papers.ssrn.com/abstract=1181442>; C.G. Jeppesen de Boer., 'Parental Relocation: Free Movement Rights and Joint Parenting' (2008) 4 *Utrecht Law Review* 73. For a discussion in the European context see K. Boele-Woelki and D. Martiny, 'The Commission on European Family Law (CEFL) and its Principles of European Family Law Regarding Parental Responsibilities' (2007) 8 *ERA-Forum* 125, 132.

9 The difficulty of collecting data on child relocation stems from the fact that in many jurisdictions they are not treated as a separate category of parental disputes. See also C. González Beilfuss, 'Evaluation of Recommendation CM/Rec(2015)4 on Preventing and Resolving Disputes on Child Relocation' (2022) Council of Europe <https://rm.coe.int/cdcj-2021-27e/1680a72905>, para. 21.

10 J. Herring and R. Taylor, 'Relocating Relocation' (2006) 18 *Child and Family Law Quarterly* 517, 523.

11 e.g. R. George, *Relocation Disputes: Law and Practice in England and New Zealand*, Hart Publishing, Oxford 2014, pp. 10–12; A. Worwood and L. Cummin, 'International Family Law Report: Can We Go or Must We Stay? The International Child Relocation Rankings' (2016) <http://www.familylaw.co.uk/news_and_comment/new-international-child-relocation-rankings-reveal-that-belgian-courts-are-the-least-likely-to-grant-a-relocation-order#.WOs4-y-Ywj8>; Family Law Council, 'Relocation: A Report to the Attorney General' (2006) <https://www.ag.gov.au/FamiliesAndMarriage/FamilyLawCouncil/Documents/Relocation%20report.pdf>.

relocation disputes have given rise to questions about the possible interactions of child relocation laws and EU law, concerning equal access to free movement rights across the Union.[12] There is, therefore, an increasing interest, from both practitioners and scholars alike, in child relocation and the role played by EU law in such disputes.

Second, child relocation is currently characterised by the lack of specific legislation or jurisprudence on the EU level, and – as will be shown – arguably only limited guidance from the European Court of Human Rights (ECtHR) exists. No legislative proposals are in sight, despite some scholarly discussion on their prospects.[13] Simultaneously, EU Member States remain bound by the broader free movement and EU citizenship framework, seen as the main origin of indirect doctrinal pressures on the national level.[14] The Treaty on the Functioning of the European Union (TFEU) provides EU citizens, adults and children alike, with the right to freely move and reside across EU Member States.[15] The development of the jurisprudence of the Court of Justice of the European Union (CJEU) has led to the expansion of the scope of cross-border free movement and EU citizenship rights over new areas of national prerogatives. However, while these (indirect) pressures are increasingly recognised in family law scholarship, the exact scope of EU legal obligations in child relocation matters remains unclear – at least until such pronouncements from the EU legislator or judicial actors are made. And, more broadly, the various ways in which EU law interacts with family law are also far from obvious.

The interactions of EU law and family law emerge from a particular normative nexus, contributing to their complex relationship. The engagement with family matters was prompted by the 'mobility reasoning' of the EU,[16] by its 'free movement' or 'internal market' imperatives[17] that required preservation

---

12 See in particular Y.M. Bérénos, 'Time to Move On: The International State of Affairs with Respect to Child Relocation Law' (2012) 8 *Utrecht Law Review* 1; R. Lamont, 'Free Movement of Persons, Child Abduction and Relocation within the European Union' (2012) 34 *Journal of Social Welfare and Family Law* 231; T. Scott 'Leave to Remove Children from the Jurisdiction: Does English Law Comply with the Treaty of Rome?' in The Society for Advanced Legal Studies (ed), 'Report on The Cross-Border Movement of Children' (1999) <http://sas-space.sas.ac.uk/4294/1/SALS_Report_on_Cross_Border_Movement_of_Children.pdf>; and the discussion in Chapter 2.

13 Y.M. Bérénos, above n. 12.

14 K. Carr, above n. 3; S. Ninatti, above n. 3; see also E. Pataut, 'A Family Status for the European Citizen?' in L. Azoulai, S. Barbou des Places and E. Pataut (eds), *Constructing the Person in EU Law: Rights, Roles, Identities*, Hart Publishing, Oxford 2016.

15 Consolidated Version of the Treaty on the Functioning of the European Union [2012] OJ C326/47.

16 E. Pataut, above n. 14, pp. 313–15.

17 H. Stalford, 'For Better, For Worse: The Relationship between EU Citizenship and the Development of Cross-Border Family Law' in M. Dougan, N.N. Shuibhne and E. Spaventa (eds), *Empowerment and Disempowerment of the European Citizen*, Hart Publishing, Oxford 2012, pp. 225–26; see also broader discussions in K. Carr, above n. 3.

of certain family law entitlements across the Union. The introduction of EU citizenship brought an expansion of this mobility reasoning that was particularly visible in cases concerning family relationships.[18] This revealed a close connection – certainly closer than initially anticipated – between EU family justice, the commitment of the EU to children's rights,[19] and other EU law provisions on freedom of movement or EU citizenship.[20] At the same time, the EU intervention in family matters was itself said to be 'a product of progressive "normalization" of cross-national migration among young adults in particular'.[21] Even if only a relatively small number of EU citizens actually makes use of their free movement rights, such assessment of social reality is often given as 'requir[ing] in some cases a reconsideration of the assumptions underlying legal systems and the substance of their rules, and necessitate[ing] an adaptation of the law'.[22] With the EU family law competence being limited, the CJEU has become the 'real engine' of the process,[23] exerting subtle indirect pressures on national family laws.[24]

The third observation is both substantive and methodological in nature. The EU legal pressures have been recognised to go beyond their functional origin and produce effects beyond the formal distribution of rights.[25] As EU law creates statuses that enable the exercise of individual rights, it also conveys ideas of who EU citizens are, how they live their lives, and what expectations they hold.[26] The EU citizen status has been described as an 'emancipatory force',[27]

---

18 S. Coutts, *Citizenship, Crime and Community in the European Union*, Hart Publishing, Oxford 2019, p. 32.

19 One of the general objectives of the EU is to promote protection of the rights of the child (Article 3(3) of the Treaty on European Union), further strengthened by the guarantees provided in the Charter of Fundamental Rights of the EU (Articles 7 and 24 of the CFR).

20 H. Stalford, above n. 17, p. 250.

21 ibid., p. 225.

22 Opinion of the Advocate General in Case C-335/17, *Neli Valcheva v Georgios Babanarakis*, ECLI:EU:C:2018:242, paras. 28–29.

23 S. Ninatti, above n. 3, 7.

24 e.g. E. Pataut, above n. 14, pp. 311–12; K. Carr, above n. 3.

25 L. Azoulai, S. Barbou des Places and E. Pataut, 'Being a Person in the European Union' in L. Azoulai, S. Barbou des Places and E. Pataut (eds), *Constructing the Person in EU Law: Rights, Roles, Identities*, Hart Publishing, Oxford 2016, p. 10.

26 See ibid., describing statuses as carrying 'an "underlying idea" of what it means to be a citizen, a student or a child in relation to others within society'; L. Azoulai, 'The European Individual as Part of Collective Entities (Market, Family, Society)' in L. Azoulai, S. Barbou des Places and E. Pataut (eds), *Constructing the Person in EU Law: Rights, Roles, Identities*, Hart Publishing, Oxford 2016, p. 218.

27 F. de Witte, 'Kick off contribution: Freedom of Movement Under Attack: Is It Worth Defending as the Core of EU Citizenship?' in F. de Witte, R. Bauböck and J. Shaw (eds), 'Freedom of Movement Under Attack: Is It Worth Defending as the Core of EU Citizenship?', (2016) RSC Working Paper, European University Institute, p. 1 <https://cadmus.eui.eu//handle/1814/44567>; see also Coutts' characterisation of EU citizenship as a status of autonomy: S. Coutts, above n. 18, pp. 31–43.

as a 'transnational status of autonomy'.[28] This emancipatory potential is said to lie not only in actual free movement, but also in its 'reflexive virtue', reorienting individuals towards new visions of autonomy and self-realisation that could remain 'unavailable but for [EU law]'.[29] The general framework of free movement in the EU constructs hence not only specific policies and laws, but also broader visions of social interactions that subsequently shape the allocation of rights and obligations, and do so in a relational way.[30] These reconfigurations – albeit not necessarily concerned with family law entitlements directly – put pressure on the conceptualisations of individual scopes of autonomy and familial obligations, and might have repercussions also for national laws. If this is indeed the case and their effects are to be observed in national family laws, cross-border child relocation seems to be one of the most suitable areas of law for their investigation. However, such investigations call for a new analytical approach, one going beyond doctrinal legal research.

The present book explores this – arguably multidimensional – influence of EU law on child relocation and its effects on national laws. It provides an in-depth analysis of how EU law already does or prospectively could influence national approaches to cross-border child relocation, conditioning its Europeanisation. The book opens with an investigation of the EU competence and legislative prospects of harmonisation of child relocation laws. It further analyses child relocation within the framework of supranational fundamental rights and freedoms in the EU, exploring the nature and scope of obligations that EU law can legitimately impose on national child relocation laws. While the focus remains on the EU, the European Convention on Human Rights (ECHR)[31] and the jurisprudence of the ECtHR are also discussed, given their importance for the protection of fundamental rights in the EU legal system. Further, the influence of EU law is conceptualised constructively.[32] The focus of the analysis shifts to EU law's legal constructions of desirable ways of life and contextual legal subjects that might be methodologically and normatively relevant for child relocation law. Finally, analysing case law in England and Wales, Germany, and Poland, the book qualitatively investigates how national judges encounter EU law and draw from its legal and contextual features, assessing the dynamics of Europeanisation of national child relocation law. This book demonstrates how EU law and its normatively inflicted methodology

---

28 S. Coutts, above n. 18, p. 29.

29 F. de Witte, above n. 27, pp. 1–2.

30 F. de Witte, 'EU Citizenship, Free Movement, and Emancipation: A Rejoinder' in F. de Witte, R. Bauböck and J. Shaw (eds), above n. 27, p. 43.

31 European Convention for the Protection of Human Rights and Fundamental Freedoms (Rome, 4 November 1950), 312 ETS 5.

32 See Section 1.3.1. below.

(can) influence national approaches to child relocation law, but – as of now – do not (yet) seem to fundamentally challenge the established conceptualisations and consistently reorient them towards the EU.

1.2. CORE ISSUES AND RESEARCH OBJECTIVES

The main objective of this book is analysis of EU law's influence on national child relocation law and its consequences at national level. In order to determine how EU law influences national child relocation law, it is first necessary to analyse the EU constitutional legal framework in reference to questions raised by child relocation.[33] The few existing contributions discuss the topic either in the context of potential harmonisation[34] or the influence that EU freedom of movement provisions and the judicial activity of the CJEU might have on national family laws.[35] Some authors assume that the EU possesses competence in cross-border child relocation matters,[36] but others reject such a possibility.[37] The exact scope of EU competence remains, therefore, unclear. From this perspective, the first key issue addressed in this book concerns the EU competence in child relocation. Answers to the competence question are highly relevant in understanding the scope and nature of any EU action concerning child relocation. If the EU competence is said to exist, it provides an opening for future action and invites a discussion on its potential scope and form. The book discusses, therefore, whether the EU could adopt a legal instrument on child relocation. This question focuses on the interpretation of available legal bases for prospective legislation, but – given the sensitivity of harmonisation measures in family law – engages also with the political feasibility and normative desirability of any such measure. Even if the EU does not have competence in this field, child relocation might come within the scope of application of EU law due to its free movement dimension. In such a case, the lack of competence must have consequences for any analysis of the scope of obligations imposed by EU law in child relocation matters.[38] In that, the determination of the competence issue is crucial for any subsequent analysis of the scope of obligations imposed by EU law on Member States in child relocation matters.

---

33 K. Boele-Woelki, B. Braat, I. Curry-Sumner, C.J. de Boer, P. Lokin, M. Vonk, N. de Vries and W. Schrama, above n. 4, 281–82.

34 Y.M. Bérénos, above n. 12.

35 R. Lamont, above n. 12; see also R. George, above n. 11, pp. 141–42.

36 Y.M. Bérénos, above n. 12.

37 Implicitly R. Lamont, above n. 12, 242; explicitly C. Cotta, 'Is an International Consensus Possible with Regard to Child Relocation?' (2011) LLM Thesis, University of Dundee (UK), p. 30.

38 L. Boucon, 'EU Law and Retained Powers of Member States' in L. Azoulai (ed), *The Question of Competence in the European Union*, Oxford University Press, Oxford 2014, p. 171.

The analysis of the scope and nature of such obligations is the second major objective of this book. The literature recognises that restrictions of child relocation might potentially be perceived as a restriction of EU law, requiring *an* adaptation of national child relocation provisions.[39] However, the exact scope and nature of legal pressures in this regard remain underexplored. In particular, the literature does not engage with fundamental rights in detail,[40] nor scrutinises closer the justification and proportionality of such restrictions that are likely to prove crucial for the analysis.[41] The book undertakes, therefore, an in-depth analysis of both fundamental rights and fundamental freedoms in the supranational European space. While the focus of the book remains on EU law, this analysis opens with an investigation of the ECHR and the jurisprudence of the ECtHR. This is so because the European Court of Human Rights remains the major player in family law, adjudicating on matters of parental responsibilities and contact rights directly, despite the growing role of the CJEU in family law over the years. The jurisprudence of the ECtHR is also of direct relevance to EU law in light of Article 52(3) of the EU Charter of Fundamental Rights (CFR)[42] that requires the Charter to be interpreted in line with the corresponding ECHR provisions. The obligations imposed on Member States under the ECHR are therefore discussed in relation to the interpretation of fundamental rights and the CFR by the CJEU. To map out the definitive scope of EU adjustment pressures, fundamental rights and fundamental freedoms are then brought together in a holistic analysis. The analysis conceptualises child relocation under EU law and is then conducted in reference to how the CJEU could legitimately interpret EU legal provisions if a child relocation case ever came to the Court. The book discusses in detail the nature of child relocation measures as restrictions of free movement, taking account of different questions posed by different child relocation laws across Europe.

The third major objective of the book is the determination of the nature and scope of what is labelled a contextual influence of EU law. This discussion is driven by the methodological observation introduced above and takes a more constructivist take on the main subject of this book. As EU law constructs certain visions of a good life and normative standards for valuable relationships or meaningful individual autonomy, such projections might go beyond the

39 R. Lamont, above n. 12; H. Stalford, above n. 17, pp. 225–26.

40 See R. Lamont, above n. 12, 241; Y.M. Bérénos, above n. 12, 21. Both authors note that the fundamental rights of the parties in disputes affected by European law should also be protected but do not analyse them. Such an analysis is also absent in T. Scott, above n. 12.

41 T. Scott, above n. 12, conducts an analysis of justification and proportionality of English relocation provisions under the Treaty of Rome but this analysis does not correspond to the current state of EU law, in particular fundamental rights. See also R. Lamont, above n. 12, 242.

42 Charter of Fundamental Rights of the European Union [2012] OJ C326/391.

formal distribution of individual rights in particular doctrinal constructions.[43] What kind of values, realities, and subjectivities does EU law project in family contexts? To what extent can EU law's proclamations of individual autonomy and community living alter people's – or national law's – understanding of family relationships? How can these be conceptualised as a form of EU law's influence on child relocation laws? These questions allow a mapping out of how EU law can both be perceived as a subtle normative pressure and provide an opportunity to reconceptualise certain aspects of national child relocation laws beyond the reach of its doctrines.

The last objective of the book is the analysis of the consequences of different types of EU influences on national laws and the dynamics of adaptation of national child relocation laws. This analysis takes place in reference to both the scope of doctrinal obligations (prospectively) imposed by EU law and the more contextual influences projected via its methodological constructions, as discussed below. The literature has not yet systematically analysed whether EU law indeed features in national child relocation disputes and, if it does, how it influences the interpretation of national laws. This book intends therefore to fill this gap. The analysis is undertaken comparatively and encompasses Germany, Poland, and the United Kingdom (England and Wales). How do national courts in these jurisdictions shape their child relocation laws, and encounter the EU and EU law in this process? The answer to this question will offer new insights not only about the influence of EU law on national law, but also about the nature of decision-making in child relocation cases and the differences between national family laws more broadly. This selection of jurisdictions in particular, in light of the UK's departure from the European Union, is explained below, together with the discussion of the methodological aspects of the research design.

Considering these research objectives, the book does not aim to be normative. The reader will find some normative arguments introduced into the discussion, as they are implicit in questions such as whether the EU has competence in child relocation or how the CJEU could legitimately interpret EU law in the child relocation context. However, the book at large is more interested in the conceptualisation, clarification, and systematisation of the European influences under analysis. It takes Europeanisation of cross-border child relocation as a phenomenon under investigation. This project is motivated by the conviction that a more refined understanding of the nature of arguments that might need to be considered by various decision-makers is beneficial in itself for scholars and practitioners alike. It is this understanding that allows one to reflect upon and clarify how different approaches to child relocation are shaped by varying social and legal contexts, and what role is (or could be) played by European norms in this process. It is also this understanding that may serve as a foundation for

[43] L. Azoulai, above n. 26, p. 218.

new regulations or new legal interpretations, be it on the national or European level. The author's hope is therefore that the findings of this book will prove useful for future research concerned with policy- and law-making, offering a new perspective on pitfalls and opportunities of engaging with EU law in the child relocation context.

1.3. THE CONCEPTUAL AND METHODOLOGICAL FRAMEWORK

One can theorise several possible ways in which EU law influences, or could influence, national child relocation law, drawing from different conceptual and methodological repertoires. This variety of possible approaches is emphasised already in the discussion of the research objectives, drawing attention to the limits of the traditional doctrinal analysis.[44] The approach(es) adopted in this book reflect, therefore, the complex nature of the phenomena under investigation, falling within the broad categorisation of law-in-context approaches.[45] Context, however, usually refers to extra-legal normativity, but the book's contextual focus rests on EU laws' attempts to reconceptualise the legally relevant context in a way that might – via its constructions of identities, social values and norms – feed back into national family laws in different ways. The approach(es) adopted do come together under the umbrella concept of Europeanisation. In that, Europeanisation is one of the concepts most relevant for the purposes of this book and tying together its themes, but, at the same time, is taken to indicate different types of phenomena. As the methodological and conceptual frameworks of Europeanisation(s) intertwine closely, they are accordingly discussed together. This discussion is then followed by a brief explanation of the more technical aspects of the methodology – the choice of jurisdictions for the comparative part of the book and the selection of the research material – as well as clarification of selected concepts used in this book.

1.3.1. EUROPEANISATION: LEGAL DOCTRINES AND BEYOND

This book's title takes Europeanisation as a background metaconcept that draws from several understandings that can be found in the literature. Family

44 For a definition and characteristics of doctrinal research see J. Smits, 'What Is Legal Doctrine?: On The Aims and Methods of Legal-Dogmatic Research' in R. van Gestel, H. Micklitz and E. Rubin (eds), *Rethinking Legal Scholarship: A Transatlantic Dialogue*, Cambridge University Press, Cambridge 2017, pp. 209–13.

45 See W. Twining, *Law in Context: Enlarging a Discipline*, Oxford University Press, Oxford 1997; M. Loth, *Private Law in Context: Enriching Legal Doctrine*, Edward Elgar Publishing, Cheltenham 2022.

law scholarship typically conceptualises Europeanisation in reference to the process of European law-making (harmonisation),[46] with an often-blurred relationship between harmonisation and processes of convergence in domestic laws.[47] In recent years, increasing attention has been paid to the harmonisation pressures exerted by the CJEU jurisprudence and the effects that the Court's rulings – creating adjustment problems – produce in national family laws (the so-called 'judicial Europeanisation'), leading to a 'clustered convergence'.[48] Both assume, typically, that the adjustment of national laws is driven by the unidirectional 'logic of consequences' and investigated doctrinally, relying on compliance with CJEU rulings and EU legislation.[49] Europeanisation is then considered to encompass both types of EU action – turning aspects of earlier national law into European family law or subjecting national law to scrutiny of the CJEU – and effects that can be linked to them. Admittedly, many decisions on free movement, non-discrimination, or EU citizenship might be a form of indirect EU influence,[50] but they do not arise from the child relocation context nor impose any obligations regarding substantive family law directly, in a doctrinal sense.[51] Therefore, it remains unclear what the EU influence is and whether it is even perceived as such by domestic actors.[52] In that, the 'logic of consequences' and the doctrinal approach, while still important starting points,

---

46 Harmonisation is usually understood as a form of approximation of national laws to create a common standard and does not need to lead to an identity of legal provisions. See W.J. Kamba, 'Comparative Law: A Theoretical Framework' (1974) 23 *International and Comparative Law Quarterly* 485, 501. In the EU context, this flows also from the language used in Article 81(1) of the TFEU. Compare the – implicit or explicit – definitions in N.A. Baarsma, *The Europeanisation of International Family Law*, T.M.C. Asser Press, The Hague 2011; C. McGlynn, 'The Europeanisation of Family Law' (2001) 13 *Child and Family Law Quarterly* 35; M.N. Shúilleabháin, 'Ten Years of European Family Law: Retrospective Reflections From a Common Law Perspective' (2010) 59 *International and Comparative Law Quarterly* 1021; A. Fiorini, 'Rome III – Choice of Law in Divorce: Is the Europeanization of Family Law Going Too Far?' (2008) 22 *International Journal of Law, Policy and the Family* 178.

47 See the discussion in W. Pintens, 'Europeanisation of Family Law' in K. Boele-Woelki (ed), *Perspectives for the Unification and Harmonisation of Family Law in Europe*, Intersentia, Oxford 2003.

48 S. Ninatti, above n. 3.

49 U. Jaremba and J.A. Mayoral, 'The Europeanization of National Judiciaries: Definitions, Indicators and Mechanisms' (2019) 26 *Journal of European Public Policy* 386, 388.

50 See K. Carr, above n. 3.

51 J.M. Scherpe, *The Present and Future of European Family Law*, Edward Elgar Publishing, Cheltenham 2016, p. 32. For a similar line of reasoning see Opinion of the Advocate General in Case C-490/20, *VMA v Stolichna obshtina, rayon 'Pancharevo'*, ECLI:EU:C:2021:296.

52 See also A. Vauchez, 'From Close-Ups to Long Shot: In Search of the "Political Role" of the Court of Justice of the European Union' in C. Kilpatrick and J. Scott (eds), *New Legal Approaches to Studying the Court of Justice: Revisiting Law in Context*, Oxford University Press, Oxford 2020, pp. 56–57 observing that still relatively little is known about the conditions under which various legal issues are turned into EU law (claims), but core areas of EU law (such as competition law) differ significantly in this regard from those remaining at the fringes of EU law.

are only partially suitable for the investigation of child relocation, both due to the lack of explicit engagement of EU law with child relocation and the nature of decision-making in such cases.

The lack of any explicit action by the EU necessitates a reconceptualisation of the unidirectional character of European influences. At the same time, this reconceptualisation flows directly from the nature of child relocation decision-making, governed by the child's best interests principle that, by virtue of Article 24 of the CFR, binds also the EU. The best interests test is 'in essence a normative-evaluative issue' as 'rights need to be shaped and reshaped as social construction in the daily lifeworlds of children and parents'.[53] Finding solutions to challenges posed by child relocation requires, in the simplest terms, an interpretation of the child's best interests principle, but presupposes also a more implicit normative standard for mutual responsibility and valuable relationships and sets out limits on individuals' autonomy, in line with a broader purpose of family law[54] and its specific normative designs.[55] Different values or normative convictions might be recast as rights in the adjudication process, or gradually find expression in the legislation itself, a process that could be most directly brought by EU law, but often they enter judicial considerations in much more subtle ways.[56] Therefore, recognising this complexity, the investigation undertaken in this book moves beyond the typical accounts of the relationship between EU law and national family law.

The book adopts a broader, constructivist approach to the phenomenon under investigation.[57] EU law is perceived not only as a system of legal

---

53 D. Reynaert and R. Roose, 'Children's Rights: A Framework to Eliminate Social Exclusion? Critical Discussions and Tensions' in M.D. Ruck, M. Peterson-Badali and M. Freeman, *Handbook of Children's Rights: Global and Multidisciplinary Perspectives*, Routledge, New York 2016, p. 47; see also the discussion in A. Quennerstedt, 'Children's Rights Research Moving into the Future – Challenges on the Way Forward' (2013) 21 *International Journal of Children's Rights* 233, 233–47.

54 See, for example, the discussion in A. Diduck, 'What Is Family Law For?' (2011) 64 *Current Legal Problems* 287.

55 e.g. D. Bradley, 'A Note on Comparative Family Law: Problems, Perspectives, Issues and Politics' (2005) *Oxford University Comparative Law Forum* 4 <https://ouclf.iuscomp.org/a-note-on-comparative-family-law-problems-perspectives-issues-and-politics/>; D. Bradley, 'Convergence in Family Law: Mirrors, Transplants and Political Economy' (2001) *Oxford University Comparative Law Forum* 2 <https://ouclf.law.ox.ac.uk/convergence-in-family-law-mirrors-transplants-and-political-economy/>; D. Bradley, 'A Family Law for Europe? Sovereignty, Political Economy and Legitimation' in K. Boele-Woelki (ed), *Perspectives for the Unification and Harmonisation of Family Law in Europe*, Intersentia, Oxford 2003, p. 101; D. Bradley, 'Comparative Law, Family Law and Common Law' (2003) 23 *Oxford Journal of Legal Studies* 127, 145–146.

56 For an analysis of the influence of human rights language and the rights consciousness it fosters on English family law see: A. Diduck, 'Public Norms and Private Lives: Rights, Fairness and Family Law' in J. Wallbank, S. Choudhry and J. Herring (eds), *Rights, Gender and Family Law*, Routledge-Cavendish, Abingdon 2009.

57 This book's approach draws heavily from the conceptual and methodological repertoire of R. Leckey, *Contextual Subjects: Family, State, and Relational Theory*, University of Toronto

norms, but also as a meaning generating practice with a normative dimension ascribed to culture, values, ideas, or belief systems.[58] More specifically, EU law is taken to create distinct categories of 'contextual legal subjects' that emerge from the courts', legislators' and legal scholars':

> paradigmatic accounts of who human beings are and how they are connected to the social world around them; [that serve] to characterize and address the claims of actual human beings who come before [the courts].[59]

Through these (re-)constructions of legal subjects, EU law expresses normative value judgments beyond the formal distribution of individual rights.[60] Such constructions might be ambiguous and not directly intended to modify the underlying rationale of national family laws,[61] as they are interested in fundamentally different phenomena (protection of free movement as opposed to protection of good family relationships). However, despite these different commitments, EU law's contextual assumptions and distinct methodologies might constitute reconceptualisation pressures for national law in cases recognised to have an EU dimension.[62] In that, the contexts created by EU law via its 'normatively inflicted methodology' might be analytically separated from its legal norms,[63] constituting a form of influence in their own right. The conceptualisation of this influence and its relationship with national child relocation law is one of the objectives of this book.

Press, Toronto 2008, and E. Mertz, 'Conclusion: A New Social Constructionism for Sociolegal Studies' (1994) 28 *Law & Society Review* 1243, adding additional insights from the Europeanisation and EU law literature. Mertz uses the term 'moderate social *constructionism*', but Mertz's 'constructionism' draws also from several 'constructivisms' that express a common overarching paradigm, with the emphasis either on the individual or the social, or on the process of construction as opposed to its product. This is reflected in Mertz's own selection of foundational works that might equally be described as 'constructivist' (compare, for example, a short summary of different 'constructivisms' and references to Bourdieu, Habermas or Berger and Luckmann in D. Kostakopoulou, *Institutional Constructivism in Social Sciences and Law: Frames of Mind, Patterns of Change*, Cambridge University Press, Cambridge 2018, pp. 45–58. The term 'constructivism' used in the book is chosen as an umbrella term closer to the multidisciplinary research on European integration.

58 For a discussion on different conceptualisations of law in the EU integration process see B. Lange, 'How to Conceptualise Law in European Union Integration Processes? Perspectives from the Literature and Empirical Research' in V. Gessner and D. Nelken (eds), *European Ways of Law: Towards a European Sociology of Law*, Hart Publishing, Oxford 2007, pp. 263–66.

59 On that concept see Leckey, above n. 57, 5, building on K. Abrams, 'The Legal Subject in Exile' (2001) 51 Duke Law Journal 27, 27 (as quoted), and complementing Abrams' attention to courts with examination of legislatures and legal scholars.

60 L. Azoulai, above n. 26, p. 218.

61 ibid., pp. 214–21. See also the analysis in K. Carr, above n. 3.

62 L. Azoulai, above n. 26, pp. 216–19.

63 On that point in general see R. Leckey, above n. 57, pp. 21–22. Leckey builds his theoretical argument about the contextual nature of legal subjects on a juxtaposition of family and

National family law is naturally governed by different rationale than EU law. However, while normative decisions taken at the national level might concern different types of relationships, they also require the decision-makers to first define the context and systematise the relevant facts in a particular way.[64] Cross-border child relocation disputes have a well-recognised mobility dimension and concern value judgments about relationships made 'in the same institutional space and on the same territory'[65] as that occupied by EU law. As national decision-makers navigate the contextual assessments, trying to assess the child's best interests and reconcile parental claims to autonomy, they necessarily encounter a world including the EU. National legal doctrines remain important, but they are 'underdeterminate' and in the pursuit of normative responses within the 'undeterminacy' of the doctrine, legal language necessarily creates 'epistemological frames' that influence the perception of social issues in a way that might be far from neutrality.[66] Some of these 'epistemological frames' flow from EU law, coming to life via its 'normatively inflicted methodology'. In that, national contextual assessments and normative responses might emerge through various interactions with the supranational legal level and its discourses.[67] Recognition of particular contexts might, at times, lead to a change in legal doctrines.[68] However, this relationship will typically be more subtle and is unlikely to be fully captured by a strictly doctrinal analysis, calling for a more qualitative approach.

One might, naturally, wonder to what extent context flows from EU law any more than it just flows from the social environment. For example, one can say that child relocation disputes are resolved against a background of an increasingly mobile world in which technology allows people to communicate easily across the globe. Thus, increasing mobility as an empirical fact might apply to the whole world, or perhaps even in a lesser way to the EU than to some other parts of the world. This is, of course, true. It is also true that certain contextual elements might not be normatively inflicted per se (e.g. the geographical proximity of EU Member States as compared to many non-European destinations). However, many such facts are (re)framed and categorised by EU law in a particular way, creating 'an institutional language … and a grammar for social conflict'.[69] While

administrative law as two legal areas with very different rationale, as is the case for family law and EU law as well.

64 ibid., p. 22. Interestingly, one of the examples used by Leckey to illustrate this point concerns a Canadian case on relocation, *Gordon v Goertz* [1996] 2 S.C.R. 27: 'when assessing an application to vary a custody order, should the total context be assessed afresh, or can the status quo rightfully claim some priority?'. See p. 269.

65 ibid., pp. 275–76.

66 E. Mertz, above n. 57, 1250–52.

67 ibid.

68 R. Leckey, above n. 57, pp. 271–73.

69 L. Azoulai, 'The Law of European Society' (2022) 59 *Common Market Law Review* (Special Issue) 203, 210.

the interaction of legal and social norms and contexts in family law can be approached from many perspectives, the exact source of the normativity does not need to be identified specifically as long as the framing of the issue under investigation allows for a sufficiently systematised analysis.[70] In that, the book's approach assumes that when mobility and personal vulnerabilities meet, the normatively inflicted contextual layers of the world in which one lives – and this is a world with EU law – can also mean something outside the direct application of EU law and its doctrines.

The book suggests, therefore, differentiating between Europeanisation understood broadly, as a metaconcept, and Europeanisation understood sensu stricto. As a metaconcept, captured by the book's title, Europeanisation encompasses both an EU-level action in a certain area (child relocation) and the consequences such an action might have for domestic laws. From this broad perspective, Europeanisation refers then to the dynamics of EU law-making, the nature and limits of adaptation pressures that EU law might exert on national law directly, and the types of convergence they might bring. On the other hand, Europeanisation sensu stricto is conceptualised, following a proposition widely accepted in political sciences, as a dynamic process of adaptation to Europe on the national level, differentiating it from (various kinds) of EU action.[71] In that, Europeanisation does not need to depend on any specific action on child relocation and adopts a bottom-up approach to developments in national law. Europeanisation sensu stricto is naturally conditioned by the scope and nature of EU action in a given field. The book analyses, therefore, how EU legislators or the CJEU could legitimately approach child relocation, how their respective actions would impact the scope of national autonomy, and in that condition the Europeanisation of cross-border child relocation law. However, while this discussion deals with the scope of legal pressures that can be exerted by EU law and their prospective consequences for national law, Europeanisation cannot be understood as a process of adapting to a legal imperative in this narrow sense only.

Europeanisation is approached here as occurring in response to either EU legal pressures or as a 'usage of Europe' in other ways.[72] This differentiation is particularly important given the current uncertainty regarding the exact EU legal obligations in child relocation. Thus, Europeanisation does not depend on a specific EU action on child relocation, but rather draws attention to the constructive potential of EU law, including its legal uncertainty. This state of affairs creates both an opportunity to draw from EU law and a chance to 'escape'

---

70 J. Eekelaar, 'Family Law and Legal Theory' in E. Brake and L. Ferguson (eds), *Philosophical Foundations of Children's and Family Law*, Oxford University Press, Oxford 2018, pp. 42–44.

71 C.M. Radaelli, 'Europeanisation: Solution or Problem?' (2004) 8 *European Integration online Papers* <https://ssrn.com/abstract=601163>. This definition is also adopted in S. Ninatti, above n. 3, but Ninatti's approach is not explicitly constructivist.

72 ibid.

any legal pressures that might be ascribed to it.[73] The latter is particularly relevant in light of the growing opposition to Europe, and the EU in particular, that can be observed in family law and beyond.[74] This uncertainty means that relevant actors might disagree on the relevance of EU context for domestic decision-making, allowing them to use this EU (legal) context to pursue their own objectives.[75] Thus, legal uncertainty creates an 'opportunity structure'[76] for many different usages of Europe, including as a source of discourse[77] or as a reference for (legal) contextualisation for social processes.[78] Only by focusing on national developments can one ascertain whether there is any change, whether it is triggered by pressure or rather by usages,[79] and whether such usages – given the opportunity structures of legal uncertainty – indeed reorient national actors towards Europe. Europeanisation, in such a setting, strongly depends on the particularities of national law which create unique grounds for facing the constraints and opportunities of EU law,[80] and can only be captured while going beyond the narrow focus on legal pressures or pursuit of convergence claims,[81] seriously engaging with the dynamics of change on the domestic level.

A final remark concerns the approach to Europeanisation of cross-border child relocation from the perspective of the EU legal system exclusively, and the differentiation between Europe and the EU more broadly. The concepts of 'Europe' and 'the EU' are used interchangeably for stylistic purposes, unless specified otherwise. However, cross-border child relocation is naturally not a uniquely EU-ropean issue, nor is the EU legal framework – despite its strong

---

73 S.K. Schmidt, 'Beyond Compliance: The Europeanization of Member States through Negative Integration and Legal Uncertainty' (2008) 10(3) *Journal of Comparative Policy Analysis* 299 <https://doi.org/10.1080/13876980802231016>. Schmidt analyses the legal uncertainty from the perspective of national politics and regulatory interventions, but the general premise can be equally applied to national judicial process as its actors might use the uncertainty to mobilise EU law for their purposes or negate its relevance while responding to various EU law-based claims.

74 e.g. L. Vaige, *Cross-Border Recognition of Formalized Same-Sex Relationships: The Role of Ordre Public*, Intersentia, Cambridge 2022, p. 25.

75 S.K. Schmidt, above n. 73, 300–04.

76 ibid.

77 See, for example, M. Kallestrup, 'Europeanisation as a Discourse: Domestic Policy Legitimisation through the Articulation of a "Need for Adaptation"' (2002) 17 *Public Policy and Administration* 110 where the author explores how domestic policies are being changed due to the articulation of a 'need' for adaptation to EU policies, with references to an alleged inevitability of European integration as a legitimising factor of the change.

78 C.M. Radaelli, above n. 71, 4.

79 ibid., 11.

80 S.K. Schmidt, above n. 73, 300.

81 ibid., 305; see also P. Legrand, 'Public Law, Europeanisation, and Convergence: Can Comparatists Contribute?' in P. Beaumont, C. Lyons and N. Walker (eds), *Convergence and Divergence in European Public Law*, Hart Publishing, Oxford 2002, p. 225.

embedding of free movement – the only one relevant for child relocation. Nothing in this book should be seen as marginalising the global context of mobility or negating the fact that freedom of movement is also a general human right. Movement becomes the everyday reality for many family members, be they EU citizens or not, and be they moving from Berlin to Brussels or from Warsaw to New York. However, only in the European Union does cross-border movement constitute the main *raison d'être* of the political and legal entity and a defining feature of its community. In the public discourse, European identity sometimes refers to identity aspects of EU citizenship and sometimes encompasses European people more generally. This discursive puzzle can be observed in many legal acts legislated at the EU level, for example in the EU Charter of Fundamental Rights that speaks of 'the peoples of Europe'. This has an analytical relevance insofar as the distinctions of what is European, what is EU-ropean, what is global, and what is national are not always easy to draw. However, while societal developments can often be located within a broader context of transnationalism or globalisation, certain legal and political processes are unique to the EU. This book focuses on free movement as an EU fundamental freedom explicitly due to its embedding within the specific EU legal and political context. Nevertheless, it should also be recognised that many people both inside and outside the EU cannot make use of rights conferred by EU law due to their status as non-EU citizens. These are important challenges for the EU to address, but the analytical choice to focus on the position of Union citizens remains theoretically and methodologically justified, as demonstrated throughout the book, and should not be read as a normative approval of any such exclusions.

1.3.2. METHOD: THE DOCTRINAL AND THE QUALITATIVE APPROACH

The approach advocated in this book implies that one needs to look for normativity not only in doctrinal rules, but also investigate the discourses that give them meaning.[82] Legal doctrines are important both for the delineation of European influences and for the analysis of domestic effects of Europeanisation. In combination, they map out the scope of opportunity and constraint in national law that determines what considerations can enter the dispute. At the same time, however, doctrinal research is focused on reducing complexity and does not account for many 'softer' elements in law of value for the constructivist approach. This is why the research material needs to be approached also qualitatively, to account for the discursive constructions representing the normatively inflicted contexts projected by

[82] E. Mertz, above n. 57, 1245.

EU law.[83] This approach views language as a way of establishing 'a particular version of the world',[84] or a particular version of the contextual legal subject. In the EU legal context, 'mobility' and similar concepts become, then, not only objective phenomena, but can authorise a certain perspective – while excluding the other – on the empirical issue they refer to.[85] While such discursive constructions might be more or less ambiguous, they can be hypothesised to stretch over the entirety of EU law and spill over into national law as well.

This method fits well with research on court cases, as judges explicitly use language in a performative way: to resolve a case at hand and, where applicable, to influence future cases (in the form of a precedent or an impulse for a change/solidification of doctrines).[86] So far, such a methodological approach in EU law has been most frequently used to research the judgments of supranational courts.[87] But discursive approaches have been widely employed also in family law, including research on various constructions of legal subjects.[88] The analysis

---

83 On discourse analysis in legal research see J. Niemi-Kiesiläinen, P. Honkatukia and M. Ruuskanen, 'Legal Texts as Discourses' in Å. Gunnarsson, E.M. Svensson and M. Davies (eds), *Exploiting the Limits of Law: Swedish Feminism and the Challenge to Pessimism*, Ashgate Publishing, Hampshire 2007; L. Ervo, 'The Hidden Meanings in the Case Law of the European Court for Human Rights' (2016) *Semiotica* 209; H. Kalimo, T. Meyer and T. Mylly, 'Of Values and Legitimacy – Discourse Analytical Insights on the Copyright Case Law of the Court of Justice of the European Union' (2018) 81 *Modern Law Review* 282. See also S. Landefeld, 'The Evolution of Norms and Concepts in International Law: A Social Constructivist Approach' in R. Deplano (ed) *Pluralising International Legal Scholarship. The Promise and Perils of Non-Doctrinal Research Methods*, Edward Elgar Publishing, Cheltenham 2019, p. 56, suggesting that discourse analysis is 'a particularly insightful technique for empirical research' in constructively oriented investigations.

84 L. Webley, 'Qualitative Approaches to Empirical Legal Research' in P. Cane and H.M. Kritzer (eds), *The Oxford Handbook of Empirical Legal Research*, Oxford University Press, Oxford 2010, pp. 942–43.

85 See e.g. M. van Ostaijen, 'Between Migration and Mobility Discourses: The Performative Potential within "Intra-European Movement"' (2017) 11 *Critical Policy Studies* 166, 182, describing the EU discourse as one of Europe seen as a geographically borderless area where European citizens can move freely as Europeans – not as migrants – because 'mobility' reveals itself as a more comforting alternative; E. Recchi, *Mobile Europe: The Theory and Practice of Free Movement in the EU*, Palgrave Macmillan, Hampshire 2015, p. 1: 'In everyday terms, "mobility" means migration "in first class"'. See also the remarks about language in E. Mertz, above n. 57.

86 R. Harding, 'Legal Constructions of Dementia: Discourses of Autonomy at the Margins of Capacity' (2012) 34 *Journal of Social Welfare and Family Law* 425, 434.

87 H. Kalimo, T. Meyer and T. Mylly, above n. 83; L. Ervo, above n. 83; D.R. Myslinska, 'Not Quite Right: Representations of Eastern Europeans in ECJ Discourse' (2021) 34 *International Journal of Politics, Culture, and Society* 271 <https://doi.org/10.1007/s10767-020-09368-2>; R.D. Kelemen, 'Talking about the European Court: Discourses of Judging in the European Union' (2012) 58 *Studies in Law, Politics and Society* 139.

88 See, for example, R. Harding, above n. 86; M. Fineman, 'Dominant Discourse, Professional Language, and Legal Change in Child Custody Decisionmaking' (1988) 101 *Harvard Law Review* 727; K. O'Donovan, '"Real" Mothers for Abandoned Children' (2002) 36 *Law & Society Review* 347; A. Diduck, 'The Unmodified Family: The Child Support Act and the Construction of Legal Subjects' (1995) 22 *Journal of Law and Society* 527.

undertaken in this book draws inspiration from these works and combines much of their methodological legacy in the investigation of child relocation in the EU context. For example, individuals engaged in cross-border child relocation disputes might be characterised through a reference to their status as EU citizens, or some attributes ascribed to this status (e.g. mobility). The context in which they operate might be some general context common to all child relocation litigants, but this might also be a specific space characterised by European integration and the EU legal framework. These claims might relate to these particular litigants (as, for example, European migrants wanting to move back home), or might be generalised in abstract terms.[89] In that, EU legal concepts might sometimes not be invoked directly, but EU law might nevertheless influence judicial discretion and the construction of legal arguments.[90] Discursive constructions are therefore equally important – next to doctrinal analysis – in revealing the nature of the EU influence and its effects on national legal systems.

1.3.3. COMPARISON AND SELECTION OF THE JURISDICTIONS

Another methodological feature of the research design is the choice of a comparative approach to the investigation of Europeanisation. One can, of course, study whether one legal system is Europeanised or not, regardless of what happens in another legal system. Thus, one can test if there is a Europeanisation of national child relocation laws in different systems independently. However, comparison sheds light on these attributes of legal systems (and their social contexts) that facilitate, shape or constrain the interaction between national law and European law. Its object is thus to provide 'a more nuanced understanding of law in context, on its own terms'.[91] The comparative method has been a subject of complex methodological discussions and controversies,[92] questioning comparative law's epistemological assumptions and the neutrality of its enquiry.[93] A detailed discussion of methodological

---

89 See also K. Abrams, above n. 59, 32, for analogical questions posed in her investigation of the interplay between different accounts of legal subjects and the scope of governmental powers.

90 See also the discussion on the influence of human rights language on English family law in A. Diduck, above n. 56.

91 N. Creutzfeldt, A. Kubal and F. Pirie, 'Introduction: Exploring the Comparative in Socio-Legal Studies' (2016) 12 *International Journal of Law in Context* 377, 377.

92 See, for example M. Reimann, 'The Progress and Failure of Comparative Law in the Second Half of the Twentieth Century' (2002) 50 *American Journal of Comparative Law* 671. See also K. Boele-Woelki, 'What Comparative Family Law Should Entail' (2008) 4 *Utrecht Law Review* 1, 6, emphasising that comparative analysis follows the same steps regardless of the area of law, and therefore general remarks on the method apply to comparative family law as well.

93 R. Michaels, 'The Functional Method of Comparative Law' in M. Reimann and R. Zimmermann (eds), *The Oxford Handbook of Comparative Law*, Oxford University Press, Oxford 2006, pp. 364–67, 381.

aspects of comparative research is beyond the scope of this book, and many great contributions on the topic are available elsewhere. This notwithstanding, it seems to be accepted by now that – in light of its lack of empirical objectivity (as even the most basic concepts of similarity and difference have no empirical criteria)[94] – the comparative method must become constructive rather than positivistic.[95] As such, the general construction of the research problem and the comparative aspect of the investigation are built on common theoretical and methodological premises, clearly contributing to a more nuanced understanding of the European influence in child relocation law and its effects.

Three European jurisdictions were selected for the comparative analysis of Europeanisation in child relocation law: England and Wales in the UK; Germany; and Poland. This choice, while necessarily conditioned by the language abilities and legal knowledge of the researcher, has a strong substantive justification. These three jurisdictions are characterised by interesting legal, political, and socio-cultural differences, while at the same time they all belong(ed) to the EU Member States with biggest migration flows. The UK (before Brexit) and Germany have consistently featured in the top five destination countries of mobile EU citizens,[96] and Poland remains one of the biggest countries of origin of EU migrants.[97] The high number of EU citizens crossing the borders of these three jurisdictions is hypothesised to correlate with the number of relocation disputes, providing rich material for a comparative analysis. At the same time, they represent varying socio-political outlooks on European integration that can be observed in public discourses. The UK was considered to be a 'reluctant European' long before Brexit,[98] while Germany is regularly classified as one

94 ibid.; N. Jansen, 'Comparative Law and Comparative Knowledge' in M. Reimann and R. Zimmermann (eds), *The Oxford Handbook of Comparative Law*, 2nd ed., Oxford University Press, Oxford 2019, pp. 297–98. This is particularly so in a project looking at law discursively.

95 R. Michaels, above n. 93, p. 363.

96 T. Castro-Martín and C. Cortina, 'Demographic Issues of Intra-European Migration: Destinations, Family and Settlement' (2015) 31 *European Journal of Population* 109. In the mid-2000s, there was a significant increase in the UK's net migration that coincided with the 2004 enlargement of the EU, and then fell sharply after the June 2016 Brexit referendum. See Migration Observatory, 'Net Migration to the UK' (2023) <https://migrationobservatory.ox.ac.uk/resources/briefings/long-term-international-migration-flows-to-and-from-the-uk/>.

97 Romania is the Member State with the highest number of citizens living in another Member State, followed by Poland and then Italy. Interestingly, over two-thirds (68%) of Polish citizens living in another EU country used to choose the United Kingdom (before Brexit) or Germany, which potentially might generate interesting observations on different dynamics of relocation between these chosen jurisdictions. For a detailed analysis of the demographic data on intra-EU migrations see T. Castro-Martín and C. Cortina, above n. 96. For a recent overview, see European Commission, 'Annual Report on Intra-EU Labour Mobility 2022' (2023) <https://data.europa.eu/doi/10.2767/560178>.

98 e.g. S. Wall, *Reluctant European: Britain and the European Union from 1945 to Brexit*, Oxford University Press, Oxford 2020.

of the Member States most strongly committed to the EU.[99] Poles, as well, are among the most Euro-enthusiastic nations in Europe, but at the same time, the increasing Polish Euroscepticism is heavily identity-based.[100] While it is not suggested that this necessarily has any substantive consequences for family law, the focus of this research on the diffusion of ideational aspects of European law nevertheless approaches it as a potentially relevant factor, influencing the scope of acceptable interpretative choices.

The choice of these jurisdictions is justified also in reference to family law and child relocation law specifically. England and Wales, as the largest jurisdiction in the UK, was chosen for the project due to its explicit provisions on child relocation that have been extensively discussed, both nationally and in a global comparative context. It represents a common law jurisdiction that has regularly been classified as pro-relocation. Germany and Poland are both civil law jurisdictions that do not have any specific regulations on relocation; relocation is treated as part of the broader area of parental responsibilities. Germany has been classified as either 'pro-relocation' or a 'neutral' country regarding the ease of obtaining permission to relocate.[101] Poland remains understudied when it comes to relocation and has not yet been discussed in any comparative work on child relocation.[102] At the same time, the general models of the exercise of parental responsibilities in these jurisdictions are different from each other. The English model of parental responsibilities is classified in comparative literature as an autonomy-with-objection model, Poland is said to follow a weaker version of the autonomy-with-objection model, while Germany represents a strong consensus model.[103] This different attention ascribed to parental autonomy is potentially relevant to research on child relocation in the EU context, in

99 See Pew Research Center's Global Attitudes Project, 'Views on the European Union across Europe' (14 October 2019) <https://www.pewresearch.org/global/2019/10/14/the-european-union/> on the public opinion surveys regarding views on European integration and benefits of EU membership; see also C. Lemke, 'Germany's EU Policy: The Domestic Discourse' (2010) 33 *German Studies Review* 503, noting that 'the Euro-polity is firmly entrenched in German political life'.

100 e.g. S. Riishøj, 'Europeanization and Euroscepticism: Experiences from Poland and the Czech Republic' (2007) 35 *Nationalities Papers* 503, 512–15; N. Lázár, 'Euroscepticism in Hungary and Poland: A Comparative Analysis of Jobbik and the Law and Justice Parties' (2015) 12 *Politeja* 215, 217–22.

101 Australian research classifies Germany as neutral, see Family Law Council, above n. 11, p. 58. On the other hand, it has also been described as pro-relocation in R. George, above n. 11, p. 11.

102 In one report, Poland is classified in the middle of the scale ranging from most likely to allow relocation to least likely to allow relocation, placing it tenth out of 22 countries. It is, however, unclear how this assessment was made as the report cites only one Polish case in which the court refused relocation. See A. Worwood and L. Cummin, above n. 11.

103 K. Scheiwe, 'Parental Conflicts over the Exercise of Joint Parental Responsibility from a Comparative Perspective: From Daily Matters to Relocation' in H. Willekens, K. Scheiwe, T. Richarz and E. Schumann (eds), *Motherhood and the Law*, Göttingen University Press, Göttingen 2019, pp. 157–64.

particular if one understands freedom of movement in the EU as, essentially, a status of autonomy.[104]

At this point, the reader probably wonders about the inclusion of the UK in this research project after the 2016 Brexit referendum. When this project was originally designed, the United Kingdom was still a Member State of the European Union. However, the choice to retain England and Wales in the analysis after the Brexit referendum was made not only for convenience. Brexit has offered a chance to observe whether the legal and social implications of the process could be reflected in child relocation cases. On a socio-political level, Brexit confirmed the UK's status as a 'reluctant European'. Additionally, the number of EU citizens leaving the UK increased after the referendum, and thus the process did not remain neutral to the life choices of the many EU citizens in the UK. Regarding law specifically, Brexit has meant that the legal framework of intra-EU mobility was about to be lost, with significant uncertainty surrounding the post-Brexit reality. Considering the contextual embedding of child relocation within the EU, this was a priori deemed to potentially provide a different (and perhaps unique) type of material with relevance for the analysis.

1.3.4. SELECTION OF THE RESEARCH MATERIAL

The analysis of supranational law conducted in this book relies predominantly on statutory rules and case law of the two supranational courts in Europe and the relevant academic literature. Although the discussion of relevant provisions of the ECHR is of value in itself, the main focus is on the analysis of child relocation cases that reached the Strasbourg Court, as it is the case law of the ECtHR that sets out the relevant legal framework in detail. At the EU level, to provide for a more complete context of the legal developments and the full spectrum of European discourses, policy documents have been consulted as well. The analysis of EU law (both in the doctrinal and the contextual dimension) draws from a very broad landscape of European family law, EU freedom of movement frameworks, and EU citizenship law. The exhaustive discussion of all these fields is not the aim of this book, for there already exists a rich literature on all these topics. The focus lies, therefore, on developments deemed most relevant from the point of view of child relocation, as explained in the respective parts of the book.

Importantly, the analysis of the supranational legal framework of child relocation does not include a detailed discussion of child abduction, unless a certain aspect thereof proves directly relevant. There is a large body of literature on the topic and the links between child relocation and child

104 S. Coutts, above n. 18, pp. 31–43; see also E. de Witte, above n. 27.

abduction laws have also been discussed.[105] Indeed, the 1980 Hague Child Abduction Convention, complemented by the Brussels II*ter* Regulation in the EU context, puts forward a general framework regarding what constitutes a wrongful removal and – *a contrario* – in a very broad sense defines a lawful relocation.[106] The removal is considered to be wrongful if in breach of the rights of custody that, under the Convention, include 'rights relating to the care of the person of the child and, in particular, the right to determine the child's place of residence' (Articles 3 and 5 of the 1980 Hague Convention). However, this Convention neither determines in detail when and how the holders of custody rights need to give permission to relocate, nor sets substantive standards for the determination of relocation disputes. Both issues remain, in principle, a matter of national laws and the notion of 'custody rights' is to be interpreted autonomously under the Convention.[107] This is not to say that there have been no controversies regarding this autonomous interpretation of custody rights, a matter of relevance for child relocation, nor that there has been no important guidance provided by the European courts in that regard.[108] However, this book is interested more in how national laws shape the right to determine the child's place of residence, how child relocation cases are (to be) decided when they reach a national court, in the approach to the balancing of rights and interests involved, and particularly the role played by mobility factors in such disputes. A detailed consideration of the approach of European courts to child abduction is therefore not necessary. However, as can be seen in Chapter 7, national pronouncements under Article 15 of the Convention might contribute to interesting clarifications of national child relocation doctrines, as the provision allows judicial authorities of the state of habitual residence to declare, in reference to national law, whether a removal was wrongful within the meaning of Article 3 of the Convention.

The comparative analysis of national jurisdictions undertaken in this book includes research material from various legal sources: statutory rules;

---

105 Permanent Bureau, 'Conclusions and Recommendations of the Fourth Meeting of the Special Commission to Review the Operation of the Hague Convention of 25 October 1980 on the Civil Aspects of International Child Abduction' (2001) <https://assets.hcch.net/upload/concl28sc4_e.pdf>; R. Schuz, *The Hague Child Abduction Convention: A Critical Analysis*, Hart Publishing, Oxford 2013, pp. 84–90.

106 K. Scheiwe, above n. 103, p. 162. The 1980 Hague Child Abduction Convention is the 1980 Hague Convention on the Civil Aspects of International Child Abduction; the Brussels II*ter* Regulation is Council Regulation (EU) 2019/1111 of 25 June 2019 on jurisdiction, the recognition and enforcement of decisions in matrimonial matters and the matters of parental responsibility, and on international child abduction (recast) [2019] OJ L178/1.

107 See, for example, Case C-400/10 PPU, *J. McB. v L. E.*, ECLI:EU:C:2010:582, para. 41.

108 Questions of consent for the move under Article 13(1)(a) of the Convention or treatment of *ne exeat* orders or inchoate rights might be particularly relevant from this perspective. See also the discussion in P.J. Blanco, 'Unmarried Fathers and Child Abduction in European Union Law' (2012) 8 *Journal of Private International Law* 135.

case law;[109] and doctrinal (scholarly) writings. Where available and relevant, additional sources – such as political discussions – are used as supplementary material to provide more context to the discussion. Due to the constructive orientation of the research question, the focus of the analysis is on published child relocation case law in the three chosen jurisdictions.[110] Additionally, in Germany and Poland, where relocation falls under general provisions on parental responsibilities, issues substantively relevant for child relocation (e.g. freedom afforded to a parent while deciding on relocation) have been, at times, raised in cases regarding contact, travel documents, or similar. Such cases are also included in the sample, but their different nature is made explicit in the analysis.

There are certain methodological challenges flowing from this research design. First, the data vary both qualitatively and quantitatively, as different sources were differently available. This challenge can, however, be turned into an opportunity as the availability of sources helps to formulate a legislative and adjudicative profile of a given jurisdiction. Second, reported cases, while in principle capturing meaningful doctrinal considerations, are reported in a discretionary way by editors of law reports, judges, or court administration, and the reasons for their publication are not always known to the public.[111] Relying on published cases means that only a percentage of all cases resolved by courts can be accessed, the majority of which may be suspected to depart

---

109 Y.M. Bérénos, above n. 12, 21, explicitly draws attention to the need to analyse the case law of civil law countries to fully account for their approaches to child relocation.

110 The Boolean search strings used for the collection of case law were designed to capture all cases included in chosen legal databases as of 30 December 2022. For England and Wales, the search was conducted in BAILII (British and Irish Legal Information Institute) and Westlaw Classic with the use of 'child AND relocation' and 'leave AND to AND remove AND child'; for Germany in Juris and Beck with 'Aufenthaltsbestimmungsrecht AND Ausland', 'Umzug AND Ausland', and 'Wohnortwechsel AND Ausland'; for Poland in Portal Orzeczeń Sądów Powszechnych (POSP), Legalis and LEX with 'wyjazd z dzieckiem za granicę' 'wyjazd na stałe AND dziecko', 'przeprowadzka dziecka'. All the cases were read to determine their relevance, but only cases discussing child relocation were retained in the final research sample. This sample includes all relocation cases, not only intra-European ones. This was necessary to fully appreciate the relative relevance of European factors for the development of the doctrine.

111 For a discussion on the nature of reported child relocation cases in the UK, see R. George, above n. 11, p. 6. For German considerations on the inter alia publication of judgments see *BVerwG, Urteil vom 26.02.1997* – 6 C 3.96, ECLI:DE:BVerwG:1997:260297U6C3.96.0; D. Eßer, 'Die Veröffentlichungspflicht der Gerichte und das Internet', *JurPC-Web-Dok* 119/2001 <https://www.jurpc.de/jurpc/show?id=20010119>; J. Berkemann, 'Freie Rechtsprechung für freie Bürger ?!' JurPC-*Web-Dok* 354/2002, paras. 10–13 <https://www.jurpc.de/jurpc/show?id=20020354>. For the Polish context, see M. Jagielski and M. Niedużak, 'Publiczna Dostępność Orzeczeń Sądowych' (2010) Forum Obywatelskiego Rozwoju, Helsińska Fundacja Praw Człowieka, Akademia Leona Koźmińskiego; E. Świętochowska, 'Temida Wciąż Uczulona Na Jawność. Nie Wszystkie Sądy Chcą Publikować Wyroki' (2018) *Dziennik Gazeta Prawna* <https://prawo.gazetaprawna.pl/artykuly/1150353,dlaczego-sady-nie-publikuja-wyrokow.html>.

in some way from the usual cases, preventing claims about the frequency of the experience they capture or its influence on everyday litigation.[112] However, the fact that sometimes casually decided and casually reported cases might be influential in legal development is not necessarily a controversial finding.[113] Published cases are additionally important 'communication devices', intended as communication not only to the parties of a particular dispute, but also other 'actual and potential participants in the legal system'.[114] The focus on the construction of meaning allows them to be seen as representative in the sense of capturing the range or variation in the phenomenon:[115] the interaction with Europe in child relocation cases.[116]

In respect to both the supranational and the national case law, the analysis focuses on judicial arguments, with less attention given to how exactly arguments are created. At times, where possible and relevant, the fact that a given argument originates, for example, from a particular remark made by the intervening Member States in front of the CJEU or parties' claims, will be acknowledged. On the national level, one needs to be aware also of the role of social workers and children's own views in the discursive constructions and substantive outcomes of the cases. While the exact competences and role of a social worker in all three jurisdictions vary, in all of them their reports carry significant weight and reflect on the language and the substance of judicial decisions.[117] The legal relevance of children's views is also widely acknowledged. However, they do not call the methodological approach into question. The strong wishes of a child or clear recommendations from a social worker might influence the construction of the judgment, but they do not

112 In the context of the UK, see R. George, above n. 11, p. 6.

113 See ibid., p. 31, regarding the influential English relocation case *Poel v Poel* [1970] 1 WLR 1469. See also, as cited by R. George, F.H. Newark, 'Twine V. Bean's Express, Ltd.' (1954) 17 *Modern Law Review* 102: 'All lawyers are familiar with half a dozen or so cases which must have appeared to the judges who tried them to be so straightforward and lacking in novelty that they were doubtless surprised when the case was reported at all, and would be astounded to learn later that they were supposed to have played a part in the formulation of new doctrines'.

114 B. Trujillo, 'Patterns in a Complex System: An Empirical Study of Valuation in Business Bankruptcy Cases' (2005) 53 *UCLA Law Review* 356, 364–65.

115 L. Webley, above n. 84, p. 935; J. Niemi-Kiesiläinen, P. Honkatukia and M. Ruuskanen, above n. 83, p. 10.

116 That said, many cases were analysed during the research process. While it is not possible to discuss every case in detail, the book presents all cases referring to the European context or legal instruments explicitly. Other cases are referenced based on how well they illustrate a particular trend or type of argumentation, and where alternative explanations can be raised, they are discussed in the context of the characteristics of the research design.

117 In the UK context, however, Rob George notes that the reports are not always ordered and have long been thought to be less influential in relocation cases than elsewhere. See R. George, above n. 11, p. 103; R. George, 'How Do Judges Decide International Relocation Cases' (2015) 27 *Child and Family Law Quarterly* 377, 396.

dispose of the obligation to determine and discuss the outcome.[118] The judicial framing of the argumentation, or the selection of facts given legal relevance, cannot therefore be seen as meaningless, even if they draw on a social worker's assessment or the child's wishes.

Lastly, the legal frameworks and developments discussed in this book are hardly static. EU law is an ever-growing field, and national courts face child relocation disputes on a daily basis, making it necessary to choose a cut-off date for the analysis. Since this research was commenced in 2016, many important changes have occurred at both the national and the European level (Brexit; the new Brussels II*ter* Regulation; and the rule of law crisis in some of the Member States, to mention but a few). The analysis of the supranational legal framework covers developments until mid-2023, while the comparative analysis of the national legal systems accounts for materials and cases published until the end of 2022. Accordingly, all the observations and conclusions of this book are based on the research material available at that time but reflect – where possible and relevant – on possible future developments.

1.3.5. EXPLANATION OF SELECTED FAMILY LAW CONCEPTS USED IN THE BOOK

The book uses several family law concepts, of which understanding does not need to be universal across different jurisdictions. Most importantly, cross-border child relocation is not a well-defined legal notion in the first place. The book understands it as a cross-border change of the child's habitual residence, following a cross-border move by a parent with his or her child, notwithstanding any variations of the definition of child relocation that might be found in national legal systems. Such variations will be highlighted where relevant for the analysis. The understanding suggested here corresponds to the definition accepted by international organisations such as the Hague Conference on Private International Law or the Council of Europe.[119] Other terms, such as

---

118 In the UK context, it is suggested that children's views have direct influence on the minority of relocation cases and in many cases, they are not sought due to the child's age, or are set aside for other reasons, e.g. that children could not possibly fully envisage what is at stake in a relocation case. See R. George, above n. 117, 398. Similar observations were made in the context of the German judicial practice: J.A. Hirth, *Internationale 'Relocation': Eine rechtsvergleichende Untersuchung über den grenzüberschreitenden Wohnortwechsel eines Elternteils mit dem Kind gegen den Willen des anderen Elternteils*, Peter Lang, Berlin 2018, pp. 101–03.

119 See Permanent Bureau, 'Preliminary Note on International Family Relocation', Hague Conference on Private International Law 2012 <https://assets.hcch.net/upload/wop/abduct2012pd11e.pdf> and the Appendix to the Recommendation CM/Rec(2015)4 of the Committee of Ministers to Member States on preventing and resolving disputes on child relocation (adopted by the Committee of Ministers of the Council of Europe on 11 February 2015).

'international child relocation', 'child relocation', and 'relocation', will be used interchangeably and refer to cross-border child relocation as the focus of this book, unless specified otherwise.

The reader will encounter also other concepts, such as: 'parental responsibilities'; 'custody'; 'resident' or 'custodial parent'; 'family courts'; etc. When juxtaposing national family laws and supranational legal systems, one touches upon a complex combination of family law terminology that occasionally is governed by autonomous concepts, occasionally by national peculiarities, and often by a mixture of both. Even the concept of 'family law' does not always have to encompass the same catalogue of issues. In this book, 'family law' is understood as national, substantive family law. Child relocation is considered to be such a family law issue. This contrasts with some research on EU law, where family law can signify 'measures concerning family law with cross-border implications' in line with the competence of the EU established in Article 81(3) of the TFEU. Where relevant, this distinction will be made explicit. The term 'parental responsibility' is used to describe rights and responsibilities that parents have in respect of their children.[120] A 'resident' or 'custodial parent' signifies a parent with whom the child resides most of the time, with the generalised a priori possibility of both parents being resident parents (although the actual possibility of such a construction depends on national law). Whether this parent needs to obtain permission to relocate is a matter of construction of national laws, but due to its focus the book concentrates mostly on cases where authorisation for relocation is needed. The word 'parent' is used for convenience but might naturally describe also other individuals recognised legally as holders of parental responsibilities. The notion of 'family courts' is understood in reference to courts having jurisdiction to hear and decide child relocation cases in their respective legal systems. In light of this, all these concepts are used in a generalised manner, unless explicitly stated that the issue under discussion concerns a specific legal system or instrument.

1.4. OVERVIEW OF THE BOOK

Beyond this introduction, the book comprises seven further chapters. Chapter 2 introduces, in more detail, those features of national child relocation laws that raise interesting questions in the EU legal context,

---

[120] On various constructions of parental responsibility across Europe, also in the context of determining the child's residence, see J. Ferrer-Riba, 'Parental Responsibility in a European Perspective' in J.M. Scherpe (ed), *European Family Law (Volume III): Family Law in a European Perspective*, Edward Elgar Publishing, Cheltenham 2016.

equally substantive and methodological. Child relocation as a separate legal issue remains relatively unknown to many jurisdictions and this chapter is aimed at readers interested in an overview of the topic, but also provides a general background for the whole book. A more in-depth discussion of many issues raised there can be found in other relevant chapters. Chapter 3 analyses the competence of the EU in child relocation and the prospects of harmonisation on the EU level. Chapters 4 and 5 taken together provide for the analysis of the supranational legal framework of child relocation. Chapter 4 examines child relocation from the perspective of the European fundamental rights. It focuses on relevant provisions of the ECHR and the jurisprudence of the ECtHR, but also explains the relationship between the Convention system and EU law. Chapter 5 investigates child relocation as a potential restriction of EU free movement law, including the analysis of its justification and proportionality. Chapter 6 focuses on the conceptualisation of the contextual influence of EU law. It demonstrates how EU law, via its normatively inflicted methodology, creates its legal subjects and projects these constructions both within and beyond the doctrinal distribution of its rights and obligations. This subjectivity might not be normatively neutral from the point of view of national family laws. Chapter 7 then moves to the analysis of child relocation law in three European jurisdictions (England and Wales, Germany, and Poland) to investigate how national courts engage with EU law and what this engagement says about the scope and nature of European influences. The chapter offers an interpretation and a comparative discussion of these findings in the three jurisdictions under analysis. Chapter 8 – the concluding chapter – brings together the questions discussed in this book, in that it sheds light on the nature of EU law's influence on cross-border child relocation and its effects on the national legal systems under analysis. The chapter provides several observations regarding the development of child relocation law within the EU and the uneasy relationship between EU law and national family laws. It highlights the relevance of the book's findings for broader discussions in the two fields respectively and raises questions that remain to be explored.

CHAPTER 2

SETTING THE SCENE

Child Relocation, Best Interests of the Child and the EU Context

2.1. INTRODUCTION

In most jurisdictions, the residence of a child is one of the main issues on which parents must agree jointly.[121] Where this agreement is lacking, a court decision allowing relocation is usually needed to guarantee the lawfulness of the move. Although most jurisdictions resolve relocation disputes with reference to the child's best interests principle, the assessment of the child's best interests is a well-recognised challenge. While the principle is embedded in Article 3 of the United Nations Convention on the Rights of the Child (the CRC) and considered to be one of the general principles underpinning the Convention,[122] the most widely ratified human rights treaty in the world, it generates a significant variety of approaches in different contexts.[123] This can also be said about child relocation. It is not the objective of this book to discuss the nature and content of the principle in detail, and many excellent commentaries on the topic can be found elsewhere.[124] However, certain features of the debate are substantively

---

121 e.g. K. Scheiwe, above n. 103, p. 157; see also J. Ferrer-Riba, above n. 120, p. 288.

122 See Article 3(1) of the Convention on the Rights of the Child (New York, 20 November 1989), 1577 UNTS 3. For a discussion on general principles of the CRC see K. Hanson and L. Lundy, 'Does Exactly what it Says on the Tin?: A Critical Analysis and Alternative Conceptualisation of the so-called "General Principles" of the Convention on the Rights of the Child' (2017) 25 *International Journal of Children's Rights* 285.

123 The principle precedes the Convention and nowadays can be commonly found on national levels, in family laws or even national constitutions. While there is a great variety of interpretations of the child's best interests across jurisdictions and legal areas, the Convention has become an important point of reference for interpretation of the principle due to its quasi-universal recognition and general character. For a general discussion see O. Cvejić Jančić, 'Rights of the Child in a Changing World' in O. Cvejić Jančić (ed) *The Rights of the Child in a Changing World*, Springer, Cham 2016, pp. 1–36.

124 e.g. M. Freeman (ed), *Article 3: The Best Interests of the Child (A Commentary on the United Nations Convention on the Rights of the Child)*, Martinus Nijhoff, Leiden 2007. See also the UN Committee on the Rights of the Child, 'General comment No. 14 (2013) on the right of the child to have his or her best interests taken as a primary consideration (art. 3, para. 1)' (29 May 2013), CRC/C/GC/14.

and methodologically relevant for the broader analysis undertaken in this book. As the CRC's understanding of the principle underpins national family laws across the EU and many EU legal instruments, including the EU Charter of Fundamental Rights (CFR) and the Brussels II*ter* Regulation,[125] the pertinent features of the principle and methodologies for best interests assessments are discussed in reference to the CRC. These broader discussions intertwine with controversies raised by child relocation cases more specifically and help to explain the origins of varying approaches to relocation that can be observed around the globe. This chapter provides, therefore, an overview of the relevant themes and sets the scene for the discussion of the nature and limits of the European influence on child relocation laws undertaken in the book.

2.2. THE GUIDING PRINCIPLE OF CHILD RELOCATION: THE BEST INTERESTS OF THE CHILD

The UN Committee on the Rights of the Child, the main guardian of the implementation of the CRC, recognises three dimensions of the principle of the best interests of the child: it is simultaneously a substantive right, a fundamental interpretative principle, and a rule of procedure.[126] The child has the substantive right to have his or her interests assessed and taken into account as a primary consideration in all actions concerning the child. The interpretative character of the principle means that if a legal provision is open to more than one interpretation, the interpretation which most effectively serves the child's best interests shall be chosen. As a rule of procedure, the principle requires assessing and determining the best interests of a child as an obligatory part of the proceedings. These legal obligations apply to all decisions and actions directly or indirectly affecting children,[127] including, thus, parental disputes in general and child relocation disputes in particular. The UN Committee recognises that this multidimensional and open-ended nature of the principle allows it to be responsive but, at the same time, makes it vulnerable to manipulation.[128] This is, indeed, where the principle has been met with major criticism from scholars and practitioners alike, both in the context of the Convention and national legal systems. The child's best interests principle has been characterised as 'vague'

---

125 See the Explanations Relating to the Charter of Fundamental Rights [2007] OJ C303/17, Explanation on Article 24; or Recital 19 of the Brussels II*ter* Regulation (Council Regulation (EU) 2019/1111 of 25 June 2019 on jurisdiction, the recognition and enforcement of decisions in matrimonial matters and the matters of parental responsibility, and on international child abduction (recast) [2019] OJ L178/1).

126 'General comment No. 14' (2013), above n. 124, paras. 3–4.

127 ibid., para. 4.

128 ibid., para. 9.

or 'indeterminate',[129] or 'an aspiration rather than a rule'.[130] It has even been compared to tossing a coin.[131] Others have noted that it leaves a lot of space for judges' personal biases and unjustified arbitrariness,[132] and encourages strategic litigation.[133] In light of these criticisms, scholarly and professional literature across disciplines has widely discussed what a correct approach to the assessment of child's best interests might be, both in general and in the context of child relocation.

2.2.1. THE BEST INTERESTS OF THE CHILD AND THEIR ASSESSMENT

The assessment of the child's best interests is challenging. In individual decisions it must be conducted on a case-by-case basis, taking into consideration the specific situation of each child and his or her personal context. The principle should be interpreted in light of the evolving capacities of the child, considering the possible scenarios for the child's development in a given moment in time as well as in the short- and long-term.[134] It should also be interpreted in recognition of the obligation to ensure effective enjoyment of other rights recognised in the CRC.[135] This obligation might refer to, for example, the right of the child to be heard – another of the fundamental principles enshrined in the Convention. The child's views are not only a substantive element of the assessment of the child's interests, but also a separate guarantee recognised in Article 12 of the CRC.[136] The provision requires the state parties to ensure that children are given an opportunity to freely express their views in all matters that affect them and obliges national authorities to give due weight to those views, according to their age and maturity. This concerns every child 'capable of forming his or her own views', a capacity that should generally be presumed.[137] Although the age

129 R.H. Mnookin, 'Child-Custody Adjudication: Judicial Functions in the Face of Indeterminacy' (1975) 39 *Law and Contemporary Problems* 226.

130 I.M. Ellman, 'Why Making Family Law Is Hard' (2003) 35 *Arizona State Law Journal* 699, 707.

131 J. Elster, 'Solomonic Judgments: Against the Best Interest of the Child' (1987) 54 *University of Chicago Law Review* 1.

132 In the context of disability see M. Lanci, 'In the Child's Best Interests? Rethinking Consideration of Physical Disability in Child Custody Disputes' (2018) 118 *Columbia Law Review* 875.

133 e.g. M.A. Glendon, 'Fixed Rules and Discretion in Contemporary Family Law and Succession Law' (1986) 60 *Tulane Law Review* 1165, 1181.

134 'General comment No. 14' (2013), above n. 124, para. 10.

135 ibid., para. 17.

136 The child's right to be heard is also recognised in Article 24 of the CFR and the Brussels II*ter* Regulation.

137 UN Committee on the Rights of the Child, 'General comment No. 12 (2009): The right of the child to be heard' (Geneva, 20 July 2009), CRC/C/GC/12, paras. 9–10.

and maturity of the child will influence the weight given to their views, and so will the nature of the disputed matter, the child's opinion needs to be seriously considered as part of the decision-making process.[138] This is naturally also the case for all divorce and separation matters by which children are affected.[139]

Article 9 of the CRC foresees that a child should not be separated from their parents against their will, except when competent authorities subject to judicial review determine that such separation is necessary for the best interests of the child. Where parents live separately, a decision on the child's place of residence is explicitly recognised by Article 9(1) as a situation in which such determination may be necessary, reflecting the relocation context.[140] The child retains, in any case, the right to maintain personal relations and direct contact with both parents on a regular basis, unless it is contrary to the child's best interests (Article 9(3)).[141] Article 3 emphasises the crucial importance of the best interests of the child in all sorts of circumstances, and Article 12 makes it clear that any best interests assessment needs to be conducted in light of the child's views: the two articles complement and reinforce each other.[142] However, while these provisions highlight the crucial nature of the (process of the) best interests assessment, they are not blind to the rights and duties of the child's parents either (Article 3(2) of the CRC).

The issue of weighing the child's best interests against other considerations is one of the main points of criticism voiced against the principle's open-ended nature.[143] According to the UN Committee on the Rights of the Child, such conflicts have to be resolved on a case-by-case basis, in an attempt to harmonise all the rights. If, after a careful balancing exercise, the harmonisation of different rights and interests is not possible, decision-makers have to analyse and weigh them up, bearing in mind that the views and rights of the child have a high priority and are not just one of several considerations.[144] Authors approaching children's rights or family law from a relational perspective suggest that thinking in terms of conflicting individual rights does not fully capture the essence

---

[138] ibid., para. 11.

[139] ibid., para. 15. National legislators implement the right in diverging ways which can cause difficulties in the cross-border context, see e.g. Case C-491/10 PPU, *Joseba Andoni Aguirre Zarraga v Simone Pelz*, ECLI:EU:C:2010:828.

[140] See also the analysis of children's rights in the relocation context in U. Kilkelly, 'Relocation: A Children's Rights Perspective' (2010) 1 *Journal of Family Law and Practice* 23.

[141] Article 10(2) of the CRC makes it explicit, in the context of family reunification, that this applies also to children whose parents reside in different states.

[142] 'General comment No. 12' (2009), above n. 137, para. 18.

[143] See, for example J. Herring, 'The welfare principle and the rights of parents' in S. Gilmore (ed), *Parental Rights and Responsibilities*, Routledge, Abingdon 2017, for a discussion on the approach to parental rights in English law; or D. Archard, 'Children, Adults, Best Interests and Rights' (2013) 13 *Medical Law International* 55 introducing a distinction between a 'threshold' and 'weighting' view of a child's capacities.

[144] 'General comment No. 14' (2013), above n. 124, para. 10.

of disputes involving children in the first place.[145] This contributes to the overall perception of indeterminacy of the principle, in particular in contexts where parental interests behind a dispute are not directly child-related, such as in child relocation cases. Therefore, the literature has suggested multiple conceptualisations of the principle that should help with its interpretations and assist in the resolution of specific disputes. Of particular relevance for further discussion on child relocation is a distinction between decisions about children and decisions affecting children.[146]

Decisions affecting children are said to require a decision-maker to focus on the best solution to the issue at large rather than on what outcome would be best for the child, although this best solution needs to be weighed against the child's best interests. Decisions about children, on the other hand, require the focus to be on the best outcome for the child.[147] They require a direct and broad investigation into what options are available and what is best for the child, but also presuppose a balancing of other interests involved.[148] This suggestion seems to correspond to accounts differentiating between a weak and a strong version of the principle.[149] For example, decisions about whether to enforce a foreign custody order would be classified as decisions indirectly affecting children, whereas decisions about custody would be decisions about children directly. As such, the distinction does not change the weight to be given to the child's interests but rather the structure of the reasoning employed, which depends on the legal context of the case, and is said to contribute to more consistent interpretations.[150]

Regarding the interpretation of the child's best interests as such, it has been suggested that the best interests of the child should be interpreted in light of subjective as well as objective aspects of the child's life.[151] The differences between the short-, medium- and long-term interests of children have been

145 e.g. P. Laufer-Ukeles, 'The Relational Rights of Children' (2016) 48 *Connecticut Law Review* 741; R. Zafran, 'Children's Rights as Relational Rights: The Case of Relocation' (2010) 18 *Journal of Gender, Social Policy & the Law* 163; J. Herring, above n. 143.

146 J. Eekelaar, 'Two Dimensions of the Best Interests Principle: Decisions About Children and Decisions Affecting Children' in E.E. Sutherland and L.-A. Barnes Macfarlane (eds), *Implementing Article 3 of the United Nations Convention on the Rights of the Child: Best Interests, Welfare and Well-being*, Cambridge University Press, Cambridge 2016; J. Eekelaar, 'The Role of the Best Interests Principle in Decisions Affecting Children and Decisions about Children' (2015) 23 *International Journal of Children's Rights* 3.

147 J. Eekelaar, 'Two Dimensions of the Best Interests Principle', above n. 146, pp. 99–100.

148 ibid., p. 102.

149 See R. Chisholm, 'The Paramount Consideration' (Conference Paper) (18 March 2002) *10th National Family Law Conference*, Melbourne, Australia, in the context of Australian law.

150 J. Eekelaar, 'The Role of the Best Interests Principle in Decisions Affecting Children and Decisions about Children', above n. 146, 5.

151 J. Eekelaar, 'The Importance of Thinking That Children Have Rights' (1992) 6 *International Journal of Law, Policy and the Family* 221.

discussed, noting the potential conflict between them.[152] The child's interests have also been classified into 'basic interests' (e.g. physical, emotional and intellectual care), 'developmental interests' (the right to enter adulthood without disadvantage), and 'autonomy interests' (in particular, the freedom to choose a lifestyle of their own).[153] The common theme running through all conceptualisation is that any assessment of the best interests of the child necessarily takes into account the child's views and familial context as well as broader social and cultural contexts (in the end, both the freedom to choose a lifestyle and the right to enter adulthood without disadvantage are highly contextual). This is not to say that individualised assessments of familial situations or children's wishes are replaced or marginalised by some generalised contextual observations, but rather that they do not take place in a contextual vacuum. As the child's best interests principle calls for a contextualisation of the child's situation, decision-makers must regularly make more or less implicit normative choices on the relevant contexts and the normative decisions to be derived from them – a particular normatively inflicted methodology in itself.

As such, the interpretation of the best interests principle at times involves, in light of individual circumstances of the case, a closer scrutiny of what empirically is, or at least is perceived to be, the most common, or 'normal', form of life for children.[154] The principle can be seen as normativising the perceived 'normal' or 'viable', or as 'the legal system integration of social consensus'.[155] This is not to suggest that 'normality' is universal, or always assessed in an evidence-based manner.[156] At times, it might also lead to results that can be evaluated as normatively undesirable,[157] and it should in no way be used at the expense of individualised assessments. Any such legal constructions should be approached critically. However, some of the most basic and widely accepted features of contemporary family law, such as joint custody, can be perceived through this lens.[158] Therefore, the perceptions of the social context and the respective ideas of a normalised parenthood or normalised childhood play a role in the construction

152 M. Freeman, above n. 124, p. 39.

153 J. Eekelaar, above n. 151, 231.

154 J. Schiratzki, 'The Best Interests of the Child: In the Light of Normality and Exceptions' (2013) 1 *International Family Law, Policy and Practice* 8, 11.

155 ibid.

156 ibid., 13.

157 See, for example, H. Reece, 'The Paramountcy Principle: Consensus or Construct?' (1996) 49 *Current Legal Problems* 267, arguing that the perceived lack of acceptance of same-sex parenting and 'the child's need to be protected from teasing has led, not just to the subordination of, but to the total negation of, a far more important and socially significant value, the equal right of lesbian and gay men to be parents'.

158 See K. Kurki-Suonio, 'Joint Custody as an Interpretation of the Best Interests of the Child in Critical and Comparative Perspective' (2000) 14 *International Journal of Law, Policy and the Family* 183, describing joint custody as a 'cultural consensus'.

of the best interests of the child.[159] The choices that are available to and made by children and their parents, what sort of parenting arrangements are plausible, and what prioritisations of interests are to be allowed, in particular when confronted with the child's best interests, depend here on a social-normative equilibrium.[160] These features of the child's best interests principle provide an important background for the analysis of child relocation in the EU, as contextualisation in reference to cross-border mobility and the EU territory is a known feature of EU law, potentially overlapping with family law's own methodologies.[161] This discussion should, therefore, be read with a methodological objective in mind rather than as a normative appraisal of any particular contextuality.

2.2.2. THE CHILD'S BEST INTERESTS PRINCIPLE IN THE RELOCATION CONTEXT

The criticism of the principle intensifies in contexts where decisions are perceived as irreversible and rest on many unknowns, such as relocation cases.[162] The child's best interests principle has been criticised here for ignoring, conflating or diluting the complex issues that are at the heart of relocation disputes.[163] Depending on how a given jurisdiction approaches the assessment of the best interests of the child, the open-ended nature of the principle might also lead to a lack of transparency as to what considerations are relevant in the context of the child's family life.[164] According to some, the 'child-centric' approach in individual cases has brought mixed experiences and mixed results, disguising some of the core issues related to parental interests and the dynamics of parental relationships under the child's best interest analysis.[165] This applies in particular to the role played by the relocating parent's interests, with their

---

159 For a discussion of a 'normalized parenthood' in child contact disputes see: M.H. Ottosen, 'In the Name of The Father, The Child and The Holy Genes: Constructions of "The Child's Best Interest" in Legal Disputes Over Contact' (2006) 49 *Acta Sociologica* 29.

160 On this point see also S.B. Boyd, 'Autonomy for Mothers? Relational Theory and Parenting Apart' (2010) 18 *Feminist Legal Studies* 137, 146–49.

161 See Chapter 6.

162 See, for example, W.D. Duggan, 'Rock-Paper-Scissors: Playing the Odds with the Law of Child Relocation' (2007) 45 *Family Court Review* 193; L. McGough, 'Starting Over: The Heuristics of Family Relocation Decision Making' (2003) 77 *St. John's Law Review* 291; A.S. Rotman, R. Tompkins, L. Linzer Schwartz and M.D. Samuels, 'Reconciling Parents' and Children's Interests in Relocation: In Whose Best Interest?' (2000) 38 *Family Court Review* 341.

163 e.g. J. Herring and R. Taylor, above n. 10, 537; T. Glennon, 'Divided Parents, Shared Children: Conflicting Approaches to Relocation Disputes in the USA' (2008) 4 *Utrecht Law Review* 55, 55; W.D. Duggan, above n. 162, 198–99; see also K. Scheiwe, above n. 103, p. 170.

164 e.g. J. Eekelaar, 'The Role of the Best Interests Principle in Decisions Affecting Children and Decisions about Children', above n. 146, 9–10; J. Herring and R. Taylor, above n. 10, 522–23.

165 S.B. Boyd, 'Relocation, Indeterminacy, and Burden of Proof: Lessons from Canada' (2011) 23 *Child and Family Law Quarterly* 155, 157.

mobility rights being the 'unspoken factor' of relocation cases.[166] Relocation disputes are, therefore, a prime example of the challenges posed by the best interests of the child principle in general.

From this perspective, relocation disputes illustrate also both the utility and difficulty of the differentiation between cases directly about children and indirectly affecting children.[167] Their ambiguity may result in approaches that treat relocation not as a dispute directly about the child's place of residence but rather about parental mobility, affecting the child only indirectly.[168] According to some authors, this approach is mistaken, as the decision should focus on where the child should live and how the child could maintain contact with both parents.[169] Others argue that focusing only on children's best interests 'ignores ... key aspects of relocation disputes'.[170] Thus, child relocation provides a good example of disputes in:

> which there is an uncomfortable tension between the ordinary process of family decision-making, which takes into account the interests of all family members, and the highly artificial basis for decision contained in the strong version of the ... principle.[171]

While even the strong version of the principle does not ignore matters indirectly relevant to the child's best interests, practice shows that there is a tension as to when these matters are relevant to the best interests assessment, and when they are considered as 'factors in their own right'.[172] As this brief discussion already shows, there is a great diversity of views on the right approach to child relocation.

Many have turned to empirical research in search of an answer to what is in the best interests of children in relocation cases. However, social science has so far provided no clear-cut answers in this regard.[173] In sum, relocation

---

166 *R.E.Q. v G.J.K.* 2012 BCCA 146 (CanLII), para. 59.

167 J. Eekelaar, 'Two Dimensions of the Best Interests Principle: Decisions About Children and Decisions Affecting Children', above n. 146, p. 110.

168 For this observation and criticism of such approaches see J. Eekelaar, 'The Role of the Best Interests Principle in Decisions Affecting Children and Decisions about Children', above n. 146, 5 and 9.

169 ibid., 9.

170 T. Glennon, above n. 163.

171 R. Chisholm, above n. 149, p. 31.

172 ibid., pp. 5–9.

173 Existing socio-legal research has not yet brought any conclusive results, and it is doubtful that it will ever be able to guide judicial decisions in a sufficiently coherent way. See, with varying conclusions, the following contributions: Family Law Council, above n. 11; J.B. Kelly, 'Children's Living Arrangements Following Separation and Divorce: Insights from Empirical and Clinical Research' (2007) 46 *Family Process* 35; M. Freeman, 'Abduction and Relocation – Links and Messages' (2013) 38 *Children Australia* 143; P. Parkinson and J. Cashmore, 'Reforming Relocation Law: An Evidence-Based Approach' (2015) 53 *Family Court Review* 23.

can have both negative and positive outcomes, depending on the individual child, circumstances of the move, and the overall family situation.[174] While this may lead to courts becoming more receptive and aware of issues involved in relocation disputes, it does not in itself guide the decision-making. Broadly, the child's interests usually speak in favour of staying in proximity to his or her parents, and potentially their wider families and friends, possibly within environments that provide familiarity and stability. The added difficulty of relocation cases is, therefore, that while in many other disputes decisions are made between options that are real, concrete, and known at the time of the decision, this is usually not the case in relocation cases that require a determination about future circumstances and future behaviours. This all makes relocation cases particularly difficult to resolve, leaving some with the conclusion that one 'can't prove these cases by any type of evidence'.[175]

It is in this context that considerations that might not be directly child-centred, in particular, parental rights and interests, enter the disputes. A parent rarely moves, especially abroad, for reasons that are solely child-oriented.[176] There is a plethora of motivations behind a parent's move with the child: to return home or to be close to family and friends (support networks); to pursue a career or educational opportunity; to join a new partner; or to enable the partner to pursue career or educational opportunities. There are also moves that are described as 'lifestyle choices' and stem from personal preferences as to where to live, in particular, to 'have a fresh start' and other – less typical – reasons. Reasons given for relocation often overlap.[177] Invariably, however, relocation cases touch upon the core financial, emotional and autonomy interests of relocating parents.[178] Such interests weigh heavily in any decisions that the parent, or the court, makes, but their relationship to the best interests of the child as a guiding principle is unclear. Others argue, therefore, that having children necessarily means that the freedom to pursue one's objectives is not absolute, and thus restrictions of mobility should be seen in this light.[179] This approach has received significant criticism from authors adopting relational perspectives on law, drawing attention to the inherently gendered dimension of relocation as a family law issue.

---

174 This overall conclusion was reached by P. Parkinson and J. Cashmore, above n. 173; see also J.A. Hirth, above n. 118, pp. 42–45.

175 W.D. Duggan, above n. 162, 198–99.

176 ibid.

177 For an overview see: R. George, above n. 117, 386–87; P. Parkinson, J. Cashmore and J. Single, 'Mothers Wishing to Relocate with Children: Actual and Perceived Reasons' (2011) 27 *Canadian Journal of Family Law* 11.

178 J. Herring and R. Taylor, above n. 10, 523.

179 e.g. R. Zafran, above n. 145, 168–69; J. Herring and R. Taylor, above n. 10, 524.

Most often, mothers are the primary caregivers who want to move together with their children.[180] Most of them will not move without them.[181] This is true also in the EU, as – although national differences are of great significance – on average mothers are typically primary caregivers after relationship breakdowns.[182] Stereotypical views on (gendered) parental roles are still present in many jurisdictions: a mother insisting on relocation might be seen as a selfish individual sidelining the interests of her children, while a mother asserting the readiness to stay if relocation is refused risks 'not having her reasons … treated with the seriousness they deserve'.[183] Some authors claim, therefore, that gender biases and imperatives of shared parenting ignore the ongoing reality of gender divisions.[184] Also, in the relocation context, the burdens are said not to be placed equally. In very few jurisdictions, courts pay attention to the issues of mobility of the non-custodial parent, in particular the fact that they are not restricted in residence choices or the possibility for them to follow the child if the child moves.[185]

Others dispute these claims, noting that non-custodial parents are factually tied to the place of residence of the child, as if they move, they cannot apply for the other parent to follow with the child.[186] On a more general level, the corollary of the right to move is seen in the non-relocating parent's right to stay.[187] However, the lack of attention to the non-relocating parent's mobility can be problematic from the point of view of the child's best interests. If courts claim to resolve the disputes according to the best interests principle, they should consider the option of the non-custodial parent moving together with the relocating parent and the child, as this might be necessary to reach the best solution in some cases.[188] These mobility discussions are of relevance particularly for this book, but the non-relocating parent's position

---

180 This is confirmed by empirical research, e.g. P. Parkinson and J. Cashmore, above n. 173, 24; M. Freeman, 'Relocation: The Reunite Research' (2009) *Reunite* <https://web.archive.org/web/20111216014043/http://www.reunite.org/edit/files/Library%20-%20reunite%20Publications/Relocation%20Report.pdf>.

181 P. Parkinson and J. Cashmore, above n. 173, 24.

182 e.g. Y. Chzhen and J. Bradshaw, 'Lone Parents, Poverty and Policy in the European Union' (2012) 22 *Journal of European Social Policy* 487, 490–91. The proportion of lone fathers (of all lone parents rather than of all parents) varies strikingly from 3% in Lithuania to 30% in Sweden.

183 See the remarks in the Australian case *U v U* [2002] HCA 36, (2002) 211 CLR 238, para. 248.

184 S.B. Boyd, above n. 165, 170 and 177; C. Smart, 'The Legal and Moral Ordering of Child Custody' (1991) 18 *Journal of Law and Society* 485, 485.

185 J. Herring and R. Taylor, above n. 10, 536.

186 P. Parkinson, above n. 8, p. 22; see also M. Freeman, above n. 180.

187 P. Parkinson, above n. 8, p. 22.

188 For a general discussion on the non-custodial parent's mobility in relocation disputes see M.H. Weiner, 'Inertia and Inequality: Reconceptualizing Disputes Over Parental Relocation' (2007) 40 *UC Davis Law Review* 1747.

is predominantly conceptualised not through the right to stay, but through the desire to have continuing contact with the child. If a relocation application is successful, the non-relocating parent risks losing frequent contact with the child – contact to which both the parent and the child are entitled as a matter of human rights.

In light of the above, some authors claim that approaching child relocation from a human rights perspective would allow for a clearer presentation of all the issues and interests involved.[189] In jurisdictions treating the child's best interests as the sole consideration, approaching child relocation from a rights perspective would allow for an independent consideration of other family members' interests.[190] This might lead to reconceptualisation of the reasoning used, even if it does not drastically transform the conclusions reached.[191] A principled balancing exercise should then focus on the values that underlie each right – values bound up with the personal autonomy of the individuals involved.[192] It has been suggested that courts should consider 'which interference will constitute a greater blight on [each parent's] vision of the good life' as a factor independent from the assessment of the position of the child.[193] This approach has been criticised for deferring the analysis to parental rights and not taking the rights of children seriously enough,[194] as children might not yet have developed their own vision of autonomy or of a good life.[195] However, this criticism has not suggested a fundamentally different approach to resolve the tensions between the rights of different individuals, but rather emphasised children's substantive rights and the corresponding procedural guarantees that result in an improved decision-making process (in particular in reference to the child's right to be heard).[196] In this context, the substantive suggestion found in the literature locates (autonomy) rights for the child in the right to an open future, with self-determination and self-fulfilment being the main underlying values of that right.[197] While the exact normative proposals under the human rights perspective differ,[198] these conceptualisations also

---

189 S. Choudhry and J. Herring, *European Human Rights and Family Law*, Hart Publishing, Oxford 2010, p. 284; see also A.B. LaFrance, 'Child Custody and Relocation: A Constitutional Perspective' (2008) 34 *University of Louisville Journal of Family Law* 1 on the constitutional perspective; R. Zafran, above n. 145, 168–71; U. Kilkelly, above n. 140 regarding children's rights; K. Scheiwe, above n. 103, pp. 166–67.

190 J. Herring and R. Taylor, above n. 10, 526; S. Choudhry and J. Herring, above n. 189, p. 285.

191 J. Herring and R. Taylor, above n. 10, 518; see also the discussion in S. Choudhry and J. Herring, above n. 189, pp. 282–85.

192 J. Herring and R. Taylor, above n. 10, 530.

193 ibid., 531.

194 U. Kilkelly, above n. 140, 34–35.

195 J. Herring and R. Taylor, above n. 10, 531.

196 U. Kilkelly, above n. 140, 35.

197 J. Herring and R. Taylor, above n. 10, 531; see also J. Millum, 'The Foundation of the Child's Right to an Open Future' (2014) 45 *Journal of Social Philosophy* 522.

198 See Chapter 4.

draw attention to the need for contextual assessments of both parental claims and children's best interests. However, in light of the complexity of child relocation disputes, different jurisdictions approach such contextual and normative assessments very differently.

2.3. DIVERGENT APPROACHES TO CHILD RELOCATION AND THE INTERNATIONAL QUEST FOR MORE COHERENCE

The contextually responsive nature of the best interests principle has led to a great variety of approaches to child relocation across different jurisdictions. This variety has prompted calls for the establishment of a common international framework on child relocation.[199] Various initiatives have aimed at developing a 'more uniform'[200] and 'comprehensive and coherent'[201] approach internationally. This international interest stemmed in particular from the alleged links between child relocation and child abduction laws.[202] The 1980 Hague Child Abduction Convention does, in a very broad sense, define circumstances under which a relocation is lawful, but does not set substantive standards for the determination of custody rights or relocation disputes.[203] The international initiatives were supposed to fill this gap, but were at times met with scepticism, be it because of competence constraints of their drafters or doubts about their effectiveness.[204] At the same time, the international efforts to provide a more coherent approach have increasingly led to the recognition of the unique EU legal dimension of child relocation disputes – not only because of their mobility dimension, but also because of the harmonisation ambitions of much of EU law. The following discussion of the diversity of national laws and the subsequent initiatives provides, therefore, unique insights also for any prospective EU intervention.

---

199 e.g. Permanent Bureau of the Hague Conference on Private International Law, 'Preliminary Document No 11 of January 2012 for the Attention of the Special Commission of January 2012 on the Practical Operation of the 1980 Hague Child Abduction Convention and the 1996 Hague Child Protection Convention' (2012) <https://assets.hcch.net/upload/wop/abduct2012pd11e.pdf>.

200 The Washington Declaration on International Family Relocation of 25 March 2010, Article 4.

201 Explanatory Memorandum to the Recommendation CM/Rec(2015)4, above n. 119, para. 6.

202 Permanent Bureau, 'Conclusions and Recommendations of the Fourth Meeting of the Special Commission to Review the Operation of the Hague Convention of 25 October 1980 on the Civil Aspects of International Child Abduction' (2001) <https://assets.hcch.net/upload/concl28sc4_e.pdf>; R. Schuz, above n. 105, pp. 84–90.

203 See also K. Scheiwe, above n. 103, p. 162.

204 R. George, 'The International Relocation Debate' (2012) 34 *Journal of Social Welfare and Family Law* 141, 148–49.

2.3.1. DIFFERENT APPROACHES TO CHILD RELOCATION

The existing approaches to child relocation are classified in the literature as pro-relocation, neutral, and anti-relocation.[205] The division is far from precise, but pro-relocation jurisdictions typically give priority to the stability of the relationship between the resident parent who intends to relocate and the child. Relocation applications made in good faith have high chances of success because either it is not seen as acceptable to restrict the general freedom of the parent who provides the most care for the child, or the unhappiness resulting from such a restriction is seen as detrimental to the child. Anti-relocation jurisdictions put more emphasis on the relationship and contact between the child and the non-relocating parent. Because relocation is seen as a significant risk to this relationship, which remains important to the child, the threshold for obtaining a permission to relocate is relatively high. Neutral countries are said to have no starting point for the analysis, while trying to assess each case individually according to the child's best interest principle, but this approach has been criticised for its unpredictability.[206]

The problem with such classification is that, often, it is the practical operation of the rules that is decisive, and not much is known about child relocation practices, in particular in continental Europe.[207] At the same time, most countries which are classified as pro- or anti-relocation 'would likely describe themselves in the same way as neutral countries – that they take into account all factors relevant to the child's welfare in deciding the best outcome'.[208] Such classification might be further blurred by broader differences in the approach to parental responsibilities.[209] It is also complicated by the fact that the construction of relocation disputes differs, with some jurisdictions approaching the issue as a modification of the existing arrangements, and others as a question whether relocation should be granted or refused.[210] Thus, different approaches to relocation might reflect a fundamental difference in the perception of post-separation parenting, the strength and indissolubility of the parents' mutual links, and the scope of autonomy resulting from such a perception.[211] While the

---

205 R. George, above n. 11; R. Schuz, above n. 105, pp. 72–76; A. Worwood and L. Cummin, above n. 11; Family Law Council, above n. 11.

206 R. George, above n. 11, pp. 11–12; R. Schuz, above n. 105, pp. 74–75.

207 R. George, above n. 11, pp. 11–12; see also Y.M. Bérénos, above n. 12, 21 calling for more case law research in civil law countries.

208 R. George, above n. 11, p. 11.

209 See e.g. K. Scheiwe, above n. 103, for a typology of different models of exercising joint parental authorities: the autonomy-with-objection model, the weak consensus model, and the strong consensus model.

210 P. Parkinson, *Family Law and the Indissolubility of Parenthood*, Cambridge University Press, Cambridge 2011, p. 154.

211 ibid., p. 157.

approaches might be classified into pro-relocation, neutral or anti-relocation, this classification depends heavily on analytical choices[212] that highlight the different elements and dynamics of national laws.

One additional aspect of the different approaches that often remains overlooked is linked to the origins and rationale of restrictions on child relocation. For example, in English law the restrictions stemmed from a judicial concern to retain oversight of the child as the ward of the state.[213] The underlying ratio of the law was a 'general distrust of the approach of courts in other jurisdictions' regarding the child's welfare and enforcement of national judgments (particularly in terms of securing the access of non-relocating parents).[214] During work on the 1996 Hague Child Protection Convention, US delegates proposed a rule that would allow the authorities of the former habitual residence of the child to retain exclusive jurisdiction for two years after relocation if one of the parents continued to reside in that state.[215] The rule was not incorporated into the final text, but the proposal

> was based on the fear of seeing the authorities of the new habitual residence, supposedly more favourable to the other parent, immediately put back in issue the measures which had just been taken by the authorities of the preceding habitual residence,[216]

confirming some sort of apprehension about domestic courts losing control over minors crossing borders. Reasons motivating relocation rules in some civil law jurisdictions seem to confirm a more universal nature of such fears.[217] The differences, therefore, might also result from jurisdictional concerns, and can be

---

212 See observations in R. George, above n. 117, 380. George notices that although traditionally New Zealand, Canada and England have been classified as anti-relocation, neutral, and pro-relocation respectively, quantitative research on case outcomes indicates that in all of these jurisdictions relocation applications have a similar success rate of around 68%.

213 R. George, above n. 11, p. 140 and cases cited there.

214 T. Scott, above n. 12, p. 13. See especially remarks on the developments within English law following the introduction of universal recognition and enforcement of orders relating to children made in all parts of the UK.

215 The 1996 Hague Child Protection Convention is the Hague Convention on Parental Responsibility and Protection of Children. For the account of the preparatory work, see P. Lagarde, 'HCCH Explanatory Report on the 1996 HCCH Child Protection Convention', Hague Conference on Private International Law, para. 41 <https://www.hcch.net/en/publications-and-studies/details4/?pid=2943&dtid=3>.

216 ibid.

217 See e.g. *Vorblatt und Erläuterungen zu dem Kindschafts- und Namensrecht-Änderungsgesetz* (2013) <https://www.parlament.gv.at/gegenstand/XXIV/I/2004>; L. Kreiner, 'Aufenthaltsbestimmungs- und Wohnortbestimmungsrecht nach §162 ABGB' (2014) Master's Thesis, University of Graz (Austria), p. 37 <http://unipub.uni-graz.at/obvugrhs/download/pdf/252083?originalFilename=true>. See also similarly motivated legal reform in Switzerland: *Botschaft zu einer Änderung des Schweizerischen Zivilgesetzbuches (Elterliche Sorge) vom 16. November 2011* [BBl 2011 9077].

mitigated by judicial trust factors and specific supranational legal frameworks. This also draws attention to a potentially unique EU dimension of child relocation disputes, given the extensive EU legislation on judicial co-operation and the role played by the principle of mutual trust within this framework.[218]

2.3.2. INTERNATIONAL DEVELOPMENTS: LOOKING FOR A MORE UNIFORM STANDARD FOR CHILD RELOCATION

Until now, four non-binding documents on child relocation have been drafted on an international level: two by international bodies (the 2010 Washington Declaration on International Family Relocation and the Recommendation CM/Rec(2015)4 of the Committee of Ministers of the Council of Europe on preventing and resolving disputes on child relocation), and two by academic communities (the London Conclusions and Resolutions on Relocation and the CEFL Principles of European Family Law Regarding Parental Responsibilities).[219]

The Principles of European Family Law Regarding Parental Responsibilities,[220] issued by the Commission on European Family Law (CEFL) in 2004, constituted the first attempt to come up with a supranational proposal on a model law on child relocation. The Principles cover rules on parental responsibilities more broadly, expressing 'what seems to be the modern common core of the international and European instruments' and the 22 national legal systems analysed in the process.[221] National reports revealed a significant divergence of relocation laws across Europe, but the drafters nevertheless saw a need to introduce specific rules on relocation in response to an increasing European mobility.[222] Principle 3:20(1) states that parents who exercise their parental responsibilities jointly should always 'agree upon with whom the child resides'. According to Principle 3:21, if one of the parents

[218] See Chapter 6.

[219] Parts of this Section are based on O. Ceran, 'Child Relocation, Soft Law, and the Quest for Uniformity at the European Court of Human Rights – Part One' (2020) 15 *Studia Prawa Prywatnego* and O. Ceran, 'Child Relocation, Soft Law, and the Quest for Uniformity at the European Court of Human Rights – Part Two' (2021) 16 *Studia Prawa Prywatnego*.

[220] Commission on European Family Law, 'CEFL Principles Regarding Parental Responsibilities' (2004) <http://ceflonline.net/wp-content/uploads/Principles-PR-English.pdf>.

[221] K. Boele-Woelki and D. Martiny, above n. 8, 136. National reports and relevant legal provisions are available on the CEFL's website: Commission on European Family Law, 'Parental Responsibility Reports by Jurisdiction' <http://ceflonline.net/parental-responsibility-reports-by-jurisdiction/>. They have also been published, together with comments and a comparative overview in K. Boele-Woelki, 'The CEFL Principles Regarding Parental Responsibilities: Predominance of the Common Core' in K. Boele-Woelki and T. Sverdrup (eds), *European Challenges in Contemporary Family Law*, Intersentia, Oxford 2008.

[222] K. Boele-Woelki and D. Martiny, above n. 8, 132.

wishes to change the child's residence within or outside the jurisdiction, he or she should inform the other parent thereof in advance. In the event of disagreement, each parent should be able to apply to the competent authority for a decision. When deciding the case, the competent authority should be guided by the best interests of the child (Principle 3:3), but should also take into consideration factors such as: the age and opinion of the child; the right of the child to maintain personal relationships with the other holders of parental responsibilities; the ability and willingness of the holders of parental responsibilities to co-operate with each other; but also their personal situations; geographical distance and accessibility; and the free movement of persons. According to the authors, the Principles tried to establish workable and pragmatic solutions to reach a compromise between different systems and to avoid unnecessary disputes. The rather general framework aims also to ensure that national legal and cultural traditions will be respected.[223]

The first global attempt to internationalise the standards on child relocation was the Washington Declaration on International Family Relocation, issued under the auspices of the Hague Conference on Private International Law during the International Judicial Conference on Cross-Border Family Relocation that took place from 23–25 March 2010. The Declaration emphasises that appropriate procedures before competent authorities should be available for parents wanting to relocate with the child, and that notice of relocation should be given to the other parent. The document also encourages mediation as well as mutual trust and communication between the states of origin and destination. In Articles 3 and 4, the Declaration puts forward a list of factors that should be considered in cross-border child relocation cases, taking into account that the best interests of the child should be the paramount consideration. This approach was endorsed in the London Conclusions and Resolutions on Relocation,[224] drafted later that year at the Conference on International Child Abduction, Forced Marriage and Relocation in London that brought together scholars and practitioners from 18 jurisdictions. The London Conclusions have not been broadly analysed in the literature,[225] but reflect the perceived need to develop 'a common international framework to guide the exercise of judicial discretion'.[226]

---

[223] ibid. For a general overview of the CEFL's objectives see K. Boele-Woelki, 'The Principles of European Family Law: Its Aims and Prospects' (2005) 1 *Utrecht Law Review* 160.

[224] See Appendix B to L.D. Elrod, 'National and International Momentum Builds for More Child Focus in Relocation Disputes' (2010) 44 *Family Law Quarterly* 341.

[225] The Conclusions are no longer available on the website of the conference organiser and there seem to be only two contributions referring to the Conclusions (one academic and one professional in nature). See L.D. Elrod, above n. 224, and D. Hodson, 'David Hodson on International Family Law: The London Conclusions and Resolutions' (2010) <http://www.familylaw.co.uk/news_and_comment/DavidHodson160810#.WQcHtMakI2w>.

[226] Preamble of the London Conclusions and Resolutions on Relocation, Appendix B to L.D. Elrod, above n. 224.

The most recent supranational instrument on child relocation is the Recommendation CM/Rec(2015)4 of the Committee of Ministers of the Council of Europe to Member States on preventing and resolving disputes on child relocation[227] drafted in February 2015. According to the Recommendation, child relocation refers to (any) change in the child's habitual residence, encompassing both domestic and cross-border relocations, and emphasises the relevance of the effect of the move in terms of contact with the non-relocating parent.[228] The best interests of the child shall be *a* primary consideration and the focus of the proceedings (Principles 2 and 8). This was a conscious choice of wording by the drafters and implies that the child's interests are leading, but not exclusively decisive.[229] It is worth noting that Article 3 of the Washington Declaration discusses the child's best interests standard as *the* paramount consideration, but in light of the broader list of factors to consider that remain largely similar under both instruments, this difference seems to be only semantic. Principle 6 of the Recommendation emphasises the right of the parents to bring any unresolved dispute on child relocation to a competent authority for decision, and the authorities should ensure that all relevant factors are taken into consideration, giving such weight to each factor as is appropriate in the circumstances of the individual case.

The Explanatory Memorandum to the Recommendation explicitly builds upon factors encompassed by the Washington Declaration[230] and Principle 3:21 of the CEFL Principles,[231] providing the broadest, yet not exhaustive, list of factors so far.[232] Without any presumptions in favour of or against relocation (Principle 9),[233] national authorities shall take into account, where relevant, the following factors:

1) the right of the child to maintain personal relationships and direct contact with the non-relocating parent;
2) the views of the child;

227 Recommendation CM/Rec(2015)4, above n. 119.

228 See the Explanatory Memorandum to the Recommendation CM/Rec(2015)4, above n. 119, paras. 10, 21–24.

229 L.M. Coenraad, 'A European Approach to Child Relocation Issues' (2015) 4 *International Family Law* 312, 316.

230 The Washington Declaration provides for a largely convergent list of factors, except for the last two.

231 See the CEFL Principle 3:21(3), above n. 220, which refers to factors such as: the age and opinion of the child; the right of the child to maintain personal relationships with the other parent; the ability and willingness of the parents to co-operate with each other; the personal situation of the parents; geographical distance and accessibility; and the free movement of persons.

232 Explanatory Memorandum to the Recommendation CM/Rec(2015)4, above n. 119, paras. 69–73.

233 See also the Washington Declaration, Article 3.

3) the proposals for practical arrangements (accommodation, employment, education, etc.) for and after the move;
4) the reasons for seeking or opposing child relocation;
5) any history of family violence or abuse;
6) the history of the family and particularly the continuity and quality of past and current care arrangements;
7) pre-existing arrangements on the child's residence and contact, including previous decisions of competent authorities;
8) the impact of the grant or refusal of the application for relocation on the child, in the whole context of the child's family and social life, and the non-relocating parent;
9) the nature of the relationship between the parents, in particular the commitment of the relocating parent to support the relationship between the child and the non-relocating parent;
10) whether the proposals for contact are realistic, having regard to their cost and burden on the child;
11) the enforceability of contact provisions in the destination state;
12) the issues of mobility for family members;
13) the existence of parenting (or similar) agreements, including provisions on relocation; and
14) the failure to inform the other parent or other holder of parental responsibilities of the proposal to relocate with the child.

The factors to be considered are, therefore, of various natures, and not all of them are directly child-centred. In particular, all existing instruments make a reference to freedom of movement or mobility issues as a relevant factor, which seems to reflect the impressions voiced in the literature that relocation disputes cannot ignore a broader familial context of the cases.

While the supranational initiatives were motivated by a need to provide more coherence in the resolution of relocation disputes across Europe and the globe, their ability to accomplish this goal has been met with some scepticism. On the one hand, the Washington Declaration was welcomed by many as 'a first step towards finding common principles which different countries might apply to relocation application'.[234] All the instruments surely draw attention to various issues that might be at stake in child relocation disputes and might not be equally recognised by all jurisdictions, in particular those that do not approach child relocation as a distinct legal problem. On the other, this diversity of national approaches, despite the shared reliance on the child's best interests principle, led some authors to the conclusion that a binding international instrument on child relocation is not possible, and in any case would not live

234 R. George, above n. 204, 145.

up to expectations.[235] Child relocation cases are already resolved in reference to the child's best interests principle, the overarching principle necessarily advocated by all supranational initiatives. The open-ended nature of the principle is what leads to diverse outcomes. As different jurisdictions can simply continue to ascribe different weight to different factors under the principle, some authors consider it unlikely that the international developments will change much in national approaches.[236] This impression might be reinforced by the fact that the European Court of Human Rights has made no references to the Recommendation (the Council of Europe's own instrument) in any of the relocation cases that reached the Court. The Washington Declaration was mentioned in one of the Court's decision as relevant international law, but does not seem to have played any particular role in the Court's argumentation.[237] The recent Evaluation of Recommendation CM/Rec(2015)4 also suggests that the Recommendation's impact on national law has been rather low, explaining this with reference to the insufficient dissemination of its principles and the fact that child relocation is often not perceived as a specific issue separate from other parental responsibility disputes.[238] Additionally, it was suggested that national lawmakers might perceive the existing national law as sufficient in light of the Recommendation's principles and non-binding nature.[239] This opens questions of whether the legal apparatus of the EU could bring more uniformity to child relocation laws across Member States, beyond what has been observed so far.

2.4. CROSS-BORDER CHILD RELOCATION IN THE EU

At the EU level, there are no specific legal provisions on cross-border child relocations sensu stricto, although the existing EU family law instruments address many issues related to the consequences of such moves (e.g. recognition and enforcement of judgments in parental matters).[240] There have, so far, been no proposals in this area of law. However, the need for research on the EU constitutional framework of relocation has been recognised in light of the divergence of approaches to child relocation, the international developments,

235 ibid. 145–150; see also C. Cotta, above n. 37, pp. 28–37. For rather cautious opinions in states' questionnaires sent and received by the Hague Conference of Private International Law, see Permanent Bureau, 'Preliminary Document No 11', above n. 199, paras. 20–22.

236 R. George, above n. 204, 148.

237 *J.A.T. and J.B.T. v United Kingdom* (dec) [2012] ECtHR, app. no. 41767/11. The case will be discussed in Chapter 4, below Section 4.3.1. See also O. Ceran, above n. 219, for a critical analysis of the ECtHR's use of the available soft law on child relocation.

238 C. González Beilfuss, above n. 9, paras. 18–19, 26–27.

239 ibid., para. 26.

240 See the Brussels II*ter* Regulation and the discussion in Chapters 5 and 6.

and freedom of movement as a possible element of the conceptualisation of child relocation disputes.[241] The existing contributions discuss the topic either in the context of potential legislative harmonisation[242] or the influence that EU freedom of movement provisions and the judicial activity of the CJEU could have on national family laws.[243] Additionally, while doctrinal analysis must be the starting point of any legal research on child relocation in the EU context, empirical legal research also provides interesting insights on the relationship between national and European law, pointing towards non-doctrinal questions about European influences on child relocation.

2.4.1. CHILD RELOCATION AND EU LAW

Several perspectives on the intersections between child relocation law and EU law have been discussed in the literature. Given the diversity of approaches and the mobility dimension of relocation, Yildiz Maria Bérénos called for harmonisation of child relocation law on the EU level.[244] However, the EU competence for harmonisation has not been discussed and, as suggested by other contributions, might be disputed.[245] In reference to the global quest for uniformity, it was also suggested that differences in the interpretation of the best interests standard might be mitigated if a superior court could control national interpretations, with an explicit reference to the CJEU.[246] However, this scenario was taken as purely hypothetical given the limited competence of the EU in family law.[247] As shall be explored in Chapter 3, the question of competence is not that straightforward and a lack of it does not exclude the judicial intervention of the CJEU. Other authors indeed noted that it is freedom of movement, rather than family law competence, that potentially brings child relocation under the scrutiny of EU law and its guardian, the CJEU.[248] Perhaps unsurprisingly, given that child relocation has generally received much more attention in common law jurisdictions,[249] this observation was first made in

241 K. Boele-Woelki, B. Braat, I. Curry-Sumner, C.J. de Boer, P. Lokin, M. Vonk, N. de Vries and W. Schrama, above n. 4, 281–82.

242 Y.M. Bérénos, above n. 12.

243 T. Scott, above n. 12; R. Lamont, above n. 12; C. Cotta, above n. 37; See also R. George, above n. 11, pp. 141–42.

244 Y.M. Bérénos, above n. 12, 2 and 21.

245 R. Lamont, above n. 12, 242; C. Cotta, above n. 37, p. 30.

246 C. Cotta, above n. 37, p. 30.

247 ibid.

248 R. Lamont, above n. 12; T. Scott, above n. 12; C. Cotta, above n. 37, p. 30.

249 For this observation see also Y.M. Bérénos, above n. 12, 21. There is an abundance of academic literature on child relocation in common law countries, and only a few articles in European civil law countries.

reference to law in England and Wales that explicitly requires the relocating parent to obtain permission for cross-border child relocation, while no such permission is needed for internal relocations.[250]

Under the Treaty of Rome, Timothy Scott argues that there is a prima facie conflict between the English international child relocation provisions and EU freedom of movement.[251] In his view, English law interferes with a worker's right to be joined by his or her family, reflecting the predominantly economic character of the EU law provisions at that time. Scott suggests that a worker wishing to relocate usually needs to accept the offer of employment promptly, and therefore is put at a disadvantage by the requirement to obtain a court's permission to do so.[252] Courts should disapply the national provisions and rather opt for an approach equivalent to the one adopted for internal relocation, where it is the non-relocating parent who needs to seek an order prohibiting the relocating parent from doing so, as a more proportionate solution.[253] While this analysis reflects the past legal framework of freedom of movement, it raises points that remain relevant.

In light of this, it is worth noting that Ruth Lamont, another author writing on English child relocation law in the EU context, reaches a significantly different conclusion years later.[254] Reflecting the changing nature of EU law, she observes that national child relocation law may be influenced by the legal framework of free movement and EU citizenship.[255] In her opinion, it is not clear whether a decision restricting relocation will always be seen as a restriction of freedom of movement, but even if it is, it should be seen as a justified and proportionate one as it seeks to protect the best interests of a child.[256] Lamont does not conduct any detailed proportionality analysis, noting that 'the relationship between the justification and free movement is opaque and unlikely to be analysed closely by the court', but rather cautions against European law eroding national concepts of domestic family law.[257]

The EU law's erosive effect seems to be recognised also by Helen Stalford analysing the relationship between the development of EU citizenship law

---

250 In simplified terms, internal relocations are not subject to statutory restrictions and, as such, are not generally prohibited. While the moves might raise other issues, e.g. in relation to contact, it is often the non-relocating parent that needs to apply to the court to stop the relocating parent's move. For a more detailed discussion see Chapter 7.

251 T. Scott, above n. 12, p. 18.

252 ibid.

253 ibid., p. 17.

254 R. Lamont, above n. 12. See also R. George, above n. 11, p. 142 agreeing with R. Lamont that 'EU law raises a potential complication' in the child relocation context.

255 R. Lamont, above n. 12, 242.

256 ibid.

257 ibid., 242–43.

and cross-border family law.[258] Stalford's analysis does not focus on child relocation, but she observes that developments in these two areas have 'paved the way for the legitimate curtailment of domestic policies which have merely a prospective rather than an actual impact on the exercise of right by the EU citizens', with child relocation used as an example.[259] She therefore suggests that the fundamental status of EU citizenship and the alignment between free movement and human rights may mean that refusals to relocate could be more easily challenged, with only the most persuasive fundamental rights arguments accepted as justifiable derogations.[260] As relocation is not the focus of this contribution, Stalford does not elaborate on the nature and scope of such a challenge to national law.

Scott, Lamont, and Stalford emphasise different aspects of the discussion on child relocation in the EU context. Scott locates the restriction on freedom of movement in the rights of the worker, which include the right to relocate with one's family.[261] The restriction is posed by the mere existence of relocation law requiring the other parent's or a court's consent.[262] He does not give any space to fundamental rights in his analysis, most strikingly not even the rights of the child, and – as he himself notes – his suggestions are not easily squared with the systemic place of child relocation laws in the international child abduction system.[263] Ruth Lamont's contribution, on the other hand, provides a comprehensive overview of the relevant EU legal framework for child relocation. She constructs the issue under investigation differently, analysing decisions refusing relocation as a restriction on the child's movement, but that might also restrict movement of the primary carer who is unlikely to consider migration without the child.[264] She also suggests that refusals of relocation might be indirectly discriminatory based on nationality, but does not further investigate this problem.[265] More importantly, while both Lamont and Stalford raise the issue of justification and proportionality as determinative for the analysis and for the nature and scope of the EU's influence on child relocation, this stage of analysis remains unexplored. Chapters 4 and 5 will take up these discussions in an attempt to clarify the remaining questions about the relationship of national child relocation laws and EU law. However, while doctrinal analysis of this relationship is the starting point of any legal research on child relocation in the EU context, it is worth observing that literature points also towards other

258 H. Stalford, above n. 17, pp. 240–41.
259 ibid.
260 ibid., p. 241.
261 T. Scott, above n. 12, p. 11.
262 ibid., p. 12.
263 ibid., p. 18.
264 R. Lamont, above n. 12, 240.
265 ibid., 241.

dimensions of this relationship, potentially calling for more complex analytical approaches.

2.4.2. CHILD RELOCATION AND EMPIRICAL LEGAL RESEARCH: WHAT PLACE FOR THE EU?

The existing literature on child relocation in general, and on child relocation in the EU context in particular, is predominantly doctrinal in approach. Doctrinal research is necessarily a starting point for any legal analysis but, given the difficulties in application of the best interest of the child standard, has some limitations. This is why the literature in common law countries has, for years now, discussed child relocation also from empirical perspectives, both quantitative and qualitative.[266] The quantitative research looks predominantly into outcomes (success rates) of child relocation cases, and the main variables and patterns that can be identified in such cases (e.g. the relationship between the child's age or the destination country and the chances of success).[267] The existing qualitative research focuses either on the legal actors and their perception of relocation law and dispute resolution,[268] or the experiences of parents and children involved in the disputes.[269] While there is no empirical research on child relocation in the European context specifically, the existing literature provides some thought-provoking material also for those interested in such investigations.

Quantitative research conducted in the UK suggests that moves within the EU might be allowed more often than elsewhere.[270] The reasons for this are

266 For a more detailed discussion of this literature see R. George, above n. 11, pp. 20–23; R. Taylor, M. Gollop and M. Henaghan, 'Relocation Following Parental Separation: The Welfare & Best Interests of Children' (2010) Centre for Research on Children and Families and Faculty of Law, University of Otago, Dunedin (New Zealand), pp. 21–39 <http://www.communityresearch.org.nz/research/relocation-following-parental-separation-the-welfare-best-interests-of-children/>.

267 e.g. R. George, above n. 117; R. George, 'Relocation Disputes in England and Wales: First Findings from the 2012 Study' Oxford Legal Studies Research Paper No. 91/2013 (2013) <https://papers.ssrn.com/sol3/papers.cfm?abstract_id=2306097>; N. Bala, A. Wheeler, J. Paetsch; L. Bertrand, 'Canadian Relocation Cases: Heading Towards Guidelines, 2011' (2013) <https://hdl.handle.net/10864/10333>.

268 e.g. R. George, above n. 11, also citing F. Mackenzie, 'Uneasy Trends in Relocation Law' (2009) unpublished LLM Thesis, Victoria University of Wellington, pp. 69–92.

269 e.g. R. George, A. Gallwey and K. Bader, 'How Do Parents Experience Relocation Disputes in the Family Courts?' (2016) 38 *Journal of Social Welfare and Family Law* 394; R. Taylor, M. Gollop and M. Henaghan, above n. 266, pp. 84–143; M. Freeman, above n. 180; P. Parkinson, J. Cashmore and J. Single, above n. 177; P. Parkinson, J. Cashmore and J. Single, 'The Need for Reality Testing in Relocation Cases' (2010) 44 *Family Law Quarterly* 1.

270 R. George, above n. 117, 386. However, it is worth noting that in this research design there were major differences in the success rate observed in the quantitative and the qualitative samples. The author concludes that the qualitative sample contained less typical cases and, as such, does not invalidate the general conclusion.

hypothesised to be primarily related to the shorter geographical distances of intra-European relocations. At the same time, while perhaps mitigated if the applicant is moving home, language and cultural differences between the UK and the destination country may be less of an issue with long-distance moves to another Commonwealth country.[271] This empirical observation raises interesting questions about explanations alternative to geographical proximity of the trends observed in the success rates of intra-EU relocation applications. The most natural one refers to the discussion above on the influence of European law. Rob George, an author of multiple studies on child relocation in England and Wales, finds it surprising that EU law has not yet been meaningfully argued before the courts, although its potential relevance was noted in one of the leading English cases on child relocation.[272] Whether or not the EU law provisions on free movement are an indicator of the qualitatively different nature of intra-EU relocations remains an open question.

The question about other possible ways of conceptualising the differences between intra-EU relocations and other relocations emerges from qualitative research on mobile families in Europe. Qualitative research conducted in a British-Italian context suggests that mothers often view a refusal to relocate back to their homelands as an exile and a limitation to their right to move freely within the EU.[273] The fact that refusals of relocation are perceived as a limitation of rights has been confirmed by qualitative research also in non-EU contexts,[274] but it is worth noting that in the European study it becomes coupled with the EU legal layer in that it is claimed that 'European migrant citizens have a different sense of belonging and are subject to a different set of legal rules'.[275] While this literature is interested primarily in the impact of the multilayered legal system on the experiences of mobile family members, it recognises the fact that laws play a role in how this (mobility) experience is lived.[276] If the child's best interests principle calls for contextual assessments, one can pose questions about how child relocation law accounts for the experiences of mobile families generated by EU law. If it can be conceptualised as normativising the perceived 'normal' or 'viable', even if 'normality' is not universal,[277] one can wonder if

---

271 ibid.

272 R. George, above n. 11, p. 141. For a detailed discussion on how EU law has been used and referred to in child relocation cases decided by national courts see Chapter 6.

273 S. Morano-Foadi, 'Problems and Challenges in Researching Bi-National Migrant Families Within the European Union' (2007) 21 *International Journal of Law, Policy and the Family* 1, 17.

274 R. Taylor, M. Gollop and M. Henaghan, above n. 266, p. 95.

275 S. Morano-Foadi, above n. 273, p. 17.

276 ibid. See also L. Ackers and H. Stalford, *A Community for Children? Children, Citizenship and Internal Migration in the EU*, Ashgate Publishing, Hampshire 2004; L. Ackers and H. Stalford, 'Children, Migration and Citizenship in the European Union: Intra-Community Mobility and the Status of Children in EC Law' (1999) 21 *Children and Youth Services Review* 987.

277 J. Schiratzki, above n. 154, 11.

the European discourses normalising mobility might reflect on the ideas of normalised parenthood or normalised childhood.[278] The doctrinal approach is seen here as insufficient to address the demands of such investigations that require more complex conceptual frameworks, combining legal, sociological and comparative approaches.[279] Child relocation cases provide an interesting case for investigation of these dynamics, as they are the only area of family law substantively and explicitly concerned with cross-border mobility, the building paradigm of the European Union. While this book cannot take up all the empirical questions that can be raised in the child relocation context, it incorporates the existing empirical insights into its constructively oriented investigations.

2.5. CONCLUDING REMARKS

Throughout, the book shall return to many of the considerations introduced in this chapter. The purpose of this discussion is, therefore, to emphasise the substantive and methodological aspects of the debates surrounding child relocation that constitute important reference points for the analysis of EU law. Mobility rights are one of the recurring themes in child relocation and the *raison d'être* of the European Union, but the EU is also bound by Article 24 of the CFR that protects children's rights and requires the child's best interests to be a primary consideration in all actions relating to children. The open-ended character of the child's best interests principle, its contextual and individualised assessment, and the struggle to account for parental interests in resolving child relocation disputes are therefore relevant also to the EU legal context. The different approaches to child relocation, rooted in the wide scope of possible interpretations of the child's best interests and in varying constructions of national laws, reflect broader differences between national family laws and their takes on parental autonomy. While these different approaches might be problematic from the point of EU law concerned with equal access to free movement rights, more uniformity in child relocation has not been easy to reach. This might be partly due to national scepticism – raising questions about harmonisation prospects on the EU level – but is largely a consequence of the nature of the disputes. The EU legal setup is admittedly unique, with the CJEU providing interpretations of EU law *de facto* binding all Member States, sometimes also in reference to soft law measures. However, the EU competence is potentially limited and so is the institutional role of its Court that cannot conduct individualised assessments of the best interests of the child. In that, the difficulties that are inherently

---

[278] For a discussion of a 'normalized parenthood' in child contact disputes see M.H. Ottosen, above n. 159.

[279] S. Morano-Foadi, above n. 273, 17–18.

embedded in child relocation debates might coincide with certain limits to the type of pressures that EU law can exert on national law. However, given the sentiments observed in the empirical research, EU law might still play a role in how child relocation cases are experienced or conceptualised, prompting inquiries into its broader effects. The following chapters will therefore return to many of the considerations of this chapter, to embed them in the analysis of EU law and draw conclusions about the nature and limits of its influence on national child relocation laws.

CHAPTER 3

EU LEGAL COMPETENCE AND HARMONISATION PROSPECTS

3.1. INTRODUCTION

Family law has always been a highly sensitive area. On the one hand, it is traditionally considered to be closely related to national identity and cultural values, subject to the so-called 'cultural constraints argument'.[280] This argument about the unique cultural character of family law provisions has often been raised as an objection against its harmonisation and has been, in principle, recognised also by EU institutions.[281] On the other hand, European family laws are said to belong to a pan-European culture that, while subject to national variations, makes family law designs rather contingent on political forces that are relatively 'fluid', leaving the question of harmonisation of family laws open.[282] Notwithstanding whether the 'cultural constraints argument' is empirically true, it causes great controversies regarding the EU intervention in family matters. These controversies are multiplied by the alleged integrationist agendas behind the EU actions, the sometimes-questioned value of the existence of separate EU regimes (along those of global reach), and the potentially far-reaching consequences of such interventions for national autonomy.[283] Critics of EU intervention in family law have always feared that this activity – formally limited to matters with cross-border implications – will

280 For a brief overview of the debate and an argument to the opposite, see M. Antokolskaia, 'Family Law and National Culture: Arguing against the Cultural Constraints Argument' (2008) 4 *Utrecht Law Review* 25.

281 European Council, 'Report on the need to approximate member states' legislation in civil matters of 16th November 2001', 13017/01 justciv 129, para. 3, recognising that family law is 'very heavily influenced by the culture and traditions of national (or even regional) legal systems, which could create a number of difficulties in the context of harmonisation'.

282 M. Antokolskaia, above n. 280, 34.

283 See e.g. P. McEleavy, 'The Brussels II Regulation: How the European Community has Moved into Family Law' (2002) 51 *International and Comparative Law Quarterly* 883, 890–94; P. Beaumont, 'International Family Law in Europe – the Maintenance Project, the Hague Conference and the EC: A Triumph of Reverse Subsidiarity' (2009) 73 *Rabels Zeitschrift für ausländisches und internationales Privatrecht* 509.

spill over into more and more areas of substantive family law.[284] This fear was not entirely unfounded, given the many voices from the scholarly community or EU institutions arguing that substantive harmonisation is not excluded, constituting both a natural follow-up and a necessary step to truly remove all the barriers to the free movement of persons.[285] Accordingly, harmonisation of family law matters has never been straightforward, with multiple doubts regarding its feasibility and desirability voiced in different contexts over the years.

Despite the controversies, numerous instruments on various family law matters with cross-border implications have been introduced on the EU level.[286] EU legislation covers rules governing the jurisdiction, recognition, and enforcement of matrimonial and parental responsibility orders,[287] orders relating to maintenance obligations,[288] and – based on the enhanced co-operation between smaller groups of Member States – law applicable to divorce and legal separation[289] as well as rules on property regimes in matters of marriage and registered partnerships.[290] Most recently, the Commission

---

284 M.N. Shúilleabháin, above n. 46, 1026–27.

285 For a summary of these discussions, see ibid., referring in particular to the Communication from the European Commission, 'Justice, Freedom and Security in Europe since 2005: An Evaluation of the Hague Programme and Action Plan' (2009), COM(2009) 263 final, that indicated that '[m]utual recognition might also consist of approximating substantive law in certain areas' and gave the example of 'standards for decisions relating to parental responsibility'.

286 All the instruments mentioned below (nn. 287–91) take Article 81(3) of the TFEU as its legal basis, in contrast to Council Regulation (EU) 650/2012 of 4 July 2012 on jurisdiction, applicable law, recognition and enforcement of decisions and acceptance and enforcement of authentic instruments in matters of succession and in the creation of a European Certificate of Succession [2012] OJ L201/107 or the European Commission, 'Proposal for a Regulation of the European Parliament and of the Council on jurisdiction, applicable law, recognition and enforcement of measures and cooperation in matters relating to the protection of adults' (2023), COM(2023) 280 final, that are sometimes considered to belong to family law at large but are not considered family law matters under EU law.

287 Council Regulation (EU) 2019/1111 of 25 June 2019 on jurisdiction, the recognition and enforcement of decisions in matrimonial matters and the matters of parental responsibility, and on international child abduction (recast) [2019] OJ L178/1.

288 Council Regulation (EC) 4/2009 of 18 December 2008 on jurisdiction, applicable law, recognition and enforcement of decisions and co-operation in matters relating to maintenance obligations [2009] OJ L7/1. The EU also ratified the Hague Conference's Protocol of 23 November 2007 on the Law Applicable to Maintenance Obligations, and authorised its Member States to ratify, or accede to, the 1996 Hague Convention on Parental Responsibility and Protection of Children.

289 Council Regulation (EU) 1259/2010 of 20 December 2010 implementing enhanced co-operation in the area of the law applicable to divorce and legal separation [2010] OJ L343/10.

290 Council Regulation (EU) 2016/1103 of 24 June 2016 implementing enhanced co-operation in the area of jurisdiction, applicable law and the recognition and enforcement of decisions in matters of matrimonial property regimes [2016] OJ L183/1 and Council Regulation (EU) 2016/1104 of 24 June 2016 implementing enhanced co-operation in the area of jurisdiction, applicable law and the recognition and enforcement of decisions in matters of the property consequences of registered partnerships [2016] OJ L183/30.

presented a proposal touching upon recognition of parenthood.[291] Legislation on EU family law is nevertheless increasingly hard to achieve. Family law instruments require a special legislative procedure and unanimity in the Council, 'which has often led to long debate with no clear outcome, or to the enactment of legislation that is less ambitious than it might have been'.[292] The legislative history clearly confirms this: some of the most recent proposals under Article 81(3) of the TFEU – originally intended to apply to all EU Member States – were ultimately adopted via the enhanced co-operation mechanism and do not apply to all Member States.[293] Therefore, while perhaps bolder at various points in time, the EU institutions have broadly accepted that substantive family law is a national competence.[294] However, while the perception of exceptionality of family law at large persists in both the Member States[295] and EU institutions,[296] European family law is still perceived as important to remove legal borders for EU citizens exercising their right to free movement.[297] This functional orientation of EU law and the controversies around the scope of EU competence in substantive family issues are also pertinent to the discussions about child relocation.

The context introduced above is equally as legal as it is political. However, there are fundamental rules on the division and exercise of competences in

291 European Commission, 'Proposal for a Council Regulation on jurisdiction, applicable law, recognition of decisions and acceptance of authentic instruments in matters of parenthood and on the creation of a European Certificate of Parenthood' (2022), COM(2022) 695 final.

292 European Commission, 'Communication from the Commission to the European Parliament and the Council: An area of freedom, security and justice serving the citizen' (2009), COM(2009) 262 final, para. 3.

293 See, for example, A. Wysocka-Bar, 'Enhanced Cooperation in Property Matters in the EU and Non-Participating Member States' (2019) 20 *ERA Forum* 187, discussing the origins of property regulations and the objections that ultimately led some Member States to reject those proposals. The Brussels II*ter* Regulation is, of course, an exception, but it does regulate matters that have been for years already regulated by the EU, and, in that sense, does not subject new areas to EU regulation.

294 See the most recent European Commission, 'Communication from the Commission to the European Parliament, the Council, the European Economic and Social Committee and the Committee of the Regions: EU strategy on the rights of the child' (2021), COM(2021) 142 final, p. 13.

295 See the so-called 'Lisbon Treaty judgment' of the German Federal Constitutional Court where the Court held that the EU Treaty must leave sufficient space to Member States for the political formation of the economic, cultural, and social living conditions, including matters shaping the circumstances of family life, and hence family law: *BVerfG, Urteil vom 30.06.2009* – 2 BvE 2/08. Family law was also explicitly mentioned in the TFEU in the Declaration by the Republic of Poland on the Charter of Fundamental Rights of the European Union [2016] OJ C202/358, proclaiming that the Charter does not affect in any way the right of Member States to legislate in this area of law.

296 See, e.g. the recent European Parliament Resolution of 5 April 2022 on the Protection of the Rights of the Child in Civil, Administrative and Family Law Proceedings [2022] OJ C434/11, Point O and the comments below.

297 A. Fiorini, 'Which Legal Basis for Family Law? The Way Forward' (2012) European Parliament Publications Office, p. 11 <https://data.europa.eu/doi/10.2861/42262>.

the EU included in the EU Treaties. Article 5(2) of the TEU stipulates that 'the Union shall act only within the limits of the competences conferred upon it by the Member States in the Treaties to attain the objectives set out therein'. Under the current legal framework, only one Treaty provision deals with family law. Article 81(3) of the TFEU gives the Union the competence to propose measures concerning family law with cross-border implications, with a special legislative procedure – requiring unanimity in the Council – foreseen for such measures. Despite some of the discussions held in the past, most experts agree, therefore, that the EU has no competence over substantive family issues in light of the core EU principle of conferral (Articles 3–4 of the TFEU *a contrario*). There are simply no Treaty provisions transferring competence in the sphere of substantive family law to the EU. Prima facie, the EU is limited to the regulation of judicial co-operation in family matters having cross-border implications as part of the area of freedom, security and justice (Article 81 of the TFEU) as a competence shared with Member States (Article 4(2)(j) of the TFEU).[298] However, the exact scope of this competence is also far from clear. The lack of agreement over how 'cross-border implications' should be interpreted is of primary importance for discussions on child relocation, considered to be one of the core issues of substantive family law. On the one hand, EU competence in child relocation is often (even if implicitly) refused,[299] as is the possibility to legislate on the matter.[300] On the other, suggestions have been made that an expansive interpretation of 'cross-border implications' under Article 81 of the TFEU could encompass (at least some) child relocation matters,[301] allowing for (at least partial) harmonisation of child relocation measures on the EU level. The EU's competence in the field requires, therefore, closer scrutiny, determining not only prospects of legislative harmonisation and its scope, but also the limits of any potential judicial intervention of the CJEU.

3.2. EU COMPETENCE AND THE LEGISLATIVE HARMONISATION OF CHILD RELOCATION

The EU competence in family matters remains controversial, and this is also the case for child relocation. However, in light of its cross-border free movement dimension, it is not surprising that calls for harmonisation of child relocation

298 For a concise overview, see D. Martiny, 'European Family Law' in J. Basedow, K.J. Hopt, R. Zimmermann and A. Stier (eds), *The Max Planck Encyclopedia of European Private Law*, Oxford University Press, Oxford 2012, pp. 595–600.

299 Implicitly R. Lamont, above n. 12, 242; explicitly C. Cotta, above n. 37, p. 30.

300 K. Boele-Woelki, 'A European Model for Harmonizing the Law on Parental Responsibilities: The Family Law Perspective' in L. Bernardi and D. Mortelmans (eds), *Shared Physical Custody: Interdisciplinary Insights in Child Custody Arrangements*, Springer Nature, Cham 2021, p. 63.

301 K. Boele-Woelki, above n. 223, 162.

measures have been made. Yildiz Maria Bérénos argues that the European Union is 'lagging behind' the global discussion, in light of both the international initiatives on child relocation and its own legislative initiatives in other areas of family law.[302] As the uniformity of approach is lacking while EU mobility increases, this might lead to inequality across the Union and insufficient protection of individual rights.[303] This state of affairs requires the development of a harmonised relocation law to meet the European Union's objective to provide for an area of freedom, security and justice, in which free movement of persons is ensured, and which would bring more legal certainty to relocating EU citizens.[304] She suggests that the first step in the harmonisation process could be a European non-binding instrument,[305] but does not elaborate on the competence of the European Union nor the potential content or form of such an instrument. An examination of the legislative competence in the field is therefore timely. As already noted, Article 81(3) of the TFEU, referring to the regulation of judicial co-operation in family matters having cross-border implications as part of the area of freedom, security and justice, constitutes the traditional legal basis for EU family law instruments.[306] However, the divergent views on the existence of EU competence in child relocation measures require a closer analysis of the substantive conditions for making use of Article 81 of the TFEU. Additionally, the Treaty includes also other provisions that could allow for the adoption of harmonisation measures. Two of these additional legal bases were raised previously in the family law literature (Articles 21(2)[307] and 352 of the TFEU),[308] albeit not in the relocation context. Their use as a legislative basis for a child relocation action should therefore also be explored.

3.2.1. HARMONISATION OF CHILD RELOCATION LAWS UNDER ARTICLE 81(3) OF THE TFEU

Article 81 of the TFEU is the cornerstone of the Union's legislative activity on judicial co-operation in civil matters, including those touching upon family law. Article 81(1) of the TFEU provides for a competence in judicial co-operation in civil matters (at large) that should be based on the principle of mutual

302 Y.M. Bérénos, above n. 12, 1–2.
303 ibid., 1–2, 20–21.
304 ibid., 2.
305 ibid., 21.
306 Family law should be understood autonomously under the EU legal framework, but child relocation would certainly fall into this category as directly concerned with parental rights and responsibilities.
307 U. Magnus and P. Mankowski, 'Introduction' in U. Magnus and P. Mankowski (eds), *European Commentaries on Private International Law: Brussels IIbis Regulation*, Otto Schmidt/De Gruyter, Berlin/Boston 2012, p. 16.
308 A. Fiorini, above n. 297, p. 18.

recognition of judgments and decisions. Such co-operation may also include the adoption of measures for approximation of the laws and regulations of the Member States, which essentially – as a far more intensive measure[309] – constitutes a harmonisation competence. Article 81 of the TFEU requires a measure to refer to: (a) judicial co-operation; and (b) in cases with cross-border implications.[310] The catalogue of judicial co-operation aims is exhaustively listed in Article 81(2)[311] and does not include substantive law. Further, Article 81(3) stipulates specifically that measures concerning family law with cross-border implications shall be established by the Council in accordance with a special legislative procedure. The key questions, then, seem to be whether child relocation cases can be said to have cross-border implications for the purposes of Article 81 and, if yes, what is the relationship between the exhaustive list included in Article 81(2) and Article 81(3)?

While the CJEU has elaborated on the cross-border dimension of many cases that it has had to face,[312] it is not clear how 'cross-border implications' should be understood in this legislative context.[313] Indeed, this phrasing has become 'the focal point of the struggle between the EU institutions regarding the potential incursion of the EU into national procedural autonomy' regarding the question of whether the interpretation of 'matters having cross-border implications' should be restrictive or expansive.[314] In particular, a broad interpretation would include, for example, two parties domiciled in the same jurisdiction where there is a potential future cross-border effect, such as subsequent enforcement of a judgment in another jurisdiction. Disputes about child relocations, although oriented at a future cross-border situation, remain, in most cases, contained to one jurisdiction and could hence be considered domestic.[315] Decisions taken in this context determine, however, whether a

---

309 M. Kotzur, 'Article 81 TFEU' in R. Geiger, D.-E. Khan and M. Kotzur, *European Union Treaties: A Commentary: Treaty on European Union, Treaty on the Functioning of the European Union, Charter of Fundamental Rights of the European Union*, C.H. Beck/Hart Publishing, Munich/Oxford 2015, p. 439.

310 Article 81(2) of the TFEU allows the EU to enact such measures 'particularly when necessary for the proper functioning of the internal market', replacing the more restrictive wording of ex-Article 65 EC ('in so far as is necessary'). M Kotzur, above n. 309, notes that the requirement of necessity in family matters 'was somewhat artificial anyway and made the market relevance appear rather arbitrary'.

311 M. Kotzur, above n. 309, p. 439.

312 See Chapter 4.

313 K. Boele-Woelki, above n. 223, 162.

314 E. Storskrubb, 'EU Civil Justice at the Harmonisation Crossroads?' in A. Nylund and M. Strandberg (eds), *Civil Procedure and Harmonisation of Law: The Dynamics of EU and International Treaties*, Intersentia, Cambridge 2019, p. 16.

315 It cannot be excluded that a relocation dispute emerges in a situation that already has a cross-border character, for example when parents live in two different Member States but one of them applies for a relocation to yet another Member State that is further away. This does not, however, render child relocation a cross-border legal issue in abstracto.

situation will 'acquire' a cross-border dimension or not,[316] and as such, these cases would also fall under the broad interpretation of this provision. This would provide for the European Union's competence in the matter and justify a potential intervention in this area of the law, despite its prima facie domestic character.

However, even if such a broader interpretation is accepted, the competence would be limited by the catalogue of aims listed in Article 81(2) of the TFEU. While Article 81(3) establishes a competence to legislate measures concerning family law with cross-border implications, without any further qualifying features, the article needs to be interpreted in its systemic context. Firstly, it can be disputed that the wording of Article 81(3) – 'notwithstanding paragraph 2' – nullifies the requirement that measures enacted under this Article must be aimed at one of the objectives listed in the exhaustive catalogue of Article 81(2), or that they must be measures of judicial co-operation in the first place (Article 81(1)). Indeed, the legislative power for measures concerning family law seems to be conferred by paragraph 2 in conjunction with paragraph 3, and not exclusively by paragraph 3.[317] Secondly, the systemic location of Article 81 in Chapter 3 on Judicial Co-operation in Civil Matters reinforces this argument and suggests that measures concerning family law with cross-border implications must be measures of judicial co-operation, as listed in paragraph 2.[318] Therefore, the competence would be constrained by the catalogue listed in Article 81(2). This might prove quite limiting to any harmonisation efforts in the field of child relocation. Rules on jurisdiction, mutual recognition, and enforcement of decisions in matters of parental responsibility, applicable also to decisions in child relocation cases, already exist on the EU level (in the Brussels II*ter* Regulation). However, child relocation could, in principle, benefit from further efforts concerned with effective access to justice, compatibility of the rules on civil procedure, or support for the training of the judiciary (Article 81(2)(e)(h)). Such judicial co-operation could encompass predominantly *procedural* aspects of child relocation, as harmonisation of *substantive* child relocation law does not fall under any of the aims listed in the catalogue. However, as shall be discussed in more detail below, the distinction between substantive and procedural aspects of child relocation is not clear-cut[319] and might create further obstacles to

316 See also K. Boele-Woelki, above n. 223, 162, arguing along similar lines that 'each internal relationship which is only connected to one national jurisdiction can – hypothetically – become a cross-border relationship'.

317 M. Kotzur, above n. 309, p. 440.

318 ibid. See also N.A. Baarsma, above n. 46, p. 113 arguing that European law, like private international law, requires '*éléments d'extranéité*' to come into play and, as such, the EU can only enact legislation on private international law aspects of family law.

319 Child relocation is best approached holistically, as reflected also in the Explanatory Memorandum to the Recommendation CM/Rec(2015)4, above n. 119, para. 8.

harmonisation of child relocation laws. In light of the ordinary meaning of these terms, substantive aspects of child relocation can be taken to include norms determining *when* a parent is required to obtain permission to relocate or *what kind of factors* a court must need to consider while determining the child's best interests in a relocation case. Procedural aspects, on the other hand, are those that determine *how* or *according to what procedural rules* the parent is to obtain permission to relocate. Before analysing the exact nature and consequences of this distinction, it is worth exploring whether there is any other legal basis in the Treaty that would justify a broader EU competence than that introduced in Article 81(3) of the TFEU.

3.2.2. ALTERNATIVE LEGAL BASES FOR HARMONISATION

Some authors suggest that Article 81(3) of the TFEU 'clearly and eventually closed the case [of alternative legislative basis] for political and practical purposes'.[320] This is because the Treaty drafters decided to unequivocally address family matters in this Treaty provision and in this specific context.[321] However, two alternative legislative bases have also been suggested in the literature – Articles 21(2)[322] and 352 of the TFEU[323] – and they will be briefly considered.[324] Article 21(1) of the TFEU provides that every citizen of the Union shall have the right to move and reside freely within the territory of the Member States, subject to the limitations and conditions laid down in the Treaties and by the measures adopted to give them effect. Article 21(2) equips the European Parliament and the Council with the competence to adopt provisions to facilitate that right if the Union's action proves necessary and the Treaties do not provide the necessary powers. Thus, Article 21 does not require a citizen to exercise any cross-border activity, and the competence stemming from this article relates to the facilitation of the right to move and reside freely in the EU directly (thus in many conceptualisations, one of the core issues at stake in relocation cases). Further, Article 352 allows the EU to

320 U. Magnus and P. Mankowski, above n. 307, p. 16.
321 ibid.
322 ibid.
323 A. Fiorini, above n. 297, p. 18.
324 One could also investigate Article 115 of the TFEU as a potential basis for harmonisation of cross-border child relocation measures. This provision allows for approximation of such laws that directly affect the functioning of the internal market. It requires unanimity in the Council (similarly to Article 81(3) of the TFEU) but is confined to the adoption of Directives. However, the provision has been rarely used and has never been mentioned in the context of family law measures. The direct link between child relocation and the functioning of the internal market cannot be taken for granted. The provision will, therefore, not be analysed in detail, but many of the arguments on the feasibility and content of the measures discussed in this chapter would remain relevant.

adopt an act necessary to attain the objectives laid down by the Treaties when the latter have not provided the powers of action necessary to attain them. Such an action must be necessary, in the context of the policies defined by the Treaties, to attain not just any objective (e.g. the general aim of promoting the wellbeing of EU citizens), but those identified under Article 3(2), (3), and (5) of the TEU.[325] As such, the Union's objective is inter alia to offer its citizens an area of freedom, security and justice without internal frontiers, and to promote gender equality and protection of the rights of a child. Prima facie, both provisions could provide a legal basis for EU intervention in child relocation.

However, the drafters of the Treaty themselves recognised that any legislative activity based on Article 352 must respect the conferral principle and the division of the competences, and, as such, must be of a subsidiary character,[326] and the same might be presumed for Article 21. This is additionally supported by the systemic interpretation in the context of Articles 21 and 81 of the TFEU; it is hard to imagine that special legislative procedure is envisaged for family matters limited merely to judicial co-operation, but ordinary procedure would be acceptable for far more intrusive substantive matters.[327] The lack of a broad legislative EU competence, one encompassing also substantive elements of child relocation law, is therefore the only systematically justified conclusion insofar as EU law is an institutional system based on the principle of conferred powers. Any other interpretation would lead to a significant change in that system without following the procedure that the Treaties provide for that purpose. The following analysis will therefore focus on the scope of EU's competence within the limits of Article 81(3) of the TFEU.

3.2.3. WHAT KIND OF HARMONISATION?

Harmonisation in EU law can have many faces, both regarding its scope and intensity.[328] Regarding its scope, harmonisation can be exhaustive

---

325 Declarations Annexed to the Final Act of the Intergovernmental Conference which adopted the Treaty of Lisbon, Signed on 13 December 2007 [2012] OJ C326/337, Declaration 41.

326 ibid., Declaration 42. See also J. Bast and K. Wetz, 'Chapter 3: System of Competences' in P.J. Kuijper, F. Amtenbrink, D. Curtin, B. De Witte, A. McDonnell and S. Van den Bogaert (eds), *The Law of the European Union*, 5th ed., Kluwer Law International, The Hague 2018, p. 77, who argue that the existence of Article 352 of the TFEU, in light of the 'advanced state of constitutional development' of the Union, leads to a conclusion that implied powers based on the EU's objectives should not be justified as incompliant with the principle of conferral.

327 Compare also para. 2 (a general competence in accordance with the ordinary legislative procedure) and para. 3 (a specific competence only in social security and protection measures in accordance with the special legislative procedure) of Article 21.

328 e.g. M. Klamert, 'What We Talk About When We Talk About Harmonisation' (2015) 17 *Cambridge Yearbook of European Legal Studies* 360, 362.

(encompassing the entirety of a given area) or partial (encompassing only certain specific aspects of the area in question).[329] The discussion of the scope of any prospective harmonisation of child relocation links, therefore, back to the distinction between its procedural and substantive aspects that needs to be clarified before any consideration of the intensity of EU action, despite the two remaining closely intertwined. Under Article 81(3) of the TFEU, this chapter argued that the EU lacks competence in substantive aspects of child relocation, but such a competence could be established for some of its procedural aspects. Substantive aspects of child relocation can be taken to include norms determining *when* a parent is required to obtain permission to relocate or *what kind of factors* a court must need to take into account while determining the child's best interests in a relocation case. Procedural aspects, on the other hand, are such that determine *how* or *according to what procedural rules* the parent is to obtain permission to relocate. However, as already noted, the decision as to what aspects of child relocation laws can be described as procedural and could be subject to harmonisation is not entirely straightforward. This is because many such aspects can be argued to closely intertwine with more substantive distribution of individual rights and obligations in the familial context, one that reflects deeper cultural or political convictions and remains outside of the EU competence.

The first – and most fundamental – example of such difficulties concerns the design of rules applicable to relocation disputes as such. The existence of more uniform, efficient procedures for child relocation rules was explicitly seen as necessary for legal certainty and equal access to mobility rights.[330] They could be, indeed, seen as imperative for the effective access to justice and the elimination of obstacles to the proper functioning of civil proceedings, if Article 81(2) is interpreted expansively.[331] Member States could be, therefore, obliged to introduce rules to that effect. While the questions of when a parent needs to obtain a permission to relocate and what kind of considerations should guide the court are clearly substantive, there are certain choices regarding how such a permission is to be obtained that can be considered more procedural. However, they remain closely related with substantive determinations. For example, the relocating parent might need to apply for permission to a court to relocate if the permission of the other parent is not given. This, however, reflects

---

329 ibid.

330 Y.M. Bérénos, above n. 12, 2, 21–22. See also the principles of the Recommendation CM/Rec(2015)4, above n. 119.

331 This interpretation might be contestable, as both access to justice and the proper functioning of civil proceedings have traditionally been interpreted in a close relationship with issues of recognition and enforcement of judgments. See the discussion in M. Wilderspin, 'Article 81 TFEU', in M. Kellerbauer, M. Klamert and J. Tomkin (eds), *The EU Treaties and the Charter of Fundamental Rights: A Commentary* (online ed.) Oxford University Press, NewYork2019<https://doi-org.ezproxy.leidenuniv.nl/10.1093/oso/9780198759393.003.170>.

a different degree of parental autonomy than the obligation to notify the other parent, with the presumption that the lack of an active objection by the non-relocating parent within a certain time presupposes approval for the move. The length of notice periods, if required, might also have varying consequences for parental autonomy and the best interests of children involved.[332] This is further reinforced by the fact that family courts, alongside their role in resolving disputes in adversary processes, are directly vested with child protection functions, and – as demonstrated by prior discussion – there is a great variety of how such functions in general, and in child relocation in particular, are understood across jurisdictions. In that, the more procedural nature of many such provisions could be disputed, revealing additionally how the question of competence intertwines with a more pragmatic (or perhaps political) question of feasibility (in particular due to the unanimity required in the Council). Nevertheless, one could imagine that certain aspects of child relocation could be less contestable and would gain acceptance across the EU Member States.[333] In fact, some of these aspects can be considered to be already (partially) regulated in the existing Brussels II*ter* Regulation, while others could be easily implemented in its future recasts or a new instrument.

One such aspect is the obligation to give the child the right to express his or her views in line with national procedural laws that is already included in Article 21 of the Regulation.[334] This obligation remains relevant and applicable also in the child relocation context, as the only prerequisite to its application is the exercise of jurisdiction by the court based on the provisions of the Regulation (which does not presuppose in itself a cross-border character of a case). Article 80 of the Regulation foresees that central authorities of the Member State where the child *was* or *is* habitually resident or present should, upon request, with supporting reasons, provide reports or information on the situation of the child or other relevant matters. Given the already existing obligations under the Regulation, and in light of the prospective nature of child relocation, it is not unthinkable that such an obligation could be extended also to central authorities of the Member State where the child *could be* habitually resident in the future, if relocation is allowed. This prospective obligation could apply also to information and assistance offered to holders of parental responsibility (Article 79 of the Brussels II*ter* Regulation). Such information could help the parents to present relevant evidence and help the deciding authorities to

[332] See also the Explanatory Memorandum to the Recommendation CM/Rec(2015)4, above n. 119, para. 56.

[333] In case of lacking unanimity, but with the support of a minimum of nine EU Member States, a new legal framework could also be put in place via the enhanced co-operation mechanism. See Article 20 of the TEU and Title III of the TFEU and the discussion below.

[334] This might not be immediately revolutionary, given the obligations of Member States under the CRC and other instruments, but should nevertheless be noted as it is included also in the Recommendation CM/Rec(2015)4, above n. 119.

assess the broader consequences of relocation for the situation of the child. It is worth observing that the provisions on the cross-border placement of a child already contain a degree of such prospective assessments (Article 82), although they are of a different nature. Further, Article 79(g) includes the obligation of central authorities to facilitate agreement between holders of parental responsibility through mediation or other alternative dispute resolution methods, and to facilitate cross-border co-operation in such contexts. The value of mediation in family matters has been widely recognised and, while the provision must be interpreted in the context of the Regulation, it could prospectively be mobilised also for cross-border child relocation cases.[335] Therefore, relatively minor changes of the Regulation could already introduce some measures facilitating efficient decision-making in the child relocation context as well.

Other procedural measures could also be seen as serving the proper functioning of civil proceedings. For example, the EU could introduce provisions on additional measures that need to accompany a relocation decision, such as decisions on contact or maintenance post-relocation.[336] Such a provision would be motivated by the need to minimise further cross-border disputes and to simplify any proceedings on recognition and enforcement that might be necessary, as well as the concern for the stability of the child's situation during and immediately after the move. Not all jurisdictions require contact agreements to be adjusted together with or prior to relocation, which might complicate such proceedings and create additional scope for (cross-border) disputes. A requirement to that end would allow for Article 8 of the Brussels II*ter* Regulation, regulating the continuing jurisdiction in relation to access rights, to truly focus on the *adjustment* of contact regimes post-relocation. As contact rights in the child's new place of residence would be determined before relocation takes place, this could also address some of the criticism levelled against the short time frame (three months) envisaged in this provision.[337] However, an

335 A general obligation to encourage alternative dispute resolution exists clearly in child abduction cases (Article 25 of the Brussels II*ter* Regulation). Additionally, the Mediation Directive (Council Directive 2008/52/EC of 21 May 2008 on certain aspects of mediation in civil and commercial matters [2008] OJ L136/3) applies also to family disputes, albeit only those of a cross-border character. The original proposal for the Directive did not include the cross-border requirement, but its introduction was requested by the Council. It remains an open question whether the inclusion of disputes such as child relocation would be met with the approval of the Member States.

336 See the Explanatory Memorandum to the Recommendation CM/Rec(2015)4, above n. 119, para. 74: 'In deciding on a request for or an objection to relocation of the child, the competent authority may need to confirm or on the contrary to modify a pre-existing decision on the custody and the personal contacts of the child'.

337 See N.V. Lowe, 'The Impact of the Revised Brussels II Regulation on Cross-Border Relocation' (2010) *The Judges Newsletter (Special Edition)* 69, 73, who suggests that this period of time might be too short, and it could be more appropriate to extend it to, e.g. six months.

obligation to decide on relocation and (some) other matters jointly might be difficult to square with procedural laws in some Member States, calling for broader reforms of often diverging procedures. Therefore, while the examples here are in no way exhaustive, they draw attention to the difficulties – legal or political – involved in the harmonisation of procedures in such a sensitive area as child relocation law. These hypotheticals demonstrate additionally that any discussion of harmonisation in abstracto remains difficult, calling rather for a detailed consideration of the rules on the exercise of the EU competence in reference to both the intensity and the form of any such measure.

3.2.4. WHAT KIND OF INSTRUMENT FOR WHAT KIND OF HARMONISATION?

While harmonisation can differ in scope, it can also differ in intensity.[338] European legislators might provide for 'maximum harmonisation', imposing fixed standards on Member States, or 'minimum harmonisation', allowing them some discretion.[339] Decisions on scope and intensity of the measure, taken together, are also determined by the rules on the exercise of the EU competence as included in Article 5(3)–(4) of the Treaty on European Union (TEU).[340] They intertwine with the determination of the instrument that is to be used in a given field, as the EU is equipped with many different tools to make its law and policy, both binding and non-binding. Article 288 of the TFEU lists Regulations, Directives, Decisions, Recommendations, and Opinions. These themes will now be investigated below. While Regulations have historically proved to be a preferred type of EU instrument for the regulation of family matters, Bérénos' emphasis on a non-binding instrument as a first step towards harmonisation[341] invites first a reflection on this type of measure, its place within the EU legal system, and its suitability to deliver the objectives sought.

From the catalogue of instruments included in Article 288 of the TFEU, only Recommendations and Opinions are non-binding, hence constituting what one might describe as 'soft law'.[342] Some authors have argued that such

---

338 M. Klamert, above n. 328, 362.

339 ibid.

340 The Treaty on European Union [2012] OJ C326/13.

341 Y.M. Bérénos, above n. 12, 21.

342 'Soft law' is not a concept used by EU Treaties. Bérénos consciously rejects the use of this term due to its ambiguity, see Y.M. Bérénos, above n. 12, 11. The concept has been nevertheless broadly employed in EU (legal) studies. See, for example, O.A. Stefan, M. Avbelj, M. Eliantonio, M. Hartlapp, E. Korkea-aho and N. Rubio, 'EU Soft Law in the EU Legal Order: A Literature Review' (2019) King's College London Law School Research Paper Forthcoming <https://papers.ssrn.com/abstract=3346629>.

acts are not subject to the principle of conferral,[343] which could indeed make them attractive for a more exhaustive – albeit less intense – regulation of child relocation. However, the non-binding nature of such instruments should not justify any extension of the competence discussed above. Soft law measures can become influential measures of governance, hence they are also bound by legitimacy requirements,[344] and it has therefore been generally accepted that rules on competence apply also to such actions on behalf of the EU.[345] The principle of conferral applies equally to other soft law instruments recognised in the practice of EU institutions, such as Guidelines or Communications of the Commission.[346] However, while the type of the instrument does not alter the scope of the EU competence per se, it becomes a relevant consideration in assessing the lawfulness of its exercise by the EU.

Where the EU competence exists, its exercise is guided by the principles of subsidiarity and proportionality. Under the subsidiarity principle (Article 5(3) of the TEU), in areas which do not fall within the exclusive competence of the Union (one of which is, without any doubt, family law), the Union should act: (1) only and insofar as the objectives of the proposed action cannot be sufficiently achieved by the Member States; and (2) can, by reason of the scale or effects of the proposed action, be better achieved at Union level.[347] The proportionality principle prescribes that the content and form of Union action shall not exceed what is necessary to achieve the objectives of the Treaties (Article 5(4) of the TEU). If these conditions are met, the EU legislator has more legal instruments to choose from, as listed in Article 288 of the TFEU. Article 296 of the TFEU stipulates that where the Treaties do not specify the type of act to be adopted, the institutions shall select it on a case-by-case

---

343 See the discussion in J. Bast and K. Wetz, above n. 326, p. 77, and the literature cited there.

344 For a general discussion of legitimacy concerns in this context see O.A. Stefan, M. Avbelj, M. Eliantonio, M. Hartlapp, E. Korkea-aho and N. Rubio, above n. 342, pp. 34–38.

345 J. Bast and K. Wetz, above n. 326, pp. 77–78; L.A.J. Senden, 'Soft Law and Its Implications for Institutional Balance in the EC' (2005) 1 *Utrecht Law Review* 79, 87–88; B. de Witte, 'The Place of the OMC in the System of EU Competences and Sources of Law' (2018) 3 *European Papers – A Journal on Law and Integration* 207, 209, noticing that the principle of conferral refers to all acts of the EU, not only (be they hard or soft) law-making acts.

346 For a general discussion of the broad category of non-binding instruments in the EU beyond the catalogue of Article 288 of the TFEU, see B. de Witte and B. Smulders, 'Chapter 6: Sources of European Union Law' in P.J. Kuijper, F. Amtenbrink, D. Curtin, B. De Witte, A. McDonnell and S. Van den Bogaert (eds), *The Law of the European Union*, 5th ed., Kluwer Law International, The Hague 2018, pp. 218–21. See also L.A.J. Senden, above n. 345, 88–89, quoting Case C-233/02, *France v Commission*, ECLI:EU:C:2004:173, para. 42, that rejected the Commission's argument '[t]hat the fact that a measure such as the Guidelines is not binding is sufficient to confer on that institution the competence to adopt it', explicitly drawing attention to the division of powers established by the Treaty.

347 This is not to say that subsidiarity is not a problematic concept in the practice of the EU institutions. For a broader discussion, see G.A. Moens and J. Trone, 'The Principle of Subsidiarity in EU Judicial and Legislative Practice: Panacea or Placebo?' (2015) 41 *Journal of Legislation* 65.

basis, in compliance with the applicable procedures and with the principle of proportionality. Another question to be addressed is, therefore, how the Treaty provisions on the exercise of EU powers reflect on the choice of a legislative measure and the nature of any potential EU action on child relocation specifically.

The necessity of the EU's action, required by the principle of subsidiarity, is a complex legal concept with an inherently political dimension.[348] In any case, because of the specificity of Union law (e.g. precedence over national law or harmonious interpretation), it cannot be denied only because the Member States could legislate some (potentially identical) domestic rules.[349] One of the principle's underlying assumptions is that decisions are taken on a level that is as close to the citizens of the Union as possible.[350] Additionally, the analysis of subsidiarity is often said to be meaningful only if coupled with proportionality in reference to a particular intended measure.[351] One could reasonably argue that the equivalence or effectiveness of some aspects of child relocation cannot be sufficiently achieved by Member States alone, and an action on the side of the EU – insofar as it is limited to these aspects – would likely remain proportionate. This would be the case particularly for any co-operation framework between the Member States, understood, for example, as the assistance offered by central authorities discussed above. The objective could be achieved by the Union itself as being better equipped to deal with such issues and for the scale of its potential action. However, other measures would call for a detailed scrutiny in light of both subsidiarity and proportionality, in particular the closer they get to or the more intertwined they are with substantive legal frameworks. National substantive rules would necessarily be affected to some extent by the introduction of the procedural measures suggested above, but not all divergences need to be removed to achieve the EU objectives and harmonisation should not become an end in itself.

---

348 See, e.g. ibid., 85, or I. Cooper, 'Is the Subsidiarity Early Warning Mechanism a Legal or a Political Procedure? Three Questions and a Typology', (2016) RSC Working Paper, European University Institute, pp. 10–11 <http://hdl.handle.net/1814/40765>.

349 R. Geiger, 'Article 352 TFEU' in R. Geiger, D.-E. Khan and M. Kotzur, *European Union Treaties: A Commentary: Treaty on European Union, Treaty on the Functioning of the European Union, Charter of Fundamental Rights of the European Union*, C.H. Beck/Hart Publishing, Munich/Oxford 2015, p. 1051.

350 Preamble, Protocol (No. 2) on the application of the principles of subsidiarity and proportionality [2008] OJ C115/206.

351 e.g. I. Cooper, 'The Watchdogs of Subsidiarity: National Parliaments and the Logic of Arguing in the EU' (2006) 44 *Journal of Common Market Studies* 281; S. Weatherill, 'The Limits of Legislative Harmonization Ten Years after Tobacco Advertising: How the Court's Case Law Has Become a "Drafting Guide"' (2011) 12 *German Law Journal* 827, 854–55; and R. Schütze, 'Subsidiarity After Lisbon: Reinforcing the Safeguards of Federalism?' (2009) 68 *Cambridge Law Journal* 525, all arguing – although from different perspectives – for benefits of coupling the subsidiarity and proportionality analysis.

The detailed discussion of subsidiarity and proportionality is beyond the scope of this analysis. It would also be more usefully conducted in the context of a specific proposal.[352] The purpose of this discussion is rather to demonstrate that proposals for EU action in child relocation require a nuanced consideration of not only *whether* the EU can act (as a question of competence, sensu stricto, in itself not necessarily clear-cut), but also *whether* it should introduce specific rules (as a question of subsidiarity) in the connection with the question of *how* to introduce them (as a question of proportionality).[353] Co-operation frameworks discussed above could – also in light of the already existing provisions – legitimately be included in a Regulation, presumably in a future recast of the Brussels II*ter* Regulation that is currently in force. However, subsidiarity and proportionality concerns would likely make a directive or perhaps even a non-binding instrument (as suggested by Bérénos) better suited for other proposals. Such provisions would nevertheless still need to be assessed in light of the proportionality and subsidiarity principles.[354] The most fundamental obligation of Member States – to have efficient (and perhaps explicit) procedures for child relocation, given their signaling value and contribution to legal certainty – could, in principle, be introduced as a directive. However, it is rather difficult to imagine that the EU could impose more specific rules in this regard, even if they are not binding, due to their close relationship with core substantive aspects of family laws and the competence limitation. In this context, it is also worth keeping in mind that measures regarding family law can be enacted under Article 20 of the TEU (enhanced co-operation). This provision allows a group of at least nine Member States to establish advanced co-operation between themselves when it has become clear that the EU, as a whole, cannot achieve the goals of such co-operation within a reasonable period. This could be a realistic attempt to accommodate various traditions and could potentially resolve some of the issues raised by the political feasibility of a child relocation instrument in light of the unanimity requirement under Article 81(3) of the TFEU.

---

352 For this argument at large see R. Schütze, above n. 351, 532–33.

353 ibid. See also I. Cooper, above n. 348, describing subsidiarity as a question of 'appropriateness' at its core.

354 As observed by B. de Witte and B. Smulders, above n. 346, p. 208, Directives can sometimes include extremely detailed provisions that functionally amount to the introduction of uniform rules, as long as they remain within the limits of their legal basis. In that, '[t]he degree of uniformity imposed by a directive will depend on the nature of the problem being regulated, and on the circumstances and the political conditions for its adoption at the EU level'. Given the nature of child relocation and the limitations of the EU's competence discussed above, it is here suggested that such a Directive should leave a rather broad autonomy to Member States. On the other hand, a higher level of detail of the standards prescribed could perhaps be accepted for a non-binding Recommendation (described by de Witte and Smulders as a 'surrogate directive') given that their adoption would take place on a voluntary basis.

3.3. CONCLUDING REMARKS

This chapter demonstrates that the EU's competence to legislate on substantive aspects of child relocation laws can be legitimately refused. However, an expansive interpretation of 'cross-border implications' under Article 81(3) of the TFEU does not exclude entirely a partial harmonisation of some of their procedural aspects. Judicial co-operation under the existing Brussels II*ter* Regulation could, in the future, be extended also to child relocation disputes. However, one can expect further debates on other potential measures that could be introduced on the EU level, due to the close relationship of procedure in substance that characterises child relocation laws. While such debates can be more usefully held in reference to specific proposals, harmonisation will likely not be straightforward. The tension between the restrictive and the broad interpretation of Article 81(3) of the TFEU in the relocation context is closely related to the constitutional question of competence that, in itself, raises many doubts. Although there are many strictly legal issues raised by the possibility of harmonisation of child relocation laws, in reality, such questions often turn out to be dependent on the political will of the Member States that need to agree to the adoption of the measures.[355] The Commission has, in the past, argued for a broad interpretation of procedural competence but the Council has refused to enact any procedural measures that would apply to purely domestic matters (even on an optional basis).[356]

In family law, the introduction of an obligation to give the child an opportunity to express his or her views in the new Brussels II*ter* Regulation can be seen as a procedural obligation going beyond the cross-border nature of this instrument, but – as rightly noticed by its drafters – it is hardly a disputable obligation, given its embedding in the human rights framework to which all Member States adhere.[357] At the same time, the Regulation does not prescribe when the child is to be heard or what weight is to be given to their views, leaving

355 See also the general discussion in E. Storskrubb, 'Civil Justice: Constitutional and Regulatory Issues Revisited' in M. Fletcher, E. Herlin-Karnell and C. Matera (eds), *The European Union as an Area of Freedom, Security and Justice*, Routledge, Abingdon 2017, pp. 325–27.

356 For an overview of the political struggle over the 'cross-border' dimension see ibid., pp. 307–10, 325. Storskrubb notes that the increasing regulation in some sector-specific areas (e.g. IP law, consumer law) leads to a circumvention of the 'cross-border implications' requirement, but all such regulations concern areas with a broad EU competence. The example of the Mediation Directive – applicable also to family matters – shows that this expansive trend is not universal, as here the Council explicitly requested the introduction of a clear definition of a 'cross-border dispute' despite the Commission's original argument towards a broader application.

357 European Commission, 'Proposal for a Council Regulation on jurisdiction, the recognition and enforcement of decisions in matrimonial matters and the matters of parental responsibility, and on international child abduction (recast)' (2016), COM(2016) 0411 final, p. 15.

these matters to national courts and legislators. One can, therefore, perceive this provision more as an exception among family law rules originating from the EU, related to the nature of the matter, than as setting a more universally applicable precedent for the future. It is generally difficult to imagine that Member States would, any time soon, accept the expansive interpretation of 'cross-border implications' in such a sensitive area as family law, where procedural and substantive issues are closely related.[358] It is also worth emphasising that any EU instrument on child relocation is unlikely to remedy the diversity of approaches in a substantive sense, and not only due to the competence limitation. Any harmonised approach would necessarily be based on the open-ended child's best interests principle which, as discussed in Chapter 2, is precisely what currently leads to this diversity.[359] The open-ended nature of the best interests principle would continue to allow different jurisdictions to put varying emphasis on different factors to be considered in relocation cases. In that, the uniformity to be achieved is clearly, at most, procedural.

Even if the EU has no legislative competence over substantive child relocation, the Luxembourg Court remains the primary interpreter of European free movement law and EU citizenship provisions. As already noted, the intertwinement of child relocation with freedom of movement, rather than family law competence per se, might bring child relocation under the scrutiny of the CJEU. The Court might, therefore, be a more likely EU actor to gradually address the alleged inequality and insufficient protection of individual rights stemming from the lack of uniformity within the EU, in particular via the 'bottom-up' enforcement of EU law within the preliminary reference procedure. In light of this, child relocation could be subject to harmonisation (pressures) beyond legislation, regardless of the variety of rules and procedures applied by different Member States. Therefore, as noted in other private law contexts, the harmonisation of certain standards of protection in reference to national child relocation measures might take place via the application of European constitutional norms on the right to family life, free movement, or

358 Many states, including EU Member States, have already argued along these lines in the context of initiatives on child relocation undertaken by the HCCH and the drafting process of the Washington Declaration. Such reservations would most likely come to the fore in the EU context as well. See the discussion in R. George, above n. 204, 149–50, who observes that Austria questioned such competence of the HCCH. It is additionally interesting to note that the European Union, while responding to the HCCH Questionnaire on the desirability and feasibility of a protocol to the 1980 Child Abduction Convention (one that included also questions on child relocation), noted that '[t]he European Union would like not to prejudge the outcome [of the feasibility study] and wishes to reserve its final position … until the results of the study are known'. In that, the EU did not make any proposals, awaiting further input that might come from the states and further recommendations of the HCCH.

359 C. Cotta, above n. 37, p. 29; R. George, above n. 204, 148.

EU citizenship.[360] Such 'non-legislative harmonisation', achieved through judgments of the CJEU, might be more sensitive to varying cultural values and differing procedures and might allow avoidance of the unnecessarily expansive, or at least contestable, interpretation of EU competences.[361] However, as already mentioned, the intensity of the Court's scrutiny depends also on the scope of the EU competence.[362] Therefore, the findings of this chapter directly bear also on the nature of the broader analysis of child relocation in the context of EU law, as will be discussed in Chapter 5.

---

360 See A. Colombi Ciacchi, 'Non-Legislative Harmonisation of Private Law under the European Constitution: The Case of Unfair Suretyships' (2005) 13 *European Review of Private Law* 285, 305–08.

361 ibid.

362 L. Boucon, above n. 38, p. 171.

CHAPTER 4

CHILD RELOCATION AND FUNDAMENTAL RIGHTS IN EUROPE

4.1. INTRODUCTION

The existing literature on child relocation in the EU does not engage with fundamental rights in detail.[363] However, with the EU Charter of Fundamental Rights becoming the EU's 'third foundational treaty',[364] the analysis of child relocation within the EU legal context must take due account of the European fundamental rights framework. The role of the CJEU as an adjudicator of fundamental rights in family matters has indeed been growing over the years,[365] but – due to the competence limitation – remains of indirect relevance for substantive family law, even if it directly influences the scope and nature of other EU law obligations. It is Europe's other supranational court – the European Court of Human Rights – that is the major player in family law, including matters of parental responsibilities and contact rights.[366] According to Article 52(3) of the EU Charter of Fundamental Rights, rights contained in the EU Charter should be interpreted in line with the ECHR provisions that correspond to them, and therefore an analysis of the ECHR and the jurisprudence of its guardian, the ECtHR, are of direct relevance for EU law.

While these themes are not prominent in the EU-focused literature on child relocation, child relocation has been framed in human rights terms at large and discussed in the context of the European Convention on Human

363 R. Lamont, above n. 12, 233 and 241, notes that the fundamental rights of the parties in disputes affected by European law should also be protected but does not analyse the framework in detail. See also Y.M. Bérénos, above n. 12, 21.

364 M. Kotzur, 'CFREU Introduction' in R. Geiger, D.-E. Khan, and M. Kotzur, *European Union Treaties: A Commentary: Treaty on European Union, Treaty on the Functioning of the European Union, Charter of Fundamental Rights of the European Union*, C.H. Beck/Hart Publishing, Munich/Oxford 2015, p. 1065.

365 e.g. S. Ninatti, above n. 3, p. 8; K. Carr, above n. 3, pp. 207–12.

366 For an overview see D. Coester-Waltjen, 'The Impact of the European Convention on Human Rights and the European Court of Human Rights on European Family Law' in J.M. Scherpe (ed), *European Family Law (Volume I): The Impact of Institutions and Organisations on European Family Law*, Edward Elgar Publishing, Cheltenham 2016. See also, e.g. U. Kilkelly, *The Child and the European Convention on Human Rights*, Routledge, Abingdon 1999.

Rights more specifically.[367] The literature has, so far, focused on the analysis of Article 8 of the ECHR (the right to respect for private and family life), under which Contracting States are typically granted a wide margin of appreciation in parental disputes.[368] However, no other provisions nor the Strasbourg Court's jurisprudence on child relocation have been discussed.[369] It is, in particular, the interplay of Article 8 of the ECHR and Article 2 of Protocol 4 to the ECHR (freedom of movement) that might be interesting in child relocation cases and relevant from the point of view of EU law. Additionally, it is useful to closely analyse the ECtHR jurisprudence in child relocation cases specifically, given that the Strasbourg Court's approach to the child's best interests principle and the respective margin of appreciation in different strands of its case law might differ.[370] As the ECHR binds all Member States and constitutes an important point of reference for EU law agents (in particular the CJEU)[371] this analysis will inevitably set minimum standards for EU law.[372]

The objective of this chapter is, therefore, to understand the margin of appreciation that Member States enjoy in child relocation cases under the ECHR and its consequences for EU law. To this end, this chapter first delineates the framework of the ECHR that could be applicable to child relocation and discusses the case law of the ECtHR concerning cross-border child relocation cases. Once the ECtHR's approach is outlined, the focus shifts onto the role of the

367 As this book is interested first and foremost in the EU legal framework, the term 'fundamental rights' is used to express the concept of 'human rights' within the EU context, as reflected also by the language of the EU Charter of Fundamental Rights. 'Human rights' is then used as referring to rights guaranteed in international law and the European Convention on Human Rights more specifically, following the language of that instrument. In general, however, they are taken to relate to a largely similar set of rights and the theoretical observations made in the literature are applicable throughout.

368 e.g. *X, Y and Z v United Kingdom* (GC) [1997] ECtHR, app. no. 21830/93, para. 44.

369 This is so because the literature precedes these developments. See, e.g. U. Kilkelly, above n. 140, 34, who notes the Court's lack of engagement with relocation directly, but points towards cases about restoring contact after child abductions as potentially relevant.

370 e.g. G. Alves de Faria, 'Sexual Orientation and the ECtHR: what relevance is given to the best interests of the child? An analysis of the European Court of Human Rights' approach to the best interests of the child in LGBT parenting cases' (2015) *Family & Law*, DOI: 10.5553/FenR/.000018; M. Sormunen, 'A Comparison of Child Protection and Immigration Jurisprudence of the European Court of Human Rights: What Role for the Best Interests of the Child?' (2019) 31 *Child and Family Law Quarterly* 249.

371 In the family law context, see for example Case C-400/10 PPU, *J. McB. v L. E.*, ECLI:EU:C:2010:582, paras. 53–56. See also the discussion in Section 4.4.3. below.

372 The relationship between the two European courts has been analysed from many different perspectives. This book focuses on this relationship insofar as necessary for subsequent analysis of child relocation in the broader EU law context. For an overview see, e.g. S. Douglas-Scott, 'A Tale of Two Courts: Luxembourg, Strasbourg and the Growing European Human Rights Acquis' (2006) 43 *Common Market Law Review* 629; F. Cherubini, 'The Relationship Between the Court of Justice of the European Union and the European Court of Human Rights in the View of the Accession' (2015) 16 *German Law Journal* 1375.

Charter of Fundamental Rights and the relationship between the jurisprudence of the two European courts: the ECtHR and the CJEU. A detailed analysis of the CJEU jurisprudence on fundamental rights falls outside the scope of this book, but the dynamics of European fundamental rights are illustrated with examples of cases touching upon family matters. The chapter then concludes with a brief assessment of the consequences of these dynamics for the analysis of child relocation in the EU legal context specifically.

4.2. CHILD RELOCATION WITHIN THE FRAMEWORK OF THE ECHR

Various issues were resolved by the ECtHR under Article 8 of the ECHR (the right to private and family life) which has become a 'nursery in which new rights are born', significantly contributing to the overall jurisprudence of the Court.[373] It is thus unsurprising that with time child relocation has also been discussed under this provision. Article 8 of the ECHR has been seen as emphasising the procedural obligations of the Contracting States in child relocation cases,[374] but not fundamentally altering the nuanced balancing exercise at the centre of the analysis.[375] As the analysis below demonstrates, this conclusion does not seem to be altered by the juxtaposition of Article 8 and other provisions of the ECHR and various protocols to the Convention (e.g. on prohibition of discrimination, the right to marry, or free movement). Due to the familial nature of the disputes, Article 8 of the ECHR is, therefore, likely to remain the main provision relevant for the analysis of child relocation cases.

4.2.1. CHILD RELOCATION UNDER ARTICLE 8 OF THE ECHR (RESPECT FOR PRIVATE AND FAMILY LIFE)

Article 8 is the first provision of the Convention that gets invoked in the context of parental disputes. The Court recognises that the mutual enjoyment, by the parent and child, of each other's company constitutes a fundamental element of family life,[376] and national authorities may be obliged to take measures

---

373 M. Burbergs, 'How the Right to Respect for Private and Family Life, Home and Correspondence Became the Nursery in Which New Rights Are Born: Article 8 ECHR' in E. Brems and J. Gerards (eds), *Shaping Rights in the ECHR: The Role of the European Court of Human Rights in Determining the Scope of Human Rights*, Cambridge University Press, Cambridge 2014.

374 U. Kilkelly, above n. 140, 35.

375 See, generally, J. Herring and R. Taylor, above n. 10; see also S. Choudhry and J. Herring, above n. 189, p. 284 for an approving view.

376 e.g. *Keegan v Ireland* [1994] ECtHR, app. no. 16969/90, para. 50.

to secure or restore it.[377] Measures regarding custody and contact taken in parental disputes are usually considered as an interference with the Article 8 rights of at least one of the individuals involved in the dispute.[378] This applies to disputes about a child's residence as well.[379] While the ECHR does not contain any provisions on children's rights specifically, the jurisprudence of the Court confirms that the best interests test falls within the scope of Article 8 and recognises the guiding role of the CRC in this area of law.[380] Any interference with Article 8 constitutes a violation of the Convention unless it is in accordance with the law, pursues aims that are legitimate under Article 8(2), and can be regarded as necessary in a democratic society. Necessity implies that the interference corresponds to a social need and is proportionate to the legitimate aim pursued, but the Court approaches the test in a context-dependent way.[381] In parental disputes, the interference is typically justified by the protection of the rights and freedoms of others, making the final judgments dependent on the proportionality test.[382]

Article 8 contains no explicit procedural requirements for securing a fair balancing of interests,[383] but the Court emphasises the close link between procedure and substance, and obliges national authorities to ensure that their decisions are based on all relevant considerations.[384] Thus, the Court often deals with procedural matters directly under Article 8, even when procedural violations can be claimed under Article 6 of the ECHR (the right to a fair trial) as well.[385] Parents need to be in a position that enables them to put forward all arguments relevant to the dispute involving their child and to have access to all relevant information which is at the disposal of the domestic courts.[386] Considerations of children's best interests are of particular importance in

---

377 e.g. *Ignaccolo-Zenide v Romania* [2000] ECtHR, app. no. 31679/96, para. 94.

378 e.g. *Hoffman v Austria* [1993] ECtHR, app. no. 12875/87.

379 e.g. *Širvinskas v Lithuania* [2019] ECtHR, app. no. 21243/17. See also the Explanatory Memorandum to the Recommendation CM/Rec(2015)4, above n. 119, para. 15.

380 See U. Kilkelly, 'The CRC in Litigation Under the ECHR' in T. Liefaard and J.E. Doek (eds), *Litigating the Rights of the Child: The UN Convention on the Rights of the Child in Domestic and International Jurisprudence*, Springer, Dordrecht 2015. See also *Nunez v Norway* [2011] ECtHR, app. no. 55597/09, paras. 78–84.

381 J. Gerards, 'Judicial Deliberations in the European Court of Human Rights' (2008) *Social Science Research Network*, SSRN Scholarly Paper ID 1114906, p. 422 <https://papers.ssrn.com/abstract=1114906>.

382 e.g. *Neulinger and Shuruk v Switzerland* [2010] ECtHR, app. no. 41615/07, paras. 134–35; *X v Latvia* (GC) [2013] ECtHR, app. no. 27853/09, para. 96.

383 e.g. *Kosmopoulou v Greece* [2004] ECtHR, app. no. 60457/00, paras. 43, 47.

384 For a more extensive discussion on procedural protection, see E. Brems, 'Procedural Protection: An Examination of Procedural Safeguards Read into Substantive Convention Rights' in E. Brems and J. Gerards (eds), *Shaping Rights in the ECHR: The Role of the European Court of Human Rights in Determining the Scope of Human Rights*, Cambridge University Press, Cambridge 2014.

385 e.g. *Diamante and Pelliccioni v San Marino* [2011] ECtHR, app. no. 32250/08, para. 151.

386 e.g. *Kosmopoulou v Greece* [2004] ECtHR, app. no. 60457/00, paras. 47–50.

parental disputes,[387] and children should in principle be heard.[388] The existing jurisprudence of the Court suggests that the conflicting parental interests must also be taken into account, but it is the best interests of the child and his or her rights under Article 8 of the Convention that will be the main axis of the analysis.[389] While the length of child care proceedings does not per se affect enjoyment of the rights, it might do so in concrete circumstances and hence is of particular importance for Article 8 assessments.[390] The ECtHR puts emphasis on the need to strike a fair balance between competing interests within a certain margin of appreciation that is typically relatively wide in parental disputes.[391] This is justified by the broad and individualised nature of such complaints, and the need to interpret the Convention 'in light of the present-day conditions'.[392] Therefore, the Convention provisions clearly give rise to positive obligations.[393]

As this discussion shows, in line with the existing literature, all parties to a relocation dispute might assert their rights under Article 8.[394] While their core will be family-related, the right to respect for private life also includes a broader right to identity, self-development or personal autonomy.[395] In that light, some authors suggest that approaching child relocation from a human rights perspective would allow for an independent consideration of all family members' interests.[396] This would modify the reasoning applied to relocation decisions[397]

387 The Court understands the principle as indicating the particular importance of children's interests rather than making them the sole consideration of the process, as confirmed, for example, by the *Nunez v Norway* case, [2011] ECtHR, app. no. 55597/09, but this approach might also differ depending on the type of the case. See also the discussion in C. Simmonds, 'Paramountcy and the ECHR: A Conflict Resolved?' (2012) 71 *Cambridge Law Journal* 498.

388 e.g. *G.B. v Lithuania* [2016] ECtHR, app. no. 36137/13, paras. 39, 84.

389 e.g. *Diamante and Pelliccioni v San Marino* [2011] ECtHR, app. no. 32250/08, para. 176; *Zawadka v Poland* [2003] ECtHR, app. no. 48542/99, para. 67. See also R. George, 'The Child's Welfare in a European Perspective' in J.M. Scherpe (ed), *European Family Law (Volume III): Family Law in a European Perspective*, Edward Elgar Publishing, Cheltenham 2016, p. 8.

390 See E. Brems, above n. 384, p. 151.

391 e.g. *Ignaccolo-Zenide v Romania* [2000] ECtHR, app. no. 31679/96, para. 94; *Keegan v Ireland* [1994] ECtHR, app. no. 16969/90, para. 49. However, the Court has been said to apply, in practice, stricter requirements for justifications and a narrower margin of appreciation in negative obligation cases. See, for example: L. Lavrysen, 'The Scope of Rights and the Scope of Obligations: Positive Obligations' in E. Brems and J. Gerards (eds), *Shaping Rights in the ECHR: The Role of the European Court of Human Rights in Determining the Scope of Human Rights*, Cambridge University Press, Cambridge 2014, p. 166.

392 *Tyrer v United Kingdom* [1978] ECtHR, app. no. 5856/72, para. 31; *X, Y and Z v United Kingdom* (GC) [1997] ECtHR, app. no. 21830/93, para. 44.

393 See also U. Kilkelly, 'Protecting Children's Rights under the ECHR: The Role of Positive Obligations' (2010) 61 *Northern Ireland Legal Quarterly* 245.

394 J. Herring and R. Taylor, above n. 10, 530.

395 European Court of Human Rights, 'Guide on Article 8 of the European Convention on Human Rights' (2022) pp. 66–67 <https://www.echr.coe.int/Documents/Guide_Art_8_ENG.pdf>.

396 J. Herring and R. Taylor, above n. 10, 526; S. Choudhry and J. Herring, above n. 189, p. 285.

397 J. Herring and R. Taylor, above n. 10, 518; see also U. Kilkelly, above n. 140, 35.

and emphasise the procedural obligations of national authorities (e.g. the child's right to be heard).[398] Others note that, despite the change in reasoning, the conflict of rights will not necessarily be made easier to resolve, requiring a nuanced, highly context-dependent balancing exercise.[399] A principled balancing exercise should then focus on the values that underlie each right, having due regard to the personal autonomy of the individuals involved.[400] In relocation cases, the analysis should then consider 'which interference will constitute a greater blight on [each parent's] vision of the good life' as a factor independent from the assessment of the child's best interests.[401] This approach has been criticised for deferring the analysis to parental rights and not taking the rights of children seriously enough,[402] as children might not yet have developed their own vision of autonomy or of a good life.[403] However, this criticism has not suggested a fundamentally different approach to resolve the tensions between the rights of different individuals, but rather emphasised children's substantive rights and the corresponding procedural guarantees that result in an improved decision-making process (in particular in reference to the child's right to be heard).[404] In this context, the substantive suggestion found in the literature locates (autonomy) rights for the child in the right to an open future, with self-determination and self-fulfilment being the main underlying values of that right.[405] However, given the subsidiary nature of the ECtHR, domestic authorities should be left with a wide margin of appreciation regarding the substantive reconciliation of conflicting interests.[406] The discussion of the ECtHR case law below confirms more empirically that Article 8 can indeed draw attention to some of the autonomy interests involved, but the jurisprudence does not lead to a fundamental reconceptualisation of child relocation disputes.

4.2.2. ARTICLE 2 OF PROTOCOL 4 TO THE ECHR (FREEDOM OF MOVEMENT) AND ITS INTERPLAY WITH ARTICLE 8 OF THE ECHR

Having clarified the obligations imposed in child relocation by Article 8 of the ECHR, one can wonder whether the analysis is altered by Article 2 of

398 U. Kilkelly, above n. 140, 35.

399 See, generally, J. Herring and R. Taylor, above n. 10; see also S. Choudhry and J. Herring, above n. 189, p. 284 for an approving view.

400 J. Herring and R. Taylor, above n. 10, 530.

401 ibid., 531.

402 U. Kilkelly, above n. 140, 34–35.

403 J. Herring and R. Taylor, above n. 10, 531.

404 U. Kilkelly, above n. 140, 35.

405 J. Herring and R. Taylor, above n. 10, 531.

406 e.g. *Diamante and Pelliccioni v San Marino* [2011] ECtHR, app. no. 32250/08, para. 176; *Zawadka v Poland* [2003] ECtHR, app. no. 48542/99, para. 67.

Protocol 4 to the Convention.[407] It is particularly the relocating parent who will claim interference with their freedom of movement, but the Court has confirmed that this Article applies also to minors, although the exercise of such freedom may depend upon parental consent. In *Diamante and Pelliccioni v San Marino*, the Strasbourg Court explicitly stated that an administrative ban on the child's travel and/or dispossessing the child of travel documents indisputably leads to an interference with the child's rights and freedoms under Article 2 of Protocol 4.[408] In this case, national courts feared that the mother would abduct the child. The fact that San Marino was not a party to the 1980 Hague Child Abduction Convention was seen as part of the analysis as of necessity of the interference.[409] Given the circumstances, the Court readily accepted that the maintenance of public order and the protection of the rights of others are legitimate aims pursued by such measures, provided their nature is temporary. In *Lolova and Popova v Bulgaria*, the Court held that a refusal to issue a passport for the child cannot in itself lead to a violation of Article 2 of Protocol 4 where the other parent's or the court's permission for the minor's travel abroad had not been obtained.[410] The Court clearly saw the issuance of a travel document and the question of parental permission to travel as separate, with the latter being a reasonable prerequisite for exercising the child's freedom of movement.[411] However, it was also confirmed that the length of the proceedings can matter for the finding of a violation under the Convention.[412]

This jurisprudence interprets Article 2 taken as a whole, but what was at stake in all these cases was Article 2(2) specifically – the right to leave any country. As such, this jurisprudence cannot be directly translated into child relocation disputes. The ban on cross-border travel that can be imposed on an individual is substantively different from a refusal of relocation that concerns residence rather than travel, although the right to leave a country is necessarily a precondition of any cross-border relocation (as was indeed the case in *Lolova and Popova*). In the relocation context, the analysis could focus on Article 2(1), which concerns the freedom to choose residence, but the wording of the Article

407 Not all Member States of the Council of Europe (or the EU) have acceded to the Protocol. See, however, remarks made in the English case *Payne v Payne* [2001] EWCA Civ 166, [2001] 1 FLR 1052 (CA): 'Although Protocol 4 has yet to be ratified by the United Kingdom, it undoubtedly lends force to the argument that a failure or refusal to recognise a right of mobility beyond the somewhat fortuitous jurisdictional boundary represents a stance of disproportionate parochialism'.

408 *Diamante and Pelliccioni v San Marino* [2011] ECtHR, app. no. 32250/08, paras. 201–14.

409 ibid., para. 213.

410 *Lolova and Popova v Bulgaria* (dec) [2015] ECtHR, app no. 68053/10, para. 47. The dispute arose against the background of a planned relocation to Canada, but the complaint was brought in reference to passport proceedings.

411 See also *Şandru v Roumanie* (dec) [2014], ECtHR, app. no. 1902/11, para. 25.

412 *Lolova and Popova v Bulgaria* (dec) [2015] ECtHR, app. no. 68053/10, para. 126.

seems to suggest that this freedom applies exclusively within the territory of a given state. International relocation cases, by definition, are concerned with a choice of residence outside such territory. However, the Court often discusses Article 2 as a whole. Reading Article 2(1) and (2) jointly, and relying on the Court's jurisprudence on Article 2(2),[413] one can argue that – if the right to leave the country concerns leaving for any other country that a person might enter – there is no reason to assume that the right to choose a residence does not include leaving a country to take up residence elsewhere, where one can legally reside. In light of this interpretation, the distinction might greatly lose significance in the EU context.

The European Court of Human Rights has not interpreted the freedom to choose one's residence under Article 2(1) of Protocol 4 in the context of cross-border parental disputes. When raised (in a decision concerning return post-abduction, found to be inadmissible), the complaints were considered under Article 8 of the ECHR.[414] This is confirmed by other relevant cases. For example, in *Penchevi v Bulgaria*, discussed below (in Section 4.3.2.), the ECtHR found the national courts' refusal to allow a child's travel abroad to join his mother in the absence of the father's consent to constitute a restriction, but did not consider the case on the merits as violation of Article 8 was found.[415] This illustrates the close relationship between these two Articles in parental disputes where their familial essence determines the provision to apply.[416] The ECtHR has even, at times, asserted that the fact that a given Contracting Party had not ratified Protocol 4 does not need to be relevant in a given case, as its circumstances – related to free movement – might give rise to claims under other provisions.[417] In particular, freedom of movement, including cross-border movement, is considered an important aspect of a person's private and family life.[418] Restrictions on the right to leave a country might need to take into account the position of foreigners, as it might not be comparable with restrictions imposed on a person in his or her own country.[419] This resonates with some of the themes raised in child relocation discussions, in particular the weight of the fact that a relocating parent might be a foreign national

---

413 European Court of Human Rights, 'Guide on Article 2 of Protocol No. 4 to the European Convention on Human Rights (Freedom of Movement)' (2022) para. 114 <https://www.echr.coe.int/documents/d/echr/Guide_Art_2_Protocol_4_ENG> and the case law cited there.

414 ibid., para. 111. See also *Lipkowsky and McCormack v Germany* (dec) [2011] ECtHR, app. no. 26755/10.

415 *Penchevi v Bulgaria* [2015] ECtHR, app no. 77818/12.

416 See J. Gerards, 'Freedom of movement' in P. van Dijk, F. van Hoof, A. van Rijn, and L. Zwaak (eds), *Theory and Practice of the European Convention on Human Rights*, 5th ed., Intersentia, Cambridge 2018, p. 938, citing *Penchevi v Bulgaria* [2015] ECtHR, app no. 77818/12 (discussed, below Section 4.3.2.) as an example.

417 *İletmiş v Turkey* [2005] ECtHR, app. no. 29871/96, para. 50.

418 ibid., para. 47.

419 *Miażdżyk v Poland* [2012] ECtHR, app. no. 23592/07, para. 39.

'going home'. When individualised assessments are needed under Article 2 of Protocol 4, the Court might draw from its jurisprudence under Article 8, and vice versa.[420] Therefore, the question about the interplay of Article 8 and Article 2 of Protocol 4 seems to be a largely theoretical one. Given the nature of child relocation disputes, both provisions could be invoked, but it can be expected that the essence of the dispute will prompt the ECtHR to consider it under Article 8 of the ECHR.

4.2.3. OTHER POTENTIALLY RELEVANT PROVISIONS OF THE ECHR

Child relocation cases, depending on circumstances, might prima facie involve an interference with other rights protected by the Convention. Considering their complexity, potential violation claims might touch upon: Article 14 of the Convention (prohibition of discrimination in the exercise of rights and freedoms established in the Convention); Article 5 of Protocol 7 to the Convention (equality between spouses); or Article 1 of Protocol 12 to the Convention (general prohibition of discrimination). These provisions might be relevant given the discussion on child relocation and gender, as relocating parents are said to be (typically) mothers who might be restricted in their residence choices in a way that non-residential parents (typically fathers) are not. Article 5 of Protocol 7 essentially imposes an obligation to provide a satisfactory legal framework of equal spousal rights and obligations concerning children.[421] However, it does not prevent national authorities from taking such measures as are necessary in the interests of children,[422] potentially justifying any such differentiation in the relocation context. Article 14 is then predominantly of a subsidiary nature.[423] In parental disputes, claims based on Article 14 have only, so far, been successful when one of the parents did not have access, as opposed to the other parent, to proceedings allowing the case to be determined according to the child's interests.[424] Hence, claims based on these provisions are unlikely to challenge the general doctrines of Article 8 or Article 2 of Protocol 4 in the relocation context.

---

420 European Court of Human Rights, 'Guide on Article 2 of Protocol No. 4 to the European Convention on Human Rights (Freedom of Movement)', above n. 413, para. 85. See also *Garib v the Netherlands* (GC) [2017] ECtHR, app. no. 43494/09, para. 140.

421 e.g. *Cernecki v Austria* (dec) [2000] ECtHR, app. no. 31061/96.

422 e.g. *Chepelev v Russia* [2007] ECtHR, app. no. 58077/00, para. 36.

423 *Marckx v Belgium* [1979] ECtHR, app no. 6833/74, para. 32. See also the European Court of Human Rights, 'Guide on Article 14 of the European Convention on Human Rights and on Article 1 of Protocol No. 12 to the Convention' (2022) para. 3 <https://www.echr.coe.int/documents/d/echr/Guide_Art_14_Art_1_Protocol_12_ENG>.

424 e.g. *Zaunegger v Germany* [2009] ECtHR, app. no. 22028/04.

Some authors suggest that when a relocation application is made because the relocating parent intends to marry their new partner who resides elsewhere, a refusal of relocation could violate the right to marry.[425] The right to marry and found a family is protected by Article 12 of the Convention. However, such an interpretation does not find confirmation in the Court's jurisprudence. The Court's case law suggests that '[t]he essence of the right to marry is the formation of a legal union of a man and a woman' and '[i]t is for them to decide whether they wish to enter such relationship in circumstances in which there are objective obstacles to their living together'.[426] Such objective obstacles were predominantly raised by immigration restrictions, where the ECtHR held that the right to live in the same country together could not be derived either from Article 8 or Article 12 of the ECHR. This interpretation can, by analogy, be applied to child relocation cases. If a parent wants to marry a new partner residing elsewhere, they cannot claim a violation of the right to marry only because the court refuses to allow them to relocate with the child. The formation of the marriage is still allowed, and it is rather the circumstance of choosing not to relocate without the child that results in the spouses living apart. Similarly, the right to found a family – which is not autonomous but rather an attribute of the right to marry – does not guarantee the right to adopt or otherwise integrate into a family a child who is not the natural child of the couple concerned.[427] Any such circumstances are to be considered under Article 8 rather than Article 12.

4.2.4. PRELIMINARY CONCLUSIONS

This analysis confirms the findings of the existing literature that, from a dogmatic point of view, the issues at stake are relatively easy to identify within the framework of the ECHR. This conclusion is not significantly altered by the consideration of Article 2 of Protocol 4 to the Convention, nor other potentially relevant provisions. While Article 2 of Protocol 4 applies also to minors and restrictions of their freedom of movement, it is to be expected that the analysis of a violation in most child relocation cases will be conducted under Article 8 of the ECHR. This is because the essence of the dispute – a parental dispute about relocation of the child – will typically lie closer to the consideration of private autonomy and family life rather than free movement issues per se. The latter might, however, be at stake where the complaint refers predominantly not to a decision about parental rights and responsibilities, but rather one about travel

---

425 A.B. LaFrance, above n. 189, 114–19. This suggestion was made in reference to the US constitutional framework.

426 e.g. *Jaremowicz v Poland* [2010] ECtHR, app. no. 24023/03, para. 60.

427 W.A. Schabas, *The European Convention on Human Rights: A Commentary*, Oxford University Press, Oxford 2015, p. 543.

documents and similar administrative acts of national authorities. Depending on the facts of the case, the two matters might be functionally related, but should not be considered as identical and subject to the same tests.[428] However, the existing jurisprudence on other matters suggests that in both categories of cases the ECtHR will likely draw from the respective doctrine on Article 8 or Article 2 of Protocol 4.

Considering the wide margin of appreciation afforded to national authorities in parental disputes under Article 8, the balancing exercise will remain complex and contextually sensitive. Hence, the general doctrine does not immediately provide guidance that could direct national authorities facing child relocation disputes or help to address their complexity. Nevertheless, given that the Court evaluates violations in individual cases, and not national law in abstracto, there is a strong factual component in the margin of appreciation doctrine.[429] The analysis can, therefore, benefit from a closer focus on the particular strand of the ECtHR's jurisprudence on cross-border child relocation disputes specifically, fleshing out the Court's approach to the child's best interest principle and the scope of the margin of appreciation in such cases.

4.3. CROSS-BORDER CHILD RELOCATION IN THE JURISPRUDENCE OF THE ECtHR

Based on the research of cases and admissibility decisions accessible via the Court's database (HUDOC),[430] three judgments and two admissibility decisions of the ECtHR that were discussed on merits can be qualified as cross-border child relocation cases for the purposes of a detailed analysis.[431]

---

428 See the decision in *Lolova and Popova v Bulgaria* [2015] ECtHR, app. no. 68053/10.

429 O. de Schutter and F. Tulkens, 'Rights in Conflict: The European Court of Human Rights as a Pragmatic Institution' in E. Brems (ed), *Conflicts Between Fundamental Rights*, Intersentia, Oxford 2008, <https://ssrn.com/abstract=2446909>, pp. 22–23.

430 The empirical research was constructed to identify all potential child relocation disputes, considering the variety of approaches existing in the Contracting Parties. It therefore followed a factual approach, based on the nature of the dispute, rather than a formal approach. As the terminology and the construction of disputes in national legal systems differ, the search was conducted using a wide variety of keywords in different combinations: 'child' and 'relocation'; 'child' and 'relocate'; 'child' and 'travel' and 'consent'; 'child' and 'move' and 'consent'; and 'child' and 'residence' and 'change'. The analysis excluded cases that were clearly irrelevant, child abduction proceedings, and parental disputes where the parent and the child lived at a distance from each other, but the dispute was not about relocation. This research is an updated version of O. Ceran, above n. 219.

431 The complaint in *Lolova and Popova v Bulgaria* [2015] ECtHR, app. no. 68053/10 (briefly discussed, above Section 4.2.2.), also concerned the length of proceedings for court permission for the child's travel abroad (that constituted, in fact, the child's relocation).

While the case law research was not limited to any particular provision of the Convention, all cases concern Article 8 of the ECHR (the right to respect for private and family life), with only one complaint brought also under Article 2 of Protocol 4.[432] The admissibility decision in *J.A.T. and J.B.T. v United Kingdom*[433] is the only case in which the ECtHR addressed what was explicitly classified as a 'child relocation case'.[434] Three other complaints, all against Bulgaria, were framed in terms of a travel abroad due to the construction of national law. They were, however, decided against a background of a planned relocation and involved law applicable to parental moves with the child to another state.[435] The most recent judgment against Romania, clearly concerned with a cross-border change of the child's residence, is therefore the first and only *judgment* issued in what was clearly a cross-border child relocation case, albeit the Strasbourg Court does not discuss the case in those terms. The following paragraphs discuss the case law in a chronological order, with particular focus on the approach to the construction of the best interests of the child, the conceptualisation and balancing of different interests, and the margin of appreciation left to national authorities.

4.3.1. THE CASE OF *J.A.T AND J.B.T v UNITED KINGDOM* (2012)

J.A.T. and J.B.T. v United Kingdom remains the only case explicitly labelled as a child relocation case, and the only complaint brought by a non-relocating parent.[436] According to the non-relocating father, the national decision allowing relocation infringed his and his son's rights under Article 8, in particular as in-force English law afforded significant weight to the relocating parent's wishes. As such, it was claimed that the law did not allow for a fair balance of interests to be reached.[437] The ECtHR recognised that a family life existed between the applicants, and that the removal of the child from the jurisdiction inevitably

However, this part of the complaint was submitted outside the six-month time limit provided for by Article 35(1) of the Convention and was declared inadmissible on formal grounds. See paras. 39–42.

432 The complaints occasionally raised also other grounds, in particular Article 6 of the ECHR (the right to a fair trial) and Article 13 of the ECHR (absence of a domestic remedy).

433 *J.A.T. and J.B.T. v United Kingdom* (dec) [2012] ECtHR, app. no. 41767/11.

434 See also L.M. Coenraad, above n. 229, 315.

435 V. Todorova, 'National Report: Bulgaria', *Commission on European Family Law* <http://ceflonline.net/wp-content/uploads/Bulgaria-Parental-Responsibilities.pdf>; 'Moving/Settling Abroad with Children: Bulgaria', *European e-Justice Portal* (2020) <https://beta.e-justice.europa.eu/289/EN/movingsettling_abroad_with_children?BULGARIA&member=1>.

436 See also L.M. Coenraad, above n. 229, 315.

437 *J.A.T. and J.B.T. v United Kingdom* (dec) [2012] ECtHR, app. no. 41767/11, para. 25.

amounted to an interference with their right to respect for their family life. The Court quickly asserted that the mother's relocation to South Africa with the son took place according to the law and pursued the aim of protecting her rights and freedoms, which is a legitimate aim under the Convention.[438] The Court recognised:

> that decisions concerning international relocation raise difficult questions for decision-makers because they involve a delicate balancing exercise between the rights of each parent and the rights of the child and any decision made will almost certainly constitute a significant interference with the rights of at least one of the parties. Consequently, the domestic authorities enjoy a wide margin of appreciation when conducting such a balancing exercise and the Court will only interfere with a domestic decision in the circumstances … where the reasons given are not relevant and sufficient, or where the decision-making process is not fair or fails to afford due respect to the rights of all of the parties.[439]

In this case, the ECtHR observed that the national court requested a social worker to prepare a report on relocation. The report revealed that the motivations for the mother's move to South Africa and her future living arrangements were unclear and that the relationship between the father and the child was very close. However, the expert thought that the child had solid foundations and parental support to deal with any potential obstacles involved in a move. Ultimately, it was recommended that the child should not relocate abroad unless there was an important reason to do so, and the evaluation of such a reason was left for the national court. The legal test applied by the English court was one set out in a leading case on international child relocation at that time, *Payne v Payne*.[440] In short, the guidance formulated in *Payne v Payne* afforded significant weight to the primary carer's reasonable request to relocate, provided that the relocation proposal is genuine and realistic. Even though the parents in the *J.A.T. and J.B.T.* case had a shared care arrangement, the national judge relied on the *Payne* guidance as the arrangement was found to be unlikely to continue, regardless of the relocation issue. The judge found the mother's plan to be well-researched, even if somewhat vague, and stated that a refusal of the relocation application would probably leave her devastated. The court also recognised the close relationship between the father and the child, and the pure intentions of the father in attempting to stop the relocation. However, after a delicate balancing of all interests involved (but against the recommendation of the social worker), the interests of the child were said to lie with relocation. In reaching this conclusion, Article 8 of the ECHR was explicitly mentioned,

---

438 ibid., para. 29.
439 ibid., para. 31.
440 *Payne v Payne* [2001] EWCA Civ 166, [2001] 1 FLR 1052 (CA).

but the interference with the father's rights was said to be justified and proportionate, also because a suitable contact arrangement was to be put in place.

The ECtHR saw the reasons behind the decision as relevant and sufficient, and the decision-making process as a fair consideration of the rights of all involved, placing the decision within the margin of appreciation afforded to national authorities.[441] The complaint was, therefore, said to be manifestly ill-founded, and hence inadmissible.[442] Despite this, the decision includes interesting interpretative clues specific for child relocation matters. The complaint referred to the characteristics of the English doctrine that could be classified as inherently pro-relocation. The ECtHR observed that it indeed gave significant weight to the reasonable proposals of the primary carer. However, there was no legal presumption in favour of relocation, and this was sufficient for the Court to find that the law affords due respect to the rights of the child or the rights of the non-relocating parent.[443] Even though the *Payne v Payne* doctrine was, already at that time, widely criticised nationally,[444] such a doctrine was seen as a legitimate exercise of the national court's margin of appreciation. Given the facts of this case, in particular the social worker's assessment that the child should not relocate abroad unless there were important reasons in favour of relocation, the Court's decision clearly recognises that parental interests may legitimately play an important role in the final determination of such finely balanced disputes. Lastly, the ECtHR recalled the Washington Declaration – the only non-binding international law instrument on child relocation at that time – as part of relevant international law.[445] However, it did not refer to the Declaration in reaching its decision. It is therefore not clear if this material was relied upon in any way, or simply consulted as potentially relevant.[446] It might be that the Declaration did not raise any new issues against the background of national law and the Court's jurisprudence. This could suggest that child relocation disputes under the

---

441 *J.A.T. and J.B.T. v United Kingdom* (dec) [2012] ECtHR, app. no. 41767/11, para. 35.

442 More on ill-foundedness: L. Zwaak, Y. Haeck and C. Burbano Herrera, 'Procedure Before the Court' in P. van Dijk, F. van Hoof, A. van Rijn, and L. Zwaak (eds), *Theory and Practice of the European Convention on Human Rights*, 5th ed., Intersentia, Cambridge 2018, pp. 165–68.

443 *J.A.T. and J.B.T. v United Kingdom* (dec) [2012] ECtHR, app. no. 41767/11, para. 32.

444 e.g. M. Hayes, 'Relocation Cases: Is the Court of Appeal Applying the Correct Principles?' (2006) 18 *Child and Family Law Quarterly* 351. This critique was not discussed in the ECtHR decision. For a broader discussion of the development of the English child relocation doctrine, see Chapter 7.

445 *J.A.T. and J.B.T. v United Kingdom* (dec) [2012] ECtHR, app. no. 41767/11, para. 24.

446 On different uses of sources by the Court see A. Nußberger, 'Hard Law or Soft Law – Does It Matter?: Distinction Between Different Sources of International Law in the Jurisprudence of the ECtHR' in A. van Aaken and I. Motoc (eds), *The European Convention on Human Rights and General International Law*, Oxford University Press, Oxford 2018, pp. 48–49.

Convention are seen as any other parental dispute about residence or custody, and do not raise any novel issues of the interpretation of Article 8.

4.3.2. THE CASE OF *PENCHEVI v BULGARIA* (2015)

The word 'relocate' does not appear even once in the text of the *Penchevi v Bulgaria* judgment.[447] The case is, however, a (temporary) cross-border child relocation case at its core. The family had been living in Germany before the dissolution of the parents' relationship. The child's father moved back to Bulgaria and subsequently retained the child there during a visit, an event that prompted the mother to go back to Bulgaria as well. The mother then initiated divorce proceedings that ended with her being granted the exercise of parental rights over the child, and contact rights being determined with a view to the child's possible residence in Germany. However, the father did not give his consent to the child's journey abroad. As the proceedings on the matter continued, the mother went to Germany alone to start university, and the child stayed with his maternal grandparents. The mother frequently travelled between the two countries to take care of the child, which negatively affected her studies. After two sets of proceedings, the mother and the son were allowed to leave for Germany, two and a half years after the mother's first application.[448] This eventually led to the complaint under Article 8 of the Convention, on behalf of both the mother and the child, and under Article 2 of Protocol 4 to the Convention in respect of the alleged violation of the child's right to freedom of movement.

The ECtHR found that the refusal of the Supreme Court of Cassation and the duration of the proceedings clearly prevented the applicants from enjoying their family life, as the mother was completing her studies in Germany. There was, therefore, a clear interference with Article 8 rights.[449] The case provided, however, an opportunity to discuss the requirement for the interference to be in accordance with the law, which is particularly interesting in light of the diversity of approaches to child relocation. The applicants claimed that the law should allow cross-border travel with the resident parent only, as this is allowed in respect to domestic travels. Alternatively, the law should differentiate between different reasons for and the duration of such travel, or in respect of which parent is the primary carer.[450] The Court found, nevertheless, that the interference was broadly in accordance with the law, even if the law was phrased in general terms. The law clearly required both parents' agreement for all questions related to the

---

447 *Penchevi v Bulgaria* [2015] ECtHR, app. no. 77818/12.
448 ibid., paras. 23–24.
449 ibid., para. 61.
450 ibid., para. 52.

exercise of parental rights, including the child's travel abroad. The Court recalled that it must confine itself to a review of the case before it, and the national law as applied in the case, and it is not its task to review national law in abstracto. The law was found to be sufficiently clear, accessible and foreseeable.[451] It was also clear to the Court that the interference pursued the legitimate aim of protecting the rights of the father.[452] As such, the national legal requirements did not impose a disproportionate or unreasonable limitation on the applicants' right to family life, given that the state needs to ensure a fair balance between the interests of a child, those of the parents, and public order – a need emphasised by the frequency of child abductions.[453]

Regarding the necessity test, the ECtHR emphasised the need to strike a fair balance between the competing interests within the margin of appreciation given to national authorities. The Court observed that the mother repeatedly sought to obtain a court's permission for the child to travel abroad. In her first application, before she started her studies, she requested permission to travel abroad freely for a period of one year, which would allow her to finish her master's degree in Germany while taking care of her son. She described her circumstances but did not limit the scope of her application to Germany specifically. That request, after being granted at first and at second instance, was refused upon a cassation appeal considered by the Bulgarian Supreme Court of Cassation. The Supreme Court of Cassation relied on its well-established and binding case law, stipulating that permission for a child's unlimited travel abroad with one parent only could not be granted because, as a matter of principle, it is never in the best interests of the child. At the same time, the Bulgarian court refused to define the boundaries of the permission as to a specified destination and time frame.[454] The mother then initiated a second set of proceedings, ultimately successful, limiting the request to Germany and other EU Member States and to a three-year time frame.

The ECtHR emphasised that the best interests of the child need to be of crucial importance.[455] Striking a fair balance under Article 8 requires national authorities to conduct an analysis considering the individual circumstances of each case, and to avoid 'the mechanical application of domestic law'.[456] The Bulgarian Supreme Court of Cassation did not discuss such circumstances, relying instead on an overly formalistic blanket approach, and held the mother's formulation of the request as too unspecified while refusing to define it of its own motion. Its decision and the assessment of the best interests of the child

451 ibid., paras. 62–64.
452 ibid., para. 65.
453 ibid., para. 67.
454 ibid., paras. 18–22.
455 ibid., para. 56.
456 ibid., para. 57.

were, therefore, clearly inadequate.[457] The ECtHR found, additionally, that the duration of the proceedings – for which there was no satisfactory explanation – clearly disrespected the applicants' rights, in particular as it was established that 'the child's healthy and harmonious development required his mother's on-going involvement'.[458] Given the finding of the violation under Article 8, the Court did not examine other complaints on their merits.[459] In particular, the Court found the complaint under Article 2 of Protocol 4 admissible, but did not think that any separate issues arose under this provision.[460] This reinforces the finding that the essence of such disputes lies closer to Article 8 of the ECHR. However, in this case, the violation of Article 2 of Protocol 4 was asserted only on behalf of the child, as the mother herself had left the country, and, therefore, her autonomy interests remained outside the analysis.

4.3.3. THE CASE OF *DIMOVA AND PEEVA v BULGARIA* (2017)

The complaint in *Dimova and Peeva v Bulgaria*[461] was brought in reference to the same domestic law as *Penchevi v Bulgaria* and concerned a refusal of relocation. The mother's intention to settle abroad with her daughter was explicitly discussed, both by the national courts and the ECtHR.[462] The mother asserted that she was in a relationship with a Bulgarian man working in the UK, intending to marry him and move there permanently. The national court refused the request in the first instance, relying on the fact that the mother could not show that she had a fixed place of residence in the UK, or any secure income, and that the move would be an obstacle to the child's contact with the father.[463] On appeal, the mother complained that the father showed no interest in the child and did not pay any child support, and his refusal to give permission to the child's travel made it impossible for the applicants to go for holidays abroad or to reside in the UK. Specifically, the child's inability to leave Bulgaria was said to make the mother's marriage impossible. The appeal court reversed the previous judgment. The strained relationship between the parents spoke in favour of granting the permission for the child to travel abroad, and constituted grounds for changing the contact regime between the father and the child. The issue of contact was not, however, decided by the court.[464]

---

457 ibid., paras. 68–71.
458 ibid., paras. 72–74.
459 ibid., paras. 77–79.
460 ibid., para. 77.
461 *Dimova and Peeva v Bulgaria* [2017] ECtHR, app. no. 20440/11.
462 ibid., para. 40.
463 ibid., paras. 7–8.
464 ibid., paras. 9–10.

Upon the cassation appeal, the Supreme Court of Cassation ultimately refused the mother's application. The Court, as in *Penchevi*, relied on its well-established case law, stipulating that unlimited permission to travel abroad is, in principle, not in the best interests of the child. However, in this case, the Court conducted an individualised assessment of the child's interests and found that the mother had not presented any proposals regarding the post-relocation contact, had not sought any change of the contact regime, and had no evidence to demonstrate the asserted facts regarding the applicants' future in the UK. The Supreme Court thought that the situation would have been different if the mother had already been married and settled in the UK – then the question would be open as to whether it would be in the best interests of the child to join her abroad.[465] Following the proceedings, the mother married her partner, and the father agreed to the daughter leaving Bulgaria with the mother. The applicants subsequently complained that the refusal by the Supreme Court of Cassation of the mother's request breached their right to respect for their private and family life (Article 8 of the Convention).

The ECtHR upheld its reasoning expressed earlier in the *Penchevi* case and relating to the justification and proportionality of the interference with family life in cases of this nature.[466] However, the ECtHR differentiated this case from the *Penchevi* case at some important points. While refusal to allow the child to travel made it impossible for the mother to leave Bulgaria for the United Kingdom, where she wished to exercise her Article 8 rights by living together with her partner and her child, the impossibility of the child following represented an interference only with the mother's Article 8 rights. This was so because in the *Penchevi* case the court's decision resulted in the applicants being separated from each other for an extensive period of time, while in this case, the mother – based on her own sense of responsibility which she expressed during the domestic proceedings – remained with her daughter the whole time, and therefore the child could enjoy her family life uninterrupted.[467] While the refusal of the Supreme Court of Cassation, as in *Penchevi*, referred to the well-established case law that, in principle, saw unlimited travel abroad as not being in the child's best interests, the judgment itself was based on the individualised assessment of this particular case, ascribing weight to the lack of stability of the living and financial situation of the mother and the child in the UK.[468]

One further difference that was discussed by the Court in a relatively extensive way was related to the contact regime in place. In *Penchevi*, the contact regime was already determined with a view to the child living in Germany at the time of the application. This was not the case in *Dimova*

---

465 ibid., paras. 11–15.
466 ibid., paras. 33–37.
467 ibid., paras. 7, 34.
468 ibid., para. 40.

and Peeva v Bulgaria. The mother did not seek any change of contact, and even during the relocation proceedings – due to a change in national law – agreed to a new and more extensive contact agreement, specifying the address from which the child was to be collected.[469] The applicants argued before the ECtHR that the determination or change of contact was not a prerequisite for allowing the relocation application, nor did the law require that the place of residence of the child was to be determined explicitly. Rather, at the time of the application it sufficed for the court to determine with which of the parents the child had to live, and the child then followed that parent.[470] However, the Court found that this notwithstanding, the law had always been explicit about the requirement of both parents agreeing to any of the child's cross-border travels, confirming its finding in *Penchevi*.[471] While a change in the contact regime was not a formal prerequisite for relocation, the move would have made it impossible to comply with. The mother did not, however, seek to modify the contact agreement, even thought she could have done so in the same proceedings. Interestingly, the Court found this fact to constitute a relevant consideration in the balancing of the competing interests.[472] Hence, the conclusion reached by national courts was within their margin of appreciation, and no violation of Article 8 was found.[473] The Court took note that the length of the proceedings might be a relevant aspect of the proportionality assessment, but – as it was not raised by any of the parties – did not consider the matter of its own motion.[474]

The case of *Dimova and Peeva v Bulgaria*, on the one hand, confirms the reasoning applied in the two cases discussed above. In particular, the Court made a reference to the procedural obligations relating to striking a fair balance between all the interests and rights involved, based on an individualised assessment, and the reasonable length of the proceedings.[475] On the other hand, it also raises some interesting points. The finding that any alleged violation of Article 8 could be considered only in reference to the mother, and not the child, seems to suggest that the child is not perceived as having an independent interest in relocation. Rather, the child's interest is related to family life and the care she or he receives from the parents. Another issue concerns the correct approach to the fact that a parent is willing to voluntarily stay behind for the sake of their child if relocation is refused, as the

469 ibid., para. 6.
470 ibid., paras. 18, 41.
471 ibid., para. 35.
472 ibid., para. 42.
473 ibid., paras. 46–47.
474 ibid., para. 45.
475 See ibid. The applicants did not complain about the length of the proceedings, and the Court did not examine this on its own motion but made a reference to the relevance of the duration of proceedings for the general question of proportionality.

mother was in the case at hand. In that, she certainly gave up plans that were relevant for other aspects of her private and family life. This issue proves to be controversial across the world,[476] but this case does not address nor resolve the controversies. For the EU context, it is particularly interesting that the Court included in its summary of relevant international law some provisions of the Brussels II*bis* Regulation concerning jurisdiction and the recognition and enforcement of judgments in matrimonial matters and matters of parental responsibility, applicable between Bulgaria and the UK at that time.[477] The inclusion of the provisions concerning recognition of judgments and the rights of access could suggest that supranational legal instruments might play a role in the balancing of rights and interests in relocation cases, as recognised under Article 2 of Protocol 4.[478] The Court did not, however, refer to the Regulation in the considerations of the merits of the case. This might be prima facie surprising given the overall significance attached to the contact arrangements in this case. Article 9 of the Regulation foresaw continuing jurisdiction of the child's former habitual residence in contact rights that could qualify the assessment. At the same time, it might be interpreted as recognition that an altered legal space plays a role in relocation disputes, but this role is secondary to core considerations such as a parent's commitment to contact. Ultimately, national authorities can balance such considerations freely within their margin of appreciation.

4.3.4. THE CASE OF *GEE AND PETZEV v BULGARIA* (2018)

Gee and Petzev v Bulgaria[479] was yet another case in which a relocating mother lodged a complaint under Article 8 on her own behalf and on the behalf of the child. The mother, who was the resident parent, lost her job in Bulgaria and moved to the UK to take up another position. In the meantime, the child was taken care of by his maternal grandmother. Subsequently, the father initiated court proceedings seeking custody of the child. In parallel, the mother initiated separate proceedings for the court's permission to issue a passport for her son, and for him to leave the country and live with her in the UK. This was refused on appeal in reference to the well-established jurisprudence discussed in *Penchevi*, prescribing that permission for a child's unlimited travel abroad with one parent could not be granted. Most importantly, however, the contact regime could not

---

476 e.g. S.B. Boyd, above n. 160, 145.

477 *Dimova and Peeva v Bulgaria* [2017] ECtHR, app. no. 20440/11, para. 24. The Brussels II*bis* Regulation is Council Regulation (EC) 2201/2003 of 27 November 2003 concerning jurisdiction and the recognition and enforcement of judgments in matrimonial matters and the matters of parental responsibility [2003] OJ L338/1.

478 *Diamante and Pelliccioni v San Marino* [2011] ECtHR, app. no. 32250/08, para. 213.

479 *Gee and Petzev v Bulgaria* (dec) [2018] ECtHR, app. no. 33535/13.

be upheld if the child was taken abroad, jeopardising the relationship between the father and the child. Therefore, the parents had to either agree on a different contact regime and a different place of residence for the child, or have the court give a ruling on these matters (which they did not explicitly apply for).[480] In the meantime, the custody proceedings initiated by the father reached the appeal level, where the court decided that it would be best for the child to reside with the mother in the UK and put in place a respective contact regime, a decision that, once final, would allow the child to lawfully join his mother.[481] The original refusal and the length of the proceedings prompted, nevertheless, the applicants' complaint under Article 8 of the Convention.[482]

The ECtHR confirmed, once again, that the jurisprudence of Bulgarian courts is overly formalistic and lacking in terms of the assessment of the child's best interests principle. However, in both sets of proceedings in this case, the courts carried out an examination of the individual circumstances, followed by a careful balancing exercise. The Court then analysed the duration of the proceedings, finding that they lasted more than three years, but this cannot be considered to be excessive in itself. The relevant custody proceedings had not been initiated by the mother, but she did benefit from their findings, and the national court ruled on the child's residence on its own motion. Additionally, the child left Bulgaria and started school in the UK before the proceedings on his residence were finalised. Consequently, there was no violation of Article 8 of either of the applicants; the application was said to be manifestly ill-founded, and hence inadmissible.[483] As such, this decision does not raise any novel points of law, but rather confirms the findings from the previous cases, reinforcing the obligations of national authorities.[484]

4.3.5. THE CASE OF *SIMONA MIHAELA DOBRE v ROMANIA* (2023)

The most recent of the judgments, *Simona Mihaela Dobre v Romania*,[485] concerns a refusal to allow the applicant and her child to move their residence abroad. The mother intended to relocate with a ten-year-old son to Canada and informed the father about her plans. The father was not in agreement with the move and subsequently applied to the court seeking custody of the child. The mother, in her counterapplication, requested the court's authorisation for the move.

480 ibid., paras. 13–18.
481 ibid., paras. 8–12.
482 ibid., para. 21.
483 ibid., paras. 29–39.
484 ibid., para. 35.
485 *Simona Mihaela Dobre v Romania* [2023] ECtHR, app. no. 8361/21.

The facts of the case suggest that the relocation application was well-argued, with the mother already having a residence permit for Canada, a good job offer, and sufficient financial means to support the move. The child had also previously visited the country and the school he would be attending. The national court heard the child as well as the court-appointed psychologist and decided to reject both the father's and the mother's applications. In particular, the court noted that the child wished to move to Canada with his mother, but that this would not be in his interests and could not be decisive, given the level of maturity of the child and the fact that the psychologist was not convinced that the boy could fully understand the consequences of the move.[486] The best interests were established in reference to the particular developmental needs of the boy as well as concern for the child's relationship with his father and older brother (who would stay in Romania). Both parents appealed, the father still seeking custody, but the decision was upheld on 7 August 2020, two years and seven months after the initial application.

The Strasbourg application was brought by the mother under Article 8 of the ECHR, on her behalf only. While recalling the relevant international law material, the Court referred to *Penchevi v Bulgaria* and, extensively, various General Comments on the CRC.[487] However, also in this case – despite being a clear relocation case – no reference has been made to the soft law instruments on child relocation. In contrast to previous cases, resting on a general notion of Article 8 rights and the right to family life, the Court explicitly recognised that both the mother's interest in choosing her place of residence and the possibility of her continuing to live with her son fall under Article 8.[488] The Court confirmed that a national decision to the opposite constitutes an interference in accordance with the law and pursues the legitimate aim of protecting the right of the child and the father to maintain contact with each other. The case was framed as a balancing exercise between the mother's interest to relocate to Canada with her child and the child's interest to maintain contact with his father and brother.[489] The ECtHR emphasised that Romanian courts were guided by the best interests analysis, relying on expert opinion and analysing the evidence and consequences of the move in detail.[490] Although the relocation plan was very well-prepared, the national court pointed out that the applicant had not presented any specific reasons for the relocation, and the ECtHR did not see it necessary to depart from this finding.[491] Simultaneously, the ECtHR did not find the length of the proceedings excessive, because there was no

---

486 ibid., paras. 27–28.

487 These references might have been prompted by an explicit reference to the CRC contained in the Romanian law on the protection of children.

488 *Simona Mihaela Dobre v Romania* [2023] ECtHR, app. no. 8361/21, para. 54.

489 ibid., para. 59.

490 ibid., paras. 64–65.

491 ibid., para. 66.

uncertainty as to the child's situation and the mother exercised her parental rights unhindered throughout their duration.[492] The fact that the mother had to suspend her relocation plans – said to express her other interests protected under Article 8 – was not explicitly taken into account. Therefore, the Court found that the national courts struck a fair balance of interests in the case and no violation of the Convention was found.

It is worth emphasising that the application was brought only by the mother and only under Article 8 of the ECHR. The Court has, however, confirmed that the choice of one's place of residence is covered by the provision, implicitly accepting that this also includes a wish to reside abroad. In that light, Article 2 of Protocol 4 does not seem to be necessary to emphasise the individual interests of the relocating parent under the Convention. The Court seems to, however, implicitly accept that in the context of such a dispute, national authorities might qualify what constitutes a good reason for a parental move abroad as part of the balancing exercise. They might also consider the status quo to be a legitimate outcome of a dispute – neither did the father obtain custody rights, nor the mother the permission to relocate. Based on the information available, it is unclear if national courts considered whether the mother would stay or leave after relocation is refused and what kind of consequences this could have for her and for the child (as it was generally considered that the interests of the child spoke in favour of continuing to live with the mother). The reasoning of both the national court and the ECtHR suggests that it might be assumed that the parent will make peace with whatever judgment is made and remain in the country following the refusal to relocate.

This implicit assumption can be seen also in the ECtHR's pronouncements on the length of proceedings (two years and seven months). The mother raised this issue in her observations, but the ECtHR believed that there was no uncertainty about the child's legal situation throughout that time and the exercise of the mother's parental rights remained undisrupted.[493] The Strasbourg Court did not see the issue as giving rise to a violation of Article 8 in itself. The Court seemed to implicitly accept that the mother's decision to stay behind for more than two years to wait for their outcome, despite her clear wish to go to Canada and a job offer already obtained, does not violate her rights under the Convention. However, if Article 8 is taken to protect her choices in terms of residence and broader private autonomy, the length of proceedings might reasonably seem to be an important factor in the analysis, as uncertainty about one's future arrangements has clear consequences for the scope of one's autonomy. In the current judgment, it seems to be implicitly assumed that – on the balancing of interests – the parent might be required to stay and await decision on the merits for as long as necessary for the protection of the child.

---

492 ibid., para. 67.
493 ibid.

4.3.6. PRELIMINARY CONCLUSIONS

While the ECtHR's case law on cross-border child relocation is still fairly limited, overall analysis of the cases reveals that the margin of appreciation afforded to national authorities remains wide. This corresponds to the broader approach followed in parental disputes resolved under Article 8 and reflects the individualised nature of the cases. While the complaints can, in principle, engage rights under Article 2 of Protocol 4, most applications are brought and resolved under Article 8. Decisions in child relocation cases will usually result in an interference with Article 8 rights which can be claimed by all individuals involved in the dispute. However, such an interference is generally in accordance with the law and pursues the legitimate aim of protecting the rights and interests of others. National authorities have procedural obligations to conduct an individualised assessment of the child's best interests as a primary consideration and allow for a fair balancing of the different rights and interests involved, and – in principle – to resolve parental disputes in a timely manner. While the ECtHR has recognised that the length of proceedings might have an impact on one's family and private life,[494] the analysis of the cases reveals that the ECtHR might be more willing to consider this factor when it is an infringement of the child's Article 8 rights that is at stake, and less so when – on the facts of the case – it is only the parent that alleges such an infringement.[495]

The balancing exercise typically conceptualises the conflict of interests as the relocating parent's and the child's interest in the continuation of the mutual enjoyment of their family life versus the interest in the mutual contact and enjoyment of family life of the non-relocating parent and the child. Interestingly, in the most recent case, *Simona Mihaela Dobre v Romania*, the ECtHR went beyond that and explicitly recognised the mother's interest in choosing her place of residence and the possibility of her continuing to live with her son as falling under Article 8.[496] While in this case the mother's interest in relocation was at some point juxtaposed with the interest of the father and the child to maintain regular contact with each other,[497] the earlier decision in *J.A.T and J.B.T v United Kingdom* suggests that the Court generally perceives the relocating parent's interests more holistically, recognising that personal autonomy and family relationships intertwine.[498] The case sample

494 European Court of Human Rights, 'Guide on Article 8 of the European Convention on Human Rights', above n. 395, pp. 79, 88, 90. See also the remarks in *Dimova and Peeva v Bulgaria* [2017] ECtHR, app. no. 20440/11.

495 Compare the cases *Penchevi v Bulgaria* [2015] ECtHR, app. no. 77818/12 and *Simona Mihaela Dobre v Romania* [2023] ECtHR, app. no. 8361/21.

496 *Simona Mihaela Dobre v Romania* [2023] ECtHR, app. no. 8361/21, para. 54.

497 ibid., para. 59.

498 ibid., para. 29.

might be too small, and the cases too fact-specific, to draw broader conclusions from this distinction, but different framings in that regard might have varying normative consequences.[499] At the same time, the cases discussed above clearly demonstrate that national approaches to relocation may vary from relatively permissive (*J.A.T and J.B.T v United Kingdom*) to relatively restrictive (*Dimova and Peeva v Bulgaria*). The pro- or anti-relocation orientation of a jurisdiction would fall within the margin of appreciation as long as there is no legal presumption and an individualised assessment is conducted in each specific case. Provided that there is a well-established legal framework to resolve such disputes, no explicit child relocation law is necessary for the law to meet requirements of clarity, accessibility, and foreseeability, as demonstrated by all the cases involving Bulgaria. As such, this seems to strongly – even if often implicitly – rely on the fact that most national laws require the parents to jointly agree on important matters such as residence, reinforced by the supranational legal framework on cross-border child abduction.

Children's rights in the relocation context, perhaps unsurprisingly, seem to be understood in reference to the relationships with their parents. The ECtHR has been regularly criticised for an adult-focused framing of private disputes involving children,[500] due to the constitutional design of the Court which turns them into public disputes against the state.[501] However, an older child could be perceived as having an independent interest in choosing her or his place of residence. Additionally, the ECtHR rightly attaches great value to an individualised assessment of the best interests, with significant weight placed on stability factors and contact after the move. The formalistic approach of Bulgarian courts was explicitly criticised by the Court. However, the Court has consistently recognised the complexity of cross-border relocation disputes since its first decision on the matter. It is also accepted that where the child expresses his or her opinion on relocation, the national courts need to consider whether their maturity allows them to fully comprehend the consequences of such a

---

499 The excessive focus on the position of the relocating parent is one of the main points of critique of relocation law in some of the existing accounts. See, for example: J. Eekelaar, 'The Role of the Best Interests Principle in Decisions Affecting Children and Decisions about Children', above n. 146, 3 and 9.

500 e.g. C. Fenton-Glynn, *Children and the European Court of Human Rights*, Oxford University Press, Oxford 2020, p. 302; A. Daly, 'The Right of Children to Be Heard in Civil Proceedings and the Emerging Law of the European Court of Human Rights' (2011) 15 *International Journal of Human Rights* 441, 454; R. Lamont, 'Article 24 – The Rights of the Child' in S. Peers, T. Hervey, J. Kenner and A. Ward (eds), *The EU Charter of Fundamental Rights: A Commentary*, 2nd ed., Hart Publishing, Oxford 2021, pp. 705–06. See also O.A. Khazova, 'International Children's Rights Law: Child and the Family' in U. Kilkelly and T. Liefaard (eds), *International Human Rights of Children*, Springer, Singapore 2020, noting that 'the family is where it is most difficult to recognize and realize the idea of a child as the rights-holder'.

501 C. Fenton-Glynn, above n. 500, p. 255.

move. Therefore, the ECtHR consistently puts emphasis on the wide margin of appreciation granted to state authorities that have the benefit of direct access to all evidence material. While generalised best interests assessment will not satisfy the obligations under Article 8 (as confirmed by *Penchevi v Bulgaria*), it remains to be seen whether there are *individualised* best interests assessments that will exceed this wide margin of appreciation.

An exhaustive critical evaluation of the current jurisprudence is beyond the scope of this book. However, this conclusion suggests that the pressure exerted by the ECtHR on child relocation law is currently rather limited. Once the procedural obligations are met and the child's best interests are assessed in an individualised manner, the margin of appreciation afforded to national legislators and judges is indeed very wide. The findings confirm the earlier suggestions that approaching child relocation from a human rights perspective might allow for a clearer structuring of all interests, in particular those of the parents, but only on a high level of abstraction. Many relocation-specific dilemmas underlying the balancing exercise will be left to domestic authorities that need to decide, for example, whether the status quo is a viable option or what weight should be attached to the child's wishes or the parent's motivations behind the wish to relocate. Therefore, in this regard, national authorities have a wide margin of appreciation to make choices in line with their own normative preferences and sensitivities.[502] This is likely to have specific implications also for the interpretation of the EU Charter of Fundamental Rights, and hence the scope of any scrutiny of child relocation measures under EU law.

4.4. FUNDAMENTAL RIGHTS AND THE EU

In today's Europe, there are two major supranational instruments concerned with the meaning and scope of fundamental rights: the ECHR and the EU Charter of Fundamental Rights. The ECtHR is vested with the protection of the rights enshrined in the former, while the CJEU is tasked with the interpretation of the latter within the broader context of EU law. Before the EU Charter entered into force in 2009, protection of fundamental rights was addressed by the CJEU as part of the general principles of EU law,[503] with the Luxembourg Court drawing from the rights enshrined in the ECHR and the ECtHR's jurisprudence

[502] See also S. Choudhry and J. Herring, above n. 189, p. 285 concluding that the human rights approach to child relocation allows different people to reach different – but equally reasonable – decisions on the matter.

[503] e.g. Case C-11/70, *Internationale Handelsgesellschaft mbH v Einfuhr- und Vorratsstelle für Getreide und Futtermittel*, ECLI:EU:C:1970:114.

as sources of interpretative guidance. After 2009, the number of references to the ECtHR's case law generally decreased.[504] However, as already mentioned, rights contained in the EU Charter should be interpreted in line with the ECHR provisions that correspond to them, and therefore an analysis of the ECHR and the jurisprudence of its guardian, the ECtHR, are of direct relevance for EU law (Article 52(3) of the CFR). This is so in particular in family matters, as the scope of application of the Charter remains limited and tied with the question of EU competences. The following sections discuss, therefore, issues of the application and interpretation of the Charter in child relocation cases, accounting for broader dynamics of fundamental rights in the European legal space.

4.4.1. PRELIMINARY REMARKS: APPLICATION AND INTERPRETATION OF THE EU CHARTER

The scope of application of the EU Charter reflects its role in the EU legal infrastructure. The Charter applies to the EU and its institution, with due regard to the principle of subsidiarity, and to Member States only when they are implementing EU law (Article 51(1) of the CFR).[505] The Charter does not extend the competences of the EU or modify its powers defined in the Treaties (Article 51(2) of the CFR). While this is prima facie clear, Article 51 raises some controversial issues, including, in particular, how to define the term 'implementing'. This discussion is particularly relevant for family law that remains outside the EU's competence. Restrictions on child relocation hardly implement EU law directly, but rather involve a potential *derogation* from its provisions. However, it has long been recognised that any derogation from EU law always needs to meet the threshold of EU law itself, and as such should be encompassed by the scope of application of the Charter.[506] Therefore, it is

---

504 For the empirical data and related analysis see G. De Búrca, 'After the EU Charter of Fundamental Rights: The Court of Justice as a Human Rights Adjudicator?' (2013) 20 *Maastricht Journal of European and Comparative Law* 168.

505 Protocol (No 30) on the Application of the Charter of Fundamental Rights of the European Union to Poland and the United Kingdom [2008] OJ C115/313, since Brexit relevant only in case of Poland, is supposed to limit the application of the Charter's provisions to this Member State and preclude the ability of the CJEU to control national laws' compliance with the Charter. However, it is generally accepted that the Protocol does not call into question the applicability of the Charter to Poland at large. Because of this, the Protocol is only of limited relevance for this discussion. For a general discussion on the protocol, see A. Arnull, 'Protocol (No 30) on the Application of the Charter of Fundamental Rights of the European Union to Poland and the United Kingdom' in S. Peers, T. Hervey, J. Kenner and A. Ward (eds), *The EU Charter of Fundamental Rights: A Commentary*, Hart Publishing, Oxford 2014.

506 A. Ward, 'Article 51 – Field of Application' in S. Peers, T. Hervey, J. Kenner and A. Ward (eds), *The EU Charter of Fundamental Rights: A Commentary*, Hart Publishing, Oxford 2014, pp. 1428–29; D. Sarmiento, 'Who's Afraid of the Charter? The Court of Justice, National Courts and the New Framework of Fundamental Rights Protection in Europe' (2013) 50 *Common*

suggested that if a dispute at hand falls within the scope of EU law, the Charter will apply.[507] In other words, the Charter can be seen as the 'shadow' of EU law provisions.[508] In light of the issues raised by child relocation disputes, any potential derogation from EU law would therefore clearly engage not only EU Treaty provisions independently, but also the provisions of the Charter.

The application of the Charter must not, however, extend the general EU competences. The scope of EU competences as such is not always clear, as already demonstrated in Chapter 3. However, in this context, the CJEU has already clarified how it interprets Article 51(2) of the CFR. When a dispute arises that is partially governed by EU law and partially by national law, Member States generally retain the freedom to interpret fundamental rights according to their own standards, as long as such interpretation does not compromise the level of protection provided by the Charter nor the effectiveness of EU law.[509] This has two main consequences for the analysis of child relocation. Assuming that child relocation falls within the scope of EU law,[510] Member States would, in principle, be free to strike their own balance of rights – with the condition that they do not compromise the level of fundamental rights protection offered by the EU, nor the primacy, unity and effectiveness of EU law. The latter safeguard is of an exceptional nature and would apply only to severe breaches of EU law.[511] The main question is, therefore, what level of protection of fundamental rights is offered by the EU in the child relocation context. As noted in the literature, any comparison of the levels of protection of fundamental rights is conceptually difficult, as values underlying such rights are perceived differently in different systems, and so is the essence of rights.[512] These conceptual considerations will, therefore, always be highly context-dependent, but the Charter elaborates on the scope and interpretation of its rights and principles in Article 52.

Market Law Review 1267, 1296–98. See also the broader discussion in K. Lenaerts, 'The Court of Justice of the European Union and the Protection of Fundamental Rights' (2011) 31 *Polish Yearbook of International Law* 79, SSRN Scholarly Paper ID 2218538 <https://papers.ssrn.com/abstract=2218538>.

507 Case C-617/10, *Åklagaren v Hans Åkerberg Fransson*, ECLI:EU:C:2013:105, paras. 18–25. See also A. Ward, above n. 506, p. 1452.

508 K. Lenaerts and J.A. Gutiérrez-Fons, 'The Place of the Charter in the EU Constitutional Edifice' in S. Peers, T. Hervey, J. Kenner and A. Ward (eds), *The EU Charter of Fundamental Rights: A Commentary*, Hart Publishing, Oxford 2014, p. 1568.

509 Case C-617/10, *Åkerberg Fransson*, ECLI:EU:C:2013:105, para. 29. For an overview of the discussion see D. Sarmiento, above n. 506, 1287–94. See also, approving, A. Ward, above n. 506, p. 1419.

510 See Chapter 5.

511 D. Sarmiento, above n. 506, 1294–95.

512 ibid., 1296. Interestingly, Sarmiento illustrates his point with the example of the right to marry. He notes that 'in some Member States, it protects values inherent to a specific conception of family life, whilst in others it is closer to an individualistic vision of the value of privacy'.

According to Article 52(2), rights which are based on the EU Treaties should be exercised under the conditions and within the limits defined by those Treaties. This applies to freedom of movement rights as well as rights deriving from Union citizenship.[513] Article 52(3) stipulates that when the Charter contains rights which correspond to rights guaranteed by the Convention for the Protection of Human Rights and Fundamental Freedoms, the meaning and scope of those rights shall be the same as those laid down by the said Convention. Further, Article 52(4) emphasises that insofar as the Charter recognises fundamental rights as they result from the constitutional traditions common to the Member States, those rights should be interpreted in harmony with those traditions.[514] Article 52(3) was meant to secure the necessary consistency between the Charter and the ECHR. This means that limitations to those rights must comply with the standards recognised by the ECHR, as interpreted in the case law of the ECtHR.[515] The level of protection should never be lower than that envisaged by the ECHR system, but the Charter does not preclude wider protection within EU law than within the ECHR system.[516] In light of this systemic relationship, the scope of the margin of appreciation that the ECtHR affords to national authorities in child relocation cases is of direct relevance for the interpretation of the Charter in such context.

4.4.2. EU CHARTER PROVISIONS RELEVANT FOR CHILD RELOCATION

Several provisions of the EU Charter are relevant for the analysis of child relocation: Article 7 (the right to private and family life); Article 24 (the rights of the child); and Article 45 (freedom of movement), with some other provisions being of a subsidiary character. Article 7 foresees that everyone has the right to respect for his or her private and family life, home and communications, and as such its scope is the same as that of Article 8 of the ECHR.[517] In the context of EU law, the right to family life has been used to reinforce free movement

---

513 Explanations Relating to the Charter of Fundamental Rights [2007] OJ C303/17, Explanation on Article 52.

514 On national traditions and potentially different interpretations, see S. Iglesias Sánchez, 'The Court and the Charter: The Impact of the Entry into Force of the Lisbon Treaty on the ECJ's Approach to Fundamental Rights' (2012) 49 *Common Market Law Review* 1565, 1605–08.

515 S. Prechal and S. Peers, 'Article 52 – Scope and Interpretation of Rights and Principles' in S. Peers, T. Hervey, J. Kenner and A. Ward (eds), *The EU Charter of Fundamental Rights: A Commentary*, Hart Publishing, Oxford 2014, p. 1456.

516 e.g. Case C-400/10 PPU, *J. McB. v L. E.*, ECLI:EU:C:2010:582, paras. 53–54, or View of the Advocate General in Case C-400/10 PPU, *J. McB. v L. E.*, ECLI:EU:C:2010:544, para. 66.

517 Explanations Relating to the Charter of Fundamental Rights [2007] OJ C303/17, Explanation on Article 7. See also Joined Cases C-133/19, C-136/19 and C-137/19, *B.M.M and Others v État belge*, ECLI:EU:C:2020:577, para. 34.

rights, in particular to strengthen the right of EU citizens to be accompanied or joined by family members when they move across the Union.[518] Article 7 of the Charter, in combination with EU law on free movement and citizenship provisions, can confer, therefore, the right to live *as a family* 'somewhere in particular'.[519] Any limitations to the exercise of Article 7 rights, as in all other rights and freedoms recognised by the Charter, must be provided for by law and respect the essence of the right (Article 52(1)). Subject to the principle of proportionality, limitations may be introduced only if they are necessary and genuinely meet objectives of general interest recognised by the Union or the need to protect the rights and freedoms of others, with the latter being particularly relevant in child relocation cases.

Article 7 is often recalled together with Article 24 of the Charter protecting the rights of the child.[520] Article 24 constitutes an evolution in comparison to the ECHR, where children and adults are protected within the same rights framework,[521] and was a highly welcomed development of EU law.[522] It recognises children's vulnerable position,[523] as well as their right to be heard and to have their best interests taken into account as a primary consideration in all action taken by public or private authorities (Article 24(2)). Article 24, as compared to Article 7 of the Charter, prioritises an individual child, but – in line with the jurisprudence of the ECtHR – does not require that the child's interests are the sole consideration in the disputes.[524] While the Strasbourg jurisprudence on Article 8 of the ECHR remains relevant for the CJEU, Article 24 does, at the same time, create an opportunity for the Court to develop its own

---

518 T. Lock, 'Article 7 CFR' in M. Kellerbauer, M. Klamert and J. Tomkin (eds), *The EU Treaties and the Charter of Fundamental Rights: A Commentary*, Oxford University Press, Oxford 2019, p. 2118.

519 ibid. The case law is, however, not fully consistent and – depending on the context – 'somewhere in particular' might refer to the territory of the Union as a whole, rather than any specific Member State. For a more detailed discussion on this, see Chapters 5 and 6.

520 e.g. Joined Cases C-133/19, C-136/19 and C-137/19, *B.M.M and Others v État belge*, ECLI:EU:C:2020:577, paras. 34–35; Case C-165/14, *Alfredo Rendón Marín v Administración del Estado*, ECLI:EU:C:2016:675, para. 81.

521 See S. Choudhry and J. Herring, above n. 189, p. 222 suggesting that this might cause their interests not to be afforded sufficient weight. See also R. Lamont, 'Article 24 – The Rights of the Child' in S. Peers, T. Hervey, J. Kenner and A. Ward (eds), *The EU Charter of Fundamental Rights: A Commentary*, Hart Publishing, Oxford 2014, pp. 705–06.

522 e.g. C. McGlynn, 'Rights for Children: The Potential Impact of the European Union Charter of Fundamental Rights' (2002) 8 *European Public Law* 387; C. McGlynn, 'Families and the European Charter of Fundamental Rights: Progressive Change or Entrenching the Status Quo?' (2001) 26 *European Law Review* 582.

523 See the general discussion in R. Forastiero, 'The Charter of Fundamental Rights and the Protection of Vulnerable Groups: Children, Elderly People and Persons with Disabilities' in G. Palmisano (ed), *Making the Charter of Fundamental Rights a Living Instrument*, Brill Nijhoff, Leiden 2014.

524 R. Lamont, above n. 521, p. 687.

child-centred standards as no corresponding provision can be found in the ECHR. In public law cases, the CJEU has already applied Article 24 in ways that strengthen children's rights.[525] The approach in private disputes seems, however, to remain more conservative.

The relation between Article 24 and Article 7 will often be crucial, especially if there is harsh conflict between the parents – which happens often in cross-border cases involving questions of freedom of movement.[526] Since EU law in this area has focused, so far, mostly on harmonising international private law on parental responsibilities as part of the area of freedom, security and justice,[527] Article 24(3) pays particular attention to the right of the child to maintain contact with both parents.[528] This right does not in itself, however, limit the competences of Member States in shaping custody and contact rights according to their own national law, as confirmed by the *J. McB* case.[529] Case law on Article 24 demonstrates that Member States retain significant discretion in the implementation of children's rights in the national context, even if a dispute falls within the scope of EU law.[530] It has been confirmed that, although the child's best interests are a primary consideration in decision-making involving children, they can be overridden by other factors in some cases.[531] As such, the Article was said to be 'changing the narratives, but not (yet) challenging the reasoning of EU law'.[532] While children's rights must be considered when assessing justifications for and proportionality of restrictions of EU free movement provisions, it is worth emphasising that the EU judicial system 'is better designed for the discovery of violations of rights through inconsistencies in law rather than failures in practice to live up to the law'.[533] The jurisdictional constraints of the CJEU, the procedural nature of many rights enshrined in Article 24 of the CFR, and the open-ended nature of the best interests of the child principle as such mean that national authorities will remain predominantly responsible for the interpretations of such rights in individual cases.[534]

---

525 See, for example, the discussion in E. Nissen, 'A Children's Rights Perspective to Ruiz Zambrano and Chavez-Vilchez: An Examination in Light of Theory, Practice and Child Development Research' (2021) 23 *European Journal of Migration and Law* 68.

526 R. Lamont, above n. 521, pp. 671–72.

527 Explanations Relating to the Charter of Fundamental Rights [2007] OJ C303/17, Explanation on Article 24.

528 R. Lamont, above n. 521, pp. 675–76.

529 See T. Lock, above n. 518, p. 2175.

530 R. Lamont, above n. 521, p. 680.

531 ibid., p. 687.

532 R. Lamont, above n. 521, p. 690.

533 H. Cullen, 'Children's Rights' in S. Peers and A. Ward (eds), *The EU Charter of Fundamental Rights: Politics, Law and Policy*, Hart Publishing, Oxford 2004, p. 345.

534 See also R. Lamont, above n. 521, p. 688.

Article 45(1) of the CFR corresponds to Article 2 of Protocol 4 in the ECHR system. It guarantees every EU citizen the right to move and reside freely within the territory of the Member States. This right might also be granted, in accordance with the Treaties, to third-country nationals (Article 45(2)). As such, Article 45 corresponds to the freedom of movement principle as protected by the Treaty (Articles 20(2)(a) and 21 of the TFEU) and secondary EU law.[535] As the application of the Charter requires an a priori link to EU law, Treaty rights continue to be of leading importance for the exercise of this freedom.[536] Therefore, it is suggested that the significance of the Article is rather symbolic.[537] Most likely, any challenges that could potentially rely on Article 45 will be brought on the basis of the Treaty,[538] and hence it is not necessary to analyse this provision separately. The same observations apply to the Charter's provisions regulating economic activity, in particular Article 15 providing for, e.g. the right to engage in work and to pursue a freely chosen or accepted occupation in any Member State. When a relocating parent wants to pursue a professional opportunity, EU law broadens legal bases available for such claims. However, as it builds on Articles 26, 45, 49 and 56 of the TFEU,[539] it merely 'reinforces the freedom' granted to EU citizens based on the Treaty.[540] The existing CJEU jurisprudence shows that the CJEU often limits itself to the analysis of the Treaty provisions as sufficient to resolve the issue at hand.[541]

Other rights included in the Charter might also be relevant for relocation disputes but will remain of a subsidiary character. Article 21 contains a prohibition of discrimination, which extends to the prohibition of discrimination based on nationality within the scope of application of the Treaties. This could prove relevant if restrictions on relocation are seen to constitute indirect discrimination on the grounds of nationality based on Article 18 of the TFEU.[542] However, insofar as the Charter provision repeats

---

535 D. Martin, 'Article 45 CFR' in M. Kellerbauer, M. Klamert and J. Tomkin (eds), *The EU Treaties and the Charter of Fundamental Rights: A Commentary*, Oxford University Press, Oxford 2019.

536 E. Spaventa, 'Article 45 – Freedom of Movement and of Residence' in S. Peers, T. Hervey, J. Kenner and A. Ward (eds), *The EU Charter of Fundamental Rights: A Commentary*, Hart Publishing, Oxford 2014, p. 1162.

537 D. Martin, above n. 535.

538 e.g. Case C-434/09, *Shirley McCarthy v Secretary of State for the Home Department*, ECLI:EU:C:2011:277, para. 27.

539 Explanations Relating to the Charter of Fundamental Rights [2007] OJ C303/17, Explanation on Article 45.

540 D. Ashiagbor, 'Article 15 – Freedom to Choose an Occupation and Right to Engage in Work' in S. Peers, T. Hervey, J. Kenner and A. Ward (eds), *The EU Charter of Fundamental Rights: A Commentary*, Hart Publishing, Oxford 2014, p. 425.

541 e.g. Case C-233/12, *Simone Gardella v Istituto nazionale della previdenza sociale (INPS)*, ECLI:EU:C:2013:449, paras. 39–41.

542 R. Lamont, above n. 12, 241.

the text of the Treaties, it also remains mostly of a symbolic character.[543] Article 23 additionally requires equality between women and men to be ensured in all areas, beyond Article 157 of the TFEU on equal treatment between sexes in matters of employment and occupation. However, the existing case law drawing from these provisions has been, so far, limited to employment conditions and social benefits.[544] Timothy Scott suggests that a worker wishing to relocate (who usually needs to accept the offer of employment promptly) is put at a disadvantage by the requirement to obtain a court's permission to do so.[545] As the majority of relocating parents are women, women might find it more difficult to access the EU employment market in such circumstances. There is also the possibility of nationality and gender grounds being raised together.[546] However, even though the CJEU has addressed some cases concerning migrant women, the intersections of gender and other grounds have not been addressed, with the Court considering only one of the grounds of discrimination.[547] Given that the Court is more likely to select a less controversial ground for its judgments, it can be expected that child relocation would rather be considered in reference to freedom of movement and discrimination based on nationality.

4.4.3. THE CJEU AS A FUNDAMENTAL RIGHTS COURT IN FAMILY-RELATED MATTERS

The discussion so far emphasises two themes: where the Charter rights correspond to Treaty rights, it is rather the 'traditional' EU law analysis that will remain of major importance; where they correspond to the ECHR, the jurisprudence of the ECtHR will significantly guide the interpretation. This does not mean that the increasing emphasis on human rights in the EU legal framework erases differences between the CJEU's and the ECtHR's systems,

---

543 See also D. Martin, 'Article 21 CFR' in M. Kellerbauer, M. Klamert and J. Tomkin (eds), *The EU Treaties and the Charter of Fundamental Rights: A Commentary*, Oxford University Press, Oxford 2019, p. 2167.

544 D. Martin, 'Article 23 CFR' in M. Kellerbauer, M. Klamert and J. Tomkin (eds), *The EU Treaties and the Charter of Fundamental Rights: A Commentary*, Oxford University Press, Oxford 2019, pp. 2171–72.

545 T. Scott, above n. 12, p. 12.

546 See R. Nielsen, 'Is European Union Equality Law Capable of Addressing Multiple and Intersectional Discrimination yet? Precautions against Neglecting Intersectional Cases' in D. Schiek and V. Chege (eds), *European Union Non-Discrimination Law: Comparative Perspectives on Multidimensional Equality Law*, Routledge-Cavendish, Abingdon 2008, p. 37.

547 ibid., p. 42; D. Schiek and S. Burri, 'Multiple Discrimination in EU Law: Opportunities for Legal Responses to Intersectional Gender Discrimination?' (2009) European Commission, Directorate-General for Employment, Social Affairs and Equal Opportunities, pp. 7–8.

particularly in light of the construction and objectives of the EU legal order.[548] The CJEU was, in the past, criticised for favouring its integrational agenda and the efficiency of the EU fundamental freedoms at the cost of fundamental human rights,[549] and for its reluctance to fully embrace some of the strands of the ECtHR jurisprudence (e.g. regarding the interpretation of what constitutes a 'family life').[550] The reasons for the divergence between the Courts might lie at a different starting point of the analysis, with the ECtHR examining restrictions on human rights (some of which might be brought by the economic fundamental freedoms), and the CJEU restrictions on free movement (with the protection of fundamental human rights being one of the potential justifications).[551] At the same time, however, some strands of the CJEU's case law grant wider protection than the ECtHR is willing to provide and are not necessarily linked to mobility. Despite the recurring criticism, the logic of fundamental rights in the Union might now be connected less to any 'internal market imperatives', but rather governed by different systemic constraints and methodological rationale from those of the ECtHR.

While the CJEU does not always fully follow interpretations put forward by the ECtHR, it is not ignorant of the standards set by the Strasbourg Court either,[552] as it also cannot be under Article 52(3) of the Charter. The Luxembourg Court has often drawn from the ECtHR's jurisprudence in its fundamental rights considerations, in particular in delicate areas such as (peripheral issues of) family law where the EU's competence is at least controversial.[553] Experiences from sensitive areas of law show that the CJEU is more likely to engage with the ECtHR's jurisprudence and is often not willing to depart from its interpretations.[554] At the same time, the CJEU's

548 W. Weiß, 'The EU Human Rights Regime Post Lisbon: Turning the CJEU into a Human Rights Court?' in S. Morano-Foadi and L. Vickers (eds), *Fundamental Rights in the EU: A Matter for Two Courts*, Hart Publishing, Oxford 2015, p. 89. See also M. Kuijer, 'The Challenging Relationship between the European Convention on Human Rights and the EU Legal Order: Consequences of a Delayed Accession' (2018) *International Journal of Human Rights* 10–11.

549 See the discussion in S.A. de Vries, 'Balancing Fundamental Rights with Economic Freedoms According to the European Court of Justice' (2013) 9 *Utrecht Law Review* 169.

550 e.g. H. Stalford, 'Concepts of Family under EU Law – Lessons from the ECHR' (2002) 16 *International Journal of Law, Policy and the Family* 410.

551 S.A. de Vries, above n. 549, 19.

552 e.g. Case C-400/10 PPU, *J. McB. v L. E.*, ECLI:EU:C:2010:582, paras. 53–56.

553 R. Wintemute, 'In Extending Human Rights, Which European Court Is Substantively "Braver" and Procedurally "Fitter"? The Example of Sexual Orientation and Gender Identity Discrimination' in S. Morano-Foadi and L. Vickers (eds), *Fundamental Rights in the EU: A Matter for Two Courts*, Hart Publishing, Oxford 2015, p. 193. See also considerations in Case C-148/02, *Carlos Garcia Avello v Belgian State*, ECLI:EU:C:2003:539 or Case C-400/10 PPU, *J. McB. v L. E.*, ECLI:EU:C:2010:582.

554 R. Wintemute, above n. 553, p. 192. See also J. Krommendijk, 'The Use of ECtHR Case Law by the Court of Justice after Lisbon: The View of Luxembourg Insiders' (2015) 22 *Maastricht Journal of European and Comparative Law* 812, 834 who, based on interviews with CJEU

engagement with fundamental rights tends to be pragmatic and conscious of the institutional implications of such engagement, in particular regarding the autonomy of EU law.[555] In light of this, some commentators note that where there is significant CJEU case law existing already, the Court is not willing to engage with the ECtHR's jurisprudence.[556] Three examples touching upon family matters can be used to illustrate this dynamic, which is constrained by and draws from the ECtHR case law, but is simultaneously shaped by the broader EU legal order.

In *J. McB.*, the CJEU had to decide whether the Brussels II*bis* Regulation, interpreted pursuant to Article 7 of the CFR, precludes a Member State:

> from requiring by its law that the father of a child who is not married to the mother shall have obtained an order of a court of competent jurisdiction granting him custody in order to qualify as having 'custody rights' which render the removal of that child ... wrongful.[557]

The Court emphasised that the Charter has the same legal value as the Treaties, and that the Court is called upon to interpret, in the light of the Charter, the law of the European Union only within the limits of the powers conferred on it, without assessing national law as such.[558] Regarding the interpretation of Article 7, the CJEU recognised that, in light of Article 52(3) of the Charter, it needs to be given the same meaning and scope as Article 8 of the ECHR.[559] Finding that the ECtHR had already considered a similar case and did not find that such a regulation violates Article 8, as long as national law provides the father with the possibility of obtaining custody, the essence of Article 7 was said to require exactly such an understanding.[560] This explicitly reaffirmed the role of the ECtHR for the interpretation of fundamental rights in the EU context.

---

agents, observes that the sensitive nature of a case is one of the factors increasing the chances for citation of the case law of the ECtHR.

555 See J. Krommendijk, above n. 554, for a very interesting analysis of the factors influencing the CJEU's engagement with ECtHR's jurisprudence, based on qualitative research involving interviews with relevant actors.

556 S. Iglesias Sánchez, above n. 514, 1604. See also S. Morano-Foadi and S. Andreadakis, 'Reflections on the Architecture of the EU after the Treaty of Lisbon: The European Judicial Approach to Fundamental Rights' (2011) 17 *European Law Journal* 595 who, based on their qualitative research, note: 'It is confirmed by the interviews that the judges' eyes first analyse the Charter, as the EU's high standard of protection, and then other sources such as the ECtHR jurisprudence and general principles of Union law, depending on the nature of the case and the wording of the questions raised by the national judge'.

557 Case C-400/10 PPU, *J. McB. v L. E.*, ECLI:EU:C:2010:582, para. 25.

558 ibid., paras. 50–52; View of the Advocate General in Case C-400/10 PPU, *J. McB. v L. E.*, ECLI:EU:C:2010:544, paras. 54–57.

559 Case C-400/10 PPU, *J. McB. v L. E.*, ECLI:EU:C:2010:582, para. 53.

560 ibid., paras. 54–57.

At the same time, the Court had a chance to deviate from this interpretation based on Article 24 – one that does not have a direct counterpart in the ECHR. It noted, however, that there exists a great variety of parent-child relationships in Member States, which is reflected in the rules on parental responsibilities. Therefore, in light of Article 24 of the Charter, national courts must have jurisdiction to protect the child's interests by a decision on custody or access that takes into account:

> all the relevant facts, ... in particular the circumstances surrounding the birth of the child, the nature of the parents' relationship, the relationship of the child with each parent, and the capacity of each parent to take the responsibility of caring for the child.[561]

Thus, it reaffirmed the wide margin of appreciation recognised in the jurisprudence of the ECtHR, taking account of its limited competence. While not framed in these terms, this assertion can also be read in light of Article 52(4), which requires that fundamental rights should be interpreted in harmony with traditions common to Member States, as the variety of family law solutions is a reflection of choices made in that regard as well.

Another illustration of this dynamic is *Garcia Avello*, a case concerning the possibility to change the surname of minor EU citizens. In his Opinion, the Advocate General made a reference to both Article 8 of the ECHR and other international instruments, including the CRC, but reached the conclusion that it is not necessary to examine fundamental rights as the case revealed discrimination on grounds of nationality that is prohibited by the Treaty.[562] In this regard, it nevertheless explicitly noted that even if the ECHR affords Contracting States a wide margin of appreciation in this field:

> the existence of a wide margin of appreciation in the context of the Convention does not ... have any direct bearing on the breadth of margin available in the different context of citizenship of the European Union.[563]

The Court indeed made no reference to fundamental rights, recognising that even if rules on names fall within the exclusive competence of the Member States, they must comply with EU law.[564] Clearly, where it is possible to resolve the case based on Treaty provisions, the Court prefers to resolve the case autonomously. This might be particularly relevant, by analogy, if restrictions on cross-border child relocation are said to constitute discrimination based on nationality.

---

561 ibid., paras. 61–63.

562 Opinion of the Advocate General in Case C-148/02, *Carlos Garcia Avello v Belgian State*, ECLI:EU:C:2003:311, para. 66.

563 ibid.

564 Case C-148/02, *Garcia Avello*, ECLI:EU:C:2003:539, para. 25.

Fundamental rights protection might also be introduced via EU Treaty provisions. In *Ruiz Zambrano*, the CJEU used Union citizenship as a new trigger for a form of fundamental rights protection.[565] Mr Ruiz Zambrano was facing expulsion from Belgium, where he resided with his children who possessed EU citizenship, but EU law did not govern his immigration situation. It was therefore 'no longer mobility [that triggered this protection], but rather a form of "vulnerability"' that seemed to deserve protection beyond doctrines available to the CJEU at that point.[566] By creating the doctrine of substance of rights of EU citizenship, the CJEU became 'the custodian of specifically European interest', which has more to do with fundamental rights than internal market or mobility.[567] At the same time, no reference was made to fundamental rights in the judgment, even though the Charter was explicitly mentioned in the questions referred to the CJEU by the national court.[568] One reason for this might be related to the fact that the ECtHR jurisprudence would not support the conclusion, as Member States have a wider margin of appreciation under the Convention.[569] Another reason might be that inclusion of fundamental rights in the substance of EU citizenship rights could create an opening towards relying on EU fundamental rights in all cases, even in those with no relation to EU law otherwise,[570] and lead to political controversies.[571] The *Dereçi*

565 Case C-34/09, *Gerardo Ruiz Zambrano v Office national de l'emploi (ONEm)*, ECLI:EU:C:2011:124; E. Dubout, 'The Protection of Fundamental Rights and the Allocation of Competences in the EU: A Clash of Constitutional Logics' in L. Azoulai (ed), *The Question of Competence in the European Union*, Oxford University Press, Oxford 2014, p. 202.

566 ibid. See also F.W. Scharpf, 'Perpetual Momentum: Directed and Unconstrained?' (2012) 19 *Journal of European Public Policy* 127 who sees the CJEU's intervention in non-discrimination cases as 'a functional explanation in a model that tries to account [not only] for active judicial law-making on economic as well as non-economic mobility rights, [but] also on fundamental rights that involve neither economic liberties nor transnational mobility'.

567 E. Dubout, above n. 565, p. 205.

568 See such remarks in K. Hailbronner and D. Thym, 'Case C-34/09, Gerardo Ruiz Zambrano v. Office National de l'emploi (ONEm), Judgment of the Court of Justice (Grand Chamber) of 8 March 2011, not yet reported' (2011) 48 *Common Market Law Review* 1253. See also M.J. van den Brink, 'EU Citizenship and EU Fundamental Rights: Taking EU Citizenship Rights Seriously?' (2012) 39 *Legal Issues of Economic Integration* 273, arguing that the concepts of citizenship and fundamental rights should be regarded as empirically, conceptually, and normatively distinct.

569 e.g. *Nunez v Norway* [2011] ECtHR, app. no. 55597/09.

570 M.J. van den Brink, above n. 568, 287.

571 e.g. S. Iglesias Sánchez, above n. 514, 1593; D. Thym, 'Towards "Real" Citizenship? The Judicial Construction of Union Citizenship and Its Limits' in M. Adams, H. de Waele, J. Meeusen and G. Straetmans (eds), *Judging Europe's Judges: The Legitimacy of the Case Law of the European Court of Justice*, Hart Publishing, Oxford 2013, p. 168; F. de Cecco, 'Fundamental Freedoms, Fundamental Rights, and the Scope of Free Movement Law' (2014) 15 *German Law Journal* 383, 403: 'The approach resonates with the constitutional orthodoxy of EU law … [and] reflects the Member States' anxieties with regard to the expansive potential of the citizenship provisions'.

case, decided soon after, clearly confirmed that fundamental rights are not part of this analysis, but the CJEU still emphasised that Member States need to meet their ECHR obligations.[572] Other cases following the *Ruiz Zambrano* doctrine all make reference to fundamental rights, but rather emphasise that the interpretation of EU law should be conducted in their light, and leave this interpretation to Member States.[573] This seems to support the conclusion that the CJEU is not blind to human rights, but constructs its own methodologies with systemic constraints in mind.

4.4.4. PRELIMINARY CONCLUSIONS

The purpose of this discussion is not to analyse the many issues raised by fundamental rights in the EU context, extensive discussion of which can be found in the literature, but rather to demonstrate three interrelated points. The first relates to the fact that the CJEU, perhaps unsurprisingly, predominantly relies on EU law. Where Charter provisions reflect Treaty provisions, the CJEU is likely to rely predominantly on the latter. Free movement and residence rights in the EU acquired the status of fundamental rights through developments preceding the Charter,[574] and as such the Charter reaffirms this status in a symbolic way and does not challenge the existing interpretations. The reliance on Treaty provisions instead of the Charter also allows the Court to approach the questions posed using a different methodology. Secondly, the CJEU is likely to rely on EU law predominantly, if it is sufficient to resolve the dispute at hand, also where the ECtHR jurisprudence on a given matter exists. Therefore, the existence of such jurisprudence in no way predetermines the exact interpretation of EU law, as the CJEU can provide more extensive protection. However, the core question about the minimum level of protection required by the ECHR is not easy to answer, in particular in areas where no clear guidance has been provided by the ECtHR.[575]

---

572 Case C-256/11, *Murat Dereci and Others v Bundesministerium für Inneres*, ECLI:EU:C:2011:734, para. 72. For a critique of this case, see M.J. van den Brink, above n. 568.

573 e.g. Case C-165/14, *Rendón Marín*, ECLI:EU:C:2016:675, para. 81, and C-133/15, *H.C. Chavez-Vilchez and Others v Raad van bestuur van de Sociale verzekeringsbank and Others*, ECLI:EU:C:2017:354, para. 70. See also M.J. van den Brink, 'Is It Time to Abolish the Substance of EU Citizenship Rights Test?' (2021) 23 *European Journal of Migration and Law* 13; P.S. Phoa and H. van Eijken, 'The Scope of Article 20 TFEU Clarified in Chavez-Vilchez: Are the Fundamental Rights of Minor EU Citizens Coming of Age?' (2018) 43 *European Law Review* 949 noting that the *Chavez-Vilchez* judgment can be read as meaning that 'a violation of a Charter right – the right to family life read in conjunction with the obligation to respect the child's best interests – causes a violation of Art. 20 TFEU in itself' but, despite the lack of clarity, should rather be seen as advocating a 'Charter-compliant' interpretation of EU law.

574 For a brief overview, see F. de Cecco, above n. 571.

575 T. Lock, 'Article 52 CFR' in M. Kellerbauer, M. Klamert and J. Tomkin (eds), *The EU Treaties and the Charter of Fundamental Rights: A Commentary*, Oxford University Press, Oxford 2019, p. 2255.

The ECtHR might test Member States' choices against the Convention, but once it affords a wide margin of appreciation, it does not prevent the EU from acting within this margin in a more directional way through its own particular methodology.

A third final point relates to the fact that the ECtHR remains an important point of reference in sensitive matters. This is perhaps best understood not in terms of the interpretation of individual rights, but in terms of legitimacy issues. The ECtHR is a human rights court with jurisdiction over all acts of Contracting Parties (Article 1 of the ECHR). It is also seen as 'procedurally fitter' to extend the protection of human rights law in controversial issues, since it allows individual applications, third-party interventions, and concurring or dissenting opinions of the judges.[576] The CJEU is not a human rights court by design, but an interpreter of EU law that needs to apply the minimum standards of the ECHR. In light of this role, and in light of its limited competence, it must be wary of limiting the Member States' powers more than the ECtHR and must ask itself what a particular extension of human rights would mean for the competence of Member States.[577] There is, therefore, an inherent tension between the competence limitations and the holistic dynamics of fundamental rights,[578] which necessarily vests national courts with 'the real ability ... to act and think European'.[579] This is why the dynamics of fundamental rights in the EU are predominantly those of accommodation of the context in which individuals (can) have ties to multiple communities, closely bound with methodological facets of 'traditional' EU law analysis.[580] When the CJEU approaches a potentially sensitive topic, and there is no clear guidance from the ECtHR, or the Court plans to extend the level of protection, it often prefers less contestable arguments of EU law.[581] All these observations need to be kept in mind when analysing child relocation in the EU context, and will be relevant for the discussions in Chapters 5 and 6.

4.5. CONCLUDING REMARKS

The objective of this chapter was to understand the margin of appreciation that Member States enjoy in child relocation cases under the ECHR and its

576 R. Wintemute, above n. 553, p. 197.

577 ibid., pp. 193–94.

578 See the discussions in E. Muir, 'Fundamental Rights: An Unsettling EU Competence' (2014) 15 *Human Rights Review* 25, or E. Dubout, above n. 565, p. 207 observing that differentiating the standards of fundamental rights protection 'makes sense in terms of respect for national competences, but much less so in terms of the protection of fundamental rights'.

579 E. Dubout, above n. 565, p. 210; Muir, above n. 578, 28.

580 See D. Sarmiento, above n. 506, 1298–1301.

581 See comments on the Case C-267/06, *Tadao Maruko v Versorgungsanstalt der deutschen Bühnen*, ECLI:EU:C:2008:179, in R. Wintemute, above n. 553, pp. 184–85.

consequences for EU law. As has been shown, national authorities retain here a wide margin of appreciation, both in terms of how they shape their relocation laws and how they resolve relocation disputes, as long as procedural obligations known from the broader jurisprudence on private disputes involving children are met. The analysis of the ECtHR case law demonstrates that such cases are indeed predominantly brought and analysed under Article 8 of the ECHR (the right to respect for private and family life) rather than Article 2 of Protocol 4 to the Convention (freedom of movement), with familial relationships considered the core of the disputes in the eyes of the Strasbourg judges. While the Court recognises that child relocation disputes might touch upon broader autonomy interests of the relocating parent, the treatment of such claims has so far been ambiguous. The Court's approach focuses rather on the context-specificity of the disputes and, unsurprisingly, the need for individualised assessments of the best interests of the child. One can, therefore, conclude that states' obligations stemming from the ECHR system are substantively limited to what is already recognised in parental disputes more broadly. This coincides with the observation that, be it consciously or accidently, the Strasbourg Court does not seem to explicitly recognise child relocation as a separate legal issue nor consistently refer to the existing soft law.

The margin of appreciation under the ECHR, as recognised by the ECtHR, has, nevertheless, certain consequences for the analysis of EU law obligations in such cases. As discussed, Article 52(3) of the EU Charter of Fundamental Rights requires that the meaning and scope of the Charter rights which correspond to rights guaranteed by the ECHR shall be the same as those laid down by the Convention. This concerns several articles of the EU Charter relevant for child relocation – in particular, Article 7 of the CFR (the right to family life). However, the dynamics of EU fundamental rights in sensitive areas, including many family-related issues involving children, are characterised by three important features that might have consequences for the CJEU's engagement with child relocation matters. The first relates to the fact that, where Charter rights correspond to Treaty rights, the CJEU might choose to resolve the dispute in reference to EU Treaty provisions only. Secondly, the CJEU will often rely on EU law only if this is sufficient to resolve the dispute at hand, also where the ECtHR jurisprudence on a given matter exists. Lastly, however, the ECtHR remains an important point of reference for fundamental rights in sensitive matters, with the CJEU wary of its jurisdictional and legitimacy constraints. While the first two observations lead to a conclusion that free movement in child relocation cases would almost certainly be approached by the CJEU in reference to Treaty rights, the last remark might suggest that the CJEU would be more likely than not to adopt the ECtHR's wide margin of appreciation in the child relocation context in its own decision-making. However, even if the CJEU decides to guide Member States towards a more specific test within the broad margin of appreciation afforded by the ECtHR, the free movement provisions of EU Treaties – intertwined with considerations of fundamental rights and EU competence – offer a more likely legal basis for such guidance. Therefore, having determined the scope and nature of EU fundamental rights obligations, it is now time to analyse child relocation within the broader context of EU law and its fundamental freedoms.

CHAPTER 5

CHILD RELOCATION AND RESTRICTION OF FREE MOVEMENT IN EU LAW

5.1. INTRODUCTION

The previous two chapters have been devoted to the discussion of the scope of EU competence in child relocation and the European framework of fundamental rights respectively. It has been shown that the EU competence is heavily limited, and the jurisprudence of the ECtHR leaves national authorities with a wide margin of appreciation in child relocation. Having highlighted how these discussions constitute an important point of reference for the analysis of child relocation as a restriction of EU free movement, it is now time to consider how the CJEU could legitimately interpret EU law if a child relocation case ever came to the Court. While family law remains among the areas of law most closely associated with national sovereignty and no legislation on child relocation exists on the EU level, EU law has long been recognised as capable of influencing such national law, with the CJEU being the 'real engine' of the process via its interpretations of the free movement provisions.[582] Free movement is, indeed, the main trigger for a closer scrutiny of national child relocation provisions and measures in the EU context. The literature recognises that restrictions on child relocation might potentially be perceived as a restriction of EU law, requiring *an* adaptation of national child relocation laws and approaches to EU legal obligations. The first discussion of child relocation in the EU context goes back to the times of workers' mobility provided by the Rome Treaty,[583] but it is, in particular, the current legal framework expanded by the EU citizenship provisions that calls for more research on the topic, as outlined by Ruth Lamont.[584] However, the exact scope and nature of legal pressures in this regard remain underexplored, in particular in reference to the analysis of their justification and proportionality.[585]

582 S. Ninatti, above n. 3, p. 7; E. Pataut, above n. 14, p. 312.

583 T. Scott, above n. 12.

584 R. Lamont, above n. 12, 232–34; see also H. Stalford, above n. 17, pp. 225–26.

585 T. Scott, above n. 12, conducts an analysis of justification and proportionality of English relocation provisions under the Treaty of Rome, but can also be criticised as not accounting for the full spectrum of EU law, in particular fundamental rights. For a discussion of the literature, see Chapter 2.

This chapter's objective is two-fold. First, it provides a doctrinal analysis of child relocation in the EU legal context. The chapter introduces the EU law framework that is potentially relevant for child relocation, discusses preliminary matters related to applicability of EU law, and draws attention to institutional constraints of the CJEU as a decision-maker, with consequences for the nature of obligations that the Court can impose. Further, it conceptualises restrictions of child relocation as restrictions of EU free movement law, taking account of different questions posed by different child relocation laws across Europe. The chapter also examines potential justifications of such measures and requirements of their proportionality, considering the particularities of this analysis in the areas of Member States' retained competences. Building on this analysis, the second objective is to explicitly draw attention to the scope and nature of legal pressures that can reasonably be exerted via the jurisprudence of the CJEU on national child relocation laws. While the CJEU can drive the 'judicial' or 'non-legislative' harmonisation, the inherent characteristics of child relocation cases in combination with the substantive and institutional constraints of EU law might render any prospective judgment less transformative than expected.

5.2. CHILD RELOCATION AND THE EU LEGAL FRAMEWORK

Freedom of movement lies at the heart of EU law. Nowadays, its provisions can be found both in the EU Treaties and in various instruments of secondary law. Freedom of movement for individuals is inherent, among others, in: Article 45 (freedom of workers); Article 49 (freedom of establishment); Article 56 (freedom to provide services); and Articles 20 and 21 of the TFEU (provisions on EU citizenship). The conditions of the exercise of these fundamental freedoms are further expressed in secondary law, in particular in the Citizens' Rights Directive.[586] Originally, movement for economic purposes was significantly privileged under EU law, but the current rules for economically non-active EU citizens can hardly be differentiated from rights granted under Articles 45 or 49

[586] Council Directive 2004/38/EC of 29 April 2004 on the right of citizens of the Union and their family members to move and reside freely within the territory of the Member States amending Regulation (EEC) No 1612/68 and repealing Directives 64/221/EEC, 68/360/EEC, 72/194/EEC, 73/148/EEC, 75/34/EEC, 75/35/EEC, 90/364/EEC, 90/365/EEC and 93/96/EEC [2004] OJ L158/77. Family rights of migrant workers can also be expressed in other acts. See for example Article 10 of Council Regulation (EU) 492/2011 of 5 April 2011 on freedom of movement for workers within the Union [2011] OJ L 141/1, the so-called 'Free Movement of Workers Regulation'.

of the TFEU.[587] While provisions on economic movement constitute *legis specialis* in relation to Article 21 of the TFEU,[588] the introduction of EU citizenship, combined with the widened aims of the EU and the commitment to fundamental rights, has been seen as 'something qualitatively different'.[589] Depending on circumstances, the Court often finds it sufficient to consider free movement rights under one of the provisions only,[590] treating the differences between different categories of movers rather flexibly according to its own 'teleologically-driven' doctrines.[591] The citizenship provisions can also be applied together with another Treaty provision, for example Article 18 of the TFEU prohibiting discrimination based on nationality.[592] Given the nature of child relocation disputes, it is, therefore, justified to focus the analysis predominantly on the EU citizenship provisions. While the contextual complexity of the cases might give rise to claims under other provisions of the Treaty, the overall analysis conducted below in reference to Articles 20 and 21 of the TFEU will remain applicable also to such claims.

Article 20 of the TFEU stipulates that every person holding the nationality of a Member State shall be a citizen of the Union, having inter alia the right to move and reside freely within the territory of the Member States. Rights provided in Article 20, including the right to free movement, shall be exercised in accordance with the conditions and limits defined by the Treaties and by the measures adopted thereunder. This means that the rights are self-executing, and it is not the core of the right, but its exercise, that should be regulated by secondary legislation.[593] The right to move and reside in the territory of Member States can be found also in Article 21 of the TFEU. The CJEU has, on multiple occasions, confirmed that these provisions establish a general right of every EU citizen to move and reside freely within the territory of the Member States, without any specific objective or dimension of their activity. Protection

---

587 D.-E. Khan and N. Wessendorf, 'Article 45 TFEU' in R. Geiger, D.-E. Khan and M. Kotzur, *European Union Treaties: A Commentary: Treaty on European Union, Treaty on the Functioning of the European Union, Charter of Fundamental Rights of the European Union*, C.H. Beck/Hart Publishing, Munich/Oxford 2015, p. 329; N.N. Shuibhne, 'Margins of Appreciation: National Values, Fundamental Rights and EC Free Movement Law' (2009) 34 *European Law Review* 230. Workers' residence rights are now regulated in the Citizens' Rights Directive.

588 e.g. Case C-457/12, *S and G v Minister voor Immigratie, Integratie en Asiel*, ECLI:EU:C:2014:136, para. 45. See also S. Henrich and D.-E. Khan, 'Article 21 TFEU' in R. Geiger, D.-E. Khan and M. Kotzur, *European Union Treaties: A Commentary: Treaty on European Union, Treaty on the Functioning of the European Union, Charter of Fundamental Rights of the European Union*, C.H. Beck/Hart Publishing, Munich/Oxford 2015, p. 254.

589 S. Weatherill, 'The Several Internal Markets' (2017) 36 *Yearbook of European Law* 125, 139 and the literature cited there. See also D. Kochenov, 'The Right to Have What Rights? EU Citizenship in Need of Clarification' (2013) 19 *European Law Journal* 502, 503.

590 e.g. Case C-457/12, *S and G*, ECLI:EU:C:2014:136, paras. 44–45.

591 S. Weatherill, above n. 589, 135.

592 S. Henrich and D.-E. Khan, above n. 588, p. 253.

593 ibid., p. 251.

includes the movement as well as the residence of EU citizens, and, as such, encompasses entry, free movement within the state, and exit.[594] The provisions prohibit national measures which preclude, hinder or discourage a Member State national from exercising his or her right to freedom of movement within the European Union, unless justified and proportionate.[595]

The distinction between Articles 20 and 21 of the TFEU has not always been entirely clear, as they both express the right to move and reside freely in the territory of the Union. The main difference between the provisions, based on the jurisprudence of the CJEU, seems to be the substance of rights test, established in *Ruiz Zambrano*. Member States are, according to the Court's interpretation of Article 20, precluded from taking measures which have the effect of depriving citizens of the Union of the genuine enjoyment of the substance of the rights conferred by virtue of their status as citizens of the Union.[596] A clear distinction between Articles 20 and 21 was drawn, based on this, in *McCarthy*.[597] The exact content of the substance of rights doctrine was broadly discussed in the literature,[598] and the utility of this distinction has since been questioned as well.[599] In general, Article 20 of the TFEU is used in 'very specific situations [when] the Union citizen concerned has not made use of his [or her] freedom of movement'[600] and Article 21 of the TFEU does not apply.[601] Therefore, as the analysis of child relocation necessarily focuses on (hinderance of) movement, the nature and relevance of this distinction is of secondary importance. Nevertheless, it is not entirely devoid of meaning. The literature suggests that the Court's jurisprudence on dependency might be interpreted in light of the 'right to care' as an essential part of EU citizenship rights.[602] Since the focus of every child relocation case is on the child – who necessarily requires care – this is an interesting conceptual question. However, the Court has not explicitly endorsed such an interpretation and, while it is worth keeping in mind, the consideration of such an option is not necessary for the purposes of the following analysis.

The rights arising from citizenship provisions are subject to limitations and conditions laid down in the Treaty and secondary provisions, in particular

594 ibid., p. 254.

595 e.g. Case C-434/09, *McCarthy*, ECLI:EU:C:2011:277, paras. 51–52.

596 e.g. Case C-34/09, *Gerardo Ruiz Zambrano v Office national de l'emploi (ONEm)*, ECLI:EU:C:2011:124, para. 42.

597 Case C-434/09, *McCarthy*, ECLI:EU:C:2011:277, para. 49.

598 See, for example, D. Kochenov, above n. 589.

599 e.g. M.J. van den Brink, above n. 573.

600 See Case C-304/14, *Secretary of State for the Home Department v CS*, ECLI:EU:C:2016:674, para. 29; Case C-165/14, *Rendón Marín*, ECLI:EU:C:2016:675, para. 74.

601 See also P.S. Phoa and H. van Eijken, above n. 573, 967–969.

602 N. Cambien, 'EU Citizenship and the Right to Care' in D. Kochenov (ed), *EU Citizenship and Federalism: The Role of Rights*, Cambridge University Press, Cambridge 2017.

the Citizens' Rights Directive.[603] Article 3(1) of the Directive clarifies that it applies to all Union citizens who move to or reside in a Member State other than that of which they are a national, and to their family members who accompany or join them, including children (Article 2(2)(c)). Therefore, not only EU citizens themselves, but also their family members (be they EU citizens themselves or not) enjoy the right of free movement and residence in the EU Member States. The Directive also specifies the conditions governing the right of exit, entry and residence for EU citizens and their family members. None of the provisions of the Directive seem to be applicable to child relocation,[604] but residence rights might still be derived from Treaty provisions directly, depending on the circumstances of the case.[605] In particular, the Directive does not apply to EU citizens returning to their Member State of origin.[606] However, the Court has previously used the case law on the interpretation of the Directive to resolve cases to which the Directive does not apply, and hence to interpret limitations of residence rights derived from EU citizenship provisions.[607] Therefore, the Directive could potentially be relevant for the analysis.

While not explicitly granting any residence or free movement rights, one can consider the Brussels II*ter* Regulation as part of the relevant legal framework.[608] The Regulation concerns the recognition and enforcement of judgments in matters of parental responsibility and obliges national authorities to respect mutual trust in this area. The discussion in Chapter 2 briefly highlighted the importance of supranational legal frameworks for child relocation disputes, in light of the composite rationale of the restrictions on relocation that

---

603 D.-E. Khan and N. Wessendorf, 'Article 49 TFEU' in R. Geiger, D.-E. Khan and M. Kotzur, *European Union Treaties: A Commentary: Treaty on European Union, Treaty on the Functioning of the European Union, Charter of Fundamental Rights of the European Union*, C.H. Beck/Hart Publishing, Munich/Oxford 2015, p. 363.

604 It is worth observing that Article 27 allows Member States to restrict the freedom of movement and residence on grounds of public policy, public security or public health, as long as restrictive measures are proportional and based exclusively on the personal conduct of the person concerned. One could imagine that restrictive decisions on child relocation could be justified in reference to public policy. For example, the general doctrine of Bulgarian courts discussed in Chapter 4 could be perceived in this light. However, as analysed in the Opinion of the Advocate General in Case C-454/19, *Staatsanwaltschaft Heilbronn v ZW*, ECLI:EU:C:2020:430, paras. 29–36, the derogation on public policy grounds provided in Article 27 of the Citizens' Rights Directive should be seen as applying only to restrictions on the right of entry sensu stricto and to measures of expulsion, and in any event cannot be used to justify measures in reliance on arguments of general nature.

605 e.g. Case C-34/09, *Ruiz Zambrano*, ECLI:EU:C:2011:124, paras. 39–42; Case C-434/09, *McCarthy*, ECLI:EU:C:2011:277, para. 28; see also Case C-127/08, *Blaise Baheten Metock and Others v Minister for Justice, Equality and Law Reform*, ECLI:EU:C:2008:449, paras. 82–84.

606 See, e.g. Case C-673/16, *Relu Adrian Coman and Others v Inspectoratul General pentru Imigrări and Ministerul Afacerilor Interne*, ECLI:EU:C:2018:385, para. 20.

607 ibid., paras. 18–26; Case C-165/14, *Rendón Marín*, ECLI:EU:C:2016:675, paras. 82–86.

608 The Regulation will be discussed in more detail in Chapter 6.

encompass also jurisdictional concerns. Also, the CJEU has previously held, in contexts encompassing family mobility, that existing instruments on cross-border recognition and enforcement should be considered in the assessment of proportionality of restrictions on freedom of movement.[609] The Regulation is, therefore, relevant also for the subsequent analysis. Having established the general legal framework of EU law, it is important to fully conceptualise to what extent child relocation falls under EU law and within the jurisdiction of the CJEU, and whose and what rights are at stake.

5.3. CHILD RELOCATION LAW AS A RESTRICTION OF FREE MOVEMENT

Cross-border child relocation remains in principle within the exclusive competence of Member States, as argued in Chapter 3. However, it has long been clear that EU law imposes limitations, via the interpretation of its free movement and citizenship provisions, on the exercise of retained competences as well.[610] The analysis of the Court traditionally follows a reasoning in which the Court first assesses the applicability of EU law, then the restrictive character of the national measure, and finally the justifications and the proportionality of the measure.[611] However, in areas which constitute retained competences of Member States, the Court conducts the analysis according to a specific legal framework that differs from the test applied in 'standard' cases as to the scope of EU law and the justification stage.[612] One of the strategies developed by the Court to justify and broaden the applicability of EU law is the process that Lena Boucon, an author writing extensively on the jurisprudence of the Court in the areas of retained competences, characterises as 'dissociation between the scope of EU law and the scope of EU powers'.[613] This results in the scope of EU law being asserted as broader than the scope of EU powers,[614] with matters involving the exercise of Treaty freedoms falling, in principle, within the scope of

609 Opinion of the Advocate General in Case C-454/19, *Staatsanwaltschaft Heilbronn v ZW*, ECLI:EU:C:2020:430, paras. 46–50. See also E. Guild, S. Peers and J. Tomkin, *The EU Citizenship Directive: A Commentary*, Oxford University Press, Oxford 2014, p. 269.

610 See, for example, the discussion in L. Boucon, above n. 38.

611 ibid., p. 171.

612 ibid.

613 ibid., p. 172.

614 ibid., p. 174. See also S. Weatherill, above n. 589, describing the days when the CJEU used to investigate whether a national measure falls within the scope of EU competences as 'long gone', or L. Azoulai, 'The Court of Justice and the Social Market Economy: The Emergence of an Ideal and the Conditions for Its Realization' (2008) 45 *Common Market Law Review* 1335, 1340 noting that the Court is given the legitimacy to identify the constraints in the pursuit of all national policies.

EU law.[615] While implicit in the existing literature,[616] this reflects more broadly on the institutional and substantive limits of any EU intervention in this area. Therefore, as highlighted in Chapter 3, the question of competence does have implications for how the CJEU approaches the interpretation of EU law. This prompts a preliminary assessment of the extent to which child relocation falls under the scope of EU law and within the jurisdiction of the CJEU.

5.3.1. PRELIMINARY REMARKS ON ADMISSIBILITY OF THE CASE

In principle, child relocation matters could be brought under scrutiny of the CJEU as a result of an infringement action (Articles 258 and 259 TFEU), requiring an a priori conceptualisation of EU legal obligations in this context that have been violated by a Member State. However, child relocation issues are – explicitly due to the unclear nature of EU obligations, the limited scope of EU competence and the political sensitivity of family law – much more likely to reach the CJEU via the preliminary reference procedure. Therefore, although the analysis undertaken here will be relevant in general, it will focus on this procedure specifically. This prompts a few additional remarks. According to Article 267 of the TFEU, the CJEU has jurisdiction to give preliminary rulings concerning the interpretation of the Treaties when such a question is raised before a court of a Member State, if the court considers that a decision on the question is necessary to enable it to give its judgment. One could legitimately dispute whether and why the interpretation of given provisions of EU law would be necessary for the court to give a judgment in a child relocation case. In the end, some voices in the literature emphasise that such cases are, at their core, about care arrangements and the child's residence, rather than free movement.[617] If the interpretation of EU law is not necessary, a preliminary reference to the CJEU would not be admissible. However, the necessity in the jurisprudence of the Court has been interpreted as meaning that the answer provided is relevant for the dispute and can be taken into account by the referring court.[618] Such circumstances should be clarified by

---

615 e.g. Case C-184/99, *Rudy Grzelczyk v Centre public d'aide sociale d'Ottignies-Louvain-la-Neuve*, ECLI:EU:C:2001:458, para. 33; Case C-224/98, *Marie-Nathalie D'Hoop v Office national de l'emploi*, ECLI:EU:C:2002:432, para. 29; Case C-148/02, *Garcia Avello*, ECLI:EU:C:2003:539, para. 24.

616 See the discussion in Chapter 3.

617 J. Eekelaar, 'The Role of the Best Interests Principle in Decisions Affecting Children and Decisions about Children', above n. 146, 9.

618 N. Wahl and L. Prete, 'The Gatekeepers of Article 267 TFEU: On Jurisdiction and Admissibility of References for Preliminary Rulings' (2018) 55 *Common Market Law Review* 511, 531.

the national court itself. The presumption of relevance of the questions posed can only be rebutted in exceptional cases.[619] At this point, briefly, it is worth recalling that references to the EU freedom of movement rights have been made in child relocation cases before.[620] The existence of academic literature on the topic suggests that EU law has been seen as potentially relevant for child relocation.[621] As confirmed by the CJEU on multiple occasions, and in the family context in the *J. McB.* case:

> it is solely for the national courts ... to determine in the light of the special features of each case both the need for a preliminary ruling ... and the relevance of the questions which they submit to the Court.[622]

As such, the Court of Justice is, in principle, bound to give a ruling on child relocation, notwithstanding the normative desirability or acceptability of placing child relocation in the EU context.

More importantly, however, part of the jurisdictional requirement of necessity is that EU rules for which interpretation is sought must be applicable to the proceedings in question.[623] In the existing literature, applicability seems to have been assumed in light of the previous expansive jurisprudence of the Court and the construction of English law. As the English provisions differentiate between internal and cross-border relocations and frame the latter as a question of permission or refusal to relocate, their EU free movement dimension becomes more tangible. However, in jurisdictions that resolve child relocation cases under the general provisions of family law and construct the disputes as a modification of custody, this is not self-evident. Therefore, a holistic analysis requires a discussion of what kind of rules or situations have a sufficient link with EU law. This assessment has also an important substantive dimension and hence deserves a separate preliminary remark.[624]

---

619 See, for example, Case C-400/10 PPU, *J. McB. v L. E.*, ECLI:EU:C:2010:582, paras. 33–34.

620 e.g. *Payne v Payne* [2001] EWCA Civ 166, [2001] 1 FLR 1052 (CA).

621 T. Scott, above n. 12; R. Lamont, above n. 12, 240–41; Y.M. Bérénos, above n. 12.

622 Case C-400/10 PPU, *J. McB. v L. E.*, ECLI:EU:C:2010:582, para. 32.

623 It goes without saying that, for the provisions on free movement to apply, a case must fall within the personal, material, and territorial scope of the Treaty provision. If these jurisdictional conditions are not satisfied, EU law does not apply. See C. Barnard, *The Substantive Law of the EU: The Four Freedoms*, 5th ed., Oxford University Press, Oxford 2016, pp. 231–32.

624 When confronted with the question of purely internal situations, the Court has used different approaches, examining the merits of a given matter or rather limiting itself to an assessment of its jurisdiction, applicability, or a mix of both. See S. Iglesias Sánchez, 'Purely Internal Situations and the Limits of EU Law: A Consolidated Case Law or a Notion to Be Abandoned?' (2018) 14 *European Constitutional Law Review* 7, 14–15. See also M.J. van den Brink, 'The Origins and the Potential Federalising Effects of the Substance of Rights Test' in D. Kochenov (ed), *EU Citizenship and Federalism: The Role of Rights*, Cambridge University Press, Cambridge 2017, p. 91 indicating that the substance of rights attached to EU

5.3.2. PRELIMINARY REMARKS ON APPLICABILITY OF EU LAW

What prima facie brings child relocation under EU law is freedom of movement. Citizenship of the Union, as the fundamental status of nationals of the Member States,[625] has broadened the scope of rights afforded to EU citizens in a way that can potentially impact on national family law.[626] However, this status is not intended to extend the scope *ratione materiae* of the Treaty, in particular to internal situations with no sufficient cross-border element and no link to EU law.[627] Nevertheless, the Court has always treated factors that bring a case within EU law as evolutive in their character. While originally one had to be exercising movement to claim EU rights, the rules have been gradually triggered by past movements, future (including potential) movements, and even the movements of other people.[628] In *Ruiz Zambrano*, decided in reference to the substance of EU citizenship rights, there was no cross-border element in the first place. This development of the jurisprudence, although often criticised for its little regard of the textual specificities of the Treaty, has led to the degradation of the actual exercise of movement as a requirement of applicability of EU law and has allowed for more and more categories of situations to be revised via the EU lens.[629] However, some cases that fall in the margin can prove difficult and their internal or cross-border context, or purely hypothetical or more tangible effect, is less clear-cut.[630] EU law is not applicable to a citizen who has never exercised his or her right of free movement, remaining in the Member State of his or her nationality, but:

> provided that the situation of that citizen does not include the application of measures that would have the effect of depriving him [or her] of the genuine enjoyment of the substance of the rights conferred by virtue of his [or her] status as a Union citizen or of impeding the exercise of his [or her] right of free movement and residence within the territory of the Member States.[631]

---

citizenship may be used as a substantive test, but it has also been used to establish the Court's jurisdiction in the first place.

625 e.g. Case C-413/99, *Baumbast and R v Secretary of State for the Home Department*, ECLI:EU:C:2002:493, para. 82; Case C-148/02, *Garcia Avello*, ECLI:EU:C:2003:539, para. 22.

626 R. Lamont, above n. 12, 231–33; H. Stalford, above n. 17, pp. 240–42.

627 e.g. Case C-148/02, *Garcia Avello*, ECLI:EU:C:2003:539, para. 1.

628 See the overview in S. O'Leary, 'The Past, Present and Future of The Purely Internal Rule in EU Law' in M. Dougan, N.N. Shuibhne and E. Spaventa (eds), *Empowerment and Disempowerment of the European Citizen*, Hart Publishing, Oxford 2012.

629 S. Weatherill, above n. 589, 135; see also S. Iglesias Sánchez, above n. 624, and S. O'Leary, above n. 628.

630 S. Weatherill, above n. 589, 136.

631 e.g. Case C-434/09, *McCarthy*, ECLI:EU:C:2011:277, para. 56.

All restrictions on cross-border child relocation can, in principle, impede these rights. However, considering various legislative solutions and legal approaches to child relocation across Member States, it is, therefore, useful to preliminarily reflect upon what kind of relocation laws and/or cases could fall within the scope of EU law.

Child relocation can be framed in many ways. For example, it can be approached as a dispute about whether permission should be granted to move with the child – based on specific relocation provisions or as a general dispute about the exercising of parental responsibilities like any other – or approached as a question of modification of the existing custody arrangement. While applicability of EU law is closely related to the substance and factual circumstances of a given dispute, one can reasonably exclude some category of disputes from the scope of EU law at the outset. Rules and disputes about allocation of custody rights by their nature have consequences for the distribution of rights related to the determination of the child's place of residence in the future. However, if no specific plan to relocate constitutes part of the dispute it should not be caught by the Treaty, as the prospects of such a move occurring are only hypothetical.[632] This assessment can, however, change, notwithstanding the statutory basis of a dispute, as soon as the case is resolved against the background of a specific relocation plan. It then engages the actual exercising of freedom of movement as one of the primary Treaty freedoms. Such Treaty rights can also be asserted against a person's Member State of origin, as might often be the case with child relocation disputes.[633] Cross-border moves to non-EU countries, as outside EU law, would not fall under the jurisdiction of the CJEU, although legal pressures exerted by EU law on intra-EU child relocation could have consequences for other international moves as well.[634] Internal moves within one's Member State of origin, would most likely fall outside the scope of the Treaty, being wholly internal.[635] Internal restrictions on relocation could, on

---

632 In a similar context, see Case C-40/11, *Yoshikazu Iida v Stadt Ulm*, ECLI:EU:C:2012:691, para. 77.

633 e.g. Case C-434/09, *McCarthy*, ECLI:EU:C:2011:277, para. 48. This is confirmed by exit cases, although they are concerned with freedom to leave a country rather than freedom to reside abroad. On that see A. Łazowski, '"Darling You Are Not Going Anywhere": The Right to Exit and Restrictions in EU Law' (2015) 40 *European Law Review* 877.

634 See, for example, the comments on the spillover of mutual trust requirements to other instruments in R. Lamont, 'Not a European Family: Implications of "Brexit" for International Family Law' (2017) *Manchester Centre for Regulation and Governance and Public Law*, p. 15 <https://research.manchester.ac.uk/en/publications/not-a-european-family-implications-of-brexit-for-international-fa>. As all cross-border relocations are typically solved under the same provisions, be they intra-EU or not, a similar process could occur here.

635 Compare, e.g. Case 175/78, *The Queen v Vera Ann Saunders*, ECLI:EU:C:1979:88, where the ECJ then held that EU law does not aim at restricting the Member State's power to

the other hand, be caught by EU law if they concerned a foreign Member State national, prompting a justification and proportionality analysis.[636] This book focuses on cross-border child relocation, and, therefore, internal relocations will not be examined in more detail, but considerations of justification and proportionality discussed in this chapter would, in principle, be applicable to all disputes falling under EU law.

Prima facie, therefore, it does not seem to be necessary for a relocation dispute to be resolved under any specific provisions dealing with relocation for EU law to apply. Notwithstanding differences in the potential constructions of child relocation laws, all disputes involving an actual plan to relocate could be caught by the Treaty. However, disputes about the allocation of parental rights and responsibilities that can hypothetically reflect on the parents' right to determine the child's place of residence are unlikely to have sufficient links with EU law. In this context, however, it is worth recalling the Court's doctrine of remoteness. Where the Court excludes a measure from the scope of a Treaty prohibition, it is because it is too uncertain or too indirect to be capable of discouraging or hindering free movement.[637] This has been confirmed also in the context of EU citizenship.[638] For the doctrine of remoteness to apply, rules in question must be non-discriminatory, must not be intended to regulate intra-EU movement or the exercise of the freedom of movement, and there must be no causal connection between the rule and the alleged barrier.[639] It is, therefore, clear that the rule, the conceptualisation of the alleged barrier, and the causal connection between them play a role in the analysis.

---

lay down restrictions, within their own territory and to their own nationals subject to its jurisdiction, in domestic criminal law. Advocate General Warner's argument to consider – instead of the existence of the cross-border element and proof of movement for the purpose of exercising economic activity – the effect which the decision would have on the individual's exercise of a right conferred by EU law, found no recognition. See the Opinion of the Advocate General in Case 175/78, *The Queen v Vera Ann Saunders*, ECLI:EU:C:1979:63, p. 1142.

636 Compare, e.g. Case 36/75, *Roland Rutili v Ministre de l'intérieur*, ECLI:EU:C:1975:137, where an Italian national was banned from moving to some parts of France. The ECJ provided a strict interpretation of the public policy reservation which may possibly restrict the free movement of workers in the Member States.

637 e.g. Case C-190/98, *Volker Graf v Filzmoser Maschinenbau GmbH*, ECLI:EU:C:2000:49, paras. 19–25.

638 Joined Cases C-11/06 and C-12/06, *Rhiannon Morgan v Bezirksregierung Köln (C-11/06) and Iris Bucher v Landrat des Kreises Düren (C-12/06)*, ECLI:EU:C:2007:626, para. 32. See also the discussion in F. Wollenschläger, 'A New Fundamental Freedom beyond Market Integration: Union Citizenship and its Dynamics for Shifting the Economic Paradigm of European Integration' (2011) 17 *European Law Journal* 1.

639 E. Spaventa, 'The Outer Limit of the Treaty Free Movement Provisions: Some Reflections on the Significance of Keck, Remoteness and Deliège' in C. Barnard and O. Odudu (eds), *The Outer Limits of European Law*, Hart Publishing, Oxford 2009, p. 251.

Most authors accept that the concept of remoteness remains at least unclear.[640] The doctrine has been said to be:

> unlikely to become of central importance, but rather remain a concept invoked on an *ad hoc* basis where the effect of the national measure is not dependent on the exercise of free movement.[641]

This may be the consequence of the mere fact that the issue is more 'practical than legal'.[642] However, in light of this, the jurisdictional assessment of applicability of EU law and the substantive assessment of the existence of a restriction are closely related. The relevance of this relationship will, therefore, be further discussed while analysing child relocation as a restriction of freedom of movement. However, as the conceptualisation of the alleged barrier has important implications for this substantive analysis, it is worth preliminarily exploring what kind of barriers might be created by child relocation laws.

5.3.3. CONCEPTUALISATION OF THE RESTRICTION: WHOSE AND WHAT FREEDOM?

The existing literature conceptualises child relocation as a restriction on movement in heterogeneous ways. Timothy Scott focuses on the position of the relocating parent who is limited by the obligation to obtain permission to relocate with the child.[643] The *mere existence of child relocation law* is hence conceptualised as restricting *the right of a working parent to relocate with his or her family*.[644] In his analysis, Scott does not discuss the rights of the child or the non-relocating parent. Ruth Lamont notes that *refusals to relocate* are a direct *restriction of the child's movement*, but they might also constitute *a restriction of the movement of the parent* who is unlikely to consider migration if they cannot migrate with the child.[645] Lamont recognises that the non-relocating

---

640 e.g. C. Costello, 'Market Access All Areas – The Treatment of Non-Discriminatory Barriers to the Free Movement of Workers' (2000) 27 *Legal Issues of Economic Integration* 267; N.N. Shuibhne, *The Coherence of EU Free Movement Law: Constitutional Responsibility and the Court of Justice*, Oxford University Press, Oxford 2013, pp. 157–88.

641 C. Costello, above n. 640, 277. See also A. Tryfonidou, 'The Notions of "Restriction" and "Discrimination" in the Context of the Free Movement of Persons Provisions: From a Relationship of Interdependence to One of (Almost Complete) Independence' (2014) 33 *Yearbook of European Law* 385.

642 N.N. Shuibhne and D. Edward, 'Continuity and Change in the Law Relating to Services' in A. Arnull, P. Eeckhout and T. Tridimas (eds), *Continuity and Change in EU Law: Essays in Honour of Sir Francis Jacobs*, Oxford University Press, Oxford 2008, p. 257.

643 T. Scott, above n. 12, p. 9.

644 ibid., p. 12.

645 R. Lamont, above n. 12, 240. See also, arguing along the same lines in other legal contexts, A.B. LaFrance, above n. 189, 68, and S.B. Boyd, above n. 160, 145.

parent could have a corresponding claim to the freedom to stay in a location, the 'right to stay'.[646] In her opinion, however, the clear focus of the EU law on the right of free movement 'may effectively obscure this analysis and subjects any restriction on free movement to a proportionality assessment which focuses solely on that right'.[647] The literature does not, therefore, provide a unanimous interpretation of whose and what right is affected by the restriction. Such conceptualisation is, however, of utter importance not only for the question of whether EU law applies, but also for any subsequent analysis of justification and proportionality.[648]

In *J. McB.*, both the Advocate General and the CJEU were of the opinion that, when the father has no custody rights, the removal of a child from a given Member State:

> represents the legitimate exercise, by the mother with custody of the child, of her own right of freedom of movement, established in Article 20(2)(a) TFEU and Article 21(1) TFEU, and of her right to determine the child's place of residence.[649]

This is noted by Ruth Lamont, who uses the case as one of the starting points for her analysis.[650] Thus, the Court confirmed that relocation engages an exercise of individual citizenship rights, even if it has repercussions for other family relationships.[651] The *J. McB.* case did not call for a clarification of the mutual relationship between the mother's rights and the rights held by the child, since the mother was the sole holder of custody rights and the dispute centred on the interpretation of the Brussels II*bis* Regulation in light of the fundamental rights of the non-custodial father. However, the phrasing used in this case might be misleading in the child relocation context, as the following paragraphs will demonstrate.

The judgment seems to suggest that when the mother relocates to another Member State, the accompanying removal of the child is a legitimate exercise of her own freedom of movement. However, neither the judgment nor the view of the Advocate General phrases the right to determine the child's place of residence as part of the mother's freedom of movement rights. As such, the child's change of residence is not an element of the exercise of the mother's freedom of movement, and therefore, removal cannot be one either. The mother can, of course, legitimately exercise her own free movement rights. Whether

646 R. Lamont, above n. 12, 240.
647 ibid.
648 The importance of a clear conceptualisation of whose and what rights are at stake was made explicit in the context of the change of the children's surname in the Opinion of the Advocate General in Case C-148/02, *Garcia Avello*, ECLI:EU:C:2003:311, paras. 46–53.
649 Case C-400/10 PPU, *J. McB. v L. E.*, ECLI:EU:C:2010:582, para. 58; View of the Advocate General in Case C-400/10 PPU, *J. McB. v L. E.*, ECLI:EU:C:2010:544, para. 69.
650 R. Lamont, above n. 12, 233–34.
651 ibid.

she can change the child's residence depends on the attribution of custody. In this case, her freedom, by virtue of her having sole custody, coincides with the right to determine the child's place of residence which can therefore be subsumed under her free movement rights. However, were custody shared, the removal of the child would clearly not be legitimate. Therefore, the change of the child's place of residence is conceptually not part of the parent's freedom of movement.

The relocation in *J. McB.* is, nevertheless, clearly framed in terms of parental rights, and not the child's rights. Neither the judgment nor the view of the Advocate General mention any independent Treaty right of the child to free movement. When refusing to grant the inchoate custody rights to the father, the Court is clear that the opposite would be incompatible with the expectation of legal certainty and 'with the need to protect the rights and freedoms of others, within the meaning of Article 52(1) of the Charter, *in this case those of the mother*' (emphasis added).[652] This confirms that the dispute was seen in terms of the competing rights of the parents, not of an independent right of the child to reside in another Member State. The dispute must be resolved in a way which respects the obligation to take into consideration the child's best interests.[653] The child's rights are, therefore, discussed only in reference to Article 24 of the Charter, interpretation of which is left to national authorities in respect for the variety of parent-child relationships across Member States.[654] Therefore, the position of the child is seen exclusively within the context of national family laws. This in itself does not negate that children have rights under EU law but reflects a perception about what constitutes the underlying interests of the child in the context of relocation and what the essence of the dispute is about.

Children – as EU citizens – have the self-standing right to move and reside within the territory of the Union.[655] Often, however, not only is the effectiveness of these rights heavily dependent on parental care,[656] but children may not have (the capacity to claim) an independent interest in movement. It can therefore be assumed that the intention on the side of one of the parents to relocate with the children – even if the child lacks the agency to claim rights independently – 'activates' their free movement rights as well. If they are dependants of this parent, as was legally the case in *J. McB.*, this fact is

---

652 Case C-400/10 PPU, *J. McB. v L. E.*, ECLI:EU:C:2010:582, para. 59.

653 ibid., paras. 60–63.

654 ibid.

655 e.g. Case C-200/02, *Kunqian Catherine Zhu and Man Lavette Chen v Secretary of State for the Home Department*, ECLI:EU:C:2004:639, para. 26; Case C-34/09, *Ruiz Zambrano*, ECLI:EU:C:2011:124, paras. 40–41. See also the personal scope of the Citizens' Rights Directive.

656 R. Lamont, above n. 12, 235. See also the discussion in H. Stalford, 'The Citizenship Status of Children in the European Union' (2000) 8 *International Journal of Children's Rights* 101.

inseparable from the exercise by their parent of his or her right to freedom of movement. The issue is then not the freedom of movement of the child as viewed independently, even if the child is able to assert agency in that regard, but in a familial context. This would correspond to the approach taken by the ECtHR as well.[657] However, adopting such an approach does not solve all questions, as interests behind the parent's and the child's rights might not be entirely the same. The issue concerns the parent, since it is in the parent's interest to move *and* to do so with the child, but it concerns the child insofar as it is in the child's interest to receive the care that might be provided by the relocating parent. Even when a child can legitimately assert their independent interests in relocation, such interests will typically blend with the familial context due to the nature of the dispute.[658] Therefore, both from the perspective of the relocating parent and the child, freedom of movement typically becomes a way to claim a general fundamental right to family life.[659]

A serious infringement of a European citizen's fundamental right could fall within the scope of EU law if fundamental rights constituted part of the substance of EU citizenship rights.[660] However, as discussed in the previous chapter, this is not currently the case. One needs, therefore, to conceptually clarify EU claims that can be raised in this context. It is worth noting that one can differentiate between two kinds of rights stemming from EU law. Primary rights stem directly from the Treaty provisions. Secondary rights are not based on the Treaty but derive from its provisions. Restrictions of primary rights – such as the right to move or reside across the Union – are always caught by EU law. On the other hand, secondary rights are protected if, *according to the particular facts of the case*, their restriction would lead to a restriction of the primary right that is intended to be exercised.[661] From this point of view, as the parent is legally free to move abroad without the child, the parent's right to move with the child will typically constitute a secondary right. It is only the child's right to move and reside abroad that engages primary Treaty rights directly.

There are two consequences of this conceptualisation. First, from the point of view of the child, child relocation restrictions necessarily constrain his or her primary free movement rights. This is so regardless of whether the child can express a desire to move or not. However, as the exercise of a minor's freedom of movement depends on their parents, and as the parents in a relocation dispute

657 See the discussion in Chapter 4.

658 These interests can also be expected to fall under Article 24 of the CFR and constitute part of the best interests analysis in reference to the child's wishes, rather than a self-standing free movement rights analysis. This is due to the delicate nature of the disputes and the competence limitation. See the discussion on the justification and proportionality below.

659 See N.N. Shuibhne, above n. 587, discussing different uses of freedom of movement.

660 M.J. van den Brink, above n. 568, 289.

661 A. Tryfonidou, *The Impact of Union Citizenship on the EU's Market Freedoms*, Hart Publishing, Oxford 2016, p. 181. See also the discussion in A. Tryfonidou, above n. 641.

have divergent views on the child's best interests that need to be addressed, the analysis is likely to conceptually resemble that seen in *J. McB.* and to focus on Article 24 of the Charter, even if the child's right to (and interest in) free movement is explicitly recognised. This familial reorientation of the focus of the dispute is also in line with the jurisprudence of the ECtHR. Second, restrictions on child relocation could lead to a restriction of the primary rights of the parent if qualified by circumstances of the case. The EU free movement framework does recognise the functional relevance of family rights at large. It has also been recognised by the CJEU that when the child's rights are involved, granting rights to the parent might be necessary for the child's claimed EU primary rights to be effective due to children's dependency.[662] While child relocation cases are not about granting a parent their right to move per se, the concept of dependency known from other cases might be useful in the analysis.[663] Most likely, the parent could not claim to be dependent on the child in a legally relevant way, nor can desirability of a particular arrangement presuppose dependency.[664] However, the restriction on relocation could, in principle, lead to a restriction of the parent's primary rights in a situation where the parent could, as a matter of the facts of the case, not leave the child behind due to the lack of sufficient care for the child in the event of the parent's migration.[665] It is clear, therefore, that regardless of the exact circumstances – prompting an emphasis on a particular set of rights – the analysis needs to focus on the position of the child. The emphasis on a particular set of rights involved will be highly fact-dependent and one can expect that this fact-dependency will significantly influence the construction of the analysis at the EU level if a child relocation case ever reached the Luxembourg Court.

5.4. CHILD RELOCATION LAWS AND DIFFERENT RESTRICTIONS OF FREE MOMENT

Measures that impose restrictions on child relocation may, within the limits discussed above, be caught by the EU Treaty. However, the exact nature of

[662] Compare the Court's jurisprudence on residence rights, e.g. Case C-34/09, *Ruiz Zambrano*, ECLI:EU:C:2011:124, Case C-200/02, *Zhu and Chen*, ECLI:EU:C:2004:639.

[663] For an overview see F. Ristuccia, 'Ties That Bind and Ties That Compel: Dependency and the Ruiz Zambrano Doctrine' (2023) 60 *Common Market Law Review* 1227.

[664] See, for example, Case C-457/12, *S and G*, ECLI:EU:C:2014:136, paras. 43–44.

[665] Compare A. Torres Pérez, 'The Right to Family Life as a Bar to the Expulsion of Third Country Nationals in the European Union' in M. González Pascual and A. Torres Pérez (eds), *The Right to Family Life in the European Union*, Routledge, London 2017, p. 162 who points out in the context of expulsion cases such as Case C-34/09, *Ruiz Zambrano*, ECLI:EU:C:2011:124 that, as a matter of both law and fact, the state can always assume responsibility for minor EU citizens, but this is not a solution that the Court is willing to accept. See also Case C-133/15, *Chavez-Vilchez*, ECLI:EU:C:2017:354, para. 72.

their restrictive effect on freedom of movement might vary depending on the construction of national family laws, with important consequences for the subsequent analysis of their justification and proportionality. The construction of most national family laws points prima facie towards a consideration of child relocation measures as non-discriminatory restrictions. However, Ruth Lamont suggests that if child relocation law adversely affects non-nationals seeking to relocate abroad, rather than nationals, restrictions on relocation could constitute indirect discrimination on the grounds of nationality in reference to Article 18 of the TFEU.[666] Article 18 of the TFEU explicitly prohibits, within its scope, any discrimination on the grounds of nationality and is also applicable in cases where EU citizenship provisions are invoked instead of a specific Treaty freedom.[667] The prohibition of discrimination is further commonly expressed as a general requirement that comparable situations must not be treated differently and different situations must not be treated in the same way, unless such treatment is objectively justified.[668] As any discrimination based on nationality is generally prohibited by the Treaty, the investigation of child relocation measures as a restriction of free movement must, therefore, start with an assessment of differences in treatment.

5.4.1. DISCRIMINATORY RESTRICTIONS

In the child relocation context, no existing rules in Europe make reference to the nationality of the parties involved. As such, they do not lead to any direct discrimination in reference to the protected grounds of Article 18 of the TFEU. However, some relocation laws differentiate between relocation within the national territory and relocation involving moves to another country.[669] Such differentiation can result from the fact that international relocations are restricted by law, while internal relocations are not, or from different substantive or procedural standards applied to international or internal relocations.[670] The notoriously alleged differences in approaches to child relocation between the Member States do not per se create any discrimination. In other words, national

---

666 R. Lamont, above n. 12, 241.

667 This provision is directly effective: Case C-413/99, *Baumbast*, ECLI:EU:C:2002:493, para. 86; see also S. Henrich and D.-E. Khan, above n. 588, p. 253.

668 See E. Muir, 'The Essence of the Fundamental Right to Equal Treatment: Back to the Origins' (2019) 20 *German Law Journal* 817, 818 describing this phrasing as the 'standard formula' of EU equality law.

669 This is, in particular, the case in the United Kingdom, as discussed further in Chapter 7, but also, e.g. Austria and Denmark.

670 Article 18 of the TFEU applies, however, only to differences in treatment between nationals of different Member States, and not nationals of Member States and non-Member States. See Joined Cases C-22/08 and C-23/08, *Athanasios Vatsouras (C-22/08) and Josif Koupatantze (C-23/08) v Arbeitsgemeinschaft (ARGE) Nürnberg 900*, ECLI:EU:C:2009:344, para. 52.

law cannot be said to be discriminatory merely because other Member States apply rules which are perceived as less strict.[671] Nevertheless, insofar as *a* differentiation between different types of situations is introduced into national law, various indirectly discriminatory scenarios need to be investigated in more detail.

In *O'Flynn*, both a milestone and a cornerstone of indirect discrimination case law, the Court distinguished four main categories of potentially discriminatory laws that, although applicable irrespective of nationality,

> affect essentially migrant workers ... or the great majority of those affected are migrant workers ..., where they are indistinctly applicable but can more easily be satisfied by national workers than by migrant workers ... or where there is a risk that they may operate to the particular detriment of migrant workers,[672]

recognising indirect discrimination as an 'effect-related' concept.[673] It is, therefore, useful to analyse child relocation laws and measures in light of these categories. Both nationals and non-nationals need to adhere to the same child relocation laws. Whether child relocation laws affect essentially non-nationals can be questioned in light of different migratory trends of different Member States. The existing empirical research suggests that relocations might be more often granted to foreigners, in particular other EU nationals, compared to other groups.[674] Whether relocation decisions constitute an indirectly discriminatory measure insofar as they *adversely* affect non-nationals[675] is also not immediately given, but one can legitimately agree that in most cases it will be less detrimental to 'be forced' to stay in one's country of origin than a foreign country, making refusals of relocation more detrimental for non-nationals. Nevertheless, this is less clear in cases where the non-national parent is not 'going home'. The disadvantage might be, therefore, highly contextual and difficult to capture, making the fact-specificity of indirect discrimination cases apparent. Notwithstanding this hypothetical discussion, the CJEU has consistently held that it is, above all, a non-national that tends to return to a Member State of origin in the event of a significant life change, such as illness or unemployment.[676] One can, therefore,

---

671 e.g. Case C-44/94, *The Queen v Minister of Agriculture, Fisheries and Food, ex parte National Federation of Fishermen's Organisations and others and Federation of Highlands and Islands Fishermen and others*, ECLI:EU:C:1995:325, paras. 44–45, where the Court held that (indirect) discrimination 'is not given in the case of unequal treatment of a foreigner that solely results from differences in national legislation of different Member States'.

672 Case C-237/94, *John O'Flynn v Adjudication Officer*, ECLI:EU:C:1996:206, para. 18.

673 J. Maliszewska-Nienartowicz, 'Direct and Indirect Discrimination in European Union Law – How to Draw a Dividing Line?' (2014) 3 *International Journal of Social Sciences* 41, 43.

674 R. George, above n. 117, 385–88.

675 As hypothesised by R. Lamont, above n. 12, 241.

676 See also the arguments in the Opinion of the Advocate General in Case C-237/94, *John O'Flynn v Adjudication Officer*, ECLI:EU:C:1996:123, para. 30.

legitimately expect that a similar reasoning would be applied to relationship breakdowns or other major family changes behind relocation.[677]

The discrimination analysis contextually closest to child relocation was conducted in the relatively recent CJEU judgment in Case C-454/19.[678] The case concerned the discriminatory effects of German criminal law provisions that foresee a harsher criminal responsibility for child abduction to another Member State as compared to child abduction within Germany. The Court held that consequences of such legislation are liable to affect, in fact, primarily Union citizens who are nationals of other Member States and who have exercised their right to move and reside freely and reside in Germany. Those citizens are more likely than German nationals to remove or send their children to another Member State, mainly their Member State of origin.[679] Naturally, in this context, the harsher consequences of such action for a migrant are apparent. However, even if there is no particular detriment in the case of a refusal of relocation, this judgment essentially confirms the suggestion put forward by Lamont that rules of such nature are liable to primarily affect mobile Union citizens.[680] Conceptually, also in light of the varied migratory patterns of other Member States, the assessment of whether non-nationals are essentially more likely to be affected could have reasonably been different, but the existing jurisprudence seems to clearly suggest that different rules on internal and international relocations would amount to discrimination, unless justified and proportionate to the legitimate aim pursued.

Additionally, the fact that the same provision applies to all (cross-border or not) relocations does not yet close the possibility of raising discrimination claims under EU law, as suggested by the *Garcia Avello* ruling in the context of laws on surnames. The law in this case was prima facie non-discriminatory, but the CJEU relied on the general non-discrimination principle to assess whether persons with double nationality are in an identical situation to persons of single nationality of the Member State in question, or whether, on the contrary, their situations are different. In the latter case, the principle of non-discrimination would mean that double nationals may assert their right to be treated in a different manner from nationals, unless the treatment in issue can be justified on objective grounds.[681] In light of the reasoning accepted in *Garcia Avello*, even

---

677 Such an assessment would be clearly grounded in empirical research. See S. Morano-Foadi, above n. 273, 9–17.

678 Case C-454/19, *ZW*, ECLI:EU:C:2020:947.

679 See, for an analogical argumentation, ibid., para. 34.

680 R. Lamont, above n. 12, 241.

681 Case C-148/02, *Garcia Avello*, ECLI:EU:C:2003:539, para. 34. See also D. Chalmers, G. Davies and G. Monti, *European Union Law Text and Materials*, 4th ed., Cambridge University Press, Cambridge 2019, p. 487 or S. Coutts, *Citizenship, Crime and Community in the European Union*, Hart Publishing, Oxford 2019, pp. 32–33. On broader contextual consequences of this judgment, see Chapter 6.

uniform rules on all relocations could amount to unequal treatment if there is a systemic refusal to grant a relocation permission to non-nationals, but only if the grounds given for the refusal were linked to the possession of a different nationality (even if indirectly), and when it could be proven that the situation of both categories of persons is, in fact, different although treated the same by law.[682] This could be the case where, for example, national law would hold that it is in the best interests of all children possessing the nationality of a given Member State to receive an upbringing in the particular socio-cultural background of this Member State, ignoring the objectively more complex situation of children with double nationality and mixed heritage.

To a contemporary family lawyer, such an example seems most likely extreme and somewhat artificial.[683] In an average relocation case, the factual circumstances and the grounds for refusal of a relocation application are much more nuanced and complex. This is a natural consequence of decisions being guided by the child's best interests assessment and accounting for a variety of situations in which individual children grow up.[684] The issue of comparability of the situations of nationals and non-nationals, therefore, would in most cases be heavily dependent on the factual background of the case and the specific argumentation used.[685] Discriminatory treatment – including cases where the discrimination would lie in treating different situations in the same way – could then be justified only based on objective considerations independent of the nationality of the individuals concerned or the exercise of cross-border mobility, and would have to be proportionate.[686] The justification and proportionality analysis in such cases is closely intertwined with the comparability analysis, and here the difficulty

682 Case C-148/02, *Garcia Avello*, ECLI:EU:C:2003:539, para. 63; Opinion of the Advocate General in Case C-148/02, *Garcia Avello*, ECLI:EU:C:2003:311, para. 75.

683 See, however, the national doctrine discussed in the ECtHR judgment in *Penchevi v Bulgaria* [2015] ECtHR, app. no. 77818/12, presented in Chapter 4, above Section 4.3.2.

684 Chapter 6 demonstrates this complexity both in reference to different approaches taken to assess the child's best interests and the variety of factual circumstances of relocation cases, as shown by the case law cited there.

685 A.P. van der Mei, 'The Outer Limits of the Prohibition of Discrimination on Grounds of Nationality: A Look through the Lens of Union Citizenship' (2011) 18 *Maastricht Journal of European and Comparative Law* 62, 77–78: 'The principle of non-discrimination rests on comparability, but in itself does not provide guidance as to which situations must be compared and when situations must be labelled as comparable … [EU citizenship] may entitle [migrant and static citizens] to equality of treatment in comparable situations but does not imply that they must be regarded as being in the same position'. See also E. Guild, *Immigration Law in the European Community*, Kluwer Law International, The Hague 2001, p. 45 noting that 'all too often situations are inherently different and inherently the same depending on the point of view from which one is looking at them', and – as such – discrimination remains difficult to 'pin down'.

686 e.g. Case C-224/98, *D'Hoop*, ECLI:EU:C:2002:432, para. 36; Case C-148/02, *Garcia Avello*, ECLI:EU:C:2003:539, para. 31.

of conducting such an analysis in abstracto becomes apparent. It is, however, not necessary to consider a full spectrum of possible circumstances due to the quasi-universal nature of the possible justifications of any discriminatory measure. The analysis conducted in the last section of this chapter will in any case demonstrate why, in most cases, claims about discrimination under EU law will be difficult to sustain.

Two final remarks can be made about discrimination claims in child relocation cases that relate to protected grounds other than nationality and could be raised also against one's Member State of origin. First, one can recall the brief discussion on potential gender discrimination involved in child relocation cases (Article 21 of the CFR). Most often, mothers are the primary caregivers who want to move together with their children.[687] Therefore, one could try to argue that restrictions on child relocation constitute also indirect gender discrimination. However, even if the Court recognised that child relocation might constitute indirect discrimination based on gender,[688] the CJEU is more likely to select a less controversial ground for its judgments, in particular if the case at hand can be argued on grounds inherently related to movement.[689] Second, the concept of indirect discrimination has been previously detached from the grounds of nationality and analysed through the general equality principle with *the prior exercise of the EU freedom of movement* becoming the protected ground.[690] However, it is hard to imagine how comparability could be established in relation to this protected ground in child relocation cases. It is also not necessary, because – as will be discussed in the following section – these types of cases could be more easily presented as non-discriminatory restrictions of free movement. In any case, both types of discriminatory restrictions discussed here could still be justified analogically to other types of discrimination. This reinforces the observation that it is the justification and proportionality stage that remains of key importance for the analysis of child relocation in the EU context.

5.4.2. NON-DISCRIMINATORY RESTRICTIONS

Discriminatory measures are always prohibited, unless justified and proportionate. However, discrimination is no longer a necessary component of a restriction.[691] To describe all sorts of non-discriminatory restrictions,

---

687 This is confirmed by empirical research, e.g. P. Parkinson and J. Cashmore, above n. 173, 24; M. Freeman, above n. 180.

688 See the reasoning in Case 170/84, *Bilka – Kaufhaus GmbH v Karin Weber von Hartz*, ECLI:EU:C:1986:204.

689 See the discussion in Chapter 4.

690 e.g. in Case C-224/98, *D'Hoop*, ECLI:EU:C:2002:432.

691 See the discussion in A. Tryfonidou, above n. 641.

the Court has used the language of 'obstacles' or 'impediments to free movement'.[692] This has led to the emergence of a general right of free movement that should be free from all measures liable to hinder, or render less attractive, its exercise,[693] or that affect access to the market of another Member State.[694] One of the core assertions made in the relocation context is that if the relocating parent is not allowed to take the child with them, the potential separation deters the parent from the move and, in that, questions the effectiveness of the parent's free movement rights.[695] The logic of importance of family relationships for the exercise of movement has indeed been recognised at the very early stages of EU law's development.[696] However, while the scope of rules that discourage movement has been interpreted in a generous way, this does not presuppose that virtually all measures making movement less attractive are caught by the Treaty.[697] The Court limits the extension of the freedom using the doctrine of remoteness that demands closer scrutiny in the child relocation context as well.

The discussion of remoteness links back to the applicability of EU law. To briefly recall the main feature of the doctrine, the Court excludes a measure from the scope of the Treaty prohibition where it is too uncertain or too indirect to be capable of discouraging or hindering free movement.[698] For the doctrine of remoteness to apply, the rules in question must be non-discriminatory, must not be intended to regulate intra-EU movement or the exercise of the freedom of movement, and there must be no causal connection between the rule and the alleged barrier.[699] The doctrine has not been fully clarified by the Court,[700] and the issue is often characterised as more 'practical than legal'.[701] In any case, as already mentioned, the rule, the conceptualisation of the alleged barrier, and the causal connection between them play a role in the analysis. Whether a measure

---

692 ibid., 393–95.

693 e.g. Case C-55/94, *Reinhard Gebhard v Consiglio dell'Ordine degli Avvocati e Procuratori di Milano*, ECLI:EU:C:1995:411, para. 37; Case C-285/01, *Isabel Burbaud v Ministère de l'Emploi et de la Solidarité*, ECLI:EU:C:2003:432, para. 95.

694 e.g. Case C-384/93, *Alpine Investments BV v Minister van Financiën*, ECLI:EU:C:1995:126, para. 38; Case C-415/93, *Union royale belge des sociétés de football association ASBL v Jean-Marc Bosman*, ECLI:EU:C:1995:463, para. 103.

695 This is what underlines the analysis in R. Lamont, above n. 12. Compare the reasoning in Case C-60/00, *Mary Carpenter v Secretary of State for the Home Department*, ECLI:EU:C:2002:434, para. 39.

696 See, for example, the Preamble of Council Regulation (EEC) 1612/68 of 15 October 1968 on freedom of movement for workers within the Community [1968] OJ L257/2 (no longer in force). See also E. Spaventa, 'From Gebhard to Carpenter: Towards a (Non-)Economic Constitution' (2004) 41 *Common Market Law Review* 743.

697 e.g. Case C-60/00, *Carpenter*, ECLI:EU:C:2002:434; see also E. Spaventa, above n. 639, p. 265.

698 e.g. Case C-190/98, *Graf*, ECLI:EU:C:2000:49, paras. 20–25.

699 E. Spaventa, above n. 639, p. 251.

700 e.g. N.N. Shuibhne, above n. 640, pp. 157–88. See also the discussions in C. Costello, above n. 640; N.N. Shuibhne and D. Edward, above n. 642.

701 N.N. Shuibhne and D. Edward, above n. 642, p. 257.

in question is too remote to be caught by the Treaty depends first on its potential discriminatory effect. If rules are discriminatory, they will be caught by the Treaty. The existence of such an effect of different relocation rules was analysed above. This step of the analysis continues, therefore, on the assumption that the rules in question are genuinely non-discriminatory, and focuses on their rationale and the causal link between the rule and the barrier.

The first question to be considered is whether the given rule is intended to regulate freedom of movement. Here, the many different constructions of national laws might contribute to different answers. Member States that resolve relocation disputes based on general provisions of custody determination and modification can legitimately claim that this is not the case, activating the doctrine of remoteness, although, and even if, the individual decisions reached are obviously capable of having an effect on movement. In Member States that have specific provisions on relocation, in particular if the issue is framed as a decision to grant or refuse relocation rather than a holistic evaluation of the custody situation, the conclusion could be different. One can draw attention to the fact that the specific relocation provisions in Austria were motivated by and involve, inter alia, references to freedom of movement.[702] In such cases, the rules – while their main rationale is not movement-related – can legitimately be claimed to regulate the exercise of free movement, and therefore, be drawn under the scrutiny of EU law. However, in most cases, the analysis would focus on the causal link between the measure and the barrier to access freedom of movement rights.

Causal connections in free movement cases, in particular when the cases touch upon free movement of persons and their family members, often seem to be assumed rather than subject to any particular legal test.[703] The *Carpenter* case, centred around care and dependence within a family, is a prime example of such an approach.[704] Mr Carpenter asserted that his cross-border provision of services was dependent on his wife's permanent residence in his home state and her provision of care for his children, but the Court did not explicitly specify the relevance of that factor to its decision. The decision was based on the reasoning according to which the absence of Mrs Carpenter would have 'detrimental effects' on the 'conditions under which Mr Carpenter exercised' his Treaty rights, going beyond the logic of non-discriminatory restrictions towards that of fundamental rights protection.[705] The case was therefore said to

[702] Article 162 of the Austrian Civil Code (ABGB). See also *Vorblatt und Erläuterungen zu dem Kindschafts- und Namensrecht-Änderungsgesetz*, above n. 217.

[703] E. Spaventa, above n. 639, p. 266; N.N. Shuibhne, above n. 640, p. 182.

[704] Case C-60/00, *Mary Carpenter v Secretary of State for the Home Department*, ECLI:EU:C:2002:434. See N.N. Shuibhne, above n. 640, p. 182; H. Toner, 'Non-Discriminatory Obstacles to the Exercise of Treaty Rights – Articles 39, 43, 49, and 18 EC' (2004) 23 *Yearbook of European Law* 275, 290–91.

[705] D. Thym, above n. 571, p. 171.

rely on the Court's 'own brand of situational empathy' rather than a solid legal test.[706] This methodological approach was criticised in the literature, even by those approving of the result.[707] As noticed in the literature, the Court could have argued that the enforced separation of a family is, in itself, a significant obstacle to freedom of movement.[708] At the same time, it would be difficult to reason that the expulsion of Mrs Carpenter *directly* affected Mr Carpenter's freedom to provide services abroad.[709] The criterion of directness is much more apt to analyse individual and concrete rights,[710] such as the primary right of the relocating parent to move his or her residence, rather than relational family rights.

In the context of family relationships, the requirement for the measure to be both direct and significant, as argued by the Court, quickly becomes problematic as factors that might deter movement might not necessarily be linked to, or be more important than the conditions of, the exercise of that movement directly.[711] Perhaps this is why some authors advocate that measures that are direct *or* significant should be caught by the Treaty.[712] Others argue, along somewhat different lines, that a restrictive reading of the scope of application of EU law in such cases is not a correct result in times when relational individuals are confronted with mobility on a daily basis.[713] Acceptance of such accounts would suggest that restrictions on child relocation are to be seen as restrictions of parental freedom of movement. However, the exact reach of the Court's scrutiny of non-discriminatory measures is still hard to delineate, with the controversies only reinforced by the EU citizenship jurisprudence.[714] Some warn that Article 21 of the TFEU should not become 'a general claim to be free from any interference with one's freedom' that can be turned 'into a

706 This expression was borrowed from M. Everson, 'A Very Cosmopolitan Citizenship: But Who Pays the Price?' in M. Dougan, N.N. Shuibhne and E. Spaventa (eds), *Empowerment and Disempowerment of the European Citizen*, Hart Publishing, Oxford 2012, p. 153, who also presents an insightful critique of this strand of case law.

707 e.g. Editorial comment, 'Freedoms Unlimited? Reflections on Mary Carpenter v. Secretary of State' (2003) 40 *Common Market Law Review* 537; N. Reich and S. Harbacevica, 'Citizenship and Family on Trial: A Fairly Optimistic Overview of Recent Court Practice with Regard to Free Movement of Persons' (2003) 40 *Common Market Law Review* 615.

708 H. Toner, above n. 704, 291.

709 J. Snell, 'The Notion of Market Access: A Concept or a Slogan?' (2010) 47 *Common Market Law Review* 437, 462–63. See also N. Reich and S. Harbacevica, above n. 707, 636, calling the link 'rather remote'.

710 J. Snell, above n. 709, 452.

711 E. Spaventa, above n. 639, p. 266.

712 For a brief overview of the literature and alternative suggestions see H. Toner, *Partnership Rights, Free Movement, and EU Law*, Hart Publishing, Oxford 2004, pp. 205–08. This does not mean that the threshold of significance is not problematic in itself. See also J. Snell, above n. 709.

713 N. Reich and S. Harbacevica, above n. 707, 629.

714 F. Wollenschläger, above n. 638, 27.

weapon directed against all restrictions on individual freedom by the Member States'.[715] Rather, a balance must be struck between the regulatory autonomy of national authorities and the practical effectiveness of Article 21 of the TFEU.[716] The recipe for reaching this balance is unclear and dependent on contextual circumstances.

Considering this discussion, one can easily anticipate a certain uneasiness if relocation rules were to be drawn into the scope of EU law. This impression can be additionally deduced from the Opinion of Advocate General Hogan in the already mentioned Case C-454/19 involving German criminal law provisions penalising child abductions. The case was decided based on the finding of discrimination, but in his Opinion, Advocate General Hogan observed:

> it seems to me that *it is not the mere decision in respect of parental authority* but rather the risk of criminal prosecution *that is actually likely to dissuade a Union citizen from leaving the host Member State* where he or she is resident and returning to his or her Member State of origin with his or her child when that person does not have the right to determine the child's place of residence.[717] (Emphasis added.)

This statement was not discussed further either by the Advocate General or the Court, perhaps unsurprisingly given the case's focus on criminal law. However, it raises some interesting questions. It might be argued that the assertion that 'it is not the mere decision in respect of parental authority' that dissuades a Union citizen from movement was used instrumentally to justify the finding of a restriction in reference to the criminal law rules. In the end, what the German criminal law provisions were said to dissuade an EU citizen from was, in the first place, an unlawful action (child abduction), whether penalised by criminal law or not, and as such, their restrictive character could be seen as secondary. But, at the same time, finding a general (non-discriminatory) restriction was not necessary since the rules were discriminatory in any case. It would also be difficult to argue that refusals of relocation, as decisions on parental authority, do not have any dissuasive effect when research clearly shows that most relocating parents decide not to move without their children. This statement becomes, therefore, interesting from the point of view of the child relocation analysis. It suggests that there are grounds for the impression that decisions about parental authority should not be drawn into the analysis of restrictions on EU law. One can hypothesise that this is so either because they do not pass the remoteness test or because of their particular inherent nature. The following paragraphs develop this discussion, putting forward arguments against drawing child relocation provisions into the scope of application of EU law.

---

715 ibid.

716 ibid., 28.

717 Opinion of the Advocate General in Case C-454/19, *ZW*, ECLI:EU:C:2020:430, para. 27.

Core aspects of national family law are rarely the direct object of the CJEU's analysis. Therefore, one needs to look to other areas of case law for arguments supporting this interpretation. It quickly becomes apparent that there are limits of free movement of persons to be found in the CJEU's jurisprudence that can be translated into family law, both in other areas of retained competences of Member States (e.g. tax law) and in incidental decisions of the Court (e.g. the *Deliège* case).[718] Taxation jurisprudence, for example, has, over the years, been extended to cover non-discriminatory restrictions of EU law. At the same time, the CJEU has on multiple occasions held that the Treaty rights do not guarantee that all forms of movement 'will be neutral from a fiscal viewpoint'.[719] The case law is not fully predictable but – even if only on facts and not as a matter of any consistent doctrine – the Court is willing to find a restriction only when discrimination is present,[720] even if it employs the language of obstacles.[721] Another outer limit of the doctrine can be derived from the *Deliège* judgment where the Court found, in the context of sporting activities, that certain rules are inherent in the conduct of certain activities and, as such, may not constitute a restriction to the Treaty freedoms.[722] The case was criticised for its unreasoned rejection of the restriction reasoning where there was clearly an obstacle to market access, and where the same final decision could be reached after the justification and proportionality assessment.[723] Nevertheless, this way the Court excluded a specific category of EU law claims from further discussion and the 'inherent nature' of certain activities can be, in principle, transposed beyond sport. In that, certain rules considered to be 'rules of the game'[724] would not be perceived as restrictions on free movement under EU law.

There are several reasons for a restrained approach in family law: the political sensitivity of family issues; its position in the EU legal framework; and the fact that EU law and family law pursue different objectives and are legitimised in

718 For an overview, see E. Spaventa, above n. 639.

719 ibid., pp. 267–68.

720 ibid., p. 269.

721 J. Snell, 'Non-Discriminatory Tax Obstacles in Community Law' (2007) 56 *International and Comparative Law Quarterly* 339, 349.

722 Joined Cases C-51/96 and C-191/97, *Christelle Deliège v Ligue francophone de judo et disciplines associées ASBL, Ligue belge de judo ASBL, Union européenne de judo (C-51/96) and François Pacquée (C-191/97)*, ECLI:EU:C:2000:199. In this case Ms Deliège, a Belgian judoka, challenged the Belgian federation-based system for selecting competitors for international competitions. Ms Deliège maintained that the Belgian rules regarding the limit to the number of athletes from each national federation obstructed her economic activity. The Court found that, although these rules inevitably have the effect of limiting the number of participants in a tournament, this is inherent in the conduct of international sports and as such may not constitute a restriction to the Treaty freedoms.

723 J. Snell, above n. 709, 461–62.

724 C. Barnard, above n. 623, p. 253.

different ways.[725] Additionally, child relocation is a particularly sensitive topic also in the national context. Legal rules and decisions should not, naturally, be beyond scrutiny only because of their sensitivity,[726] and political sensitivities can change.[727] But the different objectives of EU law and family rules in the exercise of parental responsibilities, with certain limitations being both incidental to and inherent in their operation, can call for a cautious approach. Family law has various functions: protective; facilitative; adjudicative; expressive; and channelling, and so do family courts.[728] The functions are employed to various extents in different institutions of family law but are otherwise omnipresent. The law aims to protect (in particular children); it aims to facilitate the co-operation between family members by putting in place a framework for such co-operation; it resolves disputes where co-operation fails; it expresses normative preferences and values, and with all these means it channels people towards certain institutions.[729] Parenting, as many observe, inherently requires co-operation and constrains choices; it could be questionable to see such constraints as a barrier to movement, as long as the law allows for free movement interests to be considered.[730] Thus, such rules could be argued not to constitute an obstacle to intra-EU movement because their effect on such movement is inherent in their aim – to make sure that any decision about a child's residence is made with the knowledge and approval of both parents, or national authorities, and with the child's best interests at heart. Such an aim must be a priori compatible with EU law.

When the barrier to movement coincides with the very purpose of the rules – be it, to paraphrase Spaventa, 'selecting athletes, or raising funds in taxes,' or taking care of children – and if its aim is legitimate, any effect that such a rule might have can be either disregarded as a matter of policy choice or seen as inherent in the activity in question.[731] The answer to the relocation question could therefore be, first, that most child relocation rules are, as a matter of policy choice, free from EU law scrutiny. In the case law on taxation, discriminatory choices are still prohibited unless justified. As discussed above, child relocation

---

725 Thus, there are clear parallels with taxation, despite the very different nature of the two areas of law. See J. Snell, above n. 721, 355–58. Snell mentions the practical problems of the unlimited reach of EU law as every element of national taxation could prima facie constitute a restriction, but this point seems of less importance for family law.

726 ibid., 356.

727 E. Spaventa, above n. 639, p. 270.

728 e.g. J. Doughty, 'Identity Crisis in the Family Courts? Different Approaches in England and Wales and Australia' (2009) 31 *Journal of Social Welfare and Family Law* 231; R.H. Mnookin, above n. 129; C. Schneider, 'The Channelling Function in Family Law' (1992) 20 *Hofstra Law Review* 495.

729 e.g. L.C. McClain, 'Love, Marriage, and the Baby Carriage: Revisiting the Channelling Function of Family Law' (2007) 28 *Cardozo Law Review* 2133.

730 See the brief discussion in J. Herring and R. Taylor, above n. 10, 524.

731 E. Spaventa, above n. 639, p. 270.

provisions might be discriminatory under certain circumstances as well. But as long as no discrimination is found, Member States remain free to pursue their own policy choices on a given matter. This could legitimately be the case also with child relocation. Alternatively, a rule requiring the relocating parent to obtain the other parent's agreement or the court's approval to relocate, or a decision refusing such relocation in order to find a solution that is best from the point of view of the child *must not in itself* constitute a restriction to the Treaty provisions on free movement. In *Deliège*, the Court clearly said that the rule in question does not constitute a restriction '*as long as it derives from a need inherent in the organisation of such a competition*' (emphasis added).[732] This would shift the focus onto the consideration of the 'inherent aim' and close the scope of EU law's application in child relocation cases to truly exceptional circumstances where the restrictive rule in question does not correspond to the aim it pursues.[733]

The above discussion does not fully clarify the reach of EU law. Its purpose is rather to argue that there are good reasons to leave child relocation outside this reach. However, clarification of this issue is also not strictly necessary. As a matter of dogmatic construction, child relocation measures could or could not be drawn into the scope of application of EU law – but this might have more to do with the legitimacy concerns and the situational sympathy of the Court in a given case.[734] In the end, the sensitivity of an area should not necessarily automatically exclude any situation from the scope of EU law, as many of the arguments raised above can reasonably be addressed at the justification and proportionality stage.[735] This is not to say that such a decision would be meaningless from the point of view of the EU's competences and the legitimacy of the CJEU. If the Court decides to leave child relocation measures outside EU law, this is a qualitatively different decision from drawing them under its scrutiny. In this regard, any decision would have a communicative value and significantly shape the scope of legal uncertainty under which national systems operate, reformulating the Europeanisation pressures on national courts. However, due to the nature of this area of law, any CJEU judgment might have more far-reaching consequences for the balance of powers within the Union than the substance of child relocation law as such. This assertion is supported by the analysis of justification and proportionality of any restrictive character of child relocation rules.

---

[732] Joined Cases C-51/96 and C-191/97, *Christelle Deliège*, ECLI:EU:C:2000:199, para. 69.

[733] See the analogical analysis in E. Spaventa, above n. 639, p. 270.

[734] For an interesting analysis of the different dogmatic, conceptual and legitimacy factors having a role in the Court's judgments, in particular in reference to Case C-34/09, *Ruiz Zambrano*, ECLI:EU:C:2011:124, see D. Thym, above n. 571.

[735] See also M.J. van den Brink, above n. 624, p. 325.

5.5. JUSTIFICATION AND PROPORTIONALITY

Child relocation rules and decisions might be seen, in certain circumstances, as restrictions to free movement. With the ever-growing reach of EU law and the extension of the CJEU's powers, it is the justification and proportionality stage where most interesting questions emerge.[736] The existing literature engages with these issues to a limited extent. Timothy Scott comes to the conclusion that *the requirement to apply for relocation abroad* – as opposed to there being no such requirement for internal relocations in English law – should be seen as *disproportionate*, based on arguments related to the existence of European private international law instruments.[737] Ruth Lamont concludes that *a decision which refuses relocation* taken in the child's best interests is *likely to be a proportionate* decision, but draws attention to the lack of a clear definition of proportionality review in new contexts such as family law.[738] As becomes immediately apparent, these accounts touch on two different issues: the margin of appreciation left to legislative bodies of Member States (Scott) and the scope of 'decentralized judicial review' conducted by national courts (Lamont).[739] While interdependent, these two perspectives and the intensity of the Court's scrutiny result in different doctrinal and institutional implications. This is so in particular where the Court approaches the justification and proportionality analysis in the areas of retained competences, such as family law.

Lena Boucon notes that in such legal areas the Court resolves its jurisdictional dilemma by implementing a doctrine that can be described as a 'mutual adjustment'.[740] This doctrine has two strands: first, the Court remains flexible to adapt to the peculiarities of the case and the field in question;

---

736 L. Boucon, above n. 38, p. 177; J. Zglinski, *Europe's Passive Virtues: Deference to National Authorities in EU Free Movement Law*, Oxford University Press, Oxford 2020, pp. 13–14. On the Court's receptiveness to possible justifications in the expanding legal fields, see S. Weatherill, 'The Court's Case Law on the Internal Market: "A Circumloquacious Statement of the Result, Rather than a Reason for Arriving at It"?' in M. Adams, H. de Waele, J. Meeusen and G. Straetmans (eds), *Judging Europe's Judges: The Legitimacy of the Case Law of the European Court of Justice*, Hart Publishing, Oxford 2013.

737 T. Scott, above n. 12, p. 14.

738 R. Lamont, above n. 12, 242.

739 For the clear differentiation of the two, and its doctrinal and institutional implications, see J. Zglinski, above n. 736, pp. 30–33: 'When the ECJ grants a national legislature deference in the context of justification and proportionality review, it limits judicial control over the subject matter. The Member State is given the freedom to choose how to regulate with restricted or minimal scrutiny. When the ECJ, in contrast, defers the decision on justification and proportionality to a national court, judicial review of the Member State act is not curtailed – it is merely "relocated". The relevant measure is put under full free movement scrutiny, just with the national judge acting in lieu of the Court of Justice'.

740 L. Boucon, above n. 38, p. 175.

and second, the Court imposes particular obligations upon Member States which place certain limitations on the discretionary exercise of retained competences.[741] At this stage, the Court provides criteria for the evaluation of the exercise of the retained competences of Member States 'in a wider context, the trans-national context'.[742] This has important consequences for how the Court engages with matters belonging to the retained competences of Member States, and the form of its scrutiny. The purpose of the following justification and proportionality analysis is to demonstrate that any intervention of the CJEU in this area would most likely leave a wide margin of appreciation to the legislative bodies of Member States, resulting in low adaptational pressure. At the same time, in the limited category of cases where a free movement scrutiny would be necessary, the Court would most likely defer the decision on proportionality sensu stricto to a national court (and therefore 'relocate'[743] the scrutiny under EU law to the national level). As such, even if a restriction is found, the overall adaptational pressures on national law might be more limited than initially suspected.

5.5.1. THE EXISTENCE OF A LEGITIMATE OBJECTIVE TO JUSTIFY THE RESTRICTION

Any restriction of the freedom of movement can be justified when it pursues a legitimate objective, is necessary for the protection of the interests which it intends to secure, and if the objective cannot be accomplished by less restrictive measures.[744] Also, discriminatory measures can be justified if proportionate and based on objective considerations independent of the nationality of the persons concerned.[745] This stage of the analysis must, therefore, start with the identification of a legitimate objective that child relocation measures pursue. The existence of such a legitimate objective in child relocation law does not seem to be disputed.[746] However, as its nature is relevant for the analysis of the limitations on the discretionary exercise of Member States' retained competences, it is worthwhile making it explicit.

Child relocation provisions are an expression of all the protective, facilitative, and adjudicative functions of family law. They are intrinsically

---

741 ibid.

742 L. Azoulai, above n. 614, 1342.

743 This term (as fitting for this book) was borrowed from the respective analysis of J. Zglinski, above n. 736, p. 32.

744 e.g. Case C-353/06, *Stefan Grunkin and Dorothee Regina Paul*, ECLI:EU:C:2008:559, para. 29.

745 e.g. Case C-224/98, *D'Hoop*, ECLI:EU:C:2002:432, para. 36.

746 The fact that child relocation laws pursue a legitimate objective seems to be implicit in the approach of R. Lamont, above n. 12, 240–42.

linked to the fundamental rights of both children and parents. They might additionally be justified by a legitimate public interest requiring that important decisions, such as the determination of the child's place of residence, need to be taken by parents jointly or made by the court. From a different and narrower perspective, together with child abduction laws, child relocation laws protect jurisdictional competence and procedural rights insofar as they prevent unilateral decisions leading to a change in jurisdiction. Children's rights have been, more than once, found by the Court to be a legitimate reason to restrict free movement rights.[747] They are now protected by Article 24 of the Charter. In particular, Article 24(3) protects the right of a child to maintain, on a regular basis, a personal relationship and direct contact with both parents. An exception may be made to this right only if the contact proves contrary to another interest of the child.[748] It is clear that more often than not, wrongful removal does not allow such contact and personal relationships to be maintained.[749] In line with these observations, the 1980 Hague Convention, or the Brussels II*ter* Regulation, were both adopted on the basis that the interests of children are of paramount importance in matters relating to their custody, and that children should be protected from wrongful removals.[750] Therefore, laws that aim to provide for a way to relocate lawfully pursue a legitimate objective, recognised in a broad sense by the child abduction framework,[751] and are prima facie necessary.[752]

However, child abduction instruments do not oblige the states to provide for any particular procedural or substantive provisions for lawful child relocation.[753] The CJEU has clarified on multiple occasions that measures that restrict freedom of movement might be justified by objective considerations only if they are both necessary for the protection of interests which they intend to secure, and only insofar as they are proportionate.[754] Therefore, under EU law, it is not excluded that some – in principle justified – legislative choices may go beyond what is objectively necessary and proportionate.

---

747 e.g. Case C-244/06, *Dynamic Medien Vertriebs GmbH v Avides Media AG*, ECLI:EU:C:2008:85, paras. 40–44.

748 Case C-403/09 PPU, *Jasna Detiček v Maurizio Sgueglia*, ECLI:EU:C:2009:810, paras. 58–59.

749 ibid., para. 56.

750 e.g. Case C-195/08 PPU, *Inga Rinau*, ECLI:EU:C:2008:406, paras. 48, 51–53; see also Opinion of the Advocate General in Case C-454/19, *ZW*, ECLI:EU:C:2020:430, para. 40.

751 K. Scheiwe, above n. 103, p. 162.

752 See also Opinion of the Advocate General in Case C-454/19, *ZW*, ECLI:EU:C:2020:430, para. 41: 'national legislation which seeks, inter alia, to prevent the wrongful removal or retention of children unquestionably pursues a legitimate objective under EU law'.

753 In the context of child abduction and acquisition of custody rights, see Case C-400/10 PPU, *J. McB. v L. E.*, ECLI:EU:C:2010:582, para. 52.

754 e.g. Case C-391/09, *Malgožata Runevič-Vardyn and Łukasz Paweł Wardyn v Vilniaus miesto savivaldybės administracija and Others*, ECLI:EU:C:2011:291, paras. 88–90.

5.5.2. NECESSITY AND PROPORTIONALITY OF THE NATIONAL RULE IN QUESTION

Substantive family law remains a retained competence of Member States. In such areas of law, Member States are, in principle, free to set the objectives of their policy and define the level of protection of various interests at stake.[755] The fact that some Member States might have opted for different models of protection from other Member States should not affect the justification and proportionality assessment, which should instead focus on the objectives pursued by the authorities of given Member States and the degree of protection they seek to ensure.[756] However, as Lena Boucon demonstrates, the Court requires these prerogatives to be exercised in a manner that takes into account the Treaty obligations, imposing certain 'mutual adjustment' requirements, such as mutual recognition, a substantive requirement to take into account the personal circumstances of individuals exercising their rights derived from the four freedoms of EU citizenship, and requirements of a procedural nature to enforce the principles of legal certainty and transparency.[757] The intensity of the proportionality assessment undertaken by the Court varies, therefore, in different contexts.[758]

From this perspective, one needs to keep in mind that family law, with its regulation of parental obligations towards children, is one of the areas in which there are significant cultural, moral, and/or religious differences between the Member States.[759] Hence, the Court should be sensitive not only to the need to protect children's rights but also to more specific conceptions of the family law design put forward by national laws.[760] Such conceptions would encompass, in particular, the distribution of rights and duties within a family or the reasonable 'sacrifices' that a parent might be expected to make that are channelled through national law. A key point to remember is that the obligation to obtain a court's permission to relocate is not an administrative requirement but emerges as a result of the other parent's disagreement, highlighting the facilitative and adjudicative functions of the law. As such, it is not a matter of the state regulating mobility per se but setting a standard for parental co-operation in the exercise of their rights and responsibilities, and for assessing the best

---

755 e.g. Case C-454/19, *ZW*, ECLI:EU:C:2020:947, para. 42.

756 Case C-42/07, *Liga Portuguesa de Futebol Profissional and Bwin International Ltd v Departamento de Jogos da Santa Casa da Misericórdia de Lisboa*, ECLI:EU:C:2009:519, para. 58.

757 L. Boucon, above n. 38, p. 175.

758 ibid., p. 181.

759 See Case C-454/19, *ZW*, ECLI:EU:C:2020:947, para. 42; Case C-244/06, *Dynamic Medien*, ECLI:EU:C:2008:85, paras. 44–46.

760 See the discussion on different approaches to child relocation in Chapter 2.

solution for a given child in light of the lack of uniformity of parental visions. For these reasons, and in light of the ECtHR jurisprudence analysed in the previous chapter, Member States would most likely be left with a wide regulatory autonomy in such matters.

That said, it is useful to engage with the proposal put forward by Scott in the context of English provisions on child relocation[761] to assess whether certain regulatory choices might not be necessary for the attainment of their aim. English child relocation law requires parental consent or judicial approval for all international relocations while no such general requirement exists for internal relocations.[762] Locating the reason for this in concerns about jurisdiction and enforcement, Scott notes that all EU Member States belong to the same private international law instruments and every child abducted within the EU can be swiftly returned.[763] He thus argues that these instruments are sufficient for the protection of children in the context of intra-EU relocations.[764] In light of this, Scott suggests that it should be the non-resident parent that needs to object to relocation rather than the resident parent who needs to apply for permission.[765] This reconceptualisation is said to be more proportionate from the point of view of the relocating parent's freedom of movement. The English regulation constitutes, first and foremost, a difference in treatment within the understanding advocated in this chapter, and hence would need to be justified. This notwithstanding, Scott's suggestion is worth considering as its closer scrutiny highlights the most important aspects of the analysis of necessity and proportionality in the relocation context.

Scott's analysis is not wrong insofar as he assesses the issue with reference to jurisdictional concerns only. The Court would not be convinced by an interpretation that justifies more restrictive measures by relying on the assumption that the recognition and enforcement of national judgments, or the protection of children more generally, are impossible, insufficient or too difficult in another Member State.[766] However, Scott's reliance on private international law as a guarantee for the protection of children's rights in child relocation seems to ignore the much broader objective of the law. Private international law is mostly concerned with jurisdiction and mutual recognition. Child relocation cases, on the other hand, involve a very substantive evaluation of a child's interests. In some cases, it is the substantive nature of the decision at stake

---

761 T. Scott, above n. 12.

762 For a more detailed description of English law, see Chapter 7.

763 T. Scott, above n. 12, p. 14.

764 ibid.

765 ibid., pp. 15–16. In most civil law jurisdictions both parents can apply to the court, but it is similarly only the relocating parent who has the positive obligation to obtain consent to lawfully relocate.

766 Case C-454/19, *ZW*, ECLI:EU:C:2020:947, paras. 45–48.

that leads to strong disagreement between otherwise co-operating parents, but in many it is the lack of co-operation between the parents that precedes the relocation proposal. Even if a parent were legally obliged to give notice before relocation takes place, the reversal of the procedural burden in such cases might lead to significant issues. Already now, abduction cases are sometimes disputed based on whether consent was given or not, and it could be expected that Scott's model could cause even more uncertainty and lead to an increased number of disputes.[767] Legal certainty remains an important value in this context, with parents being encouraged to always obtain consent in writing for international travel. From this perspective, placing the burden of proof on the relocating parent is better suited to providing at least some legal certainty. It is, therefore, unlikely that a solution requiring the relocating parent to assume the procedural burden of the case would be seen as unnecessary or disproportionate.

In the case of potentially discriminatory measures, some additional remarks are necessary. In principle, Member States cannot differentiate between their own territory and the territory of other Member States based on jurisdictional concerns only. Thus, different rules for internal and intra-EU relocations could constitute an unjustified discriminatory restriction. In the end, for example, if a Member State, as a matter of its regulatory choice, does not consider it necessary to restrict internal relocations, one could question why the burden for international relocation is greater. However, the fact that internal relocations do not require any special permission, or are assessed somewhat differently, does not per se render such a solution unnecessary or disproportionate. The finding of a justification in such cases is closely related to the comparability of internal and intra-EU relocations, as already highlighted earlier in this chapter. In relocation cases, the mere fact that the territory of a given Member State is much smaller (and relocation does not significantly impact the direct contact between the non-relocating parent and the child) could already question the comparability of the situations.[768] Moves abroad – even in proximity – involve many more considerations as to the language, school system, and the cultural and linguistic background of child and parents, etc. Having to integrate in another city or region in one's own country is very different from having to integrate in another Member State. Therefore, the fact that a given solution

767 Parental consent, the lack of which renders relocation unlawful, is raised as a defence in a number of child abduction cases. The difficulties are often of evidentiary nature, and the burden of proof is typically carried by the relocating parent. See, for example, many such cases on the International Child Abduction Database (INCADAT), managed by the Hague Conference on Private International Law, available at <http://www.incadat.com/>. It could be expected that the evidentiary issues would be exacerbated by Scott's proposal.

768 If it is only the geographical distance that is relevant, one could argue that the line should be drawn in reference to such geographical distance (e.g. 100 km), and not national border. Such geographical limitations feature in many US state regulations. See Appendix C in Y.M. Bérénos, above n. 12, 24–26.

for internal relocations is less restrictive does not automatically render the solution chosen for international relocations unnecessarily disproportionate. Some regulatory choices might not be justified at closer scrutiny, but such an analysis will be case-specific, and the Court should remain receptive to arguments raised in this context.

Member States would, therefore, most likely be left with a significant freedom regarding their regulatory choices in the area of child relocation. In most circumstances, their regulatory choices should be deemed necessary to achieve the objective. The Court would most likely not require Member States to introduce solutions different than those already existing in their legal systems or challenge the exclusive character of the competences that Member States enjoy in the sensitive context of substantive family law.[769] As such, the Court would rather focus, as in other fields that remain part of the retained competences of Member States, on the exercise of those competences, providing criteria for their evaluation in the EU legal context.[770]

5.5.3. PROPORTIONALITY SENSU STRICTO

When a relocation measure is deemed necessary to achieve the pursued legitimate objective, it still needs to meet certain criteria of proportionality sensu stricto. The regulation of child relocation, to be proportionate, would need to allow for an individual assessment of personal circumstances and for a transparent judicial or equivalent procedure to circumvent the lack of agreement to the other parent's relocation. The former would render all automatic impositions of refusals of relocation disproportionate while the lack of the latter would additionally amount to a violation of EU law in light of the obligation of Member States to provide for effective judicial protection of individual rights, which is both a self-standing general principle of EU law[771] and a fundamental right recognised under Article 47 of the EU Charter. Application of the principle of proportionality in an individual relocation case would additionally require the national court to ascertain the consequences that a refusal of relocation would entail for the situation of the person concerned and, if relevant, for the members of their family in light of EU law.

First and foremost, for any decision to be proportionate, it needs to be based on an individualised assessment of the situation. All relocation cases

---

769 L. Boucon, above n. 38, p. 178. Thus, the justifications might reflect 'the fundamental need to preserve the organization and/or functioning of a given policy area' that requires maintaining of certain obstacles.

770 ibid., p. 177.

771 e.g. Case C-12/08, *Mono Car Styling SA, in liquidation v Dervis Odemis and Others*, ECLI:EU:C:2009:466, para. 46.

are resolved in reference to the child's best interests principle and generally allow for such an assessment. However, in practice, national courts must indeed conduct such an individual examination in a transparent way and allow arguments referring to the overall situation of a mobile EU citizen with its particularities to be assessed in the process, taking into account the child's best interests.[772] As already mentioned in the context of discrimination, it is possible that the only way in which national law infringes EU law is a systemic refusal to recognise the situation of mobile EU parents – if deemed different – within a national framework.[773] Any blanket approach that does not allow for an individual assessment of the situation, even if only established in judicial practice and/or doctrine of a given Member State, would be disproportionate.[774] The Court has, on multiple occasions, provided guidance as to what evaluation is required to meet the threshold of an individualised assessment in expulsion and reunification cases involving children,[775] but the nature of such guidance is not fundamentally different from what family courts do on a daily basis and, in any case, the decision will likely be left to national authorities.

Secondly, the proportionality principle would require national courts, where relevant for the assessment, to take into account EU legislation on cross-border recognition and enforcement in parental matters.[776] The CJEU could oblige a national court to examine whether there are measures other than refusal of relocation that would be equally effective in achieving the objective of the child relocation law and would not encroach upon the parent's freedom of movement. But, given the competence limitation of the Court and the nature of the dispute, this obligation should be understood procedurally rather than substantively. This might be different from Ruth Lamont's suggestion that refusing relocation must also be the most appropriate way of achieving the child's best interests,[777] which seems to shift the substantive

---

772 As *Penchevi v Bulgaria* [2015] ECtHR, app. no. 77818/12, discussed in Chapter 4, above Section 4.3.2., shows, this might not always be the case. The obligation to conduct an individualised assessment was also confirmed by the ECtHR.

773 See, e.g. Opinion of the Advocate General in Case C-148/02, *Garcia Avello*, ECLI:EU:C:2003:311, para. 75; Case C-148/02, *Garcia Avello*, ECLI:EU:C:2003:539, para. 44.

774 See also R. Lamont, above n. 12, 242: 'Whilst arguments based on securing the child's best interests through protecting the relationship with both parents are likely to be legitimate, other aims may not be, especially if judicial chauvinism about relocation abroad is demonstrable'.

775 The CJEU has had a chance to hint at what kind of evaluation might matter in expulsion cases, requiring a holistic assessment, e.g. C-133/15, *Chavez-Vilchez*, ECLI:EU:C:2017:354, para. 71.

776 e.g. Case C-454/19, *ZW*, ECLI:EU:C:2020:947, paras. 48–49.

777 For example, as suggested by in R. Lamont, above n. 12, 242, if the type of contact envisaged with the non-resident parent could be achieved after relocation, the refusal of relocation is unlikely to be proportionate – unless other factors are at play. This approach seems reasonable but becomes problematic beyond a very narrow category of cases where the contact regime

standard in favour of relocation. At the same time, as the following paragraphs explain, the obligation to consider alternative measures might be of limited prescriptive value for relocation disputes in light of the different, yet open-ended, constructions of national relocation laws.

'Equal effectiveness' implies a degree of quantification of the desired outcome that is hard to achieve when the child's best interests are involved. Competing solutions might be inherently equally effective and inherently different, depending on the normative value ascribed to various factors to be taken into account in the interpretation of the child's best interests.[778] The substantive requirement that a refusal of relocation must be the most appropriate solution does, on the one hand, raise the standard higher than other competing options but, on the other, is unlikely to be of any practical significance. Courts are already obliged to make decisions choosing the most appropriate solution from a range of available alternatives. Whether one solution is inherently more appropriate than the other encounters the same difficulties as the assessment of 'equally effective' options. This is why relocation cases are so hard in the first place, and the CJEU is not in a position (both as a matter of competence and institutional design) to resolve this challenge.

The communicative value of such proposals lies, however, in the attention to the fact that national courts should consider alternatives other than a refusal of relocation. But this might be of limited prescriptive value insofar as the CJEU is not in a position to indicate what alternatives should be considered. If a national court faces a choice of whether a child is to go with the relocating parent or to stay with the same relocating parent who will give up the plan to relocate, then refusal of relocation might easily be the most appropriate solution where the child enjoys a close relationship with the non-relocating parent. But if the options are to go with the relocating parent or to stay with the non-relocating parent, this is already a different assessment that ventures into the area of the quality of personal relationships. And it is even more so if a national court starts to consider whether the parent opposing relocation could relocate as well to follow the child. These are highly context-dependent normative decisions about the substance of familial relationships. Can the relocating parent be expected to stay behind for the sake of the child's relationships? Can the other parent be expected to move for the sake of the other parent's autonomy rights? Is it a matter of alternatives put forward by

would remain unaltered *and* be the only consideration. In most cases, there are other factors that might need to be considered. At the same time, child relocation applications might spark objections more rarely if the same contact regime can be upheld after the move.

778 See also R. Mnookin, above n. 129, 255, who sees the assessment of both the best and least detrimental outcome as equivalents: 'what is least detrimental can be put in exactly the same conceptual framework. It too requires both the specification of alternative outcomes and the assessment of probabilities'.

the parties, or a balance of probabilities? In most jurisdictions, such decisions reflect the fundamental differences between competing visions about post-separation family life – one where the dissolution of the relationship ends the mutual ties and one where the family endures beyond separation[779] – and the related distribution of expectations as to mutual limitations and co-operation. None of these aspects can be legitimately addressed by the CJEU if it is to respect the retained competence of Member States and the political sensitivity of family law as such. As a result, national courts are likely to be left with the same dilemmas as they face today.

It is here that the question about the relationship between primary and secondary rights, mentioned at the beginning of this chapter, can be asked. National courts do not, in principle, restrict the freedom of movement of the relocating parent. It is thus always possible that the parent will leave the child behind if relocation is refused. The consequences for the child, if no alternative care is available, would be stark. At the same time, if there is no alternative care for the child, the parent could be (even if only as a matter of facts and not law) required to give up the exercise of their freedom of movement rights until the child reaches the age of majority. Their rights to reside across the Union in such a situation would be almost completely devoid of content. It is in such a situation that the restriction of the right to relocate with the child, *depending on the particular facts of the case*, could lead to a restriction of the primary right of the parent that is intended to be exercised and the rights of the child. Of course, the CJEU has, on many occasions, been sympathetic towards such situations. But, when enforcing such 'social justice' claims, it has always enforced them against restrictions originating from the state. In the relocation context, the main stakes concern the balancing of the conflicting rights of individuals. Is it proportionate to require a parent to stay behind for the sake of the child's relationship with the other parent where the other parent is not willing to assume everyday responsibility for the child? What is the weight of 'mere' contact rights against freedom of movement? When weighing up the interests at stake, fundamental rights will have to be taken into account by both the CJEU and a national court.[780] It cannot be excluded that in specific individual circumstances, the EU law claim would be so strongly rooted in the factual circumstances of the case that it would lead to an immediate finding of a restriction, but – for reasons discussed above – one could expect a rather deferential treatment of such cases, with the CJEU leaving interpretation of the law in a particular case to national authorities.

---

[779] P. Parkinson, above n. 210, p. 150.

[780] As already noted, when a dispute arises that falls within the scope of EU law but is (at least) partially governed by national law, Member States generally retain the freedom to interpret fundamental rights according to their own standards, as long as such interpretation does not compromise the level of protection provided by the Charter nor the effectiveness of EU law. See the discussion about the application of the EU Charter in Chapter 4.

5.6. CONCLUDING REMARKS

This chapter analyses the doctrinal aspects of the relationship between child relocation law and EU law, considering the systemic and jurisdictional constraints of the CJEU. The analysis, while self-standing, has the additional objective of identifying the nature of adaptational pressures that could reasonably be exerted by the EU legal system on national family laws. This discussion shows, first, that different legal constructions of child relocation laws across the Member States and specific circumstances of individual disputes might lead to different conclusions regarding the restrictive character of a given measure under EU law. Different rules for internal and intra-EU relocations can lead to a finding of a discriminatory restriction on EU freedom of movement. Further, while the complexity of the EU doctrines on non-discriminatory restrictions might lead to different conclusions in this regard, restrictions on child relocation can be reasonably seen as non-discriminatory restrictions of free movement under EU law. Nevertheless, one can also raise multiple arguments why child relocation measures would not be caught by the Treaty and advocate against the CJEU's intervention in this area of law. Most importantly, however, even if child relocation measures are caught by the Treaty, they will be quasi-universally justified and proportionate. As such measures significantly intertwine with broader considerations of the nature of familial relationships, a core of the retained competence of Member States, it is to be expected that Member States will remain relatively free to introduce their own child relocation laws, and any detailed justification or proportionality assessment will be left to national courts. As a more general observation, the CJEU's jurisdictional and systemic limitations make it simply 'better designed for the discovery of violations of rights through inconsistencies in law rather than failures in practice to live up to the law'.[781] It is, however, the practice that generates most controversies and discrepancies in child relocation law, particularly in light of the open-ended child's best interests principle.

These findings do not intend to suggest that an EU intervention in relocation matters would be meaningless for national law. National legislators and adjudicators would likely still be made wary of potential discrimination, the need to pay due regard to the EU instruments put in place to facilitate movement, and the procedural obligations to consider the individual situation, the features of which might be mobility-related. Rather, these findings emphasise the inherent limits of Europeanisation of child relocation understood doctrinally. It is a truism that parents enjoy as much freedom as is compatible with their parental obligations and necessary for the protection of the rights and interests of other

[781] H. Cullen, above n. 533, p. 345.

individuals involved – but questions such as to what these obligations are, how they limit freedom of movement, and how to balance them with other interests depend on normative decisions about personal relationships and personal autonomy that are unlikely to be taken at the EU level. Even if domestic law needs to be interpreted in conformity with EU law, the open-ended adjudicative standard such as the child's best interests principle both allows and requires great flexibility, and its assessments will necessarily have to be conducted by national courts in highly individualised circumstances. As such, the adaptational pressures on national law should be expected to remain highly open-ended themselves, imposing on national actors the need to 'act and think European',[782] but at the same time allowing them to do that largely on their own terms.[783] This finding does not, however, close the discussion on child relocation in the EU legal context, but rather opens it up to questions about the nature and significance of European influences perceived from the constructivist perspective.

[782] This expression is taken from E. Dubout, above n. 565, p. 210.

[783] See also P. Legrand, above n. 81, p. 253 arguing that the CJEU 'has no adjudicative power to eliminate differences [regarding] Member States' readings of European Community law itself'.

CHAPTER 6
CHILD RELOCATION AND THE CONTEXTUAL INFLUENCE OF EU LAW

6.1. INTRODUCTION

The previous three chapters have been devoted to an in-depth analysis of the nature and limits of doctrinal pressures that are, or could prospectively be, exerted by EU law on national child relocation laws. It is now time to take a closer look at the more complex and more subtle contextual influence of EU law. As noted before, the EU is generally 'not meant to constitute its own legal subjects'.[784] Due to the limitation of its competence and the institutional constraints, EU law is even less meant to do so in family law that remains interested in substantively different phenomena. However, it would be difficult to dispute the fact that EU law or the CJEU's judgments do indeed contain accounts of who human beings are, what expectations they hold, and how this presupposes normative answers to their situations.[785] As individuals 'anxious to secure their place in situations of disaffiliation, multi-affiliation or vulnerability'[786] become 'the custodian of specifically European interest',[787] EU decision-makers – and the CJEU in particular – are increasingly called upon to characterise these individuals through particular aspects of their social settings to grant them rights under EU law.[788] From this perspective, multiple authors perceive the notions of autonomy and agency as dependent on the existence of a particular (here supranational) community, within which options become available to an individual and within which the individual can develop a reasonable perception of such agency.[789] As this agency is interdependent with

---

784 L. Azoulai, S. Barbou des Places and E. Pataut, above n. 25, p. 9.
785 ibid., p. 10; L. Azoulai, above n. 26, p. 218.
786 L. Azoulai, S. Barbou des Places and E. Pataut, above n. 25, p. 9.
787 E. Dubout, above n. 565, p. 205.
788 L. Azoulai, S. Barbou des Places and E. Pataut, above n. 25, p. 9.
789 S. Coutts, above n. 18, p. 54; P.J. Neuvonen, *Equal Citizenship and its Limits in EU Law: We the Burden?*, Hart Publishing, Oxford 2016, p. 136; F. de Witte, above n. 27, p. 43, arguing that the EU is about 'the institutionalization of new relationships between citizens across borders'. See also the broader discussion in L. Azoulai, above n. 26, pp. 212–24.

social relations,[790] its constructive potential can provide a basis for rethinking 'EU citizens [as] subjects of EU law and European integration in relation to other citizens (horizontally) and not just in relation to the Member States or the Union (vertically)'.[791] This potential might, therefore, actualise itself also in cross-border child relocation cases, influencing the perceptions of parental autonomy and children's interests.

Due to the traditional economic commitment of the EU, children were rarely the direct focus of its laws and policies.[792] Children's rights were originally either based on or judicially derived from the status of their migrating parents and seen as instrumental in facilitating the economic free movement of persons.[793] But neither the EU legislator nor the CJEU have been fully blind to the relational aspects of family life, encapsulated primarily in its pronouncements on dependency in various contexts.[794] The development of case law involving children has been expandatory in effect, with the child's status gradually used to derive rights for other people, in particular in the area of residence rights.[795] This is not to deny that the CJEU has been rather ambiguous in treating children as independent agents or, at times, protected family rights through the language of the internal market only.[796] However, the Court can be perceived here as using EU law concepts to cover judgments about, inherently, the intensity and necessity of family relationships.[797] Such judgments about when (and where, and if) family members can expect to live together and when they 'can be expected to live apart' are highly contextual.[798] The exact value or real-life consequences of such contextual constructions of EU law might be questioned, in particular in family law, but they surely interact

790 P.J. Neuvonen, above n. 789, p. 136.

791 ibid., pp. 136, 168.

792 H. Stalford, *Children and the European Union: Rights, Welfare and Accountability*, Hart Publishing, Oxford 2012, p. 24. See also L. Ackers and H. Stalford, 'Children, Migration and Citizenship in the European Union: Intra-Community Mobility and the Status of Children in EC Law', above n. 276, 1007 describing children as 'invisible appendages of the breadwinning migrant family' or 'victims of derived entitlement'.

793 L. Ackers and H. Stalford, above n. 792, 991–96. See also H. Stalford, above n. 656.

794 For a discussion on whether dependency in the EU context means dependency on financial resources, care, or both, see T. Petrova, 'Children and European Citizenship: Their Autonomy and Entitlement to Care under Free Movement Law' (2013) LLM Thesis, European University Institute, pp. 18–27, or most recently F. Ristuccia, above n. 663.

795 e.g. Case C-413/99, *Baumbast*, ECLI:EU:C:2002:493; Case C-200/02, *Zhu and Chen*, ECLI:EU:C:2004:639; Case C-34/09, *Ruiz Zambrano*, ECLI:EU:C:2011:124.

796 See e.g. Case C-60/00, *Carpenter*, ECLI:EU:C:2002:434. See also F. Ristuccia, above n. 663, 1251, observing that 'the Court has yet to stress the importance of the children's right to be heard and speak their views on their ties with their family and social environment'.

797 G.T. Davies, 'The Right to Stay at Home: A Basis for Expanding European Family Rights' in D. Kochenov (ed), *EU Citizenship and Federalism: The Role of Rights*, Cambridge University Press, Cambridge 2017, p. 468.

798 ibid., p. 481.

with legal perceptions of both normality and normativity.[799] If the child's best interests principle can be conceptualised as normativising the perceived 'normal',[800] one can nevertheless ask if (and how) EU law can influence the ideas of normalised parenthood or normalised childhood,[801] the perceptions of familial mutual responsibilities, and broader value judgments made in family law.

This chapter focuses on the contextual constructions of EU law in cases involving family rights and relationships, drawing attention to the normatively inflicted methodology that governs EU law in such contexts. This analysis is conceptualised through two interrelated spheres of influence: infrastructure-oriented and principle-oriented. The former analyses the EU legal construction of a broader socio-legal framework that might impact on the future-oriented assessments of arrangements made for children in relocation cases, subtly shifting the nature of considerations and the standard of proof applicable to such disputes. The latter touches upon the assessments of the child's best interests in light of the perceived normal, 'the legal system integration of social consensus',[802] including the assessment of what kind of mobility choices might be expected from parents in their relationships with their children and each other.[803] By conceptualising the influence of EU law this way, one can not only position this influence outside of the reach of its specific doctrines, but also truly appreciate the subtle yet normative power of EU law. The discussion then brings these themes together and demonstrates what the normatively inflicted methodology of EU law, giving rise to specific contextual constructions, might mean for child relocation disputes in the Union – despite the lack of any legislation or judicial pronouncements on child relocation specifically. The chapter does not, therefore, intend to discuss the entirety of European influences seen from a constructivist perspective, but rather highlight those paradigms that might be most meaningful in the child relocation context.

---

799 See L. Azoulai, S. Barbou des Places and E. Pataut, above n. 25, pp. 6–10: 'EU law is … about the transformation of pre-established domestic socio-economic orders, … about the shifting of both governments' and individuals' preferences for the purpose of establishing a new transnational concrete order'. See also D. Kostakopoulou, *EU Citizenship Law and Policy: Beyond Brexit*, Edward Elgar Publishing, Cheltenham 2020, p. 4, noting that 'a polity organized around different principles and ideas [from a nation state] is likely to have different dynamics and can generate different experiences'.

800 J. Schiratzki, above n. 154, 11.

801 For a discussion of a 'normalized parenthood' in child contact disputes see M.H. Ottosen, above n. 159.

802 J. Schiratzki, above n. 154, 11.

803 As briefly explained in Chapter 2, the extent to which parental or other individuals' interests should or could be taken into account in the assessment of the best interests of the child is disputed. From this perspective, the notion of a 'principle-oriented' influence serves a categorisation purpose only, emphasising the subtle difference between the broader context of the cases (the broader infrastructure) and the 'softer' normative layer derived from this context.

6.2. THE INFRASTRUCTURE-ORIENTED INFLUENCE: THE SPACE OF RIGHTS

When EU citizens are granted a space of autonomy, this autonomy is exercised in a single legal space.[804] In family law, this single legal space is first and foremost created by Council Regulation (EU) 2019/1111 of 25 June 2019 on jurisdiction, the recognition and enforcement of decisions in matrimonial matters and the matters of parental responsibility, and on international child abduction (the so-called Brussels II*ter* Regulation) that fully replaced its predecessor, Council Regulation (EC) 2201/2003, in August 2022. Due to the inherently cross-border dimension of child relocation disputes, such private international law instruments might be relevant for the assessment of the situation of a child, in particular regarding the recognition and enforcement of contact rights.[805] As noted in Chapter 2, the underlying ratio of restrictions placed on international child relocation in many jurisdictions is connected with concerns regarding standards applied to parental disputes in foreign jurisdictions and enforcement issues.[806] When the decision of a national court cannot be enforced or is likely to be significantly changed due to different laws or public policies that govern parenting, there is a risk that once relocation is allowed, foreign law might be used to achieve what would otherwise not be an acceptable decision for that court.[807] Therefore, supranational legal instruments might play a role in the resolution of child relocation disputes, both in the EU and beyond.[808] In the EU legal design, the Brussels II*ter* Regulation co-creates, at the same time, the area of justice offered to EU citizens and is closely connected with the free movement of persons. While based on transnational rights of mutual recognition, it also generates a supranational point of reference with a normative dimension insofar as the transnational rights simultaneously originate from and result in

---

804 See S. Coutts, above n. 18, p. 121, in the context of criminal law.

805 e.g. M. Sattler, 'The Problem of Parental Relocation: Closing the Loophole in the Law of International Child Abduction' (2010) 67 *Washington and Lee Law Review* 1709, 1724, 1747. This was confirmed also by the drafters of the supranational soft law instruments who included recognition and enforcement as factors to consider when deciding a relocation case.

806 See in particular T. Scott, above n. 12, for remarks on changes in English law following the introduction of a uniform enforcement of contact orders in all parts of the UK. See also *Vorblatt und Erläuterungen zu dem Kindschafts- und Namensrecht-Änderungsgesetz*, above n. 217, and L. Kreiner, above n. 217, p. 37.

807 R.A. Warshak, 'In a Land Far, Far Away: Assessing Children's Best Interests in International Relocation Cases' (2013) 10 *Journal of Child Custody* 295; J.D. Morley, 'The Impact of Foreign Law on Child Custody Determinations' (2013) 10 *Journal of Child Custody* 209.

808 See A.L. Estin, 'Families Across Borders: The Hague Children's Conventions and the Case for International Family Law in the United States' (2010) 62 *Florida Law Review* 47, 99–100, recognising the 'important facilitative or channelling function' of the international family law that protects children in conflict situations.

mutual trust.[809] This section does not analyse the Regulation in detail, as many excellent commentaries can be found elsewhere.[810] Rather, it draws attention to these provisions of the Regulation that are relevant for child relocation and its broader contextual dimensions.

When the EU decided to regulate private international law matters relating to family law, it did not, however, enter a vacuum. Most importantly, the 1980 and 1996 Hague Conventions were either already in force or under construction, providing an important source of legal inspiration.[811] Nothing in this chapter should be read as disregarding these instruments, and one needs to bear in mind that there are significant overlaps between the two regimes.[812] However, the single legal space offered to EU citizens has an additional dimension insofar as the EU legal instruments intertwine with and function within a broader legal space, going functionally way beyond family law and directly shaping the life-worlds of mobile family members. Child relocation disputes rarely centre around issues of enforcement, even if relevant,[813] but various future arrangements for the child and the broader family are of crucial importance in most cases. What is unique about the EU legal framework is its level of complexity that touches upon many such arrangements directly or indirectly – education, social benefits, employment, to name but a few. As such, the normative content of the EU family law instruments cannot be divorced from their broader (legal) environment. Therefore, the last part of this section discusses, briefly, the broader legal infrastructure relevant to relocation disputes, emphasising the holistic reach of the EU legal space's contextual normativity.

---

809 In the context of criminal law, see S. Coutts, above n. 18, p. 123. See also M. Fichera, 'Sketches of a Theory of Europe as an Area of Freedom, Security and Justice' in M. Fletcher, E. Herlin-Karnell and C. Matera (eds), *The European Union as an Area of Freedom, Security and Justice*, Routledge, Abingdon 2017: 'The AFJS is an area – a space. The rhetoric of space is not to be side-lined as it contains both a territorial claim and a power of fabrication of symbols fostering legitimacy', or H. Lindahl, 'Inside and Outside the EU's "Area of Freedom, Security and Justice": Reflexive Identity and the Unity of Legal Space' (2004) 90 *ARSP: Archiv für Rechts- und Sozialphilosophie/Archives for Philosophy of Law and Social Philosophy* 478, arguing that 'in relating to a legal space as its own, a legal Community takes up a relation to itself'.

810 For a more detailed analysis on the Brussels II*bis* Regulation in the context of child relocation, see N.V. Lowe, above n. 337. For an extensive commentary on the Brussels II*ter* Regulation, see C. González Beilfuss, L. Carpaneto, T. Kruger, I. Pretelli, and M. Župan, *Jurisdiction, Recognition and Enforcement in Matrimonial and Parental Responsibility Matters: A Commentary on Regulation 2019/1111 (Brussels IIb)*, Edward Elgar Publishing, Cheltenham 2023.

811 All EU Member States are parties to both of the Conventions.

812 This concerns, in particular, the legal framework of child abduction proceedings. See, for example, Article 27 of the Brussels II*ter* Regulation.

813 See also Chapter 7.

6.2.1. MUTUAL RECOGNITION AND ENFORCEMENT

Cross-border aspects of parental responsibility matters have been a subject of EU regulation for years already. The Brussels II*ter* Regulation, as its predecessor the Brussels II*bis* Regulation did, regulates jurisdiction in matrimonial and parental responsibility matters across the Union (Articles 3–21), recognition and enforcement of judgments issued in such disputes (Articles 30–76), as well as co-operation in matters of parental responsibility (Articles 77–84). Whereas the requirements of the proper functioning of the internal market were the legislative basis for the Brussels II*bis* Regulation, in line with the wording of the Treaty at that time,[814] this instrument clearly had individual interests at heart as 'such cooperation is particularly necessary to give children a secure legal environment to maintain relations with persons who have parental responsibility over them'.[815] The underlying rationale was that the best interests of the child require stability and continuity guaranteed by the mechanisms of mutual recognition as well as contact with both parents, which should be enforced in a timely manner thanks to its special procedures.[816] Multiple recitals and provisions made references to the child's best interests and identified contact rights as priority,[817] as is also the case for the current Brussels II*ter* Regulation.[818] The Regulation explicitly recognises the value of Article 24 of the Charter of Fundamental Rights of the European Union and the United Nations Convention on the Rights of the Child.[819] These guarantees – touching upon recognition and enforcement of domestic decisions, but also children's rights – may be relevant for a national court trying to navigate the post-relocation future.

Judgments issued in parental matters are recognised without any special procedure being required (Article 30). The grounds for non-recognition are

---

814 See, e.g. Recital 1 of the Brussels II*bis* Regulation: 'The European Community has set the objective of creating an area of freedom, security and justice, in which the free movement of persons is ensured. To this end, the Community is to adopt, among others, measures in the field of judicial cooperation in civil matters that are necessary for the proper functioning of the internal market'.

815 'Report from the European Commission to the European Parliament, the Council and the European Economic and Social Committee on the Application of Council Regulation (EC) No 2201/2003 Concerning Jurisdiction and the Recognition and Enforcement of Judgements in Matrimonial Matters and the Matters of Parental Responsibility, Repealing Regulation (EC) No 1347/2000' (2014), COM(2014) 0225 final.

816 e.g. Case C-195/08 PPU, *Inga Rinau*, ECLI:EU:C:2008:406, para. 81.

817 See Recitals 12, 13 or 17, Articles 12, 15, 23 of the Brussels II*bis* Regulation. Whether preambles have the force of law is disputed. However, they have a communicative value and, as such, become part of the discursive interstices of the law. They set out a discursive context that captures a certain spirit of EU law and the vision of the EU legal subject and their way of life that EU law projects. See also the remarks on preambles in S. Ninatti, above n. 3, p. 52.

818 See Recitals 19, 39, Articles 13, 25, 39 of the Brussels II*ter* Regulation.

819 See Recitals 19, 39, 71, 84 of the Brussels II*ter* Regulation.

limited (Article 39), and courts cannot review either the jurisdiction (Article 69) or the substance of the decision (Article 71). The CJEU has always interpreted these provisions – at least until now, under the Brussels II*bis* Regulation – in a strict way, underlining that all decisions on recognition must take into account the best interests of the child and public policy exceptions can only be applied to 'a manifest breach … of a rule of law regarded as essential'.[820] After the new Brussels II*ter* Regulation entered into force, enforcement of decisions in parental responsibility matters no longer requires the exequatur.[821] Contact decisions belong to the category of 'privileged decisions' and their recognition and enforcement cannot be opposed unless a given decision is found to be irreconcilable with a later decision on the matter (Articles 42–50). If a given judgment concerns both custody and contact, the contact part is still privileged according to the Regulation's rules.[822] It is particularly the privileged treatment of access rights that is of relevance to relocation compared to other instruments.[823] An interesting innovation of the previous Regulation, upheld in its recast, is Article 8 (formerly Article 9) that foresees the continuing jurisdiction of the child's former habitual residence in contact matters for three months after a lawful change of residence.[824] The purpose of this provision is clearly relocation-oriented and offers the non-relocating parent a chance to modify any existing judgment on contact if the arrangements prove to be unworkable.[825] Similarly, the Regulation's provisions on co-operation between

820 Case C-455/15 PPU, *P v Q*, ECLI:EU:C:2015:763, paras. 37–39.

821 Compare Articles 28–36 of the Brussels II*bis* Regulation with the current Brussels II*ter* Regulation.

822 On this point, see T. Kruger, 'Article 42' in C. González Beilfuss, L. Carpaneto, T. Kruger, I. Pretelli, and M. Župan, *Jurisdiction, Recognition and Enforcement in Matrimonial and Parental Responsibility Matters: A Commentary on Regulation 2019/1111 (Brussels IIb)*, Edward Elgar Publishing, Cheltenham 2023, pp. 408–09.

823 See P. Beaumont, 'Private International Law Concerning Children in the UK after Brexit: Comparing Hague Treaty Law with EU Regulations' (2017) 29 *Child and Family Law Quarterly* 213, 227 noting that '[i]n a post-Brexit era, even if the Commission's Proposal above is adopted by the Council, it will in principle be harder to enforce access orders in other EU Member States because all of the Hague 1996 grounds for non-recognition and enforcement come into play'.

824 See N.V. Lowe, above n. 337, 73, who suggested against the background of the Brussels II*bis* Regulation that this period of time might be too short, and it could be more appropriate to extend it to, e.g. six months. This has not been implemented in the recast of the Regulation. In this context it might also be noted that current Article 7 (and previous Article 8) of the Regulation includes a *perpetuatio fori* principle in matters of parental responsibility over a child who is habitually resident in a Member State at the time the court is seized, hence jurisdiction over a dispute might continue even if the child lawfully moves to another Member State.

825 Interestingly, during the drafting of the Hague 1996 Convention, the United States delegation proposed to insert a rule into the Convention that would allow the authorities of the former habitual residence of the child who had taken, before the departure of the child, a measure

central authorities, based on methods known from the Hague Conventions, can also prove relevant in child relocation disputes, both before and after relocation takes place.[826]

The main unique feature of the EU legal system is, however, not only the substance of such rules, but rather the CJEU's control over the interpretation of the Regulation that allows consistency to be achieved beyond what is offered by other instruments. The Regulation must be interpreted within the entire system of EU law, which significantly strengthens its guarantees.[827] The underlying logic of the CJEU jurisprudence in this area has always been one of shared responsibility in the name of the best interests of the child – shared responsibility that often goes beyond what is explicitly provided for. Thanks to the mutual recognition and the broader place of the Regulation within the EU legal system, incidental issues – such as, for example, whether penalty payments imposed to enforce rights of access should be enforced in another Member State, even though none of the existing provisions explicitly allow for that – can be resolved in a consistent manner.[828] In the words of the Advocate General Maciej Szpunar:

> Such cooperation entails *the sharing of powers and responsibilities between the court of the Member State of origin and the court of the Member State of enforcement with a view to ensuring that the child receives the protection to which he is entitled under EU law*. The best interests of the child must therefore be taken into account, as a matter of priority, by the courts involved.[829] (Emphasis added.)

This sharing of powers and responsibilities, which is undefined yet controlled by the CJEU, creates, nevertheless, a certain type of legal uncertainty. This legal

concerning custody or access, to retain exclusive jurisdiction on these points after the child's departure for a period of two years, if at least one of the parents continued to reside in that state and to maintain a persisting relationship with the child. This proposal was motivated by the concerns, discussed above, that the authorities of the new habitual residence may immediately alter the measures which had just been taken by the authorities of the state of departure. This proposal was not ultimately accepted as it would lead to a division of jurisdiction in different matters concerning parental responsibilities. On this, see P. Lagarde, above n. 215, para. 41.

826 See also comments in D. Coester-Waltjen, 'Relocation – from Theory to Practice. Kindeswohl als Richtschnur bei Familiärem Auslandsumzug' (2012) *Interdisziplinäre Zeitschrift für Familienrecht* 311, 315. These provisions are coupled with other EU instruments related to judicial co-operation, such as Council Decision 2001/470/EC of 28 May 2001 establishing a European Judicial Network in civil and commercial matters [2001] OJ L174/25 or Council Regulation (EC) 1206/2001 of 28 May 2001 on cooperation between the courts of the Member States in the taking of evidence in civil or commercial matters [2001] OJ L174/1, see Recital 20. See also the discussion on the potential future of child relocation regulation in the EU in Chapter 3.

827 U. Magnus and P. Mankowski, above n. 307, p. 32.

828 Case C-4/14, *Christophe Bohez v Ingrid Wiertz*, ECLI:EU:C:2015:563.

829 Opinion of the Advocate General in Case C-4/14, *Christophe Bohez v Ingrid Wiertz*, ECLI:EU:C:2015:233, para. 83. This logic was further confirmed in the Court's judgment.

uncertainty is hardly meaningless for decisions made in national courts that are asked to anticipate the requirements of EU legal principles on a daily basis. However, it is precisely the reconfiguration of this uncertainty sanctioned by the CJEU that becomes relevant for child relocation as these cases routinely navigate all sorts of – both factual and legal – uncertainties. The common thread in much literature on child relocation, and many judgments, has been a loss of control of the national court once relocation takes place.[830] The Regulation mitigates, to some extent, such risks, but so does, naturally, the 1996 Hague Convention. However, the particularity of the Regulation system is that it directly alters the relationship between the judicial systems of Member States, and that between individuals and Member States. The area of freedom, security and justice is conceptualised as an area of shared powers and responsibilities, and the protection of the child and other family members becomes a matter of EU law. While there is always a jurisdictional loss of control involved in relocation, the protection of the child is now a common concern as a matter of EU law, relocating the responsibility to other Member States in a system in which they owe loyalty to each other.[831]

The Brussels II*bis* and now II*ter* Regulations have operated in the interests of children and their parents, but originally the regime for co-operation in parental matters came to life in reference to the internal market requirements of free movement. Since its drafting, the reasons behind the existence of a separate EU legal framework have been frequently questioned in the literature.[832] Some commentators have argued that the EU's intervention in family matters was simply 'a case of the Community staking a claim to this area'.[833] In this regard, the EU came closer to the individual citizen, but the reasons behind it were as much concerned with family law as with the pursuit of a political project of the European area of justice.[834] This co-operation in family matters undertaken by a predominantly economic supranational entity has thus been controversial from the start. These controversies are particularly visible in reference to the overriding mechanism for child abduction cases, due to the CJEU's consistent

830 See the discussion at the beginning of this chapter.

831 Article 4(3) of the TEU sets out the principle of sincere co-operation – otherwise known as the duty of loyalty – as a crucial component of the vertical relationship between the EU and the Member States. Mutual trust, underpinning the Regulation, plays a comparable role in the horizontal relationships between the Member States. See M. Klamert, 'Article 4 TEU' in M. Kellerbauer, M. Klamert and J. Tomkin (eds), *The EU Treaties and the Charter of Fundamental Rights: A Commentary*, Oxford University Press, Oxford 2019, para. 5.

832 See, e.g. P. Beaumont, above n. 283.

833 P. McEleavy, above n. 283, 890–94.

834 For a brief overview of the policy documents in this area, see M. Linton, 'Abolition of Exequatur, All in the Name of Mutual Trust!' in B. Hess, M. Bergström and E. Storskrubb (eds), *EU Civil Justice: Current Issues and Future Outlook*, Hart Publishing, Oxford 2016, pp. 262–63.

emphasis on mutual trust in highly acrimonious cases.[835] Other legal questions might not generate the same extent of controversies, but the EU's claim to this area of law is also marked by its particular normative orientation, which becomes even clearer in the conceptualisation of mutual trust.

6.2.2. MUTUAL TRUST

Mutual recognition relies on mutual trust – a concept as undefined as it is omnipresent in EU law, being seen as necessary for the creation of a truly European area of justice.[836] Mutual trust may be understood in two ways. First, it is recognised as the underlying pre-requirement of the mutual recognition of judgments, as discussed above. Second, it plays a role on its own, relating to – broadly understood – trust in qualities of judicial and administrative systems, as well as the enforcement of the rule of law, of other Member States. As such, mutual trust:

> does not mean that any of the potentially selected legal orders produces exactly the same result for the relationship in question but only – as a matter of trust, one may suggest – the expectation that different results under different legal orders will be in an acceptable range of plausibility under a common standard of justice.[837]

Thus, mutual trust is assumed both to exist as a basis for the AFSJ and to have a prospective dimension, resulting in a rather paradoxical construction. Although there are significant differences between national legal systems, questioning mutual trust as a basis for the AFSJ, the EU has 'built much on the myth of mutual trust in the past'.[838] The CJEU raised it to 'a foundational principle of the AFSJ and … of the entire EU legal order'.[839] In light of the obligations of mutual trust(!), Member States are required to accept the presumption that:

> fundamental rights have been observed by the other Member States, so that not only may they not demand a higher level of national protection of fundamental rights

---

835 S. Bartolini, 'In the Name of the Best Interests of the Child: The Principle of Mutual Trust in Child Abduction Cases' (2019) 56 *Common Market Law Review* 91. The recast of the Regulation addressed some of these issues. On that, see, for example, B. Ubertazzi, 'The Hearing of the Child in the Brussels IIa Regulation and Its Recast Proposal' (2017) 13 *Journal of Private International Law* 568.

836 See European Commission Press Release, 'Building Trust in Justice Systems in Europe: "Assises de La Justice" Forum to Shape the Future of EU Justice Policy' (Brussels, 21 November 2013) <http://europa.eu/rapid/press-release_IP-13-1117_en.htm>.

837 M. Weller, 'Mutual Trust: In Search of the Future of European Union Private International Law' (2015) 11 *Journal of Private International Law* 64, 72.

838 ibid., 67.

839 M. Moraru, '"Mutual Trust" from the Perspective of National Courts: A Test in Creative Legal Thinking' in E.R. Brouwer and D. Gerard (eds), 'Mapping Mutual Trust: Understanding

> from another Member State than that provided by EU law, but, *save in exceptional cases, they may not check* whether that other Member State has actually, in a specific case, observed the fundamental rights guaranteed by the EU.[840] (Emphasis added.)

Both elements of this paradoxical construction carry communicative and normative values. Communicatively, Member States might perhaps have different standards, but such standards are sufficient under a common (EU) standard of justice. Normatively, when features of two different systems are juxtaposed, they need to be approached as each other's functional equivalents and no negative consequences might result from their differences. This account is, naturally, simplified. Nevertheless, the ideational and contextual value of such constructions exerts pressures to reinterpret 'Europe not merely as a legal and political, but mainly as a moral space'.[841] As mutual trust is predominantly seen as the presumption of other Member States' legal systems regarding their level of compliance with fundamental rights,[842] these considerations might not be immediately relevant for child relocation cases. EU Member States are, at the same time, bound by the same international human rights instruments such as the CRC, the EU Charter of Fundamental Rights or the European Convention on Human Rights. However, such ideational pressures might spill over towards all prospective assessments of cross-border situations, including child relocation.

In the family context, the principle of mutual trust has usually been expressed in reference to recognition of judgments under the Brussels II*bis* Regulation. This will remain of relevance under the new Regulation. However, the CJEU has occasionally engaged with the prospective dimension of the principle as well. Referring to Article 15 of the Brussels II*bis* Regulation (transfer to another court), the Court has noted that:

> the court having jurisdiction may take into account, among other factors, the rules of procedure in the other Member State, such as those applicable to the taking of

---

and Framing the Role of Mutual Trust in EU Law', (2016) Working Paper MWP 2016/13, European University Institute, p. 44.

840 *Opinion 2/13 pursuant to Article 218(11) TFEU*, ECLI:EU:C:2014:2454, para. 192. See also M. Moraru, above n. 839, p. 44.

841 M. Fichera, above n. 809, p. 42; H. Lindahl, above n. 809.

842 This is not to suggest that this level is in fact the same, also in the family context. Issues arise across the Union most visibly in cases involving recognition of parenthood in cases of children growing up with same-sex parents. See, for example: A. Tryfonidou, 'EU Free Movement Law and the Children of Rainbow Families: Children of a Lesser God?' (2019) 38 *Yearbook of European Law* 220; A. Schuster, 'LGBTI Migration in Europe' in C. Ashford and A. Maine (eds), *Research Handbook on Gender, Sexuality and the Law*, Edward Elgar Publishing, Cheltenham 2020. There is, however, a visible trend in the EU towards increasingly more far-reaching regulation on various aspects of family life in the context of free movement, as also confirmed by the European Commission, 'Proposal for a Council Regulation on jurisdiction, applicable law, recognition of decisions and acceptance of authentic instruments in matters of parenthood and on the creation of a European Certificate of Parenthood' (2022), COM(2022) 695 final.

> evidence required for dealing with the case. However, the court having jurisdiction *should not take into consideration, within such an assessment, the substantive law of that other Member State which might be applicable* by the court of that other Member State, if the case were transferred to it. If the court were to take that into consideration, *doing so would be in breach of the principles of mutual trust between Member States* and mutual recognition of judgments that are the basis of Regulation No 2201/2003.[843] (Emphasis added)

The judgment followed the Opinion of the Advocate General, who based such an assessment on the existing legal provisions in reference to mutual trust:

> trust is such that it has even enabled the introduction of a specific scheme in order to facilitate enforcement of judgments on rights of access that are considered to be essential in order to protect the fundamental right of the child, laid down in Article 24(3) of the Charter of Fundamental Rights of the European Union, to maintain a relationship and direct contact with both parents.[844]

Mutual trust is built upon the assumption that Member States equally protect the rights of the child and the broader family,[845] and, at the same time, is presented as an important component of such protection and a justification of the (obligation towards) shared responsibility in that regard.

The principle of mutual trust might be argued to be artificial and to obscure differences between Member States.[846] Its operation in family matters raises many controversies, especially in the child abduction context.[847] New challenges to mutual trust are also posed by the rule of law crisis in some Member States.[848] Additionally, while mutual trust is primarily about the potential mistrust between judiciaries of Member States, in delicate family matters this mistrust is deeply intertwined with mistrust between the parties.[849]

---

843 Case C-428/15, *Child and Family Agency v J. D.*, ECLI:EU:C:2016:819, para. 57.

844 Opinion of the Advocate General in Case C-428/15, *Child and Family Agency v J. D.*, ECLI:EU:2016:458, paras. 81–83.

845 See R. Lamont, above n. 634, p. 11 noting that it encourages 'a commitment to a very high level of respect for the foreign jurisdiction'.

846 R. Lamont, 'Care Proceedings with a European Dimension under Brussels IIa: Jurisdiction, Mutual Trust and the Best Interests of the Child' (2016) 28 *Child and Family Law Quarterly* 67, 84–85.

847 See, e.g. L. Walker and P. Beaumont, 'Shifting the Balance Achieved by the Abduction Convention: The Contrasting Approaches of the European Court of Human Rights and the European Court of Justice' (2011) 7 *Journal of Private International Law* 231.

848 O. Ceran, 'Expeditiousness of child abduction proceedings, procedural autonomy, and what it has to do with sincere cooperation: *Rzecznik Praw Dziecka and Others*' (2023) 60 *Common Market Law Review* 1787.

849 V. Mitsilegas, 'The Limits of Mutual Trust in Europe's Area of Freedom, Security and Justice: From Automatic Inter-State Cooperation to the Slow Emergence of the Individual' (2012) 31 *Yearbook of European Law* 319.

It can quickly become 'public mistrust, with national courts ... potentially tending to uphold the interests of their own nationals at the expense of the system set by EU law'.[850] Mutual trust, as such, cannot be a remedy for this private mistrust or struggles in personal relationships. Even in purely national cases, there is a limit to what family courts can achieve in highly acrimonious cases. At the same time, mutual trust does provide an important degree of consistency and certainty that reduces litigation.[851] On an individual level, its two-dimensional nature has consequences also for individuals' relationships with Member States insofar as it might be seen as equalising the mutual position of EU citizens versus all Member States (which might, in the traditional view, feel less inclined to protect non-nationals rather than nationals). Serious breaches of, or threats to, fundamental rights can still be addressed, but they are addressed according to the standards of the whole Union as a community that respects fundamental rights and assumes responsibility for their protection, also in the context of its most vulnerable subjects.[852]

Child relocation cases will rarely engage with questions about application of the Regulation directly. They might, however, not be free from its impacts. Chapter 5 has already demonstrated why jurisdictional considerations would not be acceptable in relocation cases, as a matter of EU doctrine. Outside the established doctrines, mutual trust has not yet acquired the status of a self-standing standard for review, but it may gain more importance also beyond the secondary legislation within the AFSJ.[853] The prospective dimension of mutual trust in child relocation cases might, for example, limit the nature of the arguments or the scope of investigations regarding the child's future in another Member State after the move. Such an effect could potentially be observed on two levels: first, it could be generally assumed that the protection framework in the state of destination is sufficient (as a matter of factual assessment); and second, national courts could feel less inclined to conduct detailed examinations in this regard (as a matter of EU legal obligations). While such developments might seem a priori abstract or even unlikely, Chapter 7 will demonstrate that these ideational influences might indeed create both adaptational pressures and new opportunity structures for national actors, in particular if considered with the broader features of the European legal space.

---

850 ibid., 353.

851 R. Lamont, above n. 634, p. 12.

852 For a description of such a process in EU criminal law, see S. Coutts, above n. 18, pp. 148–53. In the family context, this process might be illustrated by the discussions about differences in interpretation of the child's right to be heard. See, for example, Case C-491/10 PPU, *Zarraga*, ECLI:EU:C:2010:828.

853 A. Prechal, 'Mutual Trust Before the Court of Justice of the European Union' (2017) 2 *European Papers – A Journal on Law and Integration* 75, 79, 91.

6.2.3. SINGLE (LEGAL) SPACE BEYOND FAMILY LAW

The responsibility assumed by the EU for its mobile citizens goes way beyond the provisions of the Brussels II*ter* Regulation, or the only partially tangible requirements of mutual trust. The general free movement framework built by the EU, with its many individual guarantees and state obligations, is of relevance also for child relocation cases. A variety of issues can be important for future-oriented assessments in relocation disputes, such as immigration status, visas, residence, education, employment, social benefits, etc. This broader EU legal framework is part of what prompts the voices that say that intra-EU moves have more in common with forms of interregional mobility than 'traditional' international migration.[854] As relocation disputes are inevitably concerned with cross-border movement, the EU legal guarantees limit the uncertainties related to migration. They might allow for relocation disputes to be assessed in a different light from when the destination state lies outside the EU, even where the difference might be predominantly heuristic. It is not possible, nor necessary, to analyse the EU legal framework in detail for the purposes of this chapter, but the following paragraphs will briefly outline the potential relevance of EU law for both the protection of the relationship between the child and the non-relocating parent, and the broader stability of the family's equilibrium.

Questions of nationality and migration status are rarely openly acknowledged in parenting disputes.[855] Courts hearing international relocation disputes may, however, encounter such issues. Some authors argue that, while it is often unclear what weight such arguments have in judicial proceedings, relocation to a country where the child and both parents share nationality and family ties seems much less likely to present difficulties, and courts often seem to follow this intuition.[856] Also, existing empirical research from the UK suggests that moves motivated by parental wishes to 'go home' are granted more often than moves motivated by other reasons.[857] However, as relocation disputes often occur in multinational families, it would be wrong to conflate nationality,

---

854 e.g. L. Ackers and H. Stalford, *A Community for Children?*, above n. 276, p. 165.

855 For an exception see A.L. Estin, 'Nationality and Migration Status in International Children's Law' in G. Douglas, M. Murch and V. Stephens (eds), *International and National Perspectives on Child and Family Law: Essays in Honour of Nigel Lowe*, Intersentia, Cambridge 2018.

856 ibid., pp. 222–24; M. Sattler, above n. 805, 1724 and case law cited there. See also the European case *Polidario v Switzerland* [2013] ECtHR, app. no. 33169/10, in which, following the retention of the child during a holiday period, custody of the child was awarded to the father, and the Filipina mother was granted access rights which had to be exercised in Switzerland, whereas she had no authorisation to stay in the country.

857 e.g. R. George, above n. 117, 386–87. The author rightly observes, however, that various reasons for the move often overlap and hence the finding should not be overinterpreted or approached in a simplistic way.

migration status, and destination. The territory of the EU is a clear example of a space where they often do not go hand-in-hand. A parent might go to a country of their nationality, but this does not presuppose that this is a state of the nationality of their children or former partner. Such cases raise immigration issues in practice, in particular when the remaining non-national parent wants to exercise their contact rights abroad, or potentially follow the relocating parent and the child in the future. The elements of nationality, migration status, and ties in each country – although they often go together – will also often need to be considered independently.

Such considerations can, however, be approached differently in the EU context. EU citizens have the benefit of much easier access to the mobility infrastructure, they travel visa-free across the Union, their residence rights are uniformly regulated by EU law, and they have access to many socio-economic rights in their Member State of choice based on the non-discrimination basis. This might have very tangible consequences for cross-border family life. In child relocation cases, the broader mobility infrastructure removes the risk that a parent, or a child, will not be able to (re-)enter a certain state because of administrative reasons (e.g. lack of visa), even if he or she is not a EU citizen, as long as they have a residence permit for one of the Member States.[858] In principle, an EU citizen parent might follow the child and decide to move to another Member State in the future, relatively unrestricted by any immigration law concerns. As the rights granted to EU citizens extend their scope of autonomy, this autonomy is, in principle, granted to both parents and allows the exercise of the cross-border family life to be facilitated within the whole Union.

EU law also guarantees broader stability of the child's equilibrium. Children of mobile, economically active EU citizens have automatic rights that they derive from their parents' status, such as residence and education entitlements, but also independent rights as EU citizens. Even if a parent subsequently becomes unemployed, they retain their entitlements.[859] The benefits extend beyond the economically active EU citizen and include many socio-economic rights for those who join or accompany them, and access to

858 The rights of EU nationals and third-country nationals (TCNs) vary, but TCN family members of EU citizens benefit from various EU legal guarantees. See also the Citizens' Rights Directive or Case C-40/11, *Iida*, ECLI:EU:C:2012:691, where the Court held that a third-country national who has custody rights over a minor who is an EU citizen and resides in a different Member State with another parent cannot claim right of residence derived from a Union citizen in cases that do not fall within the scope of application of the Directive, and where there is no other connection with the provisions on citizenship of European Union law.

859 e.g. Case C-480/08, *Maria Teixeira v London Borough of Lambeth and Secretary of State for the Home Department*, ECLI:EU:C:2010:83.

local services and infrastructures such as health or education systems.[860] Both in the short- and long-term, the stability of the residence of EU citizens in foreign Member States is reinforced in multiple ways. Moreover, this stability is not lost if a child decides to move back in the future, later in life. The EU has made real efforts, for example, in the area of the mutual recognition of diplomas, both through harmonisation in certain areas[861] and through judicial developments.[862] The 'European way of life' – promotion of which is one of the EU Commission's priorities for 2019–24 – encompasses free movement and absence of borders specifically, health or judicial co-operation issues, as well as cultural factors more broadly.[863] And, in the words of the Commission, '[n]othing can be more important for our way of life than protecting our children'.[864]

Of course, the existence of such extensive legal guarantees across the Union is not absolute, nor does it entirely remove more factual obstacles to movement. Geographical distance or travelling costs might still constitute significant hurdles in some cases, and specific arrangements for a prospective move might still be necessary to ensure short- and long-term stability. However, heuristically, many issues that are regularly discussed in international child relocation cases are raised in a different light in their EU context. EU citizens enjoy considerable privileges while exercising their free movement rights, which are not available to third-country nationals (TCNs) or when the destination lies outside the EU.[865] They have more (and more privileged) opportunities to maintain transnational ties or engage in reunion strategies.[866]

---

860 See, e.g. Council Directive 77/486/EEC of 25 July 1977 on the education of the children of migrant workers [1977] OJ L199/32. See also the discussion in L. Ackers, 'Citizenship, Migration and the Valuation of Care in the European Union' (2004) 30 *Journal of Ethnic and Migration Studies* 373, 376, or L. Ackers and H. Stalford, *A Community for Children?*, above n. 276, pp. 201–14, 236–37.

861 e.g. Article 53(1) of the TFEU, Council Directive 98/5/EC of 16 February 1998 to facilitate practice of the profession of lawyer on a permanent basis in a Member State other than that in which the qualification was obtained [1998] OJ L77/36, European Parliament resolution of 25 October 2018 on promoting automatic mutual recognition of diplomas [2020] OJ C345/78.

862 See a brief overview in C. Janssens, *The Principle of Mutual Recognition in EU Law*, Oxford University Press, Oxford 2013, pp. 15–17.

863 See European Commission, 'Promoting our European way of life' <https://commission.europa.eu/strategy-and-policy/priorities-2019-2024/promoting-our-european-way-life_en>.

864 Communication from the Commission to the European Parliament, the Council, the European Economic and Social Committee and the Committee of the Regions, 'A Union That Strives for More' (2020), COM(2020) 37 final <https://eur-lex.europa.eu/legal-content/EN/TXT/?qid=1581957029354&uri=CELEX:52020DC0037>.

865 It is nevertheless worth remembering that the inclusive infrastructure for EU citizens is necessarily built on the exclusion of those who do not enjoy such status.

866 L. Ryan, 'Transnational Relations: Family Migration among Recent Polish Migrants in London' (2011) 49 *International Migration* 80.

The border-free infrastructure, complementing the relative geographical proximity, both enables regular visits and increases expectations as to such visits actually taking place.[867] Of course, there are still tensions and difficulties related to mobility, and the rights are not without their limits, in particular when linked with economic activity.[868] Despite the difficulties, however, this legal infrastructure communicates the perception of the EU as a place of rights where free movement is relatively seamless, and free movers, including children, are highly privileged. This both co-creates and reinforces the symbolic shared responsibility discussed above in reference to mutual trust.

6.2.4. DISCUSSION: MUTUAL RESPONSIBILITY?

Intra-EU child relocation cases remain governed by national law. At the same time, they arise and are resolved in the specific context of a united Europe. In family law, this context is most clearly constructed by the Brussels II*ter* Regulation. This construction has two interrelated dimensions. First, it creates a specific legal reality in which parental rights and obligations function. By introducing facilitative legal regimes, it facilitates the real lives of people finding themselves in cross-border situations by recognising those situations, recalibrating the position of an individual versus Member States and the Union, and providing various forms of assistance. This legal infrastructure makes sure that, as people cross borders, both rights and obligations travel with them. At the same time, the constant emphasis on the facilitation of mobility as a *raison d'être* of the legislation and the contextual background of subsequent CJEU judgments on related matters, has a clear prospective dimension and infiltrates child relocation cases, even if only on a discursive, communicative level. To facilitate, in the end, is 'to make something possible or easier'.[869]

Second, the Regulation as part of the AFSJ is not normatively neutral. It both builds upon and projects mutual trust. This trust is no longer linked exclusively to mutual recognition but stands independently. By requiring Member States to recognise each other's judgments and participate in a shared system of their enforcement, the welfare function of family courts is conceptualised as a shared responsibility. On the one hand, the introduction of this shared responsibility is justified in reference to 'the reality of increasingly mobile citizens across the Union getting married and having children'; on the other, it is argued that it is

867 ibid., 98.

868 e.g. Case C-333/13, *Elisabeta Dano and Florin Dano v Jobcenter Leipzig*, ECLI:EU:C:2014:2358; Case C-256/11, *Dereci*, ECLI:EU:C:2011:734.

869 'facilitate', *Cambridge Dictionary online* <https://dictionary.cambridge.org/dictionary/english/facilitate>.

necessary to remove the remaining obstacles so that citizens can more easily exercise their rights across the Union, also in the best interests of the child.[870] Discursively, free movement and the realisation of the child's best interests are brought together and are dependent on the degree of compliance of national judges with the principles of the AFSJ. Different national authorities might become responsible for a child's welfare or their parents' interests at various stages of their life, and the exercise of this responsibility needs to account for the fact that (at least some) individuals experience their lives in a particular supranational space fostered by the EU.

The smooth operation of a community based on mutual trust 'is constantly promised yet undelivered'.[871] The AFSJ is a spatial construct where many different socio-legal realities function on a daily basis, and which, at the same time, brings normatively loaded concepts of freedom and justice which need to be confronted and decided upon.[872] The exact impact of the Brussels II*ter* Regulation will likely vary across Member States, as was the case for its predecessor.[873] But this impact is predominantly perceived as the application of the Regulation in national laws and its influence on the interpretation of concepts belonging inherently to private international law. EU law does not, naturally, extend jurisdiction, nor the powers of national judicial authorities, beyond borders. It does, however, create a supranational legal infrastructure in which rights and obligations can cross such borders and be enforced by national authorities in the interests of mobile individuals. The Regulation and mutual trust have become familiar features of the European legal framework and, together with the broader legal infrastructure, build upon the need to keep up with societal developments while at the same time embedding these developments in a particular context of EU integration. As such, questions about their normative value and role in creating European territoriality beyond their immediate scope of application remain open. In the EU, free movement, justice, and family rights become intertwined in a common normative framework. The EU's composite normativity normalises family mobility in a particular space of rights, but the exact limits of this normative normalisation remain unclear, as do their practical consequences. In child relocation cases, the many different instruments facilitating mobility and granting rights to EU citizens, and the socio-legal contexts they create, will not be reducible to individual norms, but rather function as a new supranational normal, perceived predominantly in their contextual (albeit not normatively neutral) dimensions.

---

870 European Commission, 'Proposal for a Council Regulation on jurisdiction, the recognition and enforcement of decisions in matrimonial matters and the matters of parental responsibility, and on international child abduction (recast)' (2016), COM(2016) 0411 final, p. 2.

871 M. Fichera, above n. 809, p. 37.

872 ibid., pp. 41–42.

873 For an overview see K. Boele-Woelki and C. González Beilfuss (eds), *Brussels II bis: Its Impact and Application in the Member States*, Intersentia, Antwerp 2007.

6.3. THE PRINCIPLE-ORIENTED INFLUENCE: EUROPEANS AS FAMILY MEMBERS

The broad space of autonomy offered to EU citizens is rooted in transnational individual rights but does not remain blind to EU citizens' relationships. Rights created by the CJEU make cross-border situations possible and feed transnational expectations, which subsequently feed back into rights. It is this norm and context conundrum, coming to life via the normatively inflicted methodology of EU law, that creates particularised normativities beyond individual norms. This dynamic is broadly described here as a principle-oriented influence. This is so because it rests less clearly on individual norms – the legal infrastructure discussed above – and more on a composite methodology of the CJEU that links norms and contexts together. The two dimensions of the influence are, however, closely intertwined. The legal infrastructures constitute a part of the context as well as including ideational and contextual elements themselves, as demonstrated by the previous section. The partially different nature of the principle-oriented influence rests in its generalised perceptions of the lives lived by EU citizens, as methodological tools of EU law, and their relational dimensions.

This methodological aspect of EU law might be relevant for child relocation disputes due to the nature of the child's best interests principle as such. The discussion of principle in Chapter 2 highlighted those of its features that allow it to be seen as normativising the perceived 'normal' or 'viable'.[874] Any such process emphasises the importance of methodological choices used to approach the context of a case, and to interpret and select the 'normality'. The legal perception of normality is never normatively neutral, and may reflect on various matters, e.g. what can be expected from parents in their relationships with their children and each other.[875] The discussion below focuses on how these processes can be conceived, via a particular juxtaposition of agency and vulnerability within personal relationships, as seen via the EU legal lens. The investigation is thematised in three strands, drawing on CJEU case law in various areas: (1) the portability of family life across the Union; (2) children's rights and the territoriality of the EU; and (3) the cosmopolitan orientation of the child in EU law. The portability of family life and the territoriality of the EU can, at the same time, be seen as two sides of the same coin, encompassing two different dimensions of a reasonable expectation (of both the EU citizen and

874 J. Schiratzki, above n. 154, 11.

875 As briefly explained in Chapter 2, the extent to which parental interests should or could be considered in the assessment of the best interests of the child is disputed. From this perspective, the notion of a 'principle-oriented' influence serves a categorisation purpose only, emphasising the subtle difference between the broader context of the cases (the broader infrastructure) and the 'softer' normative layer derived from this context. It does not suggest that parental interest should constitute part of the assessment of the child's best interests.

Member States) to be able to move. The main argument pursued here is that the transformation of the space of reference (this space being the EU rather than a state) necessarily concerns not only individual rights,[876] but also family relationships – including those enjoyed by children and their parents. The relevance of this observation is then discussed in reference to child relocation, drawing attention to how the normative methodology of EU law might intersect with national family laws and their own rationale.

6.3.1. PORTABILITY OF FAMILY LIFE ACROSS THE UNION

The EU is built on the promise of free movement. By virtue of Articles 20(2) and 21 of the TFEU, every citizen of the European Union has the primary and individual right to move and reside freely within the territory of the Member States. In principle, the exercise of such rights is not 'subject to proof of any interest whatsoever'.[877] Over the years, free movement has become much more than a citizenship right, becoming 'the element which shapes the structure of EU citizenship itself, and which to a great extent determines the relevance of EU law for individuals'.[878] Many Europeans have perceived freedom of movement as an individual right to be a more important achievement than peace between Member States.[879] But the positive effect of EU law on the freedom of movement of individuals not only consists of the extension of the geographical scope for its enjoyment, but encompasses also the right to move with one's family.[880] In light of the constructive aspects of EU law outlined at the beginning of the chapter, this 'most relevant and characteristic right'[881] extends and gives rise to a *relational* expectation of movement.[882]

---

876 See, e.g. S. Iglesias Sánchez, 'A Citizenship Right to Stay? The Right Not to Move in a Union Based on Free Movement' in D. Kochenov (ed), *EU Citizenship and Federalism: The Role of Rights*, Cambridge University Press, Cambridge 2017.

877 Case C-459/20, *X v Staatssecretaris van Justitie en Veiligheid*, ECLI:EU:C:2023:499, para. 40.

878 S. Iglesias Sánchez, above n. 876, p. 371.

879 European Commission, 'Europeans' Opinions on the European Union's Priorities' (2018) *Standard Eurobarometer Report* 90 (2215/STD90) <https://europa.eu/eurobarometer/surveys/detail/2215>.

880 This is explicitly confirmed by the Citizens' Rights Directive itself, see Article 2(2) or 3(2) and various provisions of Chapter III of the Directive. There is also an extensive body of case law asserting that if family members cannot accompany a mobile EU citizen, that citizen is discouraged from exercising his or her movement rights, e.g. Case C-60/00, *Mary Carpenter*, ECLI:EU:C:2002:434, para. 38; Case C-291/05, *Minister voor Vreemdelingenzaken en Integratie v R. N. G. Eind*, ECLI:EU:C:2007:771, paras. 35–37, 44; Case C-127/08, *Metock*, ECLI:EU:C:2008:449, paras. 56, 89; Case C-673/16, *Coman*, ECLI:EU:C:2018:385, para. 24.

881 M. Condinanzi, A. Lang and B. Nascimbene, *Citizenship of the Union and Freedom of Movement of Persons*, Brill Nijhoff, Leiden 2008, p. 20.

882 This assertion is supported by empirical research conducted by S. Morano-Foadi, above n. 273, 17. The findings suggest that mothers view a refusal to allow them to move back to their homelands as an exile and limitation to their right to move freely within the EU.

The residence rights of family members were one of the first EU law developments securing the effective exercise of free movement of persons, as their absence was considered to be a significant obstacle to the mobility of workers.[883] As already discussed in Chapter 5, these rights are now reaffirmed in Council Directive 2004/38/EC of 29 April 2004 on the right of citizens of the Union and their family members to move and reside freely within the territory of the Member States. These rights remain subject to conditions set out by the Citizens' Rights Directive, and hence are not unlimited. However, if the conditions are met, the EU citizen in question can expect to reside with their family members. When the Directive does not apply (in particular in relation to the Member State of nationality), the residence rights of a family member might additionally be protected by Article 21(1) of the TFEU or other provisions of the Treaty.[884] Even if often rooted in the functional logic of the internal market, the rich body of case law on family residence rights[885] proves and emphasises that 'from a *human point of view*' (emphasis added) family remains important for individuals, and, as such, intersections of free movement and family life need to be evaluated in the context of broader EU law and fundamental rights.[886]

Case law on family residence rights most clearly demonstrates the transnational dimension of EU citizenship.[887] The entitlements to move with one's family have been straightforwardly related to a family status acquired in the state of origin that should be recognised in the state of destination, becoming the ground for residence entitlements.[888] But family mobility for EU citizens is no longer a regime based exclusively on mutual recognition, but stems directly from free movement entitlements.[889] In recent years, when the Court adjudicates on family residence and reunification, it regularly makes references to citizenship of the Union as the fundamental status of nationals of Member States who can rely on rights related to that citizenship against both their host and origin Member States.[890] In this context, it has become a given that:

> [t]he rights which nationals of Member States enjoy under that provision include *the right to lead a normal family life*, together with their family members, both in

883 See the Preamble of Regulation (EEC) 1612/68 of 15 October 1968 on freedom of movement for workers within the Community [1968] OJ L257/2 (no longer in force).

884 e.g. Case C-457/12, *S and G*, ECLI:EU:C:2014:136, para. 34; Case C-673/16, *Coman*, ECLI:EU:C:2018:385, paras. 23–24.

885 See e.g. the categorisation in F. Ristuccia, above n. 663, 1231.

886 Case C-413/99, *Baumbast*, ECLI:EU:C:2002:493, para. 68.

887 S. Coutts, above n. 18, pp. 37–43; C. Costello, 'Metock: Free Movement and "Normal Family Life" in the Union' (2009) 46 *Common Market Law Review* 587, 616.

888 E. Pataut, above n. 14, p. 313.

889 S. Coutts, above n. 18, p. 43.

890 e.g. Case C-291/05, *Eind*, ECLI:EU:C:2007:771, para. 36; Case C-673/16, *Coman*, ECLI:EU:C:2018:385, paras. 30–31.

the host Member State and in the Member State of which they are nationals.[891] (Emphasis added.)

This guarantee no longer covers only movement to and residence in a foreign Member State,[892] but includes also return migration,[893] regardless of whether the EU citizen resided with a given family member before relocation.[894]

The right to lead a normal family life can be conceived as giving rise to a paradigm that family life is, as a matter of law, portable across the Union. This entitlement has both a material and a discursive dimension. Family arrangements established in one country are portable across both as a matter of legal status and in reference to residence rights. But the CJEU, in particular when it grants EU law protection based on the Treaty provisions, no longer refers exclusively to the individual residence rights of family members, but '*the right to lead a normal family life*' (emphasis added).[895] It sends a strong message that family situations of mobile EU citizens should not be changed only due to the fact that they make use of their free movement rights. However, when the CJEU uses the notion of 'normal family life', it remains underspecified both regarding what constitutes a *normal* life as well as what constitutes a *family*.[896] Notwithstanding discussions about the (conservative) concept of family in EU law,[897] one can surely assume that it covers parent-child relationships. The open question – relevant also for the child relocation context – is what is, in fact, normal.

In EU law, any answer to this question might have doctrinal implications as to the scope and nature of rights granted to an individual. But, as a matter of a broader normative paradigm, whatever *normal* family life is according to a given legal order, this *normal* is portable across the Union. At the same time, the EU discourse emphasises that movement is exactly part of what a normal family life entails. Even if the mere desirability of a particular familial arrangement is at stake, national courts need to balance the effects of any decision on the exercise of agency offered to EU citizens.[898] This agency is rooted in individual free

891 Case C-673/16, *Coman*, ECLI:EU:C:2018:385, para. 32, and the case law cited there.

892 These are the entitlements flowing from the Citizens' Rights Directive.

893 e.g. Case C-457/12, *S and G*, ECLI:EU:C:2014:136; Case C-673/16, *Coman*, ECLI:EU:C:2018:385.

894 e.g. Case C-127/08, *Metock*, ECLI:EU:C:2008:449, paras. 87–90.

895 This language is not exclusive to the CJEU. See, for example, *Marckx v Belgium* [1979] ECtHR, app no. 6833/74, paras. 31, 45. However, in the jurisprudence of the CJEU, it uniquely features in the context of freedom of movement.

896 C. Costello, above n. 887, 614.

897 C. McGlynn, *Families and the European Union: Law, Politics and Pluralism*, Cambridge University Press, Cambridge 2006, p. 23 argues that the 'dominant ideology of the family' is that of a 'white, heterosexual, married couple, with children, all living under the same roof, where the husband is the main breadwinner and the wife the primary carer of children and other dependants'.

898 e.g. Case C-457/12, *S and G*, ECLI:EU:C:2014:136, para. 43.

movement entitlements but is also relational insofar as family ties influence its effective scope. This not only protects migrating EU citizens, but also reorients them towards new perceptions of agency 'that remain unavailable but for EU law',[899] with potential relevance for the nature of reasonable expectations raised and assessed in child relocation cases. In the end, EU law's accounts of the legal subject structure 'the field of social possibilities' within which individuals form their identities and expectations.[900] The normative paradigm of EU law suggests that family arrangements, once established, should not be easily disturbed only because an individual decides to make use of their free movement rights and reside in another Member State. When national family courts navigate the social-normative equilibrium of family disputes, they might feel a need to account for such expectations and explicitly decide about their normative value.

6.3.2. CHILDREN'S RIGHTS AND THE TERRITORIALITY OF THE EU

The paradigm of family life's portability is transnational in nature and broadens the scope of autonomy of individuals willing to choose a cross-border life. However, EU citizenship has also a particular supranational dimension that relates to the territory of the EU and the 'European way of life' that it is supposed to offer.[901] The CJEU jurisprudence on the 'substance of the rights of Union citizenship' based on Article 20 of the TFEU, concerned with residence rights of TCNs who are parents of minor EU citizens, has increasingly positioned children and their wellbeing not in the context of individual Member States, but in the context of the whole Union.[902] While different legal frameworks apply to EU citizens and TCNs, certain methodological features of this broader paradigm shift remain interesting from the perspective of the child's best interests and familial rights and obligations.[903] This is so in particular

[899] F. de Witte, above n. 27, pp. 1–2.

[900] R. Leckey, above n. 57, pp. 6–8. See also E. Mertz, above n. 57, 1251–52.

[901] S. Coutts, above n. 18, pp. 57–68. See also D. Kostakopoulou, 'European Union Citizenship: Writing the Future' (2007) 13 *European Law Journal* 623 arguing that 'the reduction of European citizenship to a transnational citizenship downplays both the resourcefulness of EU citizenship and the supranational character of EU law'.

[902] For a more detailed discussion of the 'substance of rights' and Article 20 of the TFEU see Chapter 5, above Section 5.2.

[903] According to the Citizens' Rights Directive, Member States might in certain circumstances expel EU citizens. See Article 14(1), Article 35, or Chapter VI of the Directive. No such cases to date have, however, involved minor EU citizens or considerations of the child's best interests. While the protection of EU citizens and third-country nationals might lead to different normative results, the CJEU often draws analogies with the Citizens' Rights

when discussed in combination with the other contextual and methodological features of EU law presented in this chapter. The focal point of the following paragraphs is, therefore, to demonstrate how these EU citizenship and residence cases – which touch upon the rights of minor EU citizens – shed light on the Court's understanding of children's rights, their familial relationships, and individuals' scope of reasonable expectations regarding movement within the Union.

Ruiz Zambrano is one of the most important cases regarding EU citizenship. In this case, the CJEU relied on the status of minor EU citizens to grant the right of residence for their TCN parent. The Court held that refusing such a right to Mr Ruiz Zambrano would 'have the effect of depriving citizens of the Union of the genuine enjoyment of the substance of the rights conferred by virtue of their status as citizens of the Union' by obliging them to 'leave the territory of the Union'.[904] The *Ruiz Zambrano* case was met both with praise and criticism.[905] Many commentators noted that the CJEU opened the doors to an almost unlimited usage of EU citizenship in cases that should have been – as a matter of previous doctrine – considered purely internal and left outside the scope of EU law. But, through its construction, the *Ruiz Zambrano* judgment gave rise to the sense of a normatively inflicted territoriality of the Union, independent from any other provisions of the Treaty.[906] Seen in light of children's rights and entitlements, the Court's construction reinforced a vision of the EU as a space of values that offers a good life to minor EU citizens, presupposed by the right to stay in that space.

Commentators rightly noted that driving the Court in the *Ruiz Zambrano* case were issues of social justice, protection of family life, and children's interests rather than free movement and EU citizenship.[907] As a matter of both law and fact, the state can always assume responsibility for minor EU citizens and guarantee their right to stay in the country, for example in foster care, but this is not a solution that can be accepted – a child's right to stay in the Union

---

Directive in the latter category of cases. See the discussion in C. Neier, 'New Clarifications on Ending the Union Citizen's Right of Residence: The Grand Chamber Decisions of the European Court of Justice of 22 June 2021 in C-718/19 and C-719/19' (2021) 6 *European Papers – A Journal on Law and Integration* 941. The paradigm shifts discussed here can, therefore, also be of relevance from the constructivist perspective more broadly.

904 Case C-34/09, *Ruiz Zambrano*, ECLI:EU:C:2011:124, paras. 42–44.

905 See the brief summary of the discussion in H. Kroeze and P. Van Elsuwege, 'Revisiting Ruiz Zambrano: A Never Ending Story?' (2021) 23 *European Journal of Migration and Law* 1.

906 e.g. L. Azoulai, '"Euro-Bonds": The Ruiz Zambrano Judgment or the Real Invention of EU Citizenship' (2011) 3 *Perspectives on Federalism* 31, 34–35; K. Hailbronner and D. Thym, above n. 568, 1256–58. See also S. Coutts, above n. 18, p. 60.

907 A. Torres Pérez, 'The Right to Family Life as a Bar to the Expulsion of Third Country Nationals in the European Union' in M. González Pascual and A. Torres Pérez (eds), *The Right to Family Life in the European Union*, Routledge, Abingdon 2017, p. 166; D. Thym, above n. 571, pp. 166–69.

is not meaningful without his or her family.[908] For some commentators, this construction of the CJEU gives rise to a qualitatively new right: 'the right to stay at home'.[909] However, as the CJEU evaluates such relationships, the account of rights put forward becomes a contextual account of relational rights and obligations. *Ruiz Zambrano* and other cases involving minor EU citizens might be approached as not so much about parents and residence rights, but about children and their relationships.[910] From this perspective, *Ruiz Zambrano* was an all-or-nothing case: the children, to enjoy their family rights and depending on the residence decision, would either stay in the Union with the parents or would have to leave the Union with them. But leaving the EU in this set of circumstances was not accepted as an option under EU law. Thus, it was rightly observed that:

> the rights of the child provide a reason why states sometimes do expel their own child citizens: the interests of the child are in being with its parents, who are themselves subject to expulsion. However, *Ruiz Zambrano* effectively precludes this line of argument and moves the discussion to a different starting point. Instead of saying 'the family members must go – what is now in the interests of the child, to go with them or to stay?', the state or court which respects children's rights must say 'the child must stay – what is now in the interests of the child, that the family members go, or the family members stay?'[911]

The Court came back to the formulation used in *Ruiz Zambrano* in other cases involving minor citizens.[912] Two cases are of particular interest for the discussion undertaken in this chapter: *Alokpa* and *Rendón Marín*.[913] Both confront the right to stay at home with the possibility to move to another Member State, and, as such, go beyond the limited choice faced by the CJEU in *Ruiz Zambrano* and most other cases following its doctrine. At the same time, due to the option of intra-EU movement raised in these cases, they contain interesting contextual assessments regarding movement within the EU in the familial contexts. As will be subsequently argued in this chapter, the reasoning applied by the CJEU in these cases offers an interesting perspective on the level to which Member States need to accommodate certain parental expectations to guarantee their children's rights.

908 A. Torres Pérez, above n. 907, p. 162.
909 See G.T. Davies, above n. 797.
910 A. Torres Pérez, above n. 907, p. 162. See also the arguments in N. Cambien, above n. 602, or K. Carr, above n. 3, pp. 157, 241 observing that 'the [*Ruiz Zambrano*] decision itself was indeed motivated by the family law principle of unity of the family'.
911 See G.T. Davies, above n. 797, p. 483.
912 e.g. Case C-304/14, *Secretary of State for the Home Department v CS*, ECLI:EU:C:2016:674.
913 Case C-86/12, *Adzo Domenyo Alokpa and Others v Ministre du Travail, de l'Emploi et de l'Immigration*, ECLI:EU:C:2013:645; Case C-165/14, *Rendón Marín*, ECLI:EU:C:2016:675.

Alokpa and *Rendón Marín* can be seen as belonging to different phases of EU citizenship jurisprudence: *Alokpa* limits the application of the *Ruiz Zambrano* doctrine, while *Rendón Marín* grants protection in a similar set of circumstances and is said to effectively reverse *Alokpa*.[914] While the CJEU comes to different conclusions in these two cases, their underlying paradigms can nevertheless be seen as revealing more similarities than differences. In both, the Court recognises that minor EU citizens have the right to stay in the Union, and this right requires protection of their family relationships. In both, the Court emphasises a need for an individualised assessment. But in both, since an option to move within the Union is raised, the Court asks a slightly different question from that in *Ruiz Zambrano*: if the child will stay in the Union but might go to another Member State, what is now in the interests of the child? If the parent can go to another EU Member State both as a matter of law and fact, should they be allowed to (expect to) stay or might they be expected to go? Before elaborating on the relevance of these considerations for the child relocation context, it is, therefore, useful to first analyse closer the normatively inflicted methodology of the CJEU adopted in these cases.

In *Alokpa*, the TCN mother was residing in Luxembourg as the primary carer of two children of French nationality, born in Luxembourg. The Luxembourg authorities refused to grant her a residence permit, as neither she nor her children had sufficient means of sustenance. The authorities held that, notwithstanding the fact that the children had never resided in France, they could reside with their mother in France. The care they required could be provided in France and thus their interests would be sufficiently protected. The Court found that the substance of the rights conferred on minor EU citizens requires that state authorities need to protect their residence in the European Union, and such residence is not feasible without their parent's care. This does not, however, require the protection of their carer's right of residence as the carer can be reasonably expected to move to another Member State.[915] A national authority might, according to the circumstances, need to determine if this is indeed the case, and balance out different interests at stake. In *Alokpa*, it was not disputed that Luxembourgian authorities did indeed conduct a balanced, individualised assessment of the case. Because of this, EU law did not preclude a refusal to grant the right of residence in such a situation, unless the authorities eventually concluded that the substance of rights of the EU minor citizens in this particular case was threatened.

In *Rendón Marín*, Mr. Rendón Marín, a Colombian national, was the sole carer of two minor children born and residing in Spain – a boy of Spanish

914 S. Coutts, above n. 18, p. 64.

915 See also K. Hyltén-Cavallius, 'Who Cares? Caregivers' Derived Residence Rights from Children in EU Free Movement Law' (2020) 57 *Common Market Law Review* 399, 419–20.

nationality and a girl of Polish nationality. He had a criminal record which was the basis of the refusal of his residence permit. During the proceedings, several Member States raised the possibility of Mr Rendón Marín going to Poland, the country of nationality of his daughter, which would not result in the departure of the children from the EU. In this case, the Court held that EU law must be interpreted as precluding national legislation which requires that a TCN, who is the parent of minor children who are Union citizens in his sole care, be automatically refused the grant of a residence permit on the sole grounds that he has a criminal record, where that refusal has the consequence of requiring those children to leave the territory of the European Union. The finding was heavily motivated by the lack of any individualised assessment of the case. Such an assessment would have to consider the fundamental rights of everyone involved and the children's best interests, as well as respecting the principle of proportionality.[916]

Both cases involved TCN parents who, due to the fact that (one of) the children possessed the nationality of another Member State, could derive the right to reside in that Member State. These matters constituted the axis of the judgments in both cases but led to different conclusions, although in both cases the Court confirmed the 'substance of rights' test known from *Ruiz Zambrano*. In *Alokpa*, the Court recognised that the substance of rights did not seem to be threatened. It was not disputable that the family unit could reside in France, which was the country of nationality of the children in question, even if they did not maintain any links to the country. Implicitly, the Court probably considered that Ms Alokpa speaks French and should not encounter integration difficulties in France beyond those that she experienced in Luxembourg. But the Court still emphasised that it is for the referring court to determine whether, in the light of all of the facts of the main proceedings, Ms Alokpa and the children can '*in fact*' (emphasis added) move to France, so they are not forced out of the Union.[917] The Advocate General in this case made an interesting remark that:

> in view of the geographical proximity of the two Member States concerned, a decision to remove the persons concerned from Luxembourg would not call into question Ms Alokpa's ability to accept the job offer made by a Luxembourg employer, since she could, for example, carry out her paid employment as a frontier worker, like thousands of other French residents.[918]

Ms Alokpa could be expected to move to France with her children, a state that is not too far from Luxembourg, from where Ms Alokpa could exercise her

[916] Case C-165/14, *Rendón Marín*, ECLI:EU:C:2016:675, para. 66.
[917] Case C-86/12, *Alokpa*, ECLI:EU:C:2013:645, para. 35.
[918] Opinion of the Advocate General in Case C-86/12, *Adzo Domenyo Alokpa and Others v Ministre du Travail, de l'Emploi et de l'Immigration*, ECLI:EU:C:2013:197, para. 57.

rights as an EU resident and work as a frontier worker, if she wishes to, as many others normally do. This 'normal' is implicitly present in the norm underlying the findings, with a reference both to the space of rights and the empirical reality of EU residents making use of this space.

In *Rendón Marín*, an automatic refusal of the residence permit was said to be unlawful if it led to the children leaving the territory of the Union. The Advocate General explicitly rejected (in a footnote!) the option of the family moving to Poland as existing only in the abstract,[919] as Mr Rendón Marín stated at the hearing that he has no ties with the family of his daughter's mother (who herself does not reside in Poland) and that he does not speak Polish. But the Court did not reject such an option, as a matter of protecting the children's interests, and drew attention to the need to assess the extent to which the family could '*in fact*' go to Poland 'in the light of all the circumstances of the main proceedings', taking into account Mr Rendón Marín's apprehension about doing so.[920] This was left for national courts to assess. Such an assessment necessitates respect of the right to private and family life, as laid down in Article 7 of the Charter, read in conjunction with the obligation to take into consideration the child's best interests, recognised in Article 24(2) of the Charter.[921]

Both *Alokpa* and *Rendón Marín* make clear that Member States cannot take decisions that would lead to children's (forced) departure from the European Union against their and their parents' will. However, where what is at stake is the possibility of the children moving to another Member State, such an option can be reasonably accepted, provided that national authorities conduct an individualised assessment and consider the situation of the family and the child's best interests. The assessment of whether a decision would lead to the children's departure from the Union is based on an assessment of *plausibility* of the move to another Member State. It cannot be excluded that, with their residence rights refused, Ms Alokpa or Mr Rendón Marín would decide to leave the EU altogether instead of moving to France or Poland respectively. While it is for national courts to assess such situations, all that courts can do is balance the probabilities of all the plausible options. Children have the right to stay at home, but – where multiple connections are given – they may make a home in different Member States, depending on what their interests dictate against the broader background of a particular case. The parent can be reasonably expected to move across the Union to secure their children's rights as one of the potential scenarios. Family life can plausibly, in principle, be conducted elsewhere in

[919] See fn. 109 of the Opinion in Case C-165/14, *Alfredo Rendón Marín v Administración del Estado*, ECLI:EU:C:2016:75.

[920] Case C-165/14, *Rendón Marín*, ECLI:EU:C:2016:675, para. 79.

[921] ibid., para. 81.

the Union[922] – not only as a matter of what individuals can expect from Member States, but also what Member States can at times expect from individuals. Cases regarding minor EU citizens and the residence rights of their carers reconceptualise not only the point of reference – the territory of the Union – but also the scope of reasonable expectations and obligations regarding the effective enjoyment of family rights in the Union.

6.3.3. PARENTAGE AND THE COSMOPOLITAN CHILD IN EU LAW

The *Ruiz Zambrano* cases discussed above already highlight, albeit implicitly, a particular normative vision of life in the EU space as worthy of protection. This vision emerges from the need to protect EU citizenship rights of minor citizens and, at the same time, grounds such rights. Another strand of case law that has significantly engaged with children's rights in recent years focuses on name registration, with cases like *Garcia Avello* and *Grunkin-Paul* being the prime examples.[923] In *Garcia Avello*, the children were of double nationality (Spanish and Belgian) and had their name registered in Belgium, according to its law, by the surname borne by their father, Mr Garcia Avello. However, they were also registered at the Spanish Embassy under the surname of Garcia Weber (Weber being the mother's last name) according to the Spanish tradition, and the parents wished to have this name recognised by Belgian authorities. The authorities refused as this was not in line with the Belgian legal tradition and there were otherwise insufficient grounds for the change. The CJEU found the refusal to be disproportionate by employing a combination of non-discrimination and free movement analyses based on (then) Articles 12 and 17 of the EC Treaty.

In *Grunkin-Paul*, a similar issue emerged, although with a different set of circumstances. In this case, the child born to German parents in Denmark had his double-barrelled name registered there. The child lived in Denmark with his mother and frequently travelled to Germany to see his father, where the parents subsequently wished to register his name as well. The parents themselves never used the name *Grunkin-Paul*, and the German authorities refused the registration as Germany does not allow for double-barrelled names for its own citizens. No discrimination could be found in this case, as all the individuals concerned were German citizens, but the Court nonetheless held that based on Articles 17 and 18(1) of the EC Treaty a Member State needs to allow a citizen

922 Case C-86/12, *Alokpa*, ECLI:EU:C:2013:645, paras. 34–35; Case C-165/14, *Rendón Marín*, ECLI:EU:C:2016:675, para. 79.

923 See also E. Pataut, above n. 14, p. 316.

of the European Union, whose name has been lawfully registered in another Member State, to have that name recognised under its own laws.

These two cases derived name registration entitlements from a somewhat different reasoning, but they were similar in the perception of the EU (minor) legal subject and its (future) scope of agency. The recognition of surnames became linked not only with freedom of movement, but also with the identity of EU citizens.[924] The identity and freedom of movement cannot, however, be fully separated. In both cases, the Court recognised the practical difficulties arising from bearing different surnames under different legal systems, e.g. regarding future educational qualification diplomas.[925] While the practical difficulties that the child 'is likely to encounter' may not stem from discrimination on grounds of nationality, they constitute a clear obstacle in exercising 'the status and rights of a citizen of the European Union'.[926] The considerations of the obstacles were, however, clearly bound with the mobility reasoning of EU law. The Belgian government argued in *Garcia Avello* that its decision promotes integration. But the Court rejected this argumentation and made it clear that their situation 'cannot be assessed in reference to the framework of only one national society' but needs to be reconstructed in the broader European context.[927] In *Grunkin-Paul*, this logic was extended to cases regarding not only dual nationality, but simply a transnational (mobile) life led between the state of nationality and the state of residence. The Advocate General in *Garcia Avello* argued that:

> [t]he concept of 'moving and residing freely in the territory of the Member States' is not based on the hypothesis of a single move from one Member State to another, to be followed by integration into the latter. The intention is rather to allow free, and possibly repeated or even continuous, movement within a single 'area of freedom, security and justice', in which both cultural diversity and freedom from discrimination are ensured.[928]

This account of children as holders of transnational autonomy is future-oriented and based on a particular normative vision of a cosmopolitan or cross-border life.[929] While the Court refers to the issue of inconvenience for the children in

924 ibid., p. 318.

925 Case C-148/02, *Garcia Avello*, ECLI:EU:C:2003:539, para. 36; Opinion of the Advocate General in Case C-148/02, *Garcia Avello*, ECLI:EU:C:2003:311, para. 56.

926 Case C-353/06, *Grunkin-Paul*, ECLI:EU:C:2008:559, paras. 54–56.

927 A. Iliopoulou Penot, 'The Transnational Character of Union Citizenship' in M. Dougan, N.N. Shuibhne and E. Spaventa (eds), *Empowerment and Disempowerment of the European Citizen*, Hart Publishing, Oxford 2012, pp. 19–20.

928 Opinion of the Advocate General in Case C-148/02, *Garcia Avello*, ECLI:EU:C:2003:311, para. 72.

929 See S. Coutts, above n. 18, pp. 32–33; D. Kostakopoulou, above n. 799, p. 6, describing EU citizenship as cosmopolitan in its orientation.

the case of future movement, this relies also on the concept of the children's multiple attachments to various Member States, be it based on their origin (nationality) or migration.[930] As observed in the literature, this 'transnational life with links to both countries and to some extent autonomous of at least one of their home states' not only becomes a basis on which EU protection is granted,[931] but also constitutes a 'symbolical expression of the process of EU integration'.[932]

The *Garcia Avello* case was criticised for differentiating between those linked with only one state and those who are connected to more than one Member State,[933] creating a new kind of reverse discrimination in reference to a separate cosmopolitan group of legal subjects.[934] Indeed, the case goes beyond non-discrimination insofar as it pushes towards not a right to be treated the same as Belgian nationals, but rather a right to be treated differently than the state's own citizens.[935] Caring for children with multiple attachments is seen as requiring not only their recognition as a matter of fact, but also the facilitation of their future (potential) cross-border links, leading to rights that go beyond what they would be entitled to without the transnational connection. This account of autonomy is relational insofar as the children's multinational links are presupposed by the linkages of their parents,[936] '[creating] a far wider web of eventual connections which could be utilized in the interest of the child'.[937] In *Garcia Avello*, it was the father's link to Spain and his freedom of movement rights; in *Grunkin-Paul* it was the parent's divergent residence and subsequent cross-border ties. The Advocate General recognised in *Garcia Avello* that 'clearly such an issue concerns both generations'.[938] Subsequently, drawing a connection between the issue of names and parentage, the Court noted that:

> it is common ground that, by reason in particular of the scale of migration within the Union … parentage cannot necessarily be assessed within the social life of a Member State solely on the basis of the criterion of the system applicable to nationals of that latter State.[939]

This illustrates again a normatively inflicted methodology of the CJEU where facts and norms reinforce each other in a particular way.

---

930 T. Petrova, above n. 794, p. 37.
931 S. Coutts, above n. 18, p. 33.
932 ibid., p. 76.
933 D. Chalmers, G. Davies and G. Monti, above n. 681, p. 487.
934 T. Petrova, above n. 794, p. 36.
935 D. Chalmers, G. Davies and G. Monti, above n. 681, p. 487; see also S. Coutts, above n. 18, pp. 32–33.
936 T. Petrova, above n. 794, p. 39.
937 ibid., p. 49.
938 Opinion of the Advocate General in Case C-148/02, *Garcia Avello*, ECLI:EU:C:2003:311, paras. 50–51.
939 Case C-148/02, *Garcia Avello*, ECLI:EU:C:2003:539, para. 42.

The considerations of multiple links of EU citizens cannot be separated from their familial backgrounds and transnational choices, and these go well beyond simple considerations of legal status. EU law puts forward also a particular account of the child as a contextual legal subject – one that becomes intertwined with freedom of movement and the territory of the EU as normative references. Regarding parentage, it remains an open question to what extent and in what contexts exactly 'parentage cannot … be assessed within the social life of a Member State', and what kind of adjustment this might require from Member States. What is, however, clear is that such an adjustment might be necessary, prompting a contextualisation in reference to a broader EU-wide space. The paragraphs in the following section clarify how such projections of EU law, taken together with the paradigms discussed above, can constitute a source of reconceptualisation pressures in the context of child relocation cases specifically.

6.3.4. DISCUSSION: DELOCALISING FAMILY LIFE?

The normatively inflicted contextualism discussed here has been thematised in three different strands of the ECJ jurisprudence that discuss doctrinally different issues. What they have in common, however, is that they touch upon family relationships and the rights of minor EU citizens. Because of their vulnerable position and the intertwining interests of parents and children, adjudicating these rights always requires the CJEU to make contextual judgments.[940] These constructions combine intimate relationships, broader social links, and EU law doctrinal interpretations in accounts that are at once descriptive and prescriptive, and, as such, normatively inflicted in both dimensions.[941] However, many of the cases discussed above touch upon public law, in particular regarding immigration matters – what do they mean for child relocation? The argument pursued here is *not* that the contextualisation of child relocation cases should or will look the same. It is explicitly not normative. It is argued rather that, from a constructivist perspective focused on legal subjects and their scope of autonomy, such constructions might not be entirely irrelevant also for very different areas of law. The three strands of the case law deal with family movement, both voluntary and involuntary, and normative considerations in cases involving children. If child relocation is placed within the EU legal context, this discursive and normative repertoire might intertwine with the construction of arguments in private disputes, even if only implicitly. The distinction between private and public is itself questionable, insofar as the public determines private opportunities, and private disadvantages spill over

---

940 L. Azoulai, above n. 26, p. 218.
941 ibid., pp. 209–11.

into public entitlements.[942] In family law – considered the core of private law – the distinction hides the degree to which state authorities may impose norms on family members.[943] Because of the conceptual distinction between the norm and the context, contextual elements at play in public cases involving decisions about family relationships might spill over into other (predominantly private) domains. This is true, in particular, as the exact shape of EU legal obligations in such contexts remains unclear, pushing national actors to anticipate and navigate them independently.

The discussion above shows, first, that the European legal subject carries the expectation that he or she can move and do so with their family. The fact that such expectations are held by EU citizens seems to be confirmed by the existing, albeit scarce, empirical research.[944] Discursively, this has long been captured by the CJEU not in terms of residence rights, but in terms of the right to *lead a normal family life*. This right is, by definition, relational: it encompasses the right of the parent to have the child accompany him or her across the Union, and the right of the child to accompany the parent. These rights are, as already discussed in reference to the Citizens' Rights Directive, not unlimited. Child abduction provisions clearly require that the exercise of freedom of movement in the family context takes place according to national family law rules.[945] A desirability of a particular familial arrangement might also not be enough to grant any particular rights.[946] However, as a matter of EU law, relocation with a child 'represents the legitimate exercise, by the mother with custody of the child, of her own right of freedom of movement, established in Article 20(2)(a) TFEU and Article 21(1) TFEU'.[947] The exercise of such rights is in principle not 'subject of proof of any interest whatsoever'.[948] Family life is, and should be, portable

---

[942] N. Lacey, 'Feminist Legal Theory and the Rights of Women' in K. Knop (ed), *Gender and Human Rights*, Oxford University Press, Oxford 2004, pp. 21–22.

[943] N. Rose, 'Beyond the Public/Private Division: Law, Power and the Family' (1987) 14 *Journal of Law and Society* 61, 66, 74; A. Diduck, above n. 88. See also H.-W. Micklitz, 'Rethinking the Public/Private Divide' in M. Maduro, K. Tuori and S. Sankari (eds), *Transnational Law: Rethinking European Law and Legal Thinking*, Cambridge University Press, Cambridge 2014.

[944] S. Morano-Foadi, above n. 273, 17.

[945] Discursively, CJEU judges seem to be cautious about going beyond technicalities of the Brussels II*bis* (now II*ter*) Regulation in preliminary references on children's matters. This might naturally be because the preliminary questions touch upon such technicalities predominantly. However, other EU law cases – such as, for example, Case C-34/09, *Ruiz Zambrano*, ECLI:EU:C:2011:124 – often go in their discursive layer far beyond what is strictly necessary. When the CJEU judges are faced with more fundamental questions in the context of family matters, they tend to emphasise the limits of the Court's competences and use language that reflects such limits. See, for example, Case C-400/10 PPU, *J. McB. v L. E.*, ECLI:EU:C:2010:582.

[946] e.g. Case C-457/12, *S and G*, ECLI:EU:C:2014:136, paras. 43–44.

[947] Case C-400/10 PPU, *J. McB. v L. E.*, ECLI:EU:C:2010:582, para. 58; see also View of the Advocate General in Case C-400/10 PPU, *J. McB. v L. E.*, ECLI:EU:C:2010:544, para. 69.

[948] Case C-459/20, *X v Staatssecretaris van Justitie en Veiligheid*, ECLI:EU:C:2023:499, para. 40.

across the Union as a matter of individual free movement rights, unless there is an important reason to limit its exercise.

The difficulty of relocation cases lies, however, not in the problem of the state refusing such portability of normal family life per se. The state does not limit a voluntary movement of the child due to some administrative obstacle, but rather steps in to prevent – at least in the view of the non-relocating parent – an involuntary move that might endanger the child's best interests. A dilemma emerges, therefore, regarding how to shape the new normal family life considering this EU law portability. From a child-centred perspective, normal family life has two components corresponding to arrangements with two parents. According to the dominant conceptualisation of relocation disputes, the normal can endure only if relocation is refused, and only if one can reasonably expect the relocating parent to give up the move (in which case the stay can, in principle, become involuntary). But this conceptualisation has a very strong localising component that binds family life to a particular place. Once it is assumed that family life is portable, there is no reason why child relocation cases could not be reconceptualised with the territory of the Union being the point of reference. This paradigm does not mean that the logic of portability should prevail over other factors, as there is a plethora of circumstances that might speak in favour of preserving the child's residence in a particular place. Nor does the paradigm offer a direct suggestion as to how arrangements for children should be *normally* shaped. But it does suggest that, if one understands normal family life as the status quo that should be protected, this status quo might be understood less as where, and more as how. This is a normative push towards an expectation that care arrangements, once formed, should not easily be disrupted only because of the move – and can rightfully claim some priority when disputes arise.[949]

Second, relocation cases are commonly conceptualised as a conflict, between freedom of movement and contact rights, that needs to be resolved in the child's best interests. In some jurisdictions, however, the disputes have been reconceptualised following recognition that the issue of freedom of movement applies to both parents, since the converse of the freedom to move is the freedom to stay.[950] If a court's task is to find the best solution for a given child, the court should explore ways in which all interests can be reconciled, including the option that the non-resident parent could relocate as well.[951] In the EU context, Ruth Lamont observes that, due to the clear focus of EU law on the right of free

949 Compare R. Leckey, above n. 57, p. 269, discussing the normatively inflicted contextual methodology in reference to a Canadian child relocation case, *Gordon v Goertz* [1996] 2 S.C.R. 27: 'when assessing an application to vary a custody order, should the total context be assessed afresh, or can the status quo rightfully claim some priority?'.

950 P. Parkinson, above n. 210, p. 165.

951 ibid., pp. 169–71.

movement, a corresponding 'right to stay' has not been articulated, and hence chooses to focus her analysis solely on free movement.[952] At the same time, the rights of 'stayers' in EU law, while indeed less visible on the EU level, have received some attention in the academic literature.[953] As freedom of movement encompasses more and more positive rights, the right to stay *in a particular part of the EU* gets weakened in favour of a supranational right to stay, together with the transformation of the space of reference from a state to the EU itself.[954] This concerns individual rights, but also family relationships – including those enjoyed by children and their parents in cases such as *Alokpa* or *Rendón Marín* – and, as such, this normative climate might prompt a reconceptualisation of child relocation.

Doctrinally, expulsion cases are governed by a different rationale from relocation disputes, but relocation cases have been, at times, conceptualised as their 'obverse side'.[955] In the context of intra-EU mobility, the broader supranational paradigms might, however, obscure these differences. When competing interests are at stake, the state can, at times, expect individuals to move or allow them to stay, and vice versa. In EU law, this has been observed to 'subtly' affect the positive obligation attached to the right to stay, 'understood as the obligation to secure the effective enjoyment of this right', rather than its negative side (the right not to be expelled).[956] In other words, the concept of the territoriality of the Union and the equivalence of legal spaces are functionally related to a paradigm that EU mobility is not only occurring, but should also be possible for most individuals.[957] This process takes place not exclusively on the level of rights, but on the level of the construction of normative justifications for the individuals' contextual embedding, including their relationships. Cases like *Alokpa* and *Rendón Marín* are as much about residence rights as they are about what can be reasonably expected from a parent if children's rights and interests are to be protected.

The weakening process of the national right to stay is subject to much criticism. This criticism is justified insofar as it weakens the rights of

952 R. Lamont, above n. 12, 240.

953 e.g. S. Iglesias Sánchez, above n. 876, p. 372. The literature is usually critical and argues that the rights of the 'stayers' should be taken seriously.

954 ibid., p. 377.

955 J. Eekelaar, 'The Role of the Best Interests Principle in Decisions Affecting Children and Decisions about Children', above n. 146, 9. Eekelaar is critical of such conceptualisation, as it focuses on the child only indirectly as the question in extradition cases is about the parent. However, as the discussion above indicates, in EU law the question is often predominantly about the child – the EU citizen – and therefore, the cases have been conceptualised, to some extent, differently. Additionally, child relocation disputes in the context of EU law also become, to a big extent, disputes about parental rights. This EU conceptualisation allows one, therefore, to depart from Eekelaar's criticism on a purely conceptual level, notwithstanding any normative assessment of such developments.

956 S. Iglesias Sánchez, above n. 876, p. 380.

957 ibid., pp. 380–87.

individuals versus EU Member States in a design that aims to promote equality and enhance the living conditions of citizens.[958] This objective suffers when states can factually force EU citizens out of their territories against their will. However, it might be less controversial if treated as a contextual ground for the balancing of individual rights and expectations, or expanding the scope of scenarios that can be considered in the child's best interests in some child relocation cases.[959] If EU citizens are subjects of European integration not only vertically, but also horizontally – in relation to other citizens – it can also lead to a recalibration of reasonable mutual expectations, if only as a matter of legal constructions. Naturally, mobility is not an end in itself, and free movement can only be based on free choice – which entails the right not to move.[960] A state cannot force its own citizens out any more than it can 'zone [them] in'.[961] But in a relocation context, the possibility of zoning parents in is regularly under scrutiny in a way that the option for the other parent to move is not. EU law might allow for a reorientation of legitimate expectations and legitimate sacrifices and push towards bringing both choices – to move and not to move – under the same scrutiny.

Such a normative push could lead to a change in how national courts approach relocation disputes, but this change could be less radical than immediately expected. Bringing both choices under the same scrutiny would mean investigating the possibility of the non-relocating parent moving to the same degree as the relocating parent staying. However, the investigation can be constructed in various ways: only if such options are raised or as a matter of abstract probabilities, or as the assumption that the relocating parent goes and the other parent stays. The actual starting point is different in all these scenarios. In many cases, there will be good reasons why a parent does not want to, or cannot be expected to, move. Rather, unless the child's particular needs and interests require otherwise (which will often be the case given the broader circumstances), neither the move nor the stay should a priori be considered default. As Member States are obliged to make the exercise of relational rights possible across the whole territory of the Union, relationships can be, in principle, maintained throughout it. In other words, while the dominant conceptualisation of child relocation disputes rests on the juxtaposition of freedom of movement

958 ibid., pp. 389–92.

959 In Chapter 5, above Section 5.5., it was noted that the pool of solutions to be considered in relocation cases is not universally defined. Different approaches adopted in different Member States interact differently with EU law on freedom of movement. While it is unlikely that the CJEU would take a stand on such matters, as being outside EU competence, it is not unimaginable that the conceptual interactions with EU law taking place on national levels might exert subtle pressures on national law and eventually lead to doctrinal developments redefining this pool of options.

960 S. Iglesias Sánchez, above n. 876, p. 388.

961 A.B. LaFrance, above n. 189, 71.

and contact rights as in conflict, reconceptualisation under the EU paradigm would imply a juxtaposition of freedom of movement and the right to stay. The scope of parental agency and the scope of parental obligation would go hand in hand, be rooted in the territory of the whole Union, and subjected to the child's best interests assessment.[962] The EU paradigm would not, however, provide any guidelines as to how to balance these rights in individual cases.

Lastly, it goes without saying that child relocation cases should be resolved according to the child's best interests principle. In some cases, the child may have an opinion about the desired outcome or other aspects of the dispute that will help with the interests assessment. In many others, the conceptualisation of what is in the child's interests in relocation will remain challenging. While the decision might be reached on the balancing of the parents' autonomy interests related to their visions of a good life, children often have not yet developed their own definitive vision of autonomy or of a good life that could be drawn into the process.[963] Such a vision will need to be (re-)constructed based on the child's views ascertained by the court and complemented, where necessary, by other considerations. This is so because the best interest assessment necessarily draws from such points of reference, be that explicit or implicit. In this context, it has been suggested that it is the right to an open future that is the autonomy counterpart on the side of the child and that should be accounted for by the court.[964] Such autonomy rights in EU law, based on the contextual justifications put forward by the Court, translate into a particular version of the right to an open future, one that needs to take into account the children's cross-border links and EU mobility. The CJEU does not, naturally, have any power over arrangements made for individual children in family law. But there is an important communicative layer to these judgments that goes beyond the doctrine. The choice of where a child lives often gets bundled together with cultural considerations and future opportunities, in particular as parents come from different national or cultural backgrounds. The EU clearly projects a vision

---

962 This last point is particularly emphasised in Case C-133/15, *Chavez-Vilchez*, ECLI:EU:C:2017:354, para. 71, where the Court made a direct reference to the quality of care and its relevance for the best interests assessment in the context of EU law: 'the fact that the other parent, who is a Union citizen, is actually able and willing to assume sole responsibility for the primary day-to-day care of the child is a relevant factor, but it is not in itself a sufficient ground for a conclusion that there is not, between the third-country national parent and the child, such a relationship of dependency that the child would indeed be so compelled were there to be such a refusal of a right of residence. Such an assessment must take into account, in the best interests of the child concerned, all the specific circumstances, including the age of the child, the child's physical and emotional development, the extent of his emotional ties both to the Union citizen parent and to the third-country national parent, and the risks which separation from the latter might entail for the child's equilibrium'.

963 J. Herring and R. Taylor, above n. 10, 531.

964 ibid.; see also J. Millum, above n. 197.

in which the possibility to lead a transnational life is at least a plausible (if not desirable) choice also for children.

This is a component that brings the assessment closer to cultural considerations in child custody disputes.[965] In most cultural disputes, 'we cannot say whether it is better for a child to be brought up in one culture rather than in another, or whether it is better to assimilate into one culture rather than to maintain links with more than one culture',[966] which epitomises the difficulties of future-oriented assessments experienced by courts also in relocation disputes. This is not to suggest (nor accuse) that national courts should engage in any type of social engineering. Of course, individual cases should be resolved in the interests of a given child and courts should not adopt solutions that are detrimental to children (or against their wishes) in the name of a particular vision of a good life in the future.[967] But according to the EU paradigm, national authorities owe respect to those who might want to (or need to, due to their multinational links) build a transnational life in the future, even if such a possibility for a child emerges only due to their parents' backgrounds or choices. Whether normatively desirable in this context or not, the whole legal infrastructure of the EU is built with such a future in mind, delocalising both the individual and familial lives of EU citizens. There is, of course, much nuance to this assertion. Normative decisions made to this effect in EU law more often than not protect voluntary movement (and related decisions) against restrictions emerging from the national level. The set of questions posed by child relocation cases in national law is more complex as they bring issues of voluntary and involuntary movement together, with the assessment of the interests of an individual child at the centre of each dispute. However, the judgments of EU law are derived from a particular normatively inflicted methodology that is employed in connection with the normativity embedded in each legal doctrine. In that, different (also national) doctrines do not have to generate the same normative results, but the methodology applied can nevertheless open them up to new contextual considerations.

6.4. CONCLUDING REMARKS

Seen from this perspective, it becomes clear that EU law – with its mobility infrastructures, normatively inflicted methodologies, and their contextual

965 J. Eekelaar, 'Children Between Cultures' (2004) 18 *International Journal of Law, Policy and the Family* 178. See also L. Albertus and J. Sloth-Nielsen, 'Relocation Decisions: Do Culture, Language and Religion Matter in the Rainbow Nation?' (2010) 1 *Journal of Family Law and Practice* 86.

966 J. Eekelaar, above n. 965, 187.

967 ibid.

constructions – might influence legal issues outside of its doctrinal reach, including child relocation law. This is perhaps no longer surprising at large, but rarely conceptualised in detail in family law. The European space of rights has grown over the years and has very tangible consequences for the legal and factual conditions in which cross-border mobility of parents and their children takes place. Its value is clear given the future-oriented nature of child relocation cases. However, there is also more to its normative power. The mobility infrastructure of EU law is justified in reference to a social context in which movement becomes an everyday reality. It is based on mutual trust, but also co-constructs this normative paradigm of the ASFJ. It creates conditions of certainty and stability, but these are also normatively inflicted by the broader objectives of the EU. In that, the contextual and normative layers of EU law intertwine, capable of exerting subtle pressures on national approaches to the evaluation of the social-normative equilibrium of family law cases, and hence on the assessments of the best interests of the child as well. Within the legal infrastructures, EU law takes a normative stance on European citizens' relationships and reasonable scopes of autonomy, built upon their perceived expectations and life-worlds. As shown, these constructions concern both individual rights – including those of minor EU citizens – and family relationships. When family life is discussed, the reorientation of the point of reference towards the whole territory of the EU prompts an expectation that EU citizens may move with their family, but, at the same time, might at times be reasonably expected to move for their family. This has consequences for what kind of familial choices Member States might need to accommodate. In that, EU law might influence national law not only where it applies and is taken into account in its own right, but also where it is taken as a particular context of a case, or where EU-conditioned interests are subsumed under open-ended assessments or balancing exercises conducted in reference to the child's best interests principle. Such influence of EU law is not necessarily reducible to its individual elements, but rather reveals the broader nature of EU law both as a normative power and a constructive resource.

What remains somehow surprising, however, is that the normatively inflicted methodologies of EU law and their contextual constructions can produce effects more complex than their 'internal market imperative[s]'.[968] EU law's contextual judgments, even if subtle, are hardly neutral from the point of view of national family law, but, at the same time, necessarily encounter family laws' own methodologies and normative commitments. The methodological overlaps between EU law and child relocation law can, therefore, be hypothesised to be capable of producing varying effects, some more normatively justifiable than others. As discussed, they can validate the

[968] H. Stalford, above n. 17, p. 226.

relocating parent's autonomy claims and draw attention to the qualitatively different contexts in which mobile EU citizens might organise their lives, but they might also bear the danger of generalisations of children's interests or create de facto presumptions in favour of the move. However, perhaps paradoxically, they could be employed in the child's best interests, broadening the scope of options that might be or need to be considered by the court deciding on relocation, such as mobility of the non-relocating parent. While one can disagree on the normative desirability of these developments, the increasing attention to this factor in some jurisdictions clearly shows that such considerations are not inherently foreign to family law. EU law's methodologies could be mobilised by national actors for similar purposes. However, the viability of these interactions remains an open question.

The contextuality applied by the CJEU or instrumentalised by the EU legislator can clearly constitute a form of EU law's influence, seen from a constructivist perspective. However, this conceptual discussion does not presuppose that they have immediate consequences for national child relocation law in an empirical sense. Due to the lack of competence in family law, the EU may not have the capacity to enforce this contextualism in any useful sense.[969] In light of the constructivist nature of the analysis, it is also not a given that the EU influences discussed here exhaust all possible conceptualisations of the European(ised) legal subject or of the mutual interplay between national and European law. Under such circumstances, the normative constructions of EU law might be projected onto national laws, but it will still be up to national courts to 'act and think European'.[970] However, with national judges being also European judges, it cannot be a priori excluded that the normatively inflicted methodology governing the latter will not interplay with national child relocation laws. EU law might provide a useful normative reference to address certain tensions in national doctrines. If engagement with EU-driven normative methodologies and contextual constructions can indeed be observed in national legal systems, one must be, therefore, particularly vigilant about how these are employed, how they interplay with methodologies of national laws, and what kind of normative effects they produce. The following chapter attempts to answer these questions about the real-life impacts of EU law on child relocation cases on a national level, drawing from case law in three European jurisdictions: England and Wales, Germany, and Poland. In that, it explores the nature and scope of Europeanisation of child relocation law sensu stricto.

---

[969] See, e.g. L. Azoulai, above n. 26, p. 223; D. Chalmers, 'The Persona of EU Law' in L. Azoulai, S. Barbou des Places and E. Pataut (eds), *Constructing the Person in EU Law: Rights, Roles, Identities*, Hart Publishing, Oxford 2016, p. 96.

[970] This expression is taken from E. Dubout, above n. 565, p. 210.

CHAPTER 7

CHILD RELOCATION AND NATIONAL ENCOUNTERS WITH EU LAW

7.1. INTRODUCTION

Europeanisation in family law, as a background metaconcept, has been understood and explored in many ways. Typically, it is perceived as a process of convergence driven by EU harmonisation of certain family law matters or a form of compliance with EU law obligations set out by the CJEU (the so-called 'judicial Europeanisation').[971] What the first explains are the dynamics and outcomes of European law-making, while the second focuses on the scope of legal pressures coming from Luxembourg and subsequent adjustments on the national level. The book has already discussed cross-border child relocation in reference to both understandings, but neither can reveal much about the actual domestic effects of EU law on cross-border child relocation law *at the present time*. This is so because there is no EU legislation and no CJEU judgment on child relocation, and hence the nature and scope of any adaptational pressures remain unclear. This state of legal uncertainty creates simultaneously an opportunity to draw from EU law and a chance to 'escape' any perceived legal pressures.[972] The previous chapter demonstrates, at the same time, that the influence of EU law might have a much more complex nature than its doctrinal obligations. In particular, the normatively inflicted methodology of EU law and its contextual constructions might provide relevant reference points for cases where EU mobility can constitute a legally relevant context. In that, the ways in which domestic actors engage with EU law and their patterns of adaptation might also be more complex than a simple adjustment to the 'internal market imperative'.[973] The EU legal framework might be perceived by national actors as exerting legal pressures and requiring a reorientation of national doctrines. The EU might also be used constructively to contextualise

---

971 See W. Pintens, 'Europeanisation of Family Law' in K. Boele-Woelki (ed), *Perspectives for the Unification and Harmonisation of Family Law in Europe*, Intersentia, Oxford 2003 and the discussion in Chapter 1.

972 See S.K. Schmidt, above n. 73.

973 H. Stalford, above n. 17, p. 226.

legal interpretations, legitimise certain outcomes and reorient the scope of what is possible or plausible both in terms of contextual constructions and legal argumentations. Therefore, Europeanisation sensu stricto strongly depends on the particularities of national law which create unique grounds for facing the constraints and opportunities of EU law.[974] This chapter adopts a bottom-up approach and investigates the nature of such domestic encounters with the EU and EU law.

The chapter raises three interrelated questions. First, how do national courts engage with EU law in child relocation cases, if at all? Second, what is said about Europe or EU citizens, how and why, and what does it reveal about implicit normative assumptions carried by such discursive representations? And finally, do these encounters affect legal doctrines and/or outcomes of the cases, and how? These questions are investigated in reference to both their doctrinal dimensions (references to primary and secondary EU law and the use of the CJEU jurisprudence, if any) and their contextual dimensions (discursive interstices of the judgments that construct legal subjects and their relevant social contexts in reference to the EU or EU law). From this perspective, Europeanisation can encompass not only references to EU law, but also constructive reconfigurations of the contextual methodology applied in child relocation cases. Seen in this light, EU law might or might not become a meaningful frame of reference for national law, and Europeanisation might or might not lead to convergence. The analysis takes place in close attention to national legal doctrines on child relocation, juxtaposed together for a better understanding of different dynamics of Europeanisation. It encompasses child relocation cases and discussions in three European jurisdictions: England and Wales; Germany; and Poland. The selection of the jurisdictions and respective research materials was discussed in Chapter 1, with particular attention given to the choice to include England and Wales in the comparison despite Brexit. The jurisdictions are discussed one by one, in sequence, as the discussion of each jurisdiction follows its own structure to best reflect and contextualise relevant findings. They are then discussed in comparison, drawing attention to how Europeanisation is conditioned by the gaps and tensions within national legal doctrines at relevant times.

7.2. ENGLAND AND WALES

Child relocation in England and Wales has been extensively analysed in the literature[975] and constitutes an important point of reference for global

---

974 S.K. Schmidt, above n. 73, 300.

975 For an extensive overview see, e.g. R. George, above n. 11, pp. 25–57.

discussions on the topic. What is of particular interest here, as already noted, is that English statutory law differentiates between internal and international relocations. Internal relocations are not subject to statutory restrictions and, as such, are not generally prohibited. They can, however, raise issues regarding the contact or other child's arrangements in force, requiring an agreement of both parents or a decision of the court, and can additionally be restricted by a prohibited steps order.[976] The law on international relocation, on the other hand, is statutorily governed by Section 13 of the Children Act 1989. Where a child arrangements order[977] is in force with respect to a child, no person may remove the child from the UK without either the written consent of every person who has parental responsibility for the child or the leave of the court, unless the removal is for less than one month. Section 1(1) of the Children Act specifies that the welfare of the child is the paramount consideration.[978] The statute specifies how to approach the assessment with a welfare checklist set out in Section 1(3) of the Children Act. The court should have regard, in particular, to the following factors:

(a) the ascertainable wishes and feelings of the child concerned (considered in the light of his age and understanding);
(b) his physical, emotional and educational needs;
(c) the likely effect on him of any change in his circumstances;
(d) his age, sex, background and any characteristics of his which the court considers relevant;
(e) any harm which he has suffered or is at risk of suffering;
(f) how capable each of his parents, and any other person in relation to whom the court considers the question to be relevant, is of meeting his needs;
(g) the range of powers available to the court in the proceedings in question.[979]

While this brief description of the current legal framework already demonstrates some particularities of the law in comparison with other jurisdictions, it is the historical development of the doctrine that allows a

976 ibid., pp. 28–29, 46–49. See also the discussion below.

977 A child arrangements order regulates, in particular, the arrangements concerning with whom the child is to live and/or when the child is to live with any person.

978 See, for example, *Re C (Internal Relocation)* [2015] EWCA Civ 1305, para. 51, where it was said that: 'There is no doubt that it is the welfare principle in section 1 (1) of the [Children Act] which dictates the result in internal relocation cases, just as it is now acknowledged that it does in external relocation cases'.

979 For a discussion of the law applicable to international child relocation see, e.g. *Re C (A Child)* [2019] EWHC 131 (Fam), paras. 15 and 16, emphasising the relevance of the welfare checklist in international relocations. See also *Re F (A Child) (International Relocation Cases)* [2015] EWCA Civ 882; *K v K (Relocation: Shared Care Arrangement)* [2011] EWCA Civ 793; and *Re C (Internal Relocation)* [2015] EWCA Civ 1305.

full appreciation of those features of the law that have created (or closed) opportunities to encounter EU law.

The first truly significant development of modern English relocation law was *Poel v Poel*, decided in 1970.[980] The mother, the primary carer of the child, wished to emigrate to New Zealand with her new husband with whom she was expecting another child. The father, on the other hand, had weekly contact with the child and opposed the move. The key aspect of the reasoning in *Poel* was that an interference with the reasonable decisions of the primary carer would likely bring repercussions for the child that would be more adverse than the loss of contact. Despite an initial mixed reception, this approach became the leading authority in the years to follow:

> What Sachs LJ was saying [in *Poel*], I think, is that if the court interferes with the way of life which the custodial parent is proposing to adopt so that he or she and the new spouse are compelled to adopt a manner of life which they do not want, and reasonably do not want, the likelihood is that the frustrations and bitterness which would result from such an interference with any adult whose career is at stake would be bound to overflow on to the children. ... Consequently, in ordinary sensible human terms the court should not do something which is, prima facie, unreasonable unless there is some compelling reason to the contrary.[981]

The approach developed in *Poel*, and employed in subsequent cases, emphasised that reasonable plans to relocate internationally should not be stopped lightly, as the primary carer's wellbeing and the stability of the new family unit were important factors in promoting the child's welfare. Discursively, opting for relocation was framed as being a component of choosing a way of life, and hence an aspect of the autonomy of the residential parent and their (new) family. As *Poel* proved to be influential, notwithstanding the controversies,[982] this could have opened, in the years to follow, the doors to discursively frame relocation not only as *a* way of life in general, but as a *European* way of life in particular – drawing from the normative discourses flowing from the EU (regardless of any desirability of such a development). The following sections demonstrate that the potential foundation for such framing was laid in *Payne v Payne*, decided in 2001, which became the then-leading case in relocation, but the development of the doctrine eventually followed a different path.

---

980 *Poel v Poel* [1970] 1 WLR 1469. See the analysis in R. George, above n. 11, pp. 31–33. See also R. Taylor, 'Poels Apart: Fixed Principles and Shifting Values in Relocation Law' in S. Gilmore, J. Herring and R. Probert (eds), *Landmark Cases in Family Law*, Hart Publishing, Oxford 2011, for a discussion of this case in particular.

981 *Chamberlain v de la Mare* [1983] 4 FLR 434 (CA), 442–43.

982 See M. Hayes, above n. 444, 352, who notices that some contemporary cases continue to make references to the decision.

7.2.1. *PAYNE v PAYNE* AND THE FIRST ENCOUNTERS WITH THE EU

Payne v Payne was a relocation dispute following abduction proceedings that ended in the child's return to England. The mother wished to return home to New Zealand with her four-year-old child while the father strongly opposed the move, given his close relationship with the child. Leave was granted to the mother, but the father appealed, claiming that the approach adopted by English courts in relocation cases amounts to a presumption in favour of the move and, as such, is contrary to the child's best interests principle and human rights. The court in *Payne* rejected any presumptions, but also took the view that discussing relocation in terms of presumptions is mistaken.[983] Summarising the law, the judge noted that:

> relocation cases have been consistently decided upon the application of the following two propositions:
>
> (a) the welfare of the child is the paramount consideration; and
> (b) refusing the primary carer's reasonable proposals for the relocation of her family life is likely to impact detrimentally on the welfare of her dependent children. Therefore her application to relocate will be granted unless the court concludes that it is incompatible with the welfare of the children.[984]

While explicitly rejecting presumptions, this conclusion was seen by many as a de facto presumption itself.[985] The judge formulated guidelines for child relocation that emphasised the welfare of the child as the paramount consideration in any application but drew attention to broader contextual factors. How genuine and realistic is the relocation application? How genuine is the opposition to the move and what is the extent of detriment to the relationship between the child and the parent? What would be the detrimental impact of the refusal on the relocating parent?[986] As a result, the pro-relocation stance of English law was said to be strengthened.

While important for the development of the relocation doctrine in England in general, *Payne* is particularly interesting for the investigation of

---

983 *Payne v Payne* [2001] EWCA Civ 166, [2001] 1 FLR 1052 (CA), paras. 25–26.

984 ibid., para. 26.

985 R. George, above n. 11, p. 38; M. Hayes, above n. 444, 356.

986 *Payne v Payne* [2001] EWCA Civ 166, [2001] 1 FLR 1052 (CA), paras. 40–41. See, however, paras. 85–86 of the judgment where another judge sitting on the case, Butler-Sloss P, rephrased the guidelines in a different manner that was suggested to be the main source of guidance in some subsequent cases, e.g. *Re D (Leave to Remove: Appeal)* [2010] EWCA Civ 50. However, it was the discipline quoted above that dominated the approach in subsequent years – see R. George, above n. 11, p. 40.

the Europeanisation of relocation law, as it explicitly located child relocation within the European legal context in more than one way. In *Payne*, the appealing father asserted that the English approach was incompatible with the subsequent entry into force of the Human Rights Act 1998 incorporating the European Convention on Human Rights into the British legal system. However, while the judges recognised that Convention rights stemming from Articles 6 (right to a fair trial) and 8 (right to family life) might be engaged, they took the view that the Convention does not ask for another approach to child relocation.[987] Fundamentally, both English law and the Convention were said to require taking the child's welfare as the paramount consideration, with the focus on supporting the reasonable proposal of the primary carer as no more than an important factor in its holistic assessment.[988] As such, 'each member of the fractured family has rights to assert and that in balancing them the court must adhere to the paramountcy of the welfare principle'.[989] This approach seems to have forejudged the matter and was not subsequently questioned. English courts frequently refer to Article 8 of the ECHR, noting that in most cases there will be *an* infringement of the Convention rights and the court should conduct a proportionality assessment.[990] At the same time, domestic and European jurisprudence were said to cumulatively lead to the same principles.[991] This conclusion now seems to

---

987 *Payne v Payne* [2001] EWCA Civ 166, [2001] 1 FLR 1052 (CA), para. 57: 'the advent of the Human Rights Act 1998 … requires no re-evaluation of the judge's primary task to evaluate and uphold the welfare of the child as the paramount consideration, despite its inevitable conflict with adult rights'. For a critique of this approach see A. Bainham, 'Taking Children Abroad: Human Rights, Welfare and the Courts' (2001) 60 *Cambridge Law Journal* 489, 492. See also J. Herring and R. Taylor, above n. 10.

988 *Payne v Payne* [2001] EWCA Civ 166, [2001] 1 FLR 1052 (CA), paras. 37–45.

989 ibid., para. 37; *Re H (Children: Relocation)* [2019] EWHC 2881 (Fam), para. 4, quoting *Re C (A Child)* [2019] EWHC 131 (Fam), para. 15: 'There remains some degree of uncertainty as to how the proportionality evaluation is to be applied in relocation cases. In *Re F* it was said one should be undertaken, In *Re Y* [2015] 1 FLR 1350 it was said in private law cases it doesn't need to be, The Court of Appeal in *Re C (Internal Relocation)* expressed doubts about how it was to be undertaken. I consider that in most cases in practice the proportionality issue will be subsumed within the overall holistic evaluation in particular when considering effect of change and risk of harm'.

990 See, e.g. *Re VB & LB (Children)* [2022] EWFC 60, *SB v M* [2021] EWFC 49, or the internal relocation case *Ms D v Mr D* [2022] EWFC 164.

991 In *E (Female Genital Mutilation and Permission to Remove)* [2016] EWHC 1052 (Fam), 'domestic and European jurisprudence' was said to cumulatively lead to the following principles: (1) recognition that it is almost always in the child's interests to have contact with both parents; (2) the state has a positive obligation to protect contact as a fundamental element of family life; (3) the court must take both a medium-term and long-term view to facilitate contact; (4) the child's best interests remain the paramount consideration, and the reduction in contact will not necessarily lead to the conclusion that permission to remove should be refused. English judges noted also other developments of international law on relocation, namely the Washington Declaration. It was seen as an interesting development that may become a foundation for future reform, insofar as it advocated a more balanced and neutral non-presumptive approach. However, at that moment it had no binding effect and as

be confirmed by the ECtHR decision in *J.A.T v J.B.T*,[992] but no English judgment in the sample mentions this development.

More importantly, *Payne v Payne* was also the first judgment to mention relocation cases in the context of freedom of movement as protected both by the ECHR and EU law:[993]

> This right [parent's right to determine their place of residence] was recognised by the decision of this court in *Re E (Imposition of Conditions)* [1997] 2 FLR 638 within the confines of the jurisdiction of the court and indeed beyond within the United Kingdom. But why should the same right not extend to anywhere within the European Union (having regard to Article 48 of the Treaty of Rome) or, beyond that, within wider Europe? From that point to a right to world-wide mobility seems but a short step. The European Convention does specifically recognise this right of mobility in Article 2 of Protocol 4. … Although Protocol 4 has yet to be ratified by the United Kingdom, it undoubtedly lends force to the argument that a failure or refusal to recognise a right of mobility beyond the somewhat fortuitous jurisdictional boundary represents a stance of disproportionate parochialism.[994]

This excerpt clearly links the right to mobility with the scope of autonomy of the resident parent. However, the observation was used primarily to demonstrate that each member of the family has rights to assert, and it is the welfare of the child that should be decisive.[995] EU law was not analysed beyond the mention of Article 48 of the Treaty of Rome (freedom of movement for workers), most likely as the dispute concerned a relocation to New Zealand. One can observe, however, that the court recognised a certain gradation of the scope of autonomy in reference to mobility rights within different (legal and geographical) spaces. This did not, however, immediately result in a fundamentally different normative assessment, rather providing a stepping stone towards an argument in favour of mobility rights in general.

Despite its scarce engagement with EU law, *Payne* raised, therefore, the broader question of justification behind differentiation between internal and external relocations. Interviews with practitioners conducted by Rob George revealed that some saw this as a positive aspect of the case in light of the general

---

such did not lead to a change in the approach. In other cases, the conclusion reached was said to be the same, whatever the path followed. See also *Re H (A Child)* [2010] EWCA Civ 915; *Re AR (A Child: Relocation)* [2010] EWHC 1346 (Fam); *Re H (A Child)* [2010] EWCA Civ 789.

992 *J.A.T. and J.B.T. v United Kingdom* (dec) [2012] ECtHR, app. no. 41767/11.

993 The first English article on EU freedom of movement and child relocation, T. Scott, above n. 12, was published in 1999, two years before the judgment in *Payne v Payne* [2001] EWCA Civ 166, but it does not seem to have been taken up in any subsequent scholarly articles.

994 *Payne v Payne* [2001] EWCA Civ 166, [2001] 1 FLR 1052 (CA), paras. 36–37.

995 ibid., para. 37.

lack of restrictions on relocation within the UK, considering, in particular, the fact that internal travels could often be longer than international ones.[996] This assessment, while having a clear legal (scope of freedom to move) and factual (distance or length of travels) dimension was, however, felt also on a somewhat deeper level and framed particularly in reference to the EU, captured by one of the interviewees: 'we can't go back to a stage where people are imprisoned within one EU country as opposed to another EU country – that's clearly not *the drift of history*' (Emphasis added.).[997]

One view on the substance of the drift of history was elaborated on in *Re H (Children)*, another judgment by Lord Justice Thorpe (the judge deciding in *Payne*), dealing with internal relocation to Northern Ireland.[998] It is, therefore, worth recalling that intra-UK relocations are not explicitly restricted by the statute, but can be prevented by a court order directly or indirectly, in particular by imposing conditions on a residence order.[999] An imposition of such restrictions was initially considered exceptional.[1000] It is against this background that the diverging scope of parental autonomy was raised in *Payne*. Elevation of 'exceptionality' to the level of principle has, however, since then been criticised,[1001] and the broad welfare analysis underpins the current approach.[1002] However, as will be demonstrated below, this change of approach can also be read as brought partially by the juxtaposition of internal and international relocations.

In *Re H (Children)*, the appeal against a decision de facto refusing relocation to Northern Ireland by changing the residence order was dismissed. The court dealt with the threshold of exceptionality of restrictions to internal relocation as opposed to international relocations by bringing the two together in the following way:

> What then is the rationalisation for freer movement of the primary carer within the United Kingdom? It seems to me to be obvious. Within the same sovereignty there will be the same system of laws, with the same rights of the citizen, rights for instance to education, health care and statutory benefits. Equally, it can be said that *within Europe, whilst perhaps the burden on the applicant may be greater, it is equally mitigated by the fact that within the Community there is the same fundamental approach to social issues and a real endeavour to achieve harmonisation, obviously in social policy but also in family justice*. If, moving to the third alternative, the application is for relocation outside the European region, the necessary adjustment may be rationalized on the

[996] R. George, above n. 11, p. 99.
[997] ibid.
[998] *Re H (Children)* [2001] EWCA Civ 1338.
[999] Children Act 1989, s. 8. See also R. George, above n. 11, p. 29.
[1000] e.g. *Re E (Residence: Imposition of Conditions)* [1997] 2 FLR 638, 642.
[1001] e.g. *Re F (Children)* [2010] EWCA Civ 1428, paras. 25–26.
[1002] *Re C (Internal Relocation)* [2015] EWCA Civ 1305. See R. George, above n. 11, p. 49.

> basis that the social and other circumstances involved in relocation may require much greater adjustment for the children; alternatively, that the obstacles to contact may be enhanced. However, attempts to rationalize gradation of the hurdles that the applicant must clear are always liable to be tested by specific example, as this case suggests.[1003] (Emphasis added.)

In this passage, the court did in fact construct different dispute-relevant contexts in reference to diverse socio-legal environments. The construction drew the lines in reference to three categories: internal relocations; relocations within the European Community; and other international relocations. It did so in reference to family justice instruments ('*the same system of laws*' versus '*a real endeavour to achieve harmonisation ... in family justice*'[1004] versus '*obstacles to contact may be enhanced*' (emphasis added)), but also social issues ('*the same rights of the citizen ... to education, health care and statutory benefits*' versus '*the same fundamental approach to social issues*' versus '*the social and other circumstances involved in relocation may require much greater adjustment for the children*' (emphasis added)). This corresponds to the construction of the European space in its infrastructure-oriented dimension, as discussed in Chapter 5. The judgment makes it clear, and rightly so, that such a gradation should not overshadow the focus of every individual case: the child's best interests. However, by recognising that the burden on the applicant might be greater in intra-Community relocations, it is said to be '*equally mitigated*' by the socio-legal factors mentioned. This conceptualisation brings both internal and intra-Community relocations together. However, this does not result in a 'freer' movement within the Community but is used as an argument to reorient the approach to internal child relocation towards a stronger emphasis on individual welfare assessment. As a result, internal relocation becomes subject to a stricter test, in reference to its external counterpart.

This impression fits well with the subsequent developments of the doctrine. While the *Payne* guidelines did not introduce a formal presumption, they were often read as a de facto binding discipline.[1005] At the same time, they have been, over the years, heavily criticised for undervaluing the relationship between the child and the remaining parent while overemphasising the impact of a refusal on the relocating parent.[1006] The UK was frequently classified as a representative example of a pro-relocation jurisdiction,[1007] and

---

1003 *Re H (Children)* [2001] EWCA Civ 1338, para. 20.

1004 Family justice was, back then, the subject of Council Regulation (EC) 1347/2000 of 29 May 2000 on jurisdiction and the recognition and enforcement of judgments in matrimonial matters and in matters of parental responsibility for children of both spouses [2000] OJ L160/19.

1005 See the discussion in M. Hayes, above n. 444.

1006 ibid.

1007 e.g. R. George, above n. 11, p. 11; Family Law Council, above n. 11, pp. 52–53.

many commentators perceived the law as granting relocations too easily.[1008] In the years to follow, the Court of Appeal emphasised that the only and paramount consideration in relocation cases is the welfare of the child,[1009] and that the *Payne* guidance should be seen in this light.[1010] The welfare of the parent remains relevant insofar as it has impact on the welfare of the child. If the application to relocate is opposed by another application for a child arrangements order, the essential judicial task is to balance the competing options on where and how the child will be cared for as, in principle, equal in priority.[1011] Ultimately, the courts 'must weigh up all of the relevant factors, look at the case as a whole and determine the course that best meets the need to afford paramount consideration to the child's welfare'.[1012] This decision coincided with the development of case law on relocation applications where parents shared care over their children, as opposed to *Payne* situations where the relocating parent is the primary carer. These cases, whether said to follow the approach endorsed in *Payne* but with different weight attached to specific factors or to apply a different test, reiterated that a holistic assessment of the child's welfare remains the focus of any relocation application.[1013]

Since then, the general impression of family law practitioners seems to suggest that it is becoming increasingly difficult to relocate, or to advise on probable outcomes of relocation cases.[1014] This perhaps explains the gradual disappearance

---

1008 e.g. 'Mounting Support for a Review of Poel and Payne' (2010) <https://www.familylaw.co.uk/news_and_comment/mounting-support-for-a-review-of-poel-and-payne>; R. George 'Payne v Payne – The Long Goodbye Continues' (2015) <https://www.familylaw.co.uk/news_and_comment/payne-v-payne-the-long-goodbye-continues>.

1009 e.g. *K v K (Relocation: Shared Care Arrangement)* [2011] EWCA Civ 793; *F (A Child)* [2012] EWCA Civ 1364.

1010 J. Herring and R. Taylor, above n. 10, 524; R. George, above n. 11, p. 43 who observes that shared care relocation applications, when there is no primary carer, have been following a separate doctrine. According to some, they should not be treated differently, and therefore the *Payne v Payne* [2001] EWCA Civ 166 guidelines should be applied. The other approach says that the *Payne v Payne* guidance is premised on one of the parents being the primary carer, and hence it is not to be applied in shared care cases. However, it might be argued that there is little practical difference. The guidance is fact-sensitive in any case, so although the answers to specific sub-questions might differ, the questions remain applicable. Many factors will often be assessed differently in shared care cases, but whether this is seen as a modification of *Payne v Payne* or as a separate set of guidance remains of secondary nature.

1011 *JAL v LSW* [2017] EWHC 3699 (Fam), para. 11.

1012 *F (A Child) (International Relocation Cases)* [2015] EWCA Civ 882, para. 50.

1013 e.g. *K v K (Relocation: Shared Care Arrangement)* [2011] EWCA Civ 793; *Re C (Internal Relocation)* [2015] EWCA Civ 1305. In light of the emphasis on the non-resumptive approach in *Payne v Payne* [2001] EWCA Civ 166, R. George, above n. 11, p. 45, suggests that there might be little practical difference in opting for one approach or the other.

1014 See, for example, the comments in A. Worwood, 'International Relocation of Children in the UK (England & Wales): Overview', (2019_ *Practical Law* <http://uk.practicallaw.thomsonreuters.com/5-622-2479?transitionType=Default&contextData=(sc.Default)&firstPage=true>.

of the references to freedom of movement and the EU context. While the initial references to the EU and EU law would suggest that the approach to mobility and the scope of autonomy granted in external relocations should not be more restrictive than in internal relocations, both strands of the English doctrine that developed subsequently were based on the gradual limitation of the relevance of such claims altogether. EU law was originally raised in the context of the 'quantification' of freedom of movement with the approach to internal relocation constituting the reference point, but the law has since rejected this reference point altogether. This spirit is captured by the following judgment dealing with internal relocation:

> It is apparent from this passage that although [the judgment] postulated possible arguments for a different approach to internal and external relocation cases, Thorpe LJ did not find a particularly satisfactory foundation for it. Even the rationale which he did offer is not completely convincing. For instance, he referred to the same sovereignty within the United Kingdom meaning the same system of laws, but the United Kingdom does not have only one system of laws. Furthermore, he divided up his consideration into *three* categories, United Kingdom, the European Union and the rest of the globe, but there are only *two* categories of relocation, within the United Kingdom and outside it.
>
> I have not been any more able than was Thorpe LJ to identify a convincing explanation for the position that has been adopted, whereby the freedom of a parent to move appears to have been accorded greater weight in internal relocation cases than in external relocation cases. It might be argued that there is greater ease of enforcement of, say, an order providing for the child to spend time with the other parent after relocation if the move is within the UK than if it is not. However, I do not find this argument compelling in the light of the enforcement provisions of Brussels IIA and the 1996 Hague Convention. Enforceability of such an order may be a relevant factor in the decision whether to permit relocation outside the jurisdiction, but I am not convinced that it justifies a separate regime for internal and external relocation cases. It is equally difficult to justify a separate regime on the basis of the distances involved in the two types of relocation. …
>
> Once welfare has been identified as the governing principle in internal relocation cases, there is no reason to differentiate between those cases and external relocation cases. … Clearly, however, the outcome of that approach will depend entirely on the facts of the individual case.[1015]

Following these developments, relocation cases have been increasingly framed without any meaningful reference to freedom of movement as an individual right. However, as the above passage confirms, private international law instruments were, on multiple occasions, raised as a context that allowed internal

1015 *Re C (Internal Relocation)* [2015] EWCA Civ 1305, paras. 23–24, 54.

and international relocations to be brought together. As such, it is worthwhile investigating this 'usage of Europe' in the construction of a meaningful context for relocation disputes.

7.2.2. ENFORCEMENT MATTERS: 'AS IF IT WERE A DOMESTIC ORDER'[1016]

Enforcement provisions matter, as already suggested by the passage quoted above. Questions of private international law or alternative mechanisms to secure enforcement (e.g. mirror orders)[1017] often feature in English relocation judgments. In the passage above, the Brussels II*bis* Regulation is mentioned together with the 1996 Hague Convention, but the subsequent analysis reveals an interesting discursive difference between the courts' engagement with these two instruments. Before discussing this difference, it is worth noting that private international law is of greater importance in cases involving international travels and temporary relocations (that do not lead to a change in the habitual place of residence).[1018] This does not seem surprising insofar as the potential retention of a child is the most frequently raised objection in such disputes. If the destination state is a party to the 1980 Hague Convention, the application will typically be permitted, unless some particular circumstances of the case speak against it.[1019] Recognition and enforcement seem to weigh

---

1016 *NJ v OV* [2014] EWHC 4130 (Fam), para. 74.

1017 A mirror order is an order that 'mirrors' arrangements ordered by the judge deciding upon relocation. Mirror orders are common in English law but are generally unknown to civil law jurisdictions. See, e.g. *F v M* [2022] EWHC 2564 (Fam), paras. 20, 46; *Re VB & LB (Children)* [2022] EWFC 60, para. 98.

1018 e.g. *SR v MA (Temporary Leave to Remove from the Jurisdiction)* [2019] EWHC 435 (Fam), para. 24: 'Most of the cases cited in the advocates' skeleton arguments concern applications for temporary leave to remove a child to a country which is not a signatory to the 1980 Hague Convention. This is because it is generally accepted that a country's membership of the Convention will, in the normal course of events, provide the "left behind" parent with a swift and unequivocal means of securing the child's return in the event of a wrongful retention in that foreign jurisdiction'.

1019 e.g. *F v M (Temporary Leave to Remove: Alleged Risk of Onward Abduction to Non-Hague Country)* [2018] EWFC B90, para. 32: 'France is a Hague Convention country and were it not for the mother's objections to this trip, based on her allegations that the father is likely to use this trip for the purposes of onward travel to Lebanon, I would have little difficulty in granting the father's application'. See also similar considerations in *Re H (A Child) (Temporary Leave to Remove to Turkey) (Enforcement of Child Arrangements Order)* [2015] EWFC 39 or considerations of non-compliance in a temporary relocation case to Brazil, *SR v MA (Temporary Leave To Remove From the Jurisdiction)* [2019] EWHC 435 (Fam), paras. 23–40. Only one case dealt with travel abroad to an EU country (Slovakia), but it was unusual as it immediately followed a rejected application to relocate permanently to Turkey and, at the same time, the reasoning offered to justify a two-week holiday in Slovakia was weak: *N (A Child)* [2006] EWCA Civ 357.

relatively less in permanent relocations. In such cases, a private international law regime seems to be somewhat secondary to the willingness and ability of the relocating parent to support the child's relationship with the other parent in a long-term perspective.[1020] Even if private international law might mitigate some risks in this regard, courts might not be willing to allow relocation if the attitude of the relocating parent suggests that contact will not survive the move.[1021]

When private international law instruments are discussed, one can observe subtle differences in how the Brussels II*bis* Regulation and the 1996 Hague Convention are discursively approached in the judgments. References to the Brussels Regulation are typically brief. This itself may suggest that courts anticipate such references to be self-explanatory and uncontroversial. When the courts mention the Regulation, it is presented with a strong emphasis on its mutual equivalence logic:

> An order made here would be readily recognised and enforceable under the provisions of *BIIR* (2201/2003) as she [the mother] well knows. … I will grant the necessary certificate to confirm the authenticity of the order under the regulation.[1022]

This is the case also in highly acrimonious proceedings. In the following judgment, a note might be taken of the particular form of future-oriented

1020 e.g. *M v F* [2018] EWHC 1949 (Fam), para. 37: 'I consider that the mother will promote contact with the father whether or not an order is registered in the courts of Uganda. My conclusions on her ability to focus on the children and their need for a relationship with their father more than satisfies me that she will ensure the contact with the father takes place whether or not an order is registered in the Ugandan courts. In order to ensure that a regime is in place though I will require that the order is registered in Uganda. I do not consider that it needs to be done before the mother and children leave'. See also *FW (A Minor: Leave to Remove from Jurisdiction)* [2017] EWFC 53, para. 28.

1021 All such decisions involved non-EU or non-Convention countries, and thus it is difficult to assess to what extent this could be assessed differently where private international law instruments are in place. Compare, for example, this judgment dealing with a relocation to Hong Kong: *Re R (A Child: Relocation)* [2015] EWHC 456 (Fam), paras. 67–70: 'Do the existence of mirror orders alter this picture? Expert opinion has been taken from a Hong Kong attorney. … An English Children Act order can be mirrored in Hong Kong and is enforceable. The procedure, which I need not set out, takes between three to six weeks. … But even then it may not lead to a resolution. … Apparently the Judges there attempt to steer parents in this position towards mediation, but I have given a brief history at the progress of mediation in this country, and I personally would not regard that in an optimistic light as a way forward in the event of any problem given the mother's historical behaviour. In my view these provisions, whilst giving a modest degree of confidence as to the theory and generality of enforceability, do not give sufficient certainty or anything approaching it for a father going there (assuming for these purposes that he does) to see R for these periods'.

1022 *Re AZ (Child: Relocation to Poland)* [2016] EWFC 8, paras. 40, 43.

communication to the judiciary in the state of destination in the event of the order not being complied with:

> My order will provide on its face that this child arrangements order is expected to be recognised and enforced in Sweden pursuant to Article 23 of the Council Regulation known as Brussels II Revised, and Article 23 of the 1996 Hague Convention. Those provisions mean that it is not necessary for me to require the mother to obtain another order in Sweden before she goes, as those provisions provide that my order shall be recognised and enforced in Sweden *as if it were a domestic order*. …
>
> However, my order will state that its provisions are variable by a Swedish court if circumstances changed and B's best interests require a variation. There is one circumstance where I can envisage a variation being made. The father's counsel has raised the spectre of non-compliance with my contact order by the mother. I want to make it crystal clear that I am expecting compliance to be made to the letter. If the order is frustrated or breached without very good reason then I will expect the Swedish court to conclude that the mother's promises to me were empty and insincere. In such circumstances, a transfer of residence to the father and the return of B to live with him in London should be carefully considered.[1023] (Emphasis added.)

Interestingly, the Regulation was mentioned even in a closing paragraph of a case where relocation was refused on other grounds, and hence enforcement did not have to be discussed:

> It may be that after a year or two in the lives of these children, the father himself would, with the passage of time, come to recognise that the time has come for the relocation to take place. If anxiety persists over contact after relocation, there is every likelihood that the embryonic Brussels Regulation II BIS this will by then be in force so that the reciprocal enforcement of any contact orders between England and Spain

---

1023 *NJ v OV* [2014] EWHC 4130 (Fam), paras. 74–75. The court refers to both the Regulation and the 1996 Convention, but it was actually the Regulation that was applicable between the UK and Sweden. For a somewhat ambiguous account, see also *TJ v MS (Article 11(6–8) BIIA: Relocation: Art 24 EUCFR)* [2017] EWHC 3802 (Fam), para. 161, where the court discussed difficulties with contact after a potential move to another EU country, but not in reference to the Regulation per se, and in the specific proceedings post-abduction: 'And so even though this court might make a contact order, the Polish court will be at liberty, and quite rightly so, them then having habitual residence jurisdiction, to investigate as they see fit and if an application is made to restrict the father's contact (as I think it likely would be) there is little that I can say in an order in this court that will affect that. Having said that I think the more substantial concern is not necessarily the mother pursuing a course of litigation but simply on the ground the attitude to contact led by the family and the mother being such that it will, as I have already said, be made very difficult to work in practice with a very high risk of that fragile relationship being broken. However effective contact enforcement process may be on paper the reality as we know from domestic experience is that contact can be very vulnerable to disruption in practice and once broken can be very hard to restart'.

> would be *as straightforward and as uncomplicated as the enforcement of orders made in the Brighton County Court with both parents living in the vicinity.*[1024] (Emphasis added.)

In another case, the Court of Appeal criticised a one-sided evaluation of the mother's motivation for relocation in the lower court, but made an independent reference to the weight accorded to the Regulation:

> If I have any criticism, it is that the import of Brussels II Revised as an instrument governing the applicability, recognition and enforcement of matrimonial orders across EU member states was not given sufficient emphasis, but I would not have allowed the appeal on that ground alone.[1025]

This remark is interesting considering the existence of a strong substance-based justification for the appeal, as the consideration of the Regulation had no independent bearing on the decision (the appeal was allowed in any case). This and the previous decision seem to suggest that the Regulation has a broader signalling or communicative value beyond the main issue discussed, potentially reflecting a certain sense of EU (legal) territoriality.

The 1996 Hague Convention is, on the other hand, discussed on average in more detail than the Regulation. While its efficiency is generally accepted,[1026] more attention is occasionally paid to the actual practices in the state of destination. This might also reveal a certain differentiation between the approaches to various jurisdictions that can be perceived, perhaps, as a variation in trust. Incidentally, one can observe the equalising language of the Regulation used in reference also to the 1996 Hague Convention:

> The order which I intend to make will include an expectation that the child arrangements order will be recognised and enforced in Canada pursuant Article 23 of the 1996 Hague Convention. Those provisions mean that it is not necessary for me to require the father to obtain another order in Canada before he leaves the United Kingdom, as those provisions provide that my order shall be recognised and enforced in Canada as if it were an order made in Canada.[1027]

1024 *Re C-G (Children)* [2001] EWCA Civ 1867, para. 7.

1025 *Re P (Children)* [2014] EWCA Civ 852, para. 7.

1026 e.g. *Re MM (A Child: Relocation)* [2014] EWFC B176, para. 82: 'South Africa is a Hague Convention country where judges can be relied upon to read English and understand the terms of any order I make or any written agreement between the parties'. See also *Re C (Internal Relocation)* [2015] EWCA Civ 1305, para. 24 or *S v S (Relocation)* [2017] EWHC 2345 (Fam), para. 10.

1027 *J (A Child: Removal from the jurisdiction)* [2015] EWFC B230, para. 89. One can wonder to what extent the specific state of destination plays a role in how much certainty courts stress in this context.

It might suggest that there is no difference in the perception of the two instruments, but it might also suggest that reasoning informed by mutual trust has been 'carried over into the practice under the 1996 Hague Children Convention', as noted in the literature.[1028] The latter hypothesis might be supported by the fact that there is nevertheless more variation in how courts discuss the 1996 Hague Convention,[1029] but this variation seems to correlate to a certain extent with the level of cognitive or legal familiarity with a given legal system and the confidence in the relocating parent's co-operation after the move. In a case involving relocation to Australia, the judges on appeal were in disagreement regarding the correct approach to enforcement, with one of them raising the point that, in light of the mother's previous attitude towards contact:

> *[f]or all that both countries are parties to the Hague Convention, and that there could be mirror orders in Australia, it could be very difficult for the father to enforce obligations once the children had moved.*[1030] (Emphasis added.)

The other judge put more confidence in the enforcement:

> the judge was in my judgment wrong to assume the impotence of the court either here or in Australia. ... Equally, in these days of instant communication and internationally established liaison judges, I have more confidence than the judge (he expressed none) that neither court would sit idly by and allow the relationship to wither.[1031]

On the other hand, in a dispute about relocation to Russia, the judge made a remark about:

> the ability and willingness of the Russian judicial and civil authorities to discharge their Convention responsibilities [that] can be seen in the case of *Neustadt v Neustadt (Child Abduction)* [2014] EWHC 4307.[1032]

This might indicate that the judge felt, perhaps in light of frequent claims of Russia's non-compliance raised in the context of the 1980 Hague Child Abduction Convention, a need to emphasise the practical and not only theoretical efficacy of the Convention. At the same time, in another case, the court noted that 'any

---

[1028] See R. Lamont, above n. 634, p. 15 and the case law cited there.

[1029] Compare the different considerations in *W (Children)* [2011] EWCA Civ 345, paras. 93, 153, 160.

[1030] ibid., para. 143.

[1031] ibid., paras. 105–06.

[1032] *S v G (Relocation to Russia)* [2015] EWFC 4, para. 6. However, there is nothing self-explanatory about such an assessment.

sanction from the court in Russia is, perhaps, not the most likely way of enforcing orders' but this was less relevant to the decision insofar as the mother supported contact and the father was a frequent traveller to Moscow, the destination place.[1033] While both the Brussels II*bis* Regulation and the Hague Convention are recognised as strengthening the legal guarantees in relocation cases, none of the cases referencing the Brussels II*bis* Regulation make reference to the factual efficacy of the guarantees. Even if practical limitations were discussed, as there are limits to the courts' powers in every jurisdiction, they were discursively separated from the legal layer of this EU instrument. This observation might suggest that national courts perceived EU law as exerting pressure in that regard via its mutual trust imperative. Judgments issued post-Brexit are yet too few to juxtapose usefully against previous case law, but one can expect – at least for a certain time – a closer attention to the changed legal landscape. However, this closer scrutiny will probably not carry tangible normative consequences for child relocation cases.[1034] With all EU Member States being also signatories to the 1996 Hague Child Protection Convention, the prior practice under EU law will likely be 'carried over'[1035] into the post-Brexit era. It remains to be seen, however, whether the EU-specific mutual trust imperative will persist in the same form without EU law.

7.2.3. IDENTITY AND CITIZENSHIP: INTERNATIONAL, BUT NOT EUROPEAN?

British courts ascribe a significant value to children's heritage in relocation cases. This is easily observable as most disputes in the sample arose in mixed-heritage

1033 *Re M (Children)* [2016] EWCA Civ 1059, para. 67. See also *S v G (Relocation to Russia)* [2015] EWFC 4, para. 118 where the court held that '[t]here can be no guarantee that an order for contact will be complied with, but I consider the treaty powers to be a significant reinforcement to the already robust probability that the mother will honour her obligations'.

1034 In all such cases in the sample, relocation was permitted. *RD v TJ (Relocation – BIIA – Transitional Provisions)* [2021] EWHC 489 (Fam) concerns relocation to Poland and discusses in detail the provisions of the Withdrawal Agreement regarding the transitional provisions and the application of the EU family law instruments, paras. 19–26. The case *A Local Authority v M & Others* [2022] EWFC 82, para. 74, concerns public proceedings involving relocation to Spain and makes a mention of the Hague Convention as 'a degree of protection for the father'. On the other hand, a judgment on relocation to France (*D v S (international Relocation)* [2020] EWFC B78, para. 38) observes: 'I bear in mind D's observations as to potential obstacles in accessing justice in the event of difficulties arising if in France. I consider I do have to proceed on the basis the French system provides an equivalently satisfactory route for D to enforce his contact rights in the event of disagreement', without reference to any private international law framework. See also a (highly particular) relocation case to Ireland, *PQ v RS & Another* [2021] EWHC 572 (Fam).

1035 See R. Lamont, above n. 634, p. 15 who observes that the EU-specific reasoning based on mutual trust was already before 'carried over into the practice under to the 1996 Hague Children Convention' in respect to its non-EU signatories.

relationships. Interestingly, when one of the parents is British, the heritage is sometimes presented not as a composite, but as two somewhat opposing elements related to distinctive ways of life that go beyond the child's personal relationships:

> The outcome of the proceedings will not only determine [the child's] upbringing but also shape his identity. If the mother's application is granted, he will grow up as *an essentially Russian child* whose relationship with his father and his English family will be greatly reduced. If it is refused, his mother will have to remain here, and he will experience *a predominantly English upbringing.*[1036] (Emphasis added.)

These distinctive ways of life seem to reflect also on the discursive framing of the child's future:

> Here the judge had a very different choice. He had to choose between the mother's residence order application, which was for her responsibility as primary carer discharged in an Australian community with her new partner, and the father's competing residence order application, which proposed *an English future* and the continuation of *an English childhood* in the family created by his new relationship.[1037] (Emphasis added.)

It is, however, not always clear whether heritage factors into court decisions. In both cases quoted above, the court allowed relocation. This might suggest that this emphasis has more of a signalling value that the stakes of the dispute are fully recognised. For migrant families, the description might emphasise their limited links to the UK or a foreign identity:

> AZ is a Polish child born to Polish parents; ... While AZ happens to have been born in England, she has no English language, education, nor friends. She has not integrated here in any meaningful way; she is not a dual nationality child in the sense in which that phrase is commonly known.[1038]

This might be the case both in line with or despite any original or future plans of the parties,[1039] grounding the case in the actual level of integration rather than any particular supranational aspirations that one can at times find in EU law.

1036 *S v G (Relocation to Russia)* [2015] EWFC 4, para. 2.

1037 *Re H (A Child)* [2010] EWCA Civ 789, para. 13.

1038 *Re AZ (Child: Relocation to Poland)* [2016] EWFC 8, para. 34, or *F (A Child)* [2012] EWCA Civ 1364, para. 34.

1039 See also *D v S (international Relocation)* [2020] EWFC B78, paras. 36, 51.4: 'It is appropriate to have regard to the fact that this international couple formed their relationship outside the jurisdiction and then developed their plans in the knowledge that they were making life plans with a partner who remained strongly associated to another jurisdiction. In such circumstances I can expect they must have had regard to the potential for their partner to wish to return home and particularly so were their relationship to founder.'

Even when the court says that these factors 'have marginal relevance to the case',[1040] the interesting aspect of such assessments is, therefore, that the residence choices of migrant parents are not coupled with any identity factors. As presented in the previous chapter, the logic of EU mobility reasoning indicates that Member States should let EU citizens integrate, but at the same time should recognise their special status that goes beyond both their state of origin and their state of residence. This is not to argue that such status should lead to any doctrinal difference in the approach, as in any case the decision should be taken in the best interests of the child. However, on the level of the judicial constructions of the legal subject, there is no direct conceptual coupling of the family's choices or identities with anything remotely EU-ropean,[1041] or transcending their original cultural backgrounds.

At the same time, certain children or families can be characterised as 'international', including EU contexts. This often originates in the relatively mobile lifestyle of their parents, taken as facts of the case, that translates into children's identity factors:

> These are, as Ms Hampshire noted, truly international children for whom the world is a markedly smaller place than for others their age. … [The father] is clearly well-used to international travel to achieve his goals.[1042]

Or, similarly:

> The reality is that this little girl is an international child with parents of different nationalities who chose to settle in the UK. This child will have triple nationality and will be brought up speaking three languages. That is a huge advantage to her in the future. Being educated in an environment which reflects that international background seems to me to be the appropriate educational setting for her.[1043]

Often, the considerations of lifestyles and identity will be merged:

> This is a very international family who undertake a lot of travel. As B observed to the independent social worker, in one of his more dramatic moments, he said he had spent half his life on a plane, this was not said as any complaint but as a fact of life. Travelling is very much a feature of all their lives, both for the children, their parents and Y.[1044]

1040 *F (A Child)* [2012] EWCA Civ 1364, para. 17.

1041 See also *Re R (A Child: Relocation)* [2015] EWHC 456 (Fam), para. 27, for an interesting reference regarding the parent's job prospects framed in reference to Europe: 'She is bilingual in English and Cantonese, but she is without a second European language though historically that has not impeded her'.

1042 *SNM v TNM* [2017] EWFC B2, para. 13.

1043 *RD v TJ (Relocation – BIIA – Transitional Provisions)* [2021] EWHC 489 (Fam), para. 43.

1044 *C v D* [2011] EWHC 335 (Fam), para. 41.

The domain in which such families operate is not generic but is characterised by specific rules and the normalisation of frequent international travel or certain upbringing choices. This does not, however, necessarily lead to approval of the relocation plan, and as such the normative value of this contextualisation might be limited.

On the other hand, travel is often discussed in the context of future contact arrangements. This includes also intra-EU relocations, with remarks made about the frequency and costs of available flights that make regular visits possible.[1045] The fact that European migrant families travel regularly within Europe, and for this reason they can be more easily required to do so for contact, was recognised in some judgments, but ultimately such circumstances will be largely fact-dependent.[1046] The judgments do not seem to directly support the claim that there is a distinct European domain in which such families operate. The lack of strong pronouncements on these issues can be interpreted two-fold. It might mean that travel within Europe is normalised to the extent that it is not discussed as anything extraordinary regarding its frequency, costs and required time and effort, as opposed to cross-Atlantic travels – unless specific circumstances require otherwise. However, it might also suggest that the international domains have as much to do with resources and status as with mobility per se, encompassing concrete possibilities rather than abstract contextual potential, be it in the EU context or beyond.

Citizenship, pragmatically, can also play a role in relocation considerations. In one of the cases involving a relocation to Canada, the judge mentioned hypothetically that it would be ideal if both parents could move to Canada, noting that 'fortunately all four members of the family have Canadian and British citizenship'.[1047] This suggests that the facilitative aspect of family members sharing citizenship of the state of destination is recognised. The citizenship of the other parent often plays a role in the context of visas and prospective visits.[1048] Sadly, the precarious immigration position of the relocating parent might also be a reason for relocation.[1049] The fact that such matters were not discussed

1045 e.g. *Re AZ (Child: Relocation to Poland)* [2016] EWFC 8; *TJ v MS (Article 11(6–8) BIIA: Relocation: Art 24 EUCFR)* [2017] EWHC 3802 (Fam).

1046 e.g. *D v S (international Relocation)* [2020] EWFC B78, para. 29, regarding consideration of high costs – in respect of the father's income – of travelling to France for contact.

1047 *K v K (Relocation: Shared Care Arrangement)* [2011] EWCA Civ 793, para. 63.

1048 e.g. *Re S (A Child)* [2015] EWFC 86, para. 25: 'Both the mother and S have Pakistan nationality so there will be no immigration difficulties'; *S v G (Relocation to Russia)* [2015] EWFC 4, para. 74: 'The father for his part expresses concern about his ability to visit Moscow if [the child] lived there, being apprehensive to the point of unwillingness to travel there. The process of obtaining a family visa would require the mother's cooperation. However, … I consider it unlikely that the Russian authorities would prevent him from visiting his son there'.

1049 e.g. *H v F (Relocation)* [2014] EWFC 11, para. 36: 'The parents are not on an equal footing in relation to their immigration status. The mother has no prospect of a secure future in

in intra-EU relocations clearly suggests that the broader legal infrastructure of the EU was taken as a fact.[1050] Such considerations lost, to some extent, their importance after Brexit, but time will show the impact on this aspect of relocation cases.[1051]

7.2.4. LOCALISATION AND DELOCALISATION OF FAMILY LIFE

Following the doctrinal developments after *Payne*, references to EU law seem to have disappeared from the relocation judgments. Against this background, a case involving relocation to Spain brought such claims back in 2012. In this case, EU Treaty rights were raised on appeal to oppose the mother's proposal to relocate to Spain. The father, the carer of the child after the mother moved to Spain, claimed that his status as the primary carer should be recognised, giving due respect to his reasonable wish to remain living in the UK with no unreasonable constraints imposed on his choice of residence. The father's appeal was dismissed, with the following comments made on this point by the court:

> I quite accept that the father's right to determine his place of residence is protected both by the European Convention and by the EU Treaty: see the discussion by Thorpe LJ in *Payne v Payne* at paragraph [36]. But so too, of course, is the mother's. As Thorpe LJ went on to observe (*Payne* paragraph [37]), 'each member of the fractured family has rights to assert and … in balancing them the court must adhere to the paramountcy of the welfare principle.' Thus, this point does not of itself take the father anywhere.[1052]

The interesting feature of the case is that it was not movement per se that was said to be protected under EU law, but the choice to reside in another EU country. In light of the previous chapters, one could naturally question – as a

this country. She either has to leave immediately or remain illegally. If she remains, she has no source of income and no family support close to hand. I believe that this would carry considerable risks for her well-being with obvious likely detriment to A.'

1050 The only exception is the case *Re A (Poland)* [2009] EWCC 1 (Fam), para. 6, where the Bangladeshi father was an overstayer in the UK, and as such, present in the territory of the EU illegally: 'it would be very difficult for [the father] to exercise contact in Poland due to his very reduced financial circumstances, and more particularly because of problems with his immigration status. If he were to leave the UK he would not be allowed to re-enter'.

1051 *Re E (Relocation – choice between various options within and without the jurisdiction)* [2022] EWFC B22, para. 61, mentions that the mother had established an ability to work in the UK. While the mother is a Spanish citizen, the judgment is not fully clear as to whether the ability is meant in a legal or factual sense. If the former is true, this could have potentially had stronger relevance for the outcome (as relocation was refused in this case).

1052 *F (A Child)* [2012] EWCA Civ 1364, para. 56.

technical matter of EU law – whether the mother's right to reside in her home country was indeed protected in the same way as the father's right to reside abroad, but this is, of course, irrelevant in light of the rights that can be asserted under the ECHR. However, this aspect of the dispute's context was explicitly rejected as 'not taking the father anywhere', hence confirming the approach taken in previous cases.

The case, however, indirectly raises other interesting points linked to the scope of reasonable expectations and the localisation of family life discussed in Chapter 5. As mentioned, the father was the primary carer of the child at the time of the relocation application, as the mother decided to return to Spain after the breakup of the relationship. Nevertheless, the court decided to scrutinise the intentions and plans *of the father*. Thus, his position was approached as if the guidelines were reversed and it were his choices that were under scrutiny, and not those of the relocating parent.[1053] The lower court assessed the case in the following way:

> Applying that law to this particular case it seems to me that this case has some unique features. Both of the parties are Spanish and the intention of both parties when coming to this country was to live in this country until the father's work had been completed. Both of the parties continue to regard themselves as Spanish and not only did they regard P as Spanish but he also is of that view. What is on offer from the mother is a return to the arrangements in terms of schooling, general location and so on in which P thrived for the first six years or so of his life. And finally it is highly likely that at some point if the father has residence of P he will return to Spain, either in 2013 when this contract finishes or sometime thereafter. Having heard the father I think it is more likely than not that he will go back in 2013 but I cannot be definitive about that. *What I think I can find is that the father is, on the balance of probability, likely to return to Spain in 2013 to be nearer to P if he does not have residence of him.*[1054] (Emphasis added.)

On appeal, this judgment was upheld as no error in law could be identified. This case might not immediately seem significant, but it becomes noteworthy against the background of other cases.

The mobility of the non-relocating parent, while discussed in some jurisdictions, has not been recognised as a factor to be considered in relocation cases in England. In one case, the judge noted that the factor has risen in importance since *Payne*, but this is not reflected in the cases in the sample and the basis for such assessment remains unclear.[1055] While analysing English cases, this rise in importance seems to be predominantly theoretical. In some cases, the parent on his or her own initiative declares willingness to move if

1053 ibid., para. 25.
1054 ibid., para. 13.
1055 *K v K (Relocation: Shared Care Arrangement)* [2011] EWCA Civ 793, para. 47.

relocation is granted, which allows the court to balance out both options on the assumption that the child will not lose everyday contact with any of the parents.[1056] Courts do occasionally make references to the fact that it would *hypothetically* be the best solution for the children if both parents relocated[1057] or that the non-relocating parent themselves might feel differently about relocation in the future (which is, however, not per se related to their residence choices).[1058] In no case does the mobility of the non-relocating parent become part of the balancing exercise if this option is not raised by the parties,[1059] as captured by this passage:

> The realistic options for A's future are, I find, either to live in the care of the father in England in the mother's absence, or to live in the care of the mother in New Zealand in the father's absence. That would be mitigated if he himself relocates, but *I must for the purposes of my decision assume that he will decide to remain here.*[1060] (Emphasis added.)

Interestingly, and despite this stance, while non-relocating parents' mobility was not under scrutiny, the mobility of the new partners of relocating parents often was – regardless of whether it impaired outgoing mobility[1061] or implied immigration into the UK.[1062] This went beyond assessing the factual impact of the refusal on the new partner or family unit,[1063] as suggested by the *Payne* discipline. One of the most striking examples can be found below:

> The evidence before the judge was that her [the relocating mother's] partner would in any event go to New Zealand whether or not permission was granted. That was something on which the judge took the view that, as he had a young child, it could be thought to be evidence of lack of commitment to his new family if he were immediately to leave home and go abroad.[1064]

1056 e.g. *TC and JC (Children: Relocation)* [2013] EWHC 292 (Fam). See also *RD v TJ (Relocation – BIIA – Transitional Provisions)* [2021] EWHC 489 (Fam), where the father agreed to follow the mother and the child to Poland in the course of the proceedings.

1057 e.g. *K v K (Relocation: Shared Care Arrangement)* [2011] EWCA Civ 793, para. 63. Here, the judge clearly mentioned the possibility of the non-relocating parent moving purely hypothetically, even if recognising that such a scenario would be best for the children. It was, however, not considered whether the non-resident parent should move with the resident parent, nor scrutinised why the father does not move with them. Proposals to conduct such an assessment were put forward in the literature, e.g. K. Scheiwe, above n. 103, p. 168.

1058 e.g. *Re C-G (Children)* [2001] EWCA Civ 1867, para. 7.

1059 One potential exception could be *J (A Child: Removal from the jurisdiction)* [2015] EWFC B230, para. 62, where such an option was raised by the relocating parent. However, it seems to have played a major role in the decision-making.

1060 *H v F (Relocation)* [2014] EWFC 11, para. 41.

1061 e.g. *W (Children)* [2009] EWCA Civ 160, para. 10.

1062 e.g. *GT v RJ* [2018] EWFC 26, para. 52; *Re C (A Child)* [2011] EWCA Civ 72, para. 17.

1063 However, there are some exceptions. See, e.g. *B and S* [2003] EWCA Civ 1149.

1064 e.g. *W (Children)* [2009] EWCA Civ 160, para. 10.

Naturally, based on the assessment of facts, such circumstances might indicate a lack of commitment. Any evaluation of such commitment must take account of the scope of reasonable expectations of all the individuals involved. The courts have noted that:

> if someone forms a relationship with a woman who has children from a prior relationship where the father of those children is enjoying a stable regime of contact, then the new partner must surely be taken to enter the relationship, with all its incumbrances, with his eyes wide open. On the other hand, the father of those children must surely recognise the prospect of his former wife re-partnering and in that event a case for change being advanced. The weight to be attributed to these two general propositions will depend on the facts of the case in hand.[1065]

At the same time, a new partner might have good reasons for relocation or for not being in the position to move to the UK.[1066] But the interesting point is not whether a given adult is committed or whether their argumentation is convincing, but that the residence choice of the new partner is often discussed and scrutinised *as a matter of commitment reflecting on the relocation plan* – even when they reside and have always resided abroad – while the residence choice of the non-relocating parent is typically beyond scrutiny.[1067] The consideration of various mobility options for everyone else but the non-relocating parent indicates that the level of reasonable expectations and sacrifices is different for different people involved.[1068] The relocating parent might be reasonably expected to stay, their new partner might be reasonably expected to stay *or move to the UK*, but the non-relocating parent's residence choices are not part of the assessment, unless raised by the parent themselves. Naturally, it is the relocating parent who needs to make their case. The status quo understood as no change will also weigh heavily in any assessment,[1069] but no change in relocation cases is possible only if one assumes that the relocating parent

---

1065 *GT v RJ* [2018] EWFC 26, para. 6.

1066 e.g. *A v B* [2018] EWHC 328 (Fam), para. 23; *B and S* [2003] EWCA Civ 1149, para. 12. The reasoning of the latter case closely resembles the discourse of the earlier judgment in *Poel v Poel* [1970] 1 WLR 1469.

1067 e.g. *S v Z* [2012] EWHC 846 (Fam), para. 22: 'Second, the husband cannot realistically leave Tanzania so as to live with his wife here in England. There are many reasons for that. He has no right to live here. He is deeply connected to Tanzania, not only by his birth, upbringing and citizenship, but also by his business and home there and his other family members there. These include his own daughter, Y, whom he sees almost daily, and his own mother who currently lives with him but will move back to her own home nearby. It is, therefore, neither practical, possible nor reasonable to contemplate the husband moving from Tanzania to live in England (nor has the father suggested that he could or should do so)'.

1068 This is not to say that the possibility of the new partner relocating to the UK or forgoing their relocation plans was always accepted, even if the relocating parent accepted such a possibility in the event of refusal of relocation. See, e.g. *M v F* [2016] EWHC 3194 (Fam), para. 52.

1069 See also the comments in *GT v RJ* [2018] EWFC 26, paras. 1–2.

can reasonably be expected to stay. This contextual localisation of the point of reference for the whole family unit – old and new – in the UK is hardly normatively neutral, notwithstanding its desirability from the child-centred perspective.

This is why the Spanish case, discussed earlier, becomes interesting. It remains the only case in the sample where the court made a decision in reference *to the balance of probabilities* of *the non-relocating parent relocating as well*. The fact that the court noted that the parties' intention was originally to come to the UK for a limited period of time is not, in itself, a sufficient explanation, as the father made it clear that at the time of the application he intended to stay in the UK even if he could not outline his plans with full clarity.[1070] Intentions when coming to the UK were often not investigated for non-relocating parents who were foreign citizens, and at the same time were frequently seen as an insufficient argument in favour of relocation when raised by relocating parents.[1071] One can, therefore, wonder to what extent the fact that the case involved mobile EU citizens could have contributed to the impression that such 'reversed guidelines' were reasonably justified. In a space built on the premise of continuous movement, such an assessment gets closer to what EU normativity projects, and at the same time further from what one can observe in other English cases. It is possible, naturally, that the citizenship and identity of the parties (all of whom considered themselves Spanish) played a role in the balancing exercise, linking back to the discussion above. While this remains the only case where such a dynamic can be observed, it suggests that the delocalisation of family life might be normatively justified where particular contextual factors are at play.

7.2.5. BREXIT: 'RELUCTANT EUROPEAN' UNTIL THE END?

At the time when this research project was designed, the United Kingdom was still a Member State of the European Union. While the Brexit referendum in 2016 could have brought this design into question, Brexit offered simultaneously a chance to observe whether its socio-legal implications could be reflected in child relocation cases. The number of EU citizens leaving the UK increased after the referendum, and the legal framework of intra-EU mobility was about to be lost, complicated by the prolonged uncertainty of post-Brexit status. Additionally, this process did not remain neutral to the life choices of the many EU citizens in the UK. Social science research confirms that the events

1070 *F (A Child)* [2012] EWCA Civ 1364, para. 25.

1071 e.g. *WS v KL* [2020] EWHC 2548 (Fam), *E (Relocation – choice between various options within and without the jurisdiction)* [2022] EWFC B22, para. 22. To the contrary, see *D v S (international Relocation)* [2020] EWFC B78, paras. 36, 51.4.

leading to and the discourses surrounding Brexit focused on a particular narrative of EU migration and a specific vision of the politics of belonging.[1072] These political and legal processes had an impact on the sense of belonging of European citizens in the UK, with the uncertainty surrounding the formal recognition of rights and legal entitlements influencing their subjective sense of security.[1073] The new question emerging from these developments was, therefore, if Brexit changed the ways to approach the expectations, interests, and rights of the parties in intra-EU child relocation disputes.

Thirteen judgments in the sample concerned intra-EU relocations and were decided after the Brexit referendum, but before Brexit as such, and eight additional judgments were issued after the UK had officially left the EU. Most of them do not contain any Brexit references, which suggests that Brexit was absent from the minds of litigants and judges. In one case, Brexit was raised by the relocating mother as a source of anxiety, but the court did not deal with this assertion any further.[1074] It seems that this generalised concern about the uncertainty of the mother's own position was not seen as a relevant context for the case. In another case (relocation to Canada), Brexit was raised in the context of the employment stability of the non-relocating father, as 'with Britain leaving the EU nothing is certain about what will then happen to EU nationals working in the UK', thus meaning that the children's arrangements might need to change, notwithstanding relocation.[1075] With the father asserting that 'reassuring noises were being made generally about the post-Brexit position for EU nationals working at the university', the judge came to the conclusion that his employment was only marginally less certain than when he accepted the job.[1076] It remains an open question if the assessment could be different if the father were an unskilled worker as opposed to an Oxford professor and a member of an 'international' family.

The case that both opened and closed Brexit claims in relocation cases *as a matter of law* was, however, an application by an Italian mother who wished to take her son back to Italy. The lower court refused the mother's application. The judge allowing the appeal, while relying mostly on the alleged superficial treatment of domestic abuse allegations and their effect on the child, also made the following suggestions:

> There are arguments that should be put forward on behalf of the child in respect of his long-term welfare and location, and his heritage. This child is of Italian heritage

[1072] e.g. R. MasGiralt, 'The Emotional Geographies of Migration and Brexit: Tales of Unbelonging' (2020) 9 *Central and Eastern European Migration Review* 29.

[1073] ibid.

[1074] *TJ v MS (Article 11(6–8) BIIA: Relocation: Art 24 EUCFR)* [2017] EWHC 3802 (Fam), para. 44.

[1075] *SNM v TNM* [2017] EWFC B2, para. 13.

[1076] ibid.

> and most of his extended family live in Italy; while not a deciding factor it is one which should command some consideration by the tribunal deciding his future. The fact that as EU citizens his parents' residence and their status in the UK no longer has the certainty it previously had, and the possibility that relocation to Italy may become a necessity is a factor that should, properly, have been considered by the trial judge.[1077]

The court deciding on the appeal was not, however, convinced by this assertion:

> There are two reasons why this statement is unhelpful. In the first place, the reason why Brexit was not mentioned by the trial judge is because it was not mentioned in the evidence or submissions she heard. But secondly, and of more general application, the consequences of the UK's departure from the EU are presently unclear, and there is no sound basis on which courts can factor in the hypothetical possibility that an EU national's immigration position might at some future date become precarious. The task for trial judges of deciding these cases is difficult enough without adding imponderables of this kind.[1078]

This assessment rejects Brexit as a relevant context for the evaluation of the scope of individual autonomy. It rather sees it as an 'imponderable' that further complicates already complicated cases and does so as a matter 'of more general application'. Without suggesting that Brexit as a factor in itself should lead to different outcomes in relocation cases, such a framing suggests not only that it did not carry much weight or was seen as irrelevant for the case in question, but that it did not matter *as a particular context* in which EU citizens had to organise their lives. The desire to limit these kinds of claim is understandable, but at the same time surprising, insofar as courts in relocation cases might deal with imponderables of similar kinds on a regular basis. Compare, for example, the following statement:

> the mother [whose spousal visa was still valid for about one year at the time of the dispute] is likely to be permitted to remain in the UK as [the child's] parent [with] … the prospect of her qualifying for settlement in five or ten years depending on the level of her ability to maintain herself. … The mother would therefore be unlikely to face removal from England during [the child's] childhood, but there would be some insecurity and impermanence in her position in comparison to her position in Russia.[1079]

This is not to compare the sense of 'insecurity and impermanence' of EU citizens during Brexit negotiations with third-country nationals, but is

1077 *F v L* [2017] EWHC 1377 (Fam), para. 16.
1078 *L v F* [2017] EWCA Civ 2121.
1079 *S v G (Relocation to Russia)* [2015] EWFC 4, paras. 72–73.

rather to illustrate that the 'hypothetical possibility' of immigration positions becoming precarious (or not) often becomes a consideration in other contexts. The exclusion of Brexit as a relevant context in the transition period seems, therefore, to have had a normative dimension.[1080] The EU citizen became here *as a matter of law* partially acontextual, despite the then-ongoing transformations of their legal status. While the presence of the EU as a contextual point of reference was never particularly strong in English case law, the sample suggests that Brexit ultimately confirmed that the European influence plays a role predominantly in its more technical, infrastructure-oriented dimension, as discussed in the previous sections.

7.2.6. PRELIMINARY CONCLUSIONS

Child relocation law in England and Wales has been widely discussed, resulting in a wealth of material for analysis. The discussion originally took place against the background of different rules for internal and international relocations that traditionally afforded more autonomy to parents relocating internally. Restrictions on such relocations were, for a long time, seen as exceptional in recognition of the relocating parent's mobility rights. Hence, judges and commentators extensively engaged with the rationale and justification of such differentiation over the years. This prompted early engagement with EU law and the European socio-legal environment. However, as the subsequent developments of the doctrine demonstrate, this engagement played a role in reorienting the doctrine towards a stronger focus on the child's welfare and the holistic nature of the analysis rather than the expansion of freedom of movement or autonomy rights in the EU context. On the other hand, EU law often featured in English judgments in reference to the Brussels II*bis* Regulation. The pronouncements of courts on the nature of this legal instrument suggest a strong attachment to the guarantees that it offered, an attachment that spills over into a broader conceptualisation of the EU as a space of rights based on mutual trust. However, although one can observe certain differences in the judicial discussions of the Regulation and other private international law instruments, possibly due to the EU legal pressures and the ideational dimension of the EU legal framework, all instruments were generally seen as providing efficient guarantees. At the same time, while the EU legal infrastructure played a role in the resolution of child

---

[1080] One can, however, observe that Brexit was mentioned in some other cases concerning children, e.g. in citizenship decisions. See, for example, *K (A Child)* [2017] EWHC 2017 (Fam), para. 53: 'I bear in mind that if K remains an Indian citizen, then the mother would have to get visas for her to go abroad from England probably more often than would be necessary if K had British nationality, although this is a point of less weight since "Brexit"'.

relocation disputes, the EU did not seem to have become a meaningful point of reference in the broader contextual dimension.

As much as certain families were characterised through their (mobile) ways of life, this characterisation had more of a global than a European dimension. At the same time, the English approach seems to rely on a reasoning that has a localising effect for family life insofar as courts scrutinise the residence choices of all the individuals involved except those of the non-relocating parent. An interesting exception to this reasoning is *F (A Child) [2012] EWCA Civ 1364*, involving a Spanish family (of EU citizens), where the non-relocating father, on the balance of probabilities, was said to be likely to move back to Spain in the near future if he did not have custody of the child. This could suggest a different point of departure in some cases involving EU citizens, in particular as EU law was raised in this case, but this approach remained incidental. Such considerations in any case might be less relevant since Brexit. Brexit, simultaneously, reinforced the observation about the limited relevance of the EU context as a reference point for the construction of the scope of individuals' autonomy. It was explicitly excluded from such considerations in the transition period and, since the withdrawal of the UK from the EU, has been completely absent. This suggests that Europe mattered predominantly as a legal infrastructure, understood first and foremost in reference to its family law instruments, and did not carry any particular normative value.

Brexit will remain, however, of significance for future research interested in questions similar to those posed in this book. This is so because it influences not only the developments of English law, but also the reciprocal relationship of the UK and other EU Member States. While in the British media Brexit was systematically downplayed, the media discourses of Brexit in Europe (including Poland and Germany) have framed it as a multifaceted crisis of much significance to both the present and the future.[1081] This cannot, naturally, be directly translated into family law cases, but will continue to provide an interesting background for future discussions. It might be noted that the sample of Polish and German cases does not include any relocations to the UK that were adjudicated post-Brexit. It is, hence, impossible to ascertain whether the changing legal layer and the sense of (un)belonging played any role in the eyes of those who remain in the EU. However, as claims related to Brexit have featured already in family cases in other contexts,[1082] one cannot exclude the possibility that they will find their way into child relocation cases in other

1081 e.g. M. Krzyżanowski, 'Brexit and the Imaginary of "Crisis": A Discourse-Conceptual Analysis of European News Media' (2019) 16 *Critical Discourse Studies* 465.

1082 As a comparison, Brexit was recognised as a source of vulnerability in one Polish child abduction case. See *Wyrok Sądu Okręgowego w Suwałkach z dnia 24 kwietnia 2017 roku*, I Ca 119/17, POSP.

Member States too. Further research into such cases might shed additional light on the findings presented here. The relevance of this puzzle becomes clear if one looks at the nature of European encounters to be observed in German child relocation law.

7.3. GERMANY

Although German law does not have any specific provisions on child relocation, the issue has received some attention from scholars and practitioners in recent years.[1083] In Germany, the right to determine the child's place of residence (*das Aufenthaltsbestimmungsrecht*) is a component of the care of the person of the child (Article 1631(1) of the German Civil Code (*Bürgerliches Gesetzbuch*, BGB)) which, alongside care of the child's property, constitutes the content of parental responsibilities (*die elterliche Sorge*).[1084] German law treats relocation predominantly as a question of modification of parental responsibility rather than approval of the decision to move.[1085] It allows for the separation of different elements of parental responsibility and thus the right to determine the child's place of residence might be distributed differently from other parental rights and obligations.

If parental responsibility is vested in both parents, they both have the right to determine the child's residence and should reach agreement on relocation (Articles 1627 and 1687 of the BGB).[1086] If an agreement cannot be reached, either of them can apply to the court for a transfer of parental responsibility or the right to determine the child's residence (Article 1671 of the BGB).[1087]

1083 e.g. D. Coester-Waltjen, above n. 826; J.A. Hirth, above n. 118; P. Finger, 'Umzug mit dem Kind – Zustimmung des anderen Elternteils' (2009) *Familienrecht und Familienverfahrensrecht* 134; D. Eschelbach and U. Rölke, 'Internationale Relocation – Umzug eines Elternteils mit dem Kind ins Ausland' (2012) 6 *Das Jugendamt* 290; E. Faber, 'Sorge- und Umgangsrecht bei Umzug oder geplanter Auswanderung des betreuenden Elternteils' (2012) *Familie und Recht* 464; K. Scheiwe, above n. 103; or C. Campbell, 'Aufenthaltsbestimmungsrecht und Umzug mit dem Kind ins Ausland' (2022) *Neue Juristische Wochenschrift Spezial* 4.

1084 Article 1626(1) of the BGB. It is important to note that German family law was significantly changed following a *Gesetz zur Reform des Kindschaftsrechts* from 1997 that modified inter alia the scope of parental responsibilities. This did not remain without consequences for the resolution of relocation disputes but does not invalidate the approach followed in this book, given the focus on the discursive interstices of legal argumentation and their interplay with the doctrine. In any case, almost all decisions analysed below postdate the reform.

1085 J.A. Hirth, above n. 118, p. 67.

1086 P. Finger, above n. 1083; K. Scheiwe, above n. 103, pp. 164–65.

1087 Which basis in the statute is appropriate for relocation decisions has been discussed in the doctrine, with some other provisions suggested as well. Article 1671 seems to be the dominant view. For details of the discussion see J.A. Hirth, above n. 118, pp. 67–71. For a recent judicial remark on the difference between Articles 1628 and 1671 of the BGB see *AG Mönchengladbach-Rheydt, Beschluss vom 21.07.2021* – 18 F 85/21.

According to procedural law, the court is always bound by the parties' applications and hence can only consider solutions that have been raised during the proceedings.[1088] A parent who is the sole holder of parental responsibilities is, in principle, allowed to relocate without the consent of the other parent or the court.[1089] If the other parent wishes to prevent the relocation, they need to apply for modification of the parental responsibility.[1090] However, if one parent has an exclusive right to determine the child's place of residence but otherwise shares parental responsibility with the other parent, the situation might depend on whether it is possible for the remaining parent to exercise their other rights after relocation (e.g. regarding decisions on schooling or health matters).[1091] In light of the German law's strong emphasis on freedom of movement, this feature of the doctrine led in practice to interesting developments delineating the scope of parental autonomy according to different legal spaces, as will be discussed below.

7.3.1. FREEDOM OF MOVEMENT AS THE POINT OF DEPARTURE

Decisions on child relocation are, unsurprisingly, taken in reference to the best interests of the child (*Kindeswohl*). The best interests test developed in German law broadly encompasses the following criteria: the competence of a parent to support and foster a child, including their relationship with the other parent; the child's ties and attachment to each parent, to siblings, or to other persons playing an important role in the child's life; continuity in upbringing; and the child's will.[1092] The factors to be taken into account in relocation cases in Germany seem to be broadly similar to those in England.[1093] An interesting difference, in particular in the context of this book, is the attention to the constitutional rights of the parents, including their freedom of movement and autonomy rights. According to the German Federal Court of Justice, courts are not allowed to consider an alternative in which a parent gives up their plans to relocate, nor in principle to scrutinise the motives for

---

1088 J.A. Hirth, above n. 118, pp. 69–70.

1089 This seems to be the dominant interpretation. However, there are also divergent positions presented in the literature based on the equal relationship between contact rights and parental responsibility rights. For a brief discussion see ibid., pp. 71–72.

1090 ibid., pp. 74–75.

1091 e.g. *OLG Koblenz, Beschluss vom 09.08.2007* – 9 UF 450/07, *OLG Köln, Beschluss vom 29.10.2009* – II-21 UF 158/09. See also J.A. Hirth, above n. 118, pp. 73–74.

1092 D. Eschelbach and U. Rölke, above n. 1083; K. Scheiwe, above n. 103, p. 165; J.A. Hirth, above n. 118, pp. 80–104.

1093 K. Scheiwe, above n. 103; H. Baker, J. Hirsch and N. Sauvage, 'International Family Relocation from an English, French and German Perspective' (2012) *International Family Law* 97.

relocation.[1094] The objective of this approach is to prevent the courts from treating the status quo as the default option, which could lead to insufficient engagement with the constitutional freedoms of the relocating parent.[1095] Consequently, courts approach relocation predominantly in consideration of two basic alternatives for the child: to move with the relocating parent or to stay with the non-relocating parent (if this option has been raised).[1096]

This approach not only clearly limits the scope of judicial assessment, but also reflects what can be reasonably expected from the parents. The German Federal Court of Justice argued that, while the child's best interest remains at the centre of every decision, parental applications are to be taken at face value:

> Insofar as it would be the best solution for the child to stay with the mother in Germany and exercise the same extensive contact with the father, this is itself insufficient for not respecting the mother's reasonable wish to move to Mexico. … It is *not the general freedom of the relocating parent and the contact or care rights of the remaining parent that need to be balanced*, but the rights of both parents to care for the child. However, *the general freedom of the relocating parent is nevertheless meaningful insofar as it constitutes the factual point of departure of the balancing exercise.* … The point of departure needs to be that the relocating parent actually moves. The motives for the move cannot in principle be questioned by the court.[1097] (Emphasis added.)

This excerpt explicitly emphasises that it is not the freedom of the relocating parent and contact rights that need to be balanced out, but parental rights that need to be balanced with each other. The freedom of the relocating parent must, however, be considered, as its exercise remains at the core of the dispute, and as such is the starting point of all considerations. Further, the court argued:

> The OLG [second instance court] – differently from the AG [first instance court], and rightly so – did not consider the possibility that the mother stays in Germany.

1094 *BGH, Beschluss vom 28.04.2010* – XII ZB 81/09. See also K. Scheiwe, above n. 103, p. 166, or D. Coester-Waltjen, above n. 826, 312–14.

1095 J.A. Hirth, above n. 118, pp. 136, 154.

1096 ibid., p. 125.

1097 *BGH, Beschluss vom 28.04.2010* – XII ZB 81/09: 'Soweit es dem Kindeswohl von L. noch besser entsprechen würde, wenn sie weiterhin mit ihrer Mutter in Deutschland leben würde und engen Umgangskontakt zum Vater hätte, reicht dies allein nicht aus, um den nachvollziehbaren Wunsch der Mutter auf Übersiedlung nach Mexiko nicht zu respektieren … Für die Entscheidung sind demnach nicht die allgemeine Handlungsfreiheit des auswanderungswilligen Elternteils und das Elternrecht des im Inland verbleibenden Elternteils gegeneinander abzuwägen, sondern die beiderseitigen Elternrechte. Allerdings ist die allgemeine Handlungsfreiheit des auswanderungswilligen Elternteils gleichwohl bedeutsam, indem sie die tatsächliche Ausgangslage für die Abwägung bestimmt. … Tatsächlicher Ausgangspunkt muss vielmehr sein, dass der Elternteil seinen Auswanderungswunsch in die Tat umsetzt. Die Motive des Elternteils für seinen Auswanderungsentschluss stehen entgegen der Ansicht der Rechtsbeschwerde jedenfalls grundsätzlich nicht zur Überprüfung des FamG'.

> This applies *also in cases where, were the relocation to be refused, the mother would decide to stay to care for the child which in turn would prove to be in the best interests of the child.* In general it is to assume that the mother will follow through with her relocation plan and on this basis to decide if it is better for the child to relocate with the mother to Mexico, or to stay with the father in this country.[1098] (Emphasis added.)

This approach led the courts to formulate the parental wish to relocate as, in principle, reasonable per se. The reasonability of the move is typically beyond scrutiny and prompts a reorientation of the courts' scope of investigation of the child's best interests more broadly. Once the wish to relocate is assumed to be reasonable, the relocating parent cannot be typically expected to stay, as confirmed in other judgments:

> The alternative would be that the mother renounces the plan to move to Paris to be with her partner. This cannot however be expected of her. Her right to freely decide where she wants to live has preference – and definitely in this particular case – over the right of the father to retain the same contact regime.[1099]

The apprehension of the doctrine to engage in the assessment of respective parental plans, due to the constitutional embedding of parental rights, goes even further. The sample suggests that courts do not consider the possibility of the relocating parent staying, even when the parent declares they will do so in the event of a relocation refusal. The fact that they are willing to make such a sacrifice does not mean, *as a matter of law*, that the court can expect them to:

> The declared willingness of the [mother], in the event of [refusal of the application to relocate], to neglect her own interests and needs, possibly under certain circumstances and for a limited period of time, and to stay in Germany as abroad

---

[1098] ibid.: 'Das OLG hat – anders als das AG – zu Recht nicht auf die Möglichkeit abgestellt, dass die Mutter mit dem Kind in Deutschland verbleibt. Das gilt auch für den Fall, dass sich die Mutter, wenn ihr die Auswanderung gemeinsam mit dem Kind verwehrt wäre, für einen Verbleib in Deutschland entschließen würde und dies wiederum dem Kindeswohl im Ergebnis am besten entspräche. Insoweit ist vielmehr – wie ausgeführt – von dem Fall auszugehen, dass die Mutter ihren Auswanderungsplan verwirklicht, und auf dieser Grundlage zu entscheiden, ob es dem Kindeswohl besser dient, wenn das Kind mit der Mutter nach Mexiko übersiedelt oder aber beim Vater im Inland bleibt'.

[1099] *AG Offenburg, Beschluss vom 18.06.2008* – 2 F 423/06: 'Die Alternative bestünde darin, dass die Antragstellerin darauf verzichtet, zu ihrem Freund nach Paris zu ziehen. Dies kann von der Antragstellerin indes nicht verlangt werden. Ihr Recht darauf, frei entscheiden zu können, wo sie ihren Lebensmittelpunkt hat, hat – jedenfalls im vorliegenden Fall – Vorrang vor dem Recht des Antragsgegners, den Umgang mit in bisherigem Maß ausüben zu können'. See also, for example, *OLG Karlsruhe, Beschluss vom 27.11.2008* – 2 UF 88/08; *OLG Nürnberg, Beschluss vom 09.09.2010* – 11 WF 972/10; *AG Essen, Beschluss vom 18.02.2003* – 106 F 202/02.

> from her point of view, cannot be of any decisive importance. In fact it was only her unconditional good will, and were she to assert otherwise she could actually go to Canada. But then the child's wellbeing would in fact be much more impaired by the interruption of contact with the mother.[1100]

This emphasises that a significant value is attached to the autonomy rights of relocating parents.

As such, the court compares, from a child-centred view, the implications of the potential relocation and the implications of a potential change of the caring arrangement with the non-relocating parent as the resident parent. If relocation is deemed to be the better solution, the potential diminution in contact is to be calculated into the natural flows of life. Support for contact is an important part of the assessment of the parent's suitability,[1101] but the parent is not expected to sacrifice their autonomy and reasonable plans to secure the desired or maximum possible contact with the other parent.[1102] This is framed as the lack of obligation to secure 'effortless' contact, emphasising that while the relocating parent has to make an effort to support contact, it is also the non-relocating parent who needs to make efforts to exercise contact, which in light of relocation might reasonably require respective adjustments.[1103]

This does not mean that a relocating parent's negative attitude towards contact is irrelevant. As mentioned, this aspect constitutes an important part of the assessment of this parent's suitability. However, in relocation cases, such an attitude is framed not only as a misuse of parental rights, but also as an abuse of freedom of movement:

> The German Federal Court of Justice had decided on multiple occasions that the freedom of movement of the custodial parent entails relocation abroad. As such, it has seen this freedom as having priority over an effortless exercise of contact. … If, however, the relocating parent's sole intention was to disrupt or prevent contact,

---

1100 *OLG Zweibrücken, Beschluss vom 13.07.2004* – 5 UF 47/04: 'Der erklärten Bereitschaft der Ast., bei Nichtübertragung oder Einschränkung des Aufenthaltsbestimmungsrechtes zum Wohle des Kindes unter Hintanstellung eigener Interessen und Bedürfnisse möglicherweise unter Umständen und wenn auch nur zeitlich beschränkt in Deutschland als aus ihrer Sicht Ausland zu verbleiben, kann schlechterdings keine entscheidungserhebliche Bedeutung zukommen, bräuchte sie doch nur ihren unbedingten und auf gute Gründe gestützten anderweitigen Willen zum Ausdruck zu bringen und sich tatsächlich nach Kanada zu begeben. Dann aber wäre das Kindeswohl in der Tat durch die Unterbrechung des Kontaktes zwischen Mutter und Kind weit mehr beeinträchtigt'.

1101 See also H. Baker, J. Hirsch and N. Sauvage, above n. 1093, 102.

1102 e.g. *OLG Düsseldorf, Beschluss vom 05.08.2003* – II-6 UF 57/03; *BGH, Beschluss vom 06.12.1989* – IVb ZB 66/88.

1103 See, for example: *AG Offenburg, Beschluss vom 18.06.2008* – 2 F 423/06; *OLG Nürnberg, Beschluss vom 09.09.2010* – 11 WF 972/10; *OLG Karlsruhe, Beschluss vom 27.11.2008* – 2 UF 88/08; *OLG Frankfurt, Beschluss vom 28.11.2006* – 3 UF 238/06.

> this would be abusive and not covered by the fundamental right to freedom of movement.[1104]

Interestingly, in a case where such an abusive motivation was found, the court framed rejection of the relocation application as a matter of the mother's freedom of movement giving way to the child's interests:

> With relocation to Salerno (Italy), which means a far-reaching change for the [child], the mother would put her own interests in fleeing her conflicts over the needs of the child to have reliable and stable relationships. … In these circumstances, the freedom of movement that the mother enjoys needs to weigh less than the child's interest in enjoying contact with the father.[1105]

Autonomy and freedom of movement are explicitly protected, but only if exercised in good faith.

Parental plans to move abroad can, therefore, be restricted, if justified by the circumstances of the case, and so can the right to determine a child's place of residence as a matter of principle. In one such dispute, not involving a specific proposal to relocate abroad, this right (*das Aufenthaltsbestimmungsrecht*) was restricted to the territory of Germany only. The mother (a Turkish national) was therefore granted the exclusive right to change the children's residence, but only within the country. While justifying its decision, the court found it necessary to elaborate on the consequences of the judgment for the mother's freedom of movement:

> This limitation does not unproportionately infringe upon this parent's freedom of movement. If [the mother] does in fact decide to move with the child or children to another country, be it now or at some point in the future, [she] has the possibility to clarify in a further set of proceedings if conditions for such a move abroad are in fact met.[1106]

1104 *OLG Frankfurt, Beschluss vom 28.11.2006* – 3 UF 238/06: 'Der BGH hat mehrfach entschieden, dass es gerade zu dem Recht auf Freizügigkeit des betreuenden Elternteils gehört, auch ins Ausland zu gehen und sogar dort den Wohnsitz zu begründen. Er hat insoweit dieses Recht als vorrangig gegenüber dem Recht des anderen Elternteils auf mühelosen Umgang gesehen … Wenn man allerdings ihre Absicht unterstellte, den gewöhnlichen Aufenthalt des Kindes nur wechseln zu wollen, um ein Umgangsrecht des Vaters zu verhindern, so wäre dies missbräuchlich und nicht vom Grundrecht der Freizügigkeit gedeckt'.

1105 *OLG Koblenz, Beschluss vom 04.05.2010* – 11 UF 149/10: 'Mit einer Übersiedlung in die Provinz Salerno/Italien, die für … eine tiefgreifende Veränderung herbeiführen würde, würde die Antragstellerin ihre eigenen Interessen nach Lösung ihrer Konflikte über die Bedürfnisse des Kindes nach verlässlichen und stabilen Verhältnissen stellen. … Unter diesen Umständen muss die Freizügigkeit, die die Antragstellerin genießt, im Hinblick auf das Kindeswohl hinter das Umgangsrecht des Antragsgegners zurücktreten'.

1106 *OLG Stuttgart, Beschluss vom 08.10.2020* – 15 UF 176/20: 'Mit dieser Beschränkung wird die Freizügigkeit dieses Elternteils nicht unangemessen beeinträchtigt. Will dieser tatsächlich

This confirms that parental freedom of movement is an important value in disputes involving children's residence, notwithstanding their exact nature or outcomes.

The approach put forward by the German Federal Court of Justice and developed in the subsequent jurisprudence can be seen as delocalising family life to some extent. It does so through protecting the reasonable expectation to move, but not through taking into consideration the non-relocating parent's ability to move. The relocating parent is not expected to stay and the non-relocating parent is not expected to go, with both choices being valid, reasonable, and, in principle, beyond scrutiny.[1107] Neither of the options is the default option, and whether the child will stay or go depends on the quality of care and respective relationships in light of all circumstances. This means that primary carers will typically be allowed to relocate, while relocation in truly shared arrangements cases will often weigh towards preserving the status quo understood as the current place of residence.[1108] This approach has developed, however, fully and exclusively in reference to national law. Despite the significance attached to freedom of movement in the resolution of child relocation disputes, no case in the sample mentions this freedom in the context of the EU legal framework.

One can only hypothesise about the reasons behind this lack of engagement with EU law. It might correspond to the general scarcity of references to supranational law in relocation cases. Out of all analysed cases, only two very briefly mention the jurisprudence of the ECtHR.[1109] Other international instruments or the Washington Declaration are not mentioned at all, even though the Declaration is translated into German and discussed in the German literature.[1110] But it might also suggest that courts consciously avoid references to EU freedom of movement because they anticipate that such claims could be objectionable, or that it would let EU law into an area of law that has been consequently defended by the German judiciary as beyond EU law's scope.[1111] With the German Basic Law (*Grundgesetz für die Bundesrepublik Deutschland*)

---

jetzt oder zu einem späteren Zeitpunkt mit dem Kind bzw. den Kindern in einen anderen Staat wegziehen, verbleibt ihm die Möglichkeit, in einem weiteren Verfahren klären zu lassen, ob die Voraussetzungen für einen Wegzug ins Ausland tatsächlich vorliegen'.

1107 e.g. *AG Essen, Beschluss vom 18.02.2003* – 106 F 202/02. See also the considerations in a recent internal relocation case: *OLG Frankfurt a. M., Beschluss vom 04.01.2022* – 7 UF 117/21.

1108 J.A. Hirth, above n. 118, pp. 130–35.

1109 *OLG Frankfurt, Beschluss vom 28.11.2006* – 3 UF 238/06; *OLG München, Beschluss vom 09.05.2008* – 12 UF 1854/07.

1110 D. Eschelbach and U. Rölke, above n. 1083; D. Coester-Waltjen, above n. 826.

1111 See the judgment of the German Federal Constitutional Court where the court held that the EU Treaty must leave sufficient space to the Member States for the political formation of the economic, cultural, and social living conditions, including matters shaping the circumstances of family life, and hence family law: *BVerfG, Urteil vom 30.06.2009* – 2 BvE 2/08.

providing an independent legal ground for protection of freedom and autonomy interests, such references are not necessary and might be strategically avoided. The latter hypothesis might be supported by the fact that EU law has featured in judicial decisions in other ways, in particular in reference to the European space of rights.

7.3.2. THE EU AS A SPACE OF RIGHTS

German courts very rarely consider recognition and enforcement as a factor in relocation cases.[1112] This has been criticised in the literature,[1113] but it also explains the lack of references to the Brussels II*bis* Regulation in comparison to those that can be observed in English judgments. The EU space of rights is not, however, entirely absent from the judgments. It is employed in two different ways that represent different dimensions of this space. The first one can be associated with the space of mutual trust, as identified in the previous chapter, limiting the scope of arguments one can raise against relocation to another Member State. The other usage, while related to the first one, links the legal framework with a broader socio-legal environment. Importantly, as mentioned at the beginning of this section, this has led to a substantively different scope of autonomy offered to parents who, while having the sole right to determine the child's place of residence, otherwise share parental responsibilities with the non-relocating parent. Thus, one can suggest that engagement with Europe and EU law has led to doctrinal changes in national law.

The first usage can be observed in a judgment of the Constitutional Court of the State of Berlin, issued in response to a constitutional complaint filed by a father who wanted to relocate to Spain with his disabled daughter. The lower court decided that because of the economic crisis in Spain, good conditions for a disabled child cannot be expected, either in terms of financial support from social services or infrastructure and education opportunities, even if granted by law. At the same time, the court said that in Germany there is a very good market for care services and sufficient financial support, considering the child's lifelong situation. Such argumentation was not accepted by the Constitutional Court:

> Insofar as [the lower court] referred to the poor economic situation in Spain and the questionable realisation of social law claims there, stating that it was ultimately unable to assess such general conditions, this was – already on the basis of detailed

1112 Only two cases include such considerations: *BGH, Beschluss vom 28.04.2010* – XII ZB 81/09; *KG Berlin, Beschluss vom 05.09.2008* – 18 UF 83/08. See also J.A. Hirth, above n. 118, pp. 169–70.

1113 J.A. Hirth, above n. 118, pp. 96–100, 163.

> considerations of the social law conditions in Spain – not acceptable. Independently, [the court] should not have concluded that it is unable to make a final assessment on this, but should have determined all the necessary circumstances according to procedural rules. Furthermore, [the court] could not legitimately question the rule of law of another EU Member State.[1114]

This excerpt already suggests that the primary issue at stake was that the court failed to sufficiently investigate the situation in Spain. The assertions about the economic situation in Spain and its consequences for the child were simply not factually substantiated enough. In light of this, one can wonder about the role of the last sentence that ties such an assessment to the rule of law of another Member State. In the context of the whole judgment, it even seems contradictory – either the problem is the depth of factual assessment of the situation, or the competence of the court to make such an assessment in the first place. This phrasing clearly also carries a normative value, one that draws attention to mutual ties between EU Member States and can be linked to mutual trust. While such an EU law reference is not explicitly repeated in any other case, arguments of a similar nature to those that gave rise to this complaint were rejected in all subsequent intra-EU cases.[1115] The same outcome in that case could probably have been achieved without any reference to the EU, but the court clearly 'used' Europe to strengthen its argument, if not to put forward a normative proposal as to the acceptable scope and nature of assessment of other EU legal systems.

A related yet different usage of Europe perceives the space of rights more broadly. As already mentioned, if one parent has the sole right to determine the child's place of residence but otherwise shares parental responsibility with the other parent, the doctrine permits the parent to relocate without the other parent's approval when the remaining parent will be able to exercise their rights after relocation. The doctrine, while delineating the scope of autonomy

---

1114 *VerfGH Berlin, Beschluss vom 19.03.2013* – VerfGH 158/12: 'Soweit das Kammergericht auf die schlechte wirtschaftliche Situation in Spanien und die fragliche Realisierung von sozialrechtlichen Ansprüchen in Spanien abgestellt und hierzu ausgeführt habe, die Rahmenbedingungen in Spanien letztlich nicht beurteilen zu können, sei dies – schon aufgrund seiner ausführlichen Darlegungen zu den sozialrechtlichen Bedingungen in Spanien – nicht nachvollziehbar. Abgesehen davon hätte sich das Kammergericht nicht darauf zurückziehen dürfen, zu einer abschließenden Beurteilung nicht in der Lage zu sein, sondern hätte nach dem geltenden Amtsermittlungsgrundsatz selbst die für eine abschließende Prüfung notwendigen Umstände ermitteln müssen. Des Weiteren sei nicht nachvollziehbar, dass es rechtsstaatliche Prinzipien in dem EU-Mitgliedsland Spanien in Zweifel ziehe'.

1115 e.g. *OLG Köln, Beschluss vom 04.11.2015* – 10 UF 123/15, involving a relocation to Greece. The court shared the concerns of the first instance court regarding the health insurance status of the child but agreed with its decision that it cannot attach such weight to these concerns that would result in rejection of the application. The same applied to other concerns about school and a broader economic framework.

in relocation cases, has been understandably clarified in reference to child abduction law (and the concept of wrongful removal under the 1980 Hague Child Abduction Convention in particular). For example, the Higher Regional Court in Koblenz explained its decision on the lawfulness of relocation to the UK in the following terms:

> The dispute concerns [the father's] right to decide about the essential aspects of upbringing (e.g. religion, schooling, etc.) and health of the children. The ability to exercise these rights is not significantly reduced by relocation. It is true that the father can no longer directly supervise the wellbeing of his children as often as before. Language problems can also play a role if the father wants to obtain information about the children from third parties (e.g. at school). However, the father can continue to exercise his rights. One cannot assert that these exist only formally and in reality he is prevented from exercising them. *It must not be forgotten that the mother and the children have moved to another country of the European Community. The children's father enjoys freedom of movement there. The legal systems of the states in the Community and the living conditions there are not significantly different as far as child welfare aspects are concerned. Therefore, if a parent who has the sole right to determine the place of residence for the child changes his or her place of residence and that of the child within the states of the European Community against the will of the parent who is otherwise also a holder of parental responsibility, this is not unlawful in the sense of the Child Abduction Convention, because the other parent can sufficiently exercise his rights from home.*[1116] (Emphasis added.)

The court, to strengthen its assessment, referred also to Article 9 of the Brussels II*bis* Regulation that allowed the courts of the country of origin to retain jurisdiction in contact matters for three months after the move, to allow

1116 *OLG Koblenz, Beschluss vom 09.08.2007* – 9 UF 450/07: 'In der Sache geht es um die Mitentscheidung über die wesentlichen Aspekte der Erziehung (z. B. Religion, Entscheidung über eine weiterführende Schule usw.), aber auch um das gesundheitliche Wohl der Kinder. Die Möglichkeit, diese Rechte auszuüben, werden durch den neuen Aufenthaltsort der Kinder nicht wesentlich geschmälert. Zwar kann der Vater das Wohlergehen seiner Kinder nicht mehr durch Augeschein so häufig überprüfen wie vor dem Wechsel. Auch können Sprachprobleme eine Rolle spielen, wenn der Vater sich Informationen über die Kinder bei Dritten einholen will (z. B. bei der Schule). Jedoch kann der Vater weiter seine Rechte ausüben. Es kann keine Rede davon sein, dass diese für ihn nur noch formal bestehen, er aber tatsächlich an ihrer Ausübung gehindert ist. Es darf nicht aus dem Blick geraten, dass die Mutter mit den Kindern in ein anderes Land der europäischen Gemeinschaft übergesiedelt ist. Der Kindesvater genießt dort Freizügigkeit. Die Rechtssysteme der Staaten der Gemeinschaft und die dortigen Lebensverhältnisse sind nicht gravierend unterschiedlich, soweit Kindeswohlaspekte betroffen sind. Wechselt deshalb ein Elternteil, der das alleinige Aufenthaltsbestimmungsrecht für das Kind hat, seinen Wohnort und den des Kindes innerhalb der Staaten der europäischen Gemeinschaft gegen den Willen des im Übrigen mitsorgeberechtigten Elternteils, ist das nicht widerrechtlich i. S. von Art. 3 HKiEntÜ, weil der andere Elternteil seine Mitsorge auch von seinem Heimatland aus in ausreichendem Maße ausüben kann'.

the non-relocating parent to adjust to the contact regime if necessary.[1117] The Regulation was, however, not at the centre of the judgment. Rather, the court focused on general social and legal similarities between the Community members. The legal framework relevant for the assessment included the freedom of movement that the father himself enjoys in the UK, implying that he can go, at any time, to see the child and exercise his parental responsibilities. This decision was subsequently referenced in a case that involved relocation to Thailand where the court said:

> While a change of residence within the European Community is to be accepted against the will of the parent who otherwise shares parental responsibility, since the other parent can also sufficiently exercise their rights from their home state … , relocation from Germany to Thailand constitutes a different case due to the distance and the associated problems of adequate communication with the child and his/her caregivers in the social environment. It would factually be impossible for the other parent to exercise their rights, such as health care, property management as well as religion or schooling.[1118]

As these cases demonstrate, the doctrine was (re)constructed, at least partially, in reference to the juxtaposition of the European Community and other cases. This encounter with the European space became an orientation point for future judgments. Subsequently, the 'test' of ability to exercise parental rights post-relocation expanded into other, non-EU, cases,[1119] to some extent reflecting the spillover of the mutual trust logic observed in English cases. In a case involving relocation to Russia, the court observed:

> The Court is of the opinion that the father is not unreasonably prevented from the exercise of his rights by the relocation of the child to Moscow to the extent that would result in the move being unlawful. The dispute concerns [the father's] right to decide about the essential aspects of upbringing (e.g. religion, schooling, etc.) and health of the child. The ability to exercise these rights is not significantly reduced by the child's new place of residence, since the Russian Federation is a signatory to

---

1117 ibid. See also Article 8 of the Brussels II*ter* Regulation.

1118 *OLG Köln, Beschluss vom 29.10.2009* – II-21 UF 158/09: 'Auch wenn ein Wechsel des Wohnortes innerhalb der Staaten der europäischen Gemeinschaft gegen den Willen des im Übrigen mitsorgeberechtigten Elternteils zu akzeptieren ist, da der andere Elternteil seine Mitsorge in derartigen Fällen auch von seinem Heimatland aus in ausreichendem Maße ausüben kann …, beinhaltet eine Übersiedelung von Deutschland nach Thailand aufgrund der Entfernung und der damit zusammenhängenden Probleme einer hinreichenden Kommunikation mit dem Kind und dessen Bezugspersonen im sozialen Umfeld, dass eine Ausübung der den Kindeseltern gemeinsam zustehenden Teilbereiche der elterlichen Sorge, wie z. B. der Gesundheitsfürsorge, der Vermögenssorge sowie die Entscheidung über die Religion und den Schulbesuch, tatsächlich unmöglich gemacht würde'.

1119 *OLG Köln, Beschluss vom 29.10.2009* – II-21 UF 158/09; *KG Berlin, Beschluss vom 02.03.2015* – 3 UF 156/14.

> the 1996 Hague Convention and bound by its provisions, including the obligation to recognise German authorities' decisions in the area of parental custody to provide an authority infrastructure including the planned central authority that ensures compliance with the Convention. ... Regarding the question of whether a different decision would have to be made here if the mother had moved to a country to which Germany is not linked by international agreements in matters relating to parental custody and in which personal contacts are difficult to establish using modern means of communication, or require long and arduous journeys, the Court did not need to consider this.[1120]

The approach focuses on private international law and factual possibilities of exercising parental rights.[1121] The interplay between the factual and legal aspects of the situations remains somewhat vague, and the case sample too limited to draw any definitive conclusions. However, the construction of the relevant socio-legal context for EU destinations allows them to be perceived through a general quasi-presumption of the ability to enforce and exercise rights post-relocation, while non-EU cases might be subject to scrutiny on an individual basis. This conclusion, reflecting a particular normative layer of the European space, is supported by other cases involving children's mobility, for example imposing restrictions on international travel only on travel outside of the European Union.[1122]

1120 *KG Berlin, Beschluss vom 02.03.2015* – 3 UF 156/14: 'Der Senat ist der Auffassung, dass dem Vater die Wahrnehmung der übrigen Teilbereiche der elterlichen Sorge, die er zusammen mit der Mutter ausübt, nicht unzumutbar durch die Übersiedlung des Kindes nach Moskau in einem solchen Maße erschwert ist, dass sich damit die Mitnahme des Kindes als widerrechtlich im Sinne von Art. 7 KSÜ darstellt. In der Sache geht es um die Mitentscheidung über die wesentlichen Aspekte der Erziehung (z. B. Religion, Entscheidung über den Besuch einer Kita/eines Kindergarten und später der Schule), aber auch um das gesundheitliche Wohl des Kindes. Die Möglichkeit, diese Rechte auszuüben, werden durch den neuen Aufenthaltsort des Kindes nicht wesentlich geschmälert, zumal die Russische Föderation Vertragsstaat des KSÜ ist und an die dort geschlossenen völkerrechtlichen Vereinbarungen gebunden ist, dementsprechend die Anerkennung deutscher Behördenentscheidungen im Bereich der elterlichen Sorge (Art. 23 ff. KSÜ) im Rahmen des Abkommens sicher stellen und eine Behördeninfrastruktur einschließlich der vorgesehenen Zentralen Verbindungsbehörde (Art. 29 ff. KSÜ) zur Verfügung stellen muss, die die Erfüllung der eingegangenen internationalen Verpflichtungen sicher stellt. ... Auf die Frage, inwieweit hier anders zu entscheiden wäre, wenn die Mutter in ein Land verzogen wäre, mit dem die Bundesrepublik Deutschland nicht durch völkerrechtliche Vereinbarungen in die die elterliche Sorge betreffenden Angelegenheiten verbunden ist und in das persönliche Kontakte über moderne Kommunikationsmittel nur schwer herzustellen und weite und mühsame Reisen erforderlich sind (vgl. etwa im Fall eines nach Thailand verbrachten Kindes: OLG Köln, Beschluss vom 29.10.2009 – II-21 UF 158/09 -, zit.n.juris), brauchte der Senat hier nicht einzugehen'.

1121 Thailand is not a signatory to the 1996 Hague Convention, but the argumentation focused on broader issues of distance, difficulties in communication, and social environment rather than any private international law regime.

1122 *OLG Brandenburg, Beschluss vom 29.3.2022* – 10 UF 43/21.

7.3.3. THE EUROPEAN CHILD?

The two usages of Europe discussed above link to different aspects of mutual trust as rooted in the logic of recognising the equivalence of different EU legal systems. This normative dimension of recognition requirements can be employed much more broadly, contributing to a construction of context based on the overall mobilising logic of EU law used by the CJEU in cases involving children. Before discussing such usage of Europe, it is important to briefly mention the role of cultural considerations in German relocation cases. Heritage and culture rarely occupy a significant space in relocation cases, although multiple judgments contain strong assertions that there is no 'natural priority' of upbringing in Germany.[1123] Against this background, the judgment below contains an interesting coupling of cultural considerations and the EU both as a legal and social context:

> The fears put forward by the father that relocation to Italy will lead to an alienation of the children from their German linguistic and cultural background, and that their 'claim to national identity should not be sacrificed to a rootless utopian internationalism', were not seen by the OLG [lower instance court] as carrying significant weight. Taking into account the circumstances, *a bilingual and bicultural education in another large European country will be an advantage. Italian school-leaving qualifications will be, if necessary, recognised in the whole of the European Union.* Eventual difficulties for further studies in Germany, resulting from growing up abroad and being part of another schooling system, are therefore not so grave that they could justify refusal of relocation and require a transfer of custody to the father.[1124] (Emphasis added.)

It is perhaps unsurprising that the courts rejected claims based on the cultural identity of the child, and from this point of view the case might be seen as another example of the rejection of any priority of German upbringing. However, this case is remarkable because the socio-cultural assessment is coupled with the

---

1123 e.g. *OLG Zweibrücken, Beschluss vom 13.07.2004* – 5 UF 47/04: 'Jeder "natürliche Vorrang" für eine Erziehung des Kindes in Deutschland wäre jedenfalls völlig'.

1124 *BGH, Beschluss vom 06.12.1989* – IVb ZB 66/88: 'Der vom Vater demgegenüber in den Vordergrund gestellten Befürchtung, daß die Kinder in Italien dem deutschen Sprach- und Kulturraum entfremdet würden, jedoch ihr "Anspruch auf nationale Identität nicht einem wurzellosen utopischen Internationalismus geopfert werden" dürfe, hat das OLG kein durchschlagendes Gewicht beigemessen. … Unter diesen Umständen sei ein zweisprachiges Aufwachsen für die weitere Entwicklung der Kinder ein Gewinn. Schulabschlüsse in Italien würden auch in der Europäischen Gemeinschaft anerkannt. Mögliche Schwierigkeiten für ein späteres Studium in Deutschland infolge des Aufwachsens in einem anderen Kulturkreis und Schulsystem seien nicht derart gewichtig, daß es gerechtfertigt sei, die Kinder aus den derzeitigen günstigen Lebensverhältnissen herauszunehmen und das Sorgerecht auf den Vater zu übertragen'.

EU legal layer. The court came back to these considerations while rejecting the appeal:

> The OLG [lower court] has recognised the problems that can arise for the children from attending an Italian primary school and from growing up in an Italian environment and included them in its assessment. ... The OLG did not overlook the fact that, compared to others who grew up in Germany and only attended German schools, children may in the future be disadvantaged in areas that are based on a particular knowledge of German culture and German language. However, there is no legal ground to question its assessment not to attach decisive importance to it in the regulation of custody, especially since this disadvantage is *in the context of European development* offset by the significant advantage of growing up with links to another European – Italian – linguistic and cultural background.[1125] (Emphasis added.)

It is not only the bicultural and bilingual education that is of benefit to the children – and in any case, whether this brings a particular benefit for German children with German parents and no links to another country could in principle be questioned. But it is the bicultural and bilingual education '*in another big European country*' and '*in the context of European developments*' that is seen as an advantage that offsets the possible disadvantages. Additionally, the territoriality of the European space of rights is emphasised with the reference to the recognition of Italian school-leaving qualifications that should allow the children to continue their education and professional life in Germany if they wish to do so in the future. The consideration of cultural factors was probably brought by the father's claims and might be considered incidental. However, this framing of the issue was in no way obvious and indicates that the court saw the usage of Europe in this context as supporting the overall argumentation.[1126] In principle, this could be seen as an example of appropriation of the methodology of the CJEU. However, as this judgment precedes respective EU

[1125] ibid.: 'Das OLG hat die Probleme, die aus dem Besuch der italienischen Grundschule und aus dem Aufwachsen in einer italienischen Umwelt für die Kinder entstehen können, erkannt und in seine Würdigung einbezogen. ... Das OLG hat nicht übersehen, daß die Kinder später im Vergleich zu anderen, die in Deutschland aufgewachsen sind und nur deutsche Schulen besucht haben, auf den Gebieten benachteiligt sein können, die auf besondere Kenntnisse der deutschen Kultur und der deutschen Sprache aufbauen. Es ist aber rechtlich nicht zu beanstanden, daß es dem keine für die Regelung des Sorgerechts ausschlaggebende Bedeutung beigemessen hat, zumal diesem Nachteil, der im Hinblick auf die europäische Entwicklung hoch einzuschätzende Vorteil gegenübersteht, mit dem italienischen einem zweiten großen europäischen Sprach- und Kulturkreis besonders verbunden zu sein'.

[1126] One could investigate in more detail to what extent these pronouncements mirrored a broader discourse of that time. The decision was issued in December 1988, the year in which Germany took over the Presidency of the Council of the European Communities and on the cusp of the year that was to bring revolutionary developments in Europe. In the 1990s, overall support for the EU and European integration was also relatively high.

law developments, it should rather be seen as a usage of Europe flowing from the national level, and clearly indicates the constructive potential of the EU beyond its legal pressures.

7.3.4. PRELIMINARY CONCLUSIONS

The characteristic feature of the German law on child relocation is its consistent emphasis on the autonomy rights of the relocating parent. However, as freedom of movement is protected by the German constitution, courts have clearly not felt a need to frame it within the EU context. As this emphasis was first clearly expressed in a case about relocation to Mexico, one can reasonably see it as not EU-ropean in origin. Such a framing could come naturally, given the quasi-synonymous nature of free movement and the EU, but its absence suggests that no particular pressures of EU law are felt in this regard. This development delocalises family life in line with what the EU normativity would project, insofar as it does not treat non-relocation as a default option. Nevertheless, it remains domestic in origin and the EU does not seem to have played any role in the doctrine formation in this regard.

German judgments provide, however, rich examples of the reception and reconstruction of the more contextual and ideational influences of the EU. One such example reflects on the doctrine applied in cases where the relocating parent has the sole right to determine the child's place of residence, but otherwise shares parental rights with the non-relocating parent. In such cases, the doctrine makes the lawfulness of relocation dependent on whether the rights of the remaining parent can be exercised after the move. This doctrine is explicitly framed in reference to the EU as a space of rights and a broader relevant context. At the same time, this framing was subsequently expanded to encompass also other states, e.g. European signatories of the 1996 Hague Convention. As such, while EU law and its contextual discourses carry a particular normative value, it is not (or at least it is no longer) an exclusive trigger for the reorientation of national doctrines. This might have to do with a spillover of the logic of mutual trust, as discussed in the English context, but might also prove that all private international law instruments are more generally seen now as equivalent or that such arguments do not carry much independent weight in the first place, being rather used to support the judicial conclusion reached on other facts. The EU space of rights seems to feature in German judgments, although subtly, also to limit the extent to which national courts can scrutinise the legal systems of other Member States – a usage that can legitimately be argued to be unique to the EU space.

Incidentally, Europe was also used as a contextual point of reference in the perception of the child's best interests. This perception was closely linked to the broader European developments and the space of rights that allows

European citizens to cross borders smoothly. This space was constructed based on the EU legal infrastructures and societal values that become bound to such infrastructures. Thus, it reflected a particular cultural construction of the child, reminiscent of the discussion in Chapter 5. However, as noted, the judgment preceded most of such developments on the EU level, indicating a national origin of the construction. Despite this and the incidental nature of the judgment, its line of reasoning clearly illustrates the constructive potential of the many different usages of Europe.

7.4. POLAND

Child relocation has not been extensively analysed in the Polish literature as a specific legal issue. According to Article 95 §1 of the Family and Guardianship Code (*Kodeks rodzinny i opiekuńczy*, KRO), parental authority includes duties and rights relating to the supervision of the child and his or her property, and decisions about his or her upbringing. This catalogue is not exhaustive,[1127] and the rights and duties of parental supervision are broadly accepted as including the right to determine a child's residence.[1128] Parents sharing parental responsibilities should make joint decisions on important matters concerning the child and if there is disagreement, they can apply to family court to decide the matter.[1129] Relocation abroad has been consistently held to be an important matter concerning the child.[1130] The exercise of parental responsibility is dividable and might be left with both parents, or the court can designate one parent as the custodial parent without formally limiting the parental responsibility of the other, but by indicating the scope of their rights in relation to specific matters (including, usually, the right to co-decide on the child's residence).[1131]

If both parents share parental responsibility for the child, either of them can apply to the court to resolve the matter and/or modify existing arrangements.[1132] In practice, most such cases are framed as an application to resolve an important matter regarding the child, such as a specific application for approval of the planned relocation. If one parent has sole parental authority

1127 E. Trybulska-Skoczelas, 'Art. 95' in J. Wierciński (ed), *Kodeks Rodzinny i Opiekuńczy. Komentarz*, System Informacji Prawnej LEX, 2014; G. Jędrejek, 'Art. 95' in G. Jędrejek (ed), *Kodeks Rodzinny i Opiekuńczy. Pokrewieństwo i Powinowactwo. Komentarz*, System Informacji Prawnej LEX, 2014.

1128 *Uchwała Sądu Najwyższego z dnia 23 maja 2012 r.*, III CZP 21/12, OSNC 2012/12/140.

1129 Article 97 §2 of the KRO.

1130 See *Uchwała Sądu Najwyższego z dnia 10 listopada 1971 r.*, III CZP 69/71, OSNC 1972/3/49.

1131 Articles 58 §1a and 107 §1 of the KRO. See also E. Trybulska-Skoczelas, above n. 1127.

1132 Article 730 §1 ff. of the Civil Procedure Code (*Kodeks postępowania cywilnego*).

over a child, they are, in principle, free to relocate. A parent who does not have the right to decide on the child's residence but fears that the other parent might take the child abroad, can file a motion for an injunction (*zabezpieczenie*) to stop any potential relocation, or might apply for a modification of the parental responsibility regime. The question of whether a parent with the sole right to decide where the child resides can relocate if the other parent shares other elements of parental responsibility remains disputed,[1133] but an analysis of the case law and the literature suggests that such situations are very rare.

Parental responsibilities shall be exercised in a manner that supports the child's interests and social interests (*dobro dziecka i interes społeczny*).[1134] This is also the standard for judicial decisions. Notwithstanding the phrasing, these two elements are generally seen as overlapping and should be interpreted in line with the child's best interests principle from the CRC.[1135] The child's interests should be understood both in a subjectivised and in an objectivised way, taking into account the views and values of a given family or environment of the child, which should normally prove to be in line with the social interests.[1136] The child's welfare will normally prevail if there is a conflict with the other interests.[1137] This cannot, however, be understood as a complete disregard of parental interests insofar as mutual relationships are involved.[1138] The doctrine has not established any uniform guidelines as to how (in light of what specific factors) to assess the child's interests. There is also no specific doctrine nor commentary on the resolution of child relocation cases. Thus, the court will determine the relevant factors according to the facts of the case.

The reported case law in Poland allows limited conclusions to be drawn, compared to England and Germany, or perhaps leads to conclusions of a different kind. First of all, the sample of cases is much smaller and comprises predominantly cases decided in the last few years, and almost exclusively include intra-EU migrations. Another particularity is that all relocations in the sample involve Polish citizens. None of the relocations were, hence, motivated by a desire to move back home which characterises so many of the relocations

---

[1133] *Uchwała Sądu Najwyższego z dnia 10 listopada 1971 r.*, III CZP 69/71, suggests that prior permission is necessary when such rights would be hindered by the relocation; see also *Postanowienie Sądu Okręgowego w Zamościu z dnia 17 grudnia 2015 r.*, I Cz 585/15, LEX nr 1965222.

[1134] Article 95 §3 of the KRO.

[1135] e.g. J. Gajda, 'Art. 95 KRO' in K. Pietrzykowski (ed.), *Kodeks rodzinny i opiekuńczy. Komentarz. Wyd. 8*, C.H. Beck (Legalis), Warszawa 2023, para 7.

[1136] ibid., paras 2–3.

[1137] e.g. *Uchwała Sądu Najwyższego z dnia 14 lutego 1955 r.*, I CO 83/54, OSNCK 1955/3/52. This conclusion is strongly supported by the existing international instruments regarding children's rights, especially the UN Convention on the Rights of the Child and the EU Charter.

[1138] e.g. *Wyrok Sądu Najwyższego z dnia 17 grudnia 1965 r.*, I CR 309/65, OSNC 1966/7–8/132.

elsewhere. However, an interesting feature of the cases was the complexity of residence and mobility configurations of the family members involved in the disputes. In many cases, the non-relocating parent lived abroad or was temporarily or periodically working abroad at the time of the relocation. This allows for a different presentation of the context from that discussed so far, but at the same time the limitations of the sample might have a clear bias towards relocations and do not offer a full picture of judicial considerations.

7.4.1. CROSS-BORDER TRAVELS AND THE LEGAL CULTURE OF *FAIT ACCOMPLI* – THE EU AS PART OF THE PROBLEM?

Considering the scarce discussion on relocation in the Polish doctrinal literature, it might be surprising that as many as three studies discuss empirical data involving relocation cases. Although two of them date way back, a brief discussion of their findings proves useful to paint the profile of this jurisdiction. One article surveys all 67 cases on international travels or relocations that were resolved in Poland in 1979.[1139] Relocation cases were also discussed in another empirical study on parental disputes resolved in 1979.[1140] Both articles note that the number of relocation cases seems to be extremely low compared to the overall number of divorces, concluding that this might stem from the parents' ability to reach agreement outside the courts and a limited number of such moves in general (as in communist Poland, international travel outside the socialist bloc was not accessible to most people).[1141] One can also hypothesise that back in the 1980s, post-divorce custody was usually held by mothers and socially it was broadly accepted that the responsibility for family life was vested exclusively with women.

However, also recent research on parental disputes indicates that applications for permission to relocate or travel abroad are still extremely rare compared to the number of applications for permission to obtain a passport or an ID for the child that are implicitly or explicitly motivated by such plans.[1142] The fact

1139 W. Stojanowska and E. Hordyńska, 'Zezwolenie sądu opiekuńczego na wyjazd małoletniego dziecka za granicę z jednym z rodziców' (1982) 16 *Zeszyty Naukowe Instytutu Badania Prawa Sądowego*, 145.

1140 W. Stojanowska, 'Rozstrzyganie przez sąd na podstawie art. 24 i 97 §2 k.r.o. o istotnych sprawach rodziny w braku porozumienia między małżonkami lub rodzicami' (1985) 7–8 *Nowe Prawo*.

1141 W. Stojanowska and E. Hordyńska, above n. 1139, 151–52; W. Stojanowska, above n. 1140, 90. Interestingly, the rules regulating children's international travel – but not permanent relocation – were different for travel to the socialist countries as compared to other destinations.

1142 J. Słyk, 'Rozstrzyganie o istotnych sprawach dziecka w przypadku braku porozumienia rodziców (art. 97 §2 k.r.o.)' (2013) 14 *Prawo w działaniu* 44, 102–03. See also *Postanowienie*

that the travel document needs to be obtained with the court's permission suggests that parental agreement on the matter is lacking, as otherwise a written permission from the other parent would be sufficient. This further implies that most parents do not apply for any permission to travel or relocate, but limit themselves to obtaining a travel document (an administrative requirement in any case).[1143] When it comes to the moves, they often decide by themselves and present the other parent with *fait accompli*.[1144] Indeed, the analysis of Polish case law undertaken here seems to confirm the finding that relocation cases are rare, and many issues indirectly related to or caused by (often unlawful) relocations are raised in cases dealing with travel documents or contact rights post-relocation.[1145] However, this state of affairs creates tensions as doctrines on passports or cross-border contact rights are not suited to accommodating all the interests typically raised in relocation disputes.

These tensions lead to an increasing pressure to address the issue of the cross-border movement of children in a different way. Interestingly, they are often framed in reference to the EU and the Schengen area, as seen in the parliamentary questions from MPs.[1146] The tensions, hence, are felt in relation to Poland's membership in the Union. The competent ministries consequently assert that such matters are already regulated by family law, which remains the only area of law that can address them, in light of the lack of border controls in the Union.[1147] The long-standing jurisprudence of the Supreme Court confirms not only that every instance of travel and relocation abroad requires permission, but also that removing or retaining the child abroad against these rules can result in the restriction of parental rights and a change of the resident parent, if in the

Sądu Okręgowego we Włocławku z dnia 30 marca 2022 r., I Ca 214/21, POSP, where the court found that the proceedings to limit parental responsibilities of the father could have been initiated by the mother to be free to move abroad, despite no such plans having been made explicit nor any application in that regard lodged with the court.

1143 J. Słyk, above n. 1142.

1144 ibid., 119.

1145 e.g. *Postanowienie Sądu Rejonowego dla m.st. Warszawy z dnia 15 czerwca 2016 r.*, VI Nsm 27/15, POSP.

1146 'Interpelacja Nr 21013 – Tekst' <http://www.sejm.gov.pl/Sejm8.nsf/InterpelacjaTresc.xsp?key=57C80A3D>; 'Interpelacja Nr 6028 w Sprawie Swobodnego Przemieszczania Się Małoletnich Dzieci w Strefie Schengen' <http://orka2.sejm.gov.pl/IZ6.nsf/INTop/06028?OpenDocument>. Interestingly, one parliamentary question concerned Polish parents who cannot obtain a court's permission to move from their place of residence abroad back to Poland, see 'Interpelacja Nr 9442' <http://www.sejm.gov.pl/sejm9.nsf/interpelacja.xsp?typ=INT&nr=9442&view=null>. See also the discussion about the politicisation of EU mobility in O. Ceran, 'Expeditiousness of child abduction proceedings, procedural autonomy, and what it has to do with sincere cooperation: *Rzecznik Praw Dziecka and Others*' (2023) 60 *Common Market Law Review* 1787.

1147 Poland has a long history of emigration and as such, intra-EU migrations are definitely not the origin of the problem. However, in light of the increased migration post-accession, the problem seems to be increasingly felt and framed in this context.

best interests of the child.[1148] However, while this in principle is clear, some judgments that do not deal with relocation per se contain somewhat ambiguous assertions in this regard.

In a dispute about the issuance of a passport, the father was concerned that the mother would take the child abroad permanently to the Netherlands. The court relied on the European space of rights as reassurance in light of the father's concerns. This could be reasonable if linked with the child abduction regime, but this was not the case:

> It is noteworthy that even if the mother decided to stay abroad for longer, be it in the Netherlands or another state in Europe, the father would retain the right to exercise personal contact with his son, and it would merely be necessary to adjust the contact regime again.[1149]

This could correspond to the construction of the EU as a space of rights in German law, one that led to a reorientation of relocation law as well. However, in German law, the reference applied to cases where the left-behind parent did not have the right to determine the child's place of residence in the first place. The Polish court seemed to sideline the fact that any 'stay abroad for longer' would require separate permission independently of the decision to issue a passport or travel abroad for holidays. This was not a matter of contact rights but the right to decide about the child's residence which was shared by both parents. In another case, the appeal court had to reverse the lower's court judgment that refused to impose a financial penalty for infringing a contact agreement on a mother who (unlawfully) moved to Ireland. The lower court's argument was that the move was justified for economic and family reasons.[1150] The appeal court made it clear that, whatever the reasons, the move was unlawful as the mother did not obtain the father's or a court's permission. Such judgments leave the impression that, when the dispute itself is not about relocation, some courts ascribe to resident parents – as a matter of contextual constructions – a broad scope of autonomy, at least in the EU context. Relocation clearly requires a permission from the other parent or the

---

1148 *Uchwała Sądu Najwyższego z dnia 7 sierpnia 1982 r.*, VI KZP 18/82, OSNPG 1982/10/137. See also *Postanowienie Sądu Okręgowego w Sieradzu z dnia 17 października 2018 r.*, I Ca 389/18, LEX nr 2577035.

1149 *Wyrok Sądu Okręgowego w Słupsku z dnia 9 sierpnia 2013 r.*, IV Ca 362/13, LEX nr 1883897: 'Godzi się też zauważyć, że nawet wówczas, gdyby matka małoletniego postanowiła pozostać, czy to w Holandii, czy też w innym państwie Europy na dłużej, skarżący, jako ojciec małoletniego, zachowałby prawo do osobistych kontaktów z synem, a jedynie koniecznym byłoby ich ponowne, sądowne uregulowanie'. See also *Postanowienie Sądu Rejonowego dla m.st. Warszawy z dnia 15 czerwca 2016 r.*, VI Nsm 27/15.

1150 *Postanowienie Sądu Okręgowego w Zamościu z dnia 17 grudnia 2015 r.*, I Cz 585/15, LEX nr 1965222.

court, but such cases seem to suggest that their contexts carry some normative assumptions, even if they remain somehow implicit.

These tensions have led some authors to believe that the child's place of residence in every court decision should be indicated more precisely than just by a reference to the resident parent. Formulating the place of residence in reference to the parent is said to lead to the wrong conclusion that the custodial parent might freely move with the child wherever they want.[1151] Whether this is empirically true remains an open question, but such proposals draw attention to the signalling value of explicit regulations on child relocation. It is, nevertheless, worth observing that many judgments do indeed explicitly refer to a child's cross-border change of residence (or any long-term stay abroad) as requiring a parental agreement.[1152] Regardless of the formulation of national law, permission to relocate abroad with the child is still clearly required by the international and European legal frameworks on child abduction. The judgments above seem to suggest that the relatively strong sense of autonomy of resident parents might be both culturally and legally conditioned, and the observed issues – while the law on relocation is, in principle, clear – might be related to the broader construction of Polish law that can be classified as the autonomy-with-objection model.[1153] National courts, when drawing the limits of parental rights and responsibilities in custody judgments, often make an application for a child's passport dependent on parental agreement in explicit reference to the fact that it allows the child to travel outside of the European Union – as implicitly opposed to a national ID allowing for travels within it.[1154] This might indirectly spill over onto matters surrounding relocation. Thus, as the EU expands this scope of autonomy, it also becomes an additional irritant for the already problematic area of law.

7.4.2. MOBILE FAMILIES AND THE SPACE OF ECONOMIC OPPORTUNITIES

The characteristic features of the Polish sample reflect the complex migration trajectories of many families. Although the sample is small, three cases involve residence disputes about children already living abroad, be it because they moved with the resident parent, or following a later joint decision of both

1151 Z. Kołakowska-Halbersztadt, '1.6. Zmiana miejsca zamieszkania' in P. Gluza, Z. Kołakowska-Halbersztadt and M. Tański (ed.) *Dziecko w rozstaniu rodziców*, Wydawnictwo Prawnicze LexisNexis, Warszawa 2013 <https://sip.lex.pl/#/monograph/369312586/8>.

1152 e.g. *Postanowienie Sądu Okręgowego w Sieradzu z 30 czerwca 2022 r.*, I Ca 212/22, POSP.

1153 K. Scheiwe, above n. 103, pp. 157–158.

1154 *Postanowienie Sądu Okręgowego w Sieradzu z 30 czerwca 2022 r.*, I Ca 212/22, POSP; *Postanowienie Sądu Rejonowego dla m. st. Warszawy w Warszawie z dnia 15 czerwca 2016 r.*, VI Nsm 27/15, POSP.

parents with the remaining parent subsequently applying for their residence in Poland.[1155] One application was filed by a non-resident mother working abroad who wanted her son to join her after nine years of living apart.[1156] On the other hand, many parents opposing relocation were, at the time of the application, residing or working abroad themselves. In such circumstances, the courts often heard arguments about the long-term plans of the non-relocating parent who intended to come back to Poland once their economic situation improved.[1157] Thus, in many cases family life was already delocalised – not through any particular construction of the court or the law, but as a matter of fact.

The motivation of relocating parents in most cases was also linked to better employment opportunities and overall material conditions, often in circumstances where their new partner already worked abroad. The respective scopes of autonomy of both parents, hence, were often brought together:

> Since October 2013, [the father] has been working in Germany as a production worker. … He usually comes to Poland once a month. … He is not considering permanent relocation abroad. [The father] intends to return to the country permanently after paying off his debts, including his maintenance debts … Nevertheless, he has actually been abroad already for two years and estimates that he might stay in Germany for another two. … At the same time, he expects the mother to give up her own family life, the possibility of reuniting with the father of her youngest daughter, creating better career prospects for herself, and better material prospects for the children, only so that he can live in the same place as his daughters in an undefined future, when he decides to return to the country. In the opinion of the Court, the participant's objection in these circumstances is contrary to the children's welfare.[1158]

1155 e.g. *Postanowienie Sądu Okręgowego w Słupsku z dnia 4 października 2017 r.*, IV Ca 242/17, POSP; *Postanowienie Sądu Okręgowego w Toruniu z dnia 27 kwietnia 2016 r.*, VIII Ca 91/16, LEX nr 2040286.

1156 *Postanowienie Sądu Rejonowego w Bielsku Podlaskim z dnia 29 stycznia 2015 r.*, III Nsm 110/14, LEX nr 1866318.

1157 e.g. *Postanowienie Sądu Rejonowego w Raciborzu z dnia 7 stycznia 2016 r.*, III Nsm 361/15, POSP.

1158 ibid.: 'Od października 2013 roku M. M. pracuje w Niemczech jako pracownik produkcji. … Do Polski przyjeżdża zwykle raz w miesiącu. … Nie rozważa wyjazdu za granicę. Uczestnik zamierza powrócić na stałe do kraju, kiedy uda mu się spłacić posiadane zadłużenie, w tym zadłużenie alimentacyjne względem funduszu alimentacyjnego i małoletnich. … Niemniej jednak faktycznie przebywa tam już tam dwa lata i szacuje, że pozostanie jeszcze kolejne dwa. … Jednocześnie oczekuje, że matka małoletnich zrezygnuje z ułożenia własnego życia rodzinnego, wspólnego zamieszkania z ojcem jej najmłodszej córki i stworzenia sobie lepszych perspektyw zawodowych, a małoletnim – perspektyw materialnych, tylko z tego powodu, aby on sam mógł mieszkać w tym samym miejscu co córki w bliżej nieokreślonej przyszłości, kiedy zdecyduje się do kraju powrócić. W ocenie Sądu, sprzeciw uczestnika jest w tych okolicznościach sprzeczny z dobrem małoletnich'.

Migration was typically conceptualised as an economic opportunity for all involved. Differently from Germany or England, the courts were, however, often content with a generalised perception of European neighbours as presenting such opportunities, regardless of whether any specific employment offers have been made or were easily available. While different courts were more or less explicit about it, one can observe here a certain disillusion with the employment market in Poland over the years:

> The prospects of the [mother] are also incomparably better there. *In Poland, raising three small children, she has no real chance of employment.* Meanwhile, in Germany, she will be able to share responsibilities with her [new] husband and combine part-time work with raising her daughters. *It is a well-known fact that qualified medical carers are in demand on the German labour market.* Therefore, after acquiring a basic knowledge of German language, [the mother] can count on beneficial employment conditions. In the opinion of the Court, the decision to relocate seems therefore rational and well thought out.[1159] (Emphasis added.)

This assessment seems to correspond, in its contextual embedding, to research findings suggesting that EU citizenship rights open new opportunities for women otherwise prevented from advancing in their occupation because of certain discriminatory characteristics in their national environments.[1160] At the same time, the reliance on employment opportunities and better material conditions might, in effect, shift the disadvantage of the economic characteristics of Poland onto parents opposing relocation. The normalisation of the situation in which individuals can 'make use of the real and effective possibility to be successful in another Member State', and on the other hand need to reckon with such a scenario, leads to a particular form of the weakening of the right to stay.[1161]

1159 ibid.: 'Zamieszkanie w Niemczech oznacza stworzenie dla wnioskodawczyni i jej partnera lepszych warunków zawodowych i materialnych. Będą mogli stale przebywać oboje wraz z dziećmi, a jednocześnie zapewnić im odpowiednie warunki materialne. T. C. posiada w Niemczech stałe, dobrze płatne zatrudnienie, a także możliwości rozwoju zawodowego. Również perspektywy wnioskodawczyni są tam nieporównywalnie lepsze. W Polsce, wychowując sama trójkę małoletnich dzieci i nie ma realnej szansy na zatrudnienie. Tymczasem w Niemczech, będzie mogła dzielić obowiązki z mężem i pogodzić pracę na część etatu z wychowaniem córek. Powszechnie wiadomym jest, że na niemieckim rynku pracy poszukiwani są wykwalifikowani opiekunowie medyczni. Dlatego, po uzupełnieniu podstawowych braków w zakresie języka, wnioskodawczyni może liczyć na zatrudnienie na korzystnych warunkach. W ocenie Sądu, decyzja o wyjeździe wydaje się być zatem racjonalna i przemyślana. Wnioskodawczyni kieruje się przede wszystkim chęcią połączenia rodziny'.

1160 See the discussions in L. Ackers, *Shifting Spaces: Women, Citizenship and Migration Within the European Union*, Policy Press, London 1998, or M. Morokvasic, '"Settled in Mobility": Engendering Post-Wall Migration in Europe' (2004) 77 *Feminist Review* 7, who argues that EU migration is often more empowering for women than migration in general.

1161 S. Iglesias Sánchez, above n. 876, p. 382.

Due to the characteristics of the sample, these arguments are, however, made cautiously. The complexity of the cases cannot be reduced to one factor. In fact, in most cases the relocating mother was moving not only because of economic reasons, but also to join a new partner. The courts seem to have put a lot of emphasis on the opportunity to grow up in a reconstructed family as positively reflecting on the child's welfare,[1162] and thus these two logics significantly intertwine. These arguments should also not be read as questioning the outcomes or the court's assessment of the child's best interests. The financial situation of a given family is an important factor in the wellbeing of the child, and in most cases the maintenance obligations were not diligently met by the opposing parent. Rather, this interpretation suggests that the construction of the relevant context for relocation disputes clearly crosses Polish borders and presents relocation as a (natural) opportunity rather than a risk. Other EU countries are perceived as obvious destinations to improve one's economic opportunities, a construction that, to a great extent, corresponds to societal reality.

The factual assessments are clearly underpinned by the perception of the EU as a place of easily accessible economic opportunities, but not framed in European terms. None of the relocation cases in the sample mention freedom of movement, be it either in the national[1163] or the EU context, nor any of the international soft law instruments.[1164] In light of English and German case law, the discussion on the *fait accompli* in the EU context, and the remarks on the German labour market in the excerpt above, one can assume that such references could be present. Their absence might suggest that the EU is, at large, not a particularly meaningful point of reference for child relocation cases. The lack of such references might, however, also be related to their normatively contestable nature. Emigration, in particular as an economic opportunity, is clearly normalised in the Polish relocation judgments, and this normalisation clearly builds on the European space as well. However, as the national discussions on negative phenomena related to the cross-border movement of children regularly take place in reference to the EU context, national courts might be more sensitive towards such argumentation in an actual relocation dispute resolution.

Whether this characterisation is EU-specific cannot, unfortunately, be ascertained considering the limitations of the sample. The only relocation case outside the European Union involved Canada as a state of destination, in

---

1162 e.g. *Postanowienie Sądu Rejonowego w Raciborzu z dnia 7 stycznia 2016 r.*, III Nsm 361/15, POSP; *Postanowienie Sądu Rejonowego w Człuchowie z dnia 12 października 2017 r.*, III Nsm 91/17, POSP.

1163 Free movement is protected by Article 52 of the Polish Constitution.

1164 In Polish case law, the only reference to any international instruments was not specific to relocation cases and regarded the child's right to be heard as included in Article 12 of the CRC and in the Council of Europe Recommendation R/84/4 of the Committee of Ministers to Member States of 28 February 1984 on parental responsibilities. See *Postanowienie Sądu Okręgowego w Toruniu z dnia 27 kwietnia 2016 r.*, VIII Ca 91/16, POSP.

a significantly different set of circumstances. The mother wanted to join her own parents living abroad but had no particular plan for the move; the father enjoyed a very good relationship with the child and had exceptional (for Polish standards) resources to provide for the mother and the child financially. In this brief judgment, the court recognised that the mother's employment situation was inadequate and could be improved by relocating, but such a benefit did not justify the disruption of the very good relationship between the father and child, given the distance and cost of travel between Poland and Canada.[1165] The interplay of distance with reasons for relocation, the exceptionally good relationships of the non-relocating parent and the child, and economic factors makes it difficult to draw any comparative conclusions in relation to Polish cases on intra-EU relocations, which calls for more research on the topic.

7.4.3. PRELIMINARY CONCLUSIONS

In Poland, the sample of cases has very different characteristics than those in England and Germany: it is much smaller, encompasses relocations of exclusively Polish citizens, and almost exclusively to other EU states. At the same time, existing research suggests that the small number of relocation cases mirrors a general issue of relocations frequently taking place without the required permission. This issue – reflecting a broader problem of legal culture – is sometimes coupled with the EU layer that expands the scope of parental autonomy. As this expansion clearly builds on the EU as a space of rights, in the eyes of many it explicitly becomes part of the broader problem. The lack of direct references to the EU in relocation cases might be explained from this perspective, despite the European space being explicitly or implicitly present in various relocation-related disputes. At the same time, other Member States are frequently presented in relocation cases as part of a space of easily available economic opportunities that allows parents to take advantage of new possibilities to improve their (often difficult) situation in Poland. Since many disputes had a cross-border dimension already at the time of the relocation application, e.g. as the non-relocating parent himself or the new partner worked abroad, taking advantage of this space of economic opportunities becomes a reasonable expectation of the relocating parent as well. This expectation also carries a normative value. Due to the limitations of the sample, however, it is difficult to ascertain whether this observation is EU-specific or rather reflects a more generalised social context taken together with the Polish model of the exercise of parental responsibilities.

[1165] *Postanowienie Sądu Rejonowego dla m.st. Warszawy z dnia 30 października 2014 r.*, VI Nsm 736/14, LEX nr 1913832.

7.5. DISCUSSION: CHILD RELOCATION LAW AND ENCOUNTERS WITH EUROPE IN COMPARISON

The description of child relocation law in England and Wales, Germany, and Poland respectively reveals certain characteristic features of each jurisdiction. While all jurisdictions take a holistic evaluation of the child's best interests as a starting point of the analysis, a more in-depth comparison highlights further differences between their approaches. These differences result all from a broader variation in the approach to parental disputes, divergent socio-legal contexts, as well as from distinct ways to engage with constitutional rights at stake in relocation disputes. This confirms that, to fully account for different countries' approaches to child relocation, one needs to analyse not only their statutory law, but also their case law.[1166] The in-depth analysis reveals that courts might approach child relocation cases with a different set of possible outcomes in mind. While the status quo might weigh heavily in the assessment of an English court,[1167] this is, in principle, not the case for a German judge who will approach the assessment on the assumption that the relocating parent has the right to and will move (or, alternatively, will perceive the status quo in a different way).[1168] In that, engagement with freedom of movement rights has led to different doctrinal developments in the two jurisdictions. This difference inevitably generates also different outcomes, but – despite being heavily intertwined with freedom of movement – reflects also divergent perceptions of the scope of reasonable expectations regarding parental 'sacrifices'. This is precisely what was hypothesised to constitute a limit to any EU intervention in the field in previous chapters, despite being of crucial importance for child relocation law at large. Against this background, Polish case law has not been particularly explicit on the role played by mobility factors, leaving many questions open. Based on a consideration of a broader set of relocation-related disputes, one can cautiously perceive the scope of parental autonomy as relatively wide also in this jurisdiction.

The comparison of these three jurisdictions confirms, further, that an in-depth investigation of the domestic level is necessary to fully understand the dynamics and effects of the European influence on child relocation law. It reveals that each jurisdiction perceives European pressures differently, and 'uses' Europe differently beyond such pressures as well. The legal pressures seem to be felt almost exclusively in reference to the mutual trust imperative of the Union, be it in the narrow context of the Brussels II*bis* Regulation (as in the UK)

1166 Y.M. Bérénos, above n. 12, 21.

1167 See the comments in *GT v RJ* [2018] EWFC 26, paras. 1–2.

1168 *BGH, Beschluss vom 28.04.2010* – XII ZB 81/09.

or in the broader context of the equivalence of legal spaces (as demonstrated by the German remark on the rule of law of another Member State). In such cases, EU law is used to co-construct the context of the cases in a way that can potentially limit the need for, or legitimate scope of, investigation into matters that can be of relevance for the child's best interests. This dynamic corresponds to Europeanisation understood as the traditional, top-down adaptation of national courts to their role as EU judicial institutions but constitutes, in fact, a constructive use of EU law insofar as the nature and scope of EU legal pressures remain undetermined.

The infrastructure-oriented pressures do not, however, reveal a definitive reorientation of the normative point of reference of child relocation law towards the EU. As such remarks feature in the judgments also in relation to other private international law instruments and other relocation destinations, Europe seems to be used here in a more heuristic manner rather than being perceived as a unique normative power. The legal infrastructure grounds, however, the more principle-oriented engagements with EU law. It allows national courts to use the EU's normativity where this seems justified by other considerations in a given case or type of cases. This is demonstrated by the developments of the German doctrine on relocations where the parent has the sole right to decide the child's place of residence but otherwise shares parental responsibility. Some of the Polish cases can also be seen as confirming this interpretation. Where good reasons for relocation were given, courts justified the broader scope of autonomy of the relocating parent in reference to the contextual layers of the EU space, albeit present only implicitly. In other words, while the EU might be, to some extent, felt as exerting a normative pressure, engagement with this normativity seems to happen entirely on domestic terms when justified in the broader context of the case. The judicial considerations of Brexit or free movement in the English cases might also be seen in this light.

The discussion in this chapter provides evidence that EU law or a broader EU normativity are occasionally considered in child relocation cases. Simultaneously, engagement with the most straightforward normative proposition of EU law – free movement – remains very limited. Only English courts took note of EU free movement provisions in the relocation context, but these references were heavily constrained by the broader discussions (and contestations) of national law at that time. In Germany, although free movement is openly discussed in most cases and ascribed a significant value, it has not been framed in the EU context. Polish courts do not discuss free movement in child relocation cases at all, although (or perhaps because) in non-judicial discourses these issues are often brought together, but this does not prevent them from contextualising the cases in a way that affords relocating parents a wide scope of autonomy. The lack of direct references to EU law might, naturally, be a result of the in-built indifference (or explicit distancing) of family law towards EU law. In terms of observable effects, however, all the jurisdictions discussed seem to be far from reorienting their approaches to child relocation towards Europe or framing them in terms of European paradigms. While Europe is occasionally used to obtain a particular normative result, this has not produced a comprehensive or consistent change. Its presence in child relocation discourses might have, therefore, more to do with other normative choices to which it proves instrumental rather than with broader convergence processes.

While none of the national child relocation laws discussed seem to move towards Europe in a consistent way, this does not render the encounters with Europe meaningless. In the German or English context, a trigger for a doctrinal development came from a usage of Europe on more than one occasion and has since then been generalised for broader contexts. From a hermeneutical point of view, the presence of European discourses or arguments suggests that, in the eyes of the judiciary, the EU has become a context that might need to be addressed. This, by itself, suggests that the contextual influence of the EU is relevant for investigations of law and society, in particular if it is not perceived only as a narrow free movement imperative. However, even with Europe being recognised as a normatively inflicted context, broader normative decisions about good relationships must be taken.[1169] The reception of the EU context is then dependent on pre-existing national structures and sensitivities, as the discussion in this chapter demonstrates. It is against their background that national courts might escape the European pressures (be they real or perceived) or use Europe as an additional resource while making normative choices on family matters. This suggests that the effects of European influence in child relocation law should not be overrated and changes, if any, are predominantly domestic in origin.

7.6. CONCLUDING REMARKS

This chapter discussed various encounters with Europe that take place in child relocation cases in England and Wales, Germany, and Poland. The discussion demonstrates that national courts do occasionally engage with EU law and the European space in child relocation cases, but the effects of such engagements are less straightforward – and certainly less radical – than one might expect. EU law is most visibly present in its infrastructure-oriented dimension, but this presence does not reveal a definitive reorientation of the normative point of reference of child relocation law towards the EU. When the European space features in its principle-oriented dimension, it provides a normative frame of reference, but

[1169] On that point broadly, see R. Leckey, above n. 57, p. 264.

this frame is in no way sufficient to create change. While certain contextual features of the European legal subjects might prompt national courts to face new dilemmas (as in, for example, the case of Brexit), their normative value intertwines with, rather than supersedes, other sources of normativity at play. The way in which national courts engage with the European space is, therefore, clearly influenced by the needs, opportunities, and constraints of both national doctrines and individual cases. The different uses of Europe that can be observed in the analysed jurisdictions confirm this observation, but also strengthen the broader claim about the need to approach Europeanisation in this area of law as a dynamic, constructive process.

Looking at the findings critically, one can observe that the case law samples are characterised by a great variety and the approach is not always consistent. This is not surprising given that cross-border child relocation cases are repeatedly perceived as binary disputes posing great difficulty for decision-makers involved. Against this background, EU law is often approached as able to bring more consistency across the EU – a convergence of child relocation law. However, in light of the discussion in this book, it should be accepted that there are important limits to what EU law can achieve in this regard, even with an explicit action regarding child relocation. EU law could impose important requirements – first and foremost to consider EU free movement rights and mutual trust – but these would reconceptualise the reasoning applied to child relocation cases predominantly in a procedural sense, with a limited potential to deeply challenge national approaches substantively. This chapter demonstrates that even where EU law is considered to constitute a pressure, judges justifiably reach different conclusions on its relevance not only for general doctrines, but also for the resolution of the case at hand. In that, the conditions of broader family law structures and social contexts, as well as individual circumstances of each case, clearly take priority over any normative pressures of EU law, even when such normativity is instrumentally employed for the resolution of the case at hand. This finding should, however, be welcomed. Where the EU and EU law have become an important context of child relocation cases (be it explicit or implicit), the normatively inflicted methodology of EU law has not replaced or distorted the methodologies of national family law as such. Even where EU law becomes a resource or an irritant for national law, this is secondary to deeper contestations embedded within the national doctrine and – if anything – increases the pressures for, and allows for, its clarification. From this perspective, one can indeed have good reason to believe that 'decisions made in the best interest of the child will be unaffected'[1170] by the 'internal market imperative'[1171] of EU law.

[1170] R. Lamont, above n. 12, 242.
[1171] H. Stalford, above n. 17, p. 226.

At the same time, as Europeanisation is a dynamic process, the engagements with the EU will continue and might gradually lead to deeper changes in national laws. These can, however, be expected to occur predominantly through constructive, bottom-up interactions with the EU legal space and its contextual layers filled with societal expectations, values, and principles.

CHAPTER 8
CONCLUSIONS

8.1. CROSS-BORDER CHILD RELOCATION: THE DYNAMICS OF EUROPEANISATION

Substantive family law is a firmly established and consistently defended competence of the Member States. And yet, in more and more cases family entitlements and EU citizenship rights intersect. This is demonstrated by the growing number of judgments in which the CJEU touches upon family matters, albeit often indirectly via the EU free movement and non-discrimination frameworks. Free movement is explicitly what might bring cross-border child relocation within the scope of EU law. It is, therefore, unsurprising that scholars and practitioners alike have expressed an interest in the legal obligations that EU law does or could impose on national child relocation laws. While EU legal actors have not yet acted in this field, the literature recognises that child relocation laws, with their potential effects on free movement, might prompt an interest of EU legislators in their harmonisation.[1172] EU law, due to its power to remove obstacles to free movement, is also potentially attractive to relocating parents involved in such disputes. Some are more welcoming of change that might be brought by EU law and others fear its potentially erosive effects.[1173] At the same time, EU citizens already cross borders in a world with the EU, where social reality and the legal frameworks of mobility necessarily intersect. National family laws are, therefore, increasingly faced with the need to accommodate the trans-border and multicultural features of transformations characterising modern family life, and child relocation law is no exception – with or without any EU intervention. However, not much is known about how national decision-makers currently approach EU law in child relocation cases, if at all.

Against this background, the book has provided an in-depth analysis of the influence of EU law on cross-border child relocation law and its effects on the national level. At its very centre stood the question of how EU law does and can influence child relocation law, under what circumstances, and

1172 Y.M. Bérénos, above n. 12.

1173 Compare, for example, ibid. and R. Lamont, above n. 12, 242.

with what kind of consequences? In other words, the book has explored how different types of EU action can condition Europeanisation of cross-border child relocation law. It has discussed the relationship between child relocation and EU law considering the limited EU competence, as well as the dynamics of both the positive and negative integration processes. Finally, it has looked at this relationship from the bottom up, exploring the nature of family judges' engagement with the EU legal space in English, German, and Polish case law on child relocation – the dynamics of their Europeanisation sensu stricto. In that, the book adds a distinctive perspective on cross-border child relocation, both in the EU context and beyond, and European family law research. The main theme that emerges here is that interactions of cross-border child relocation law and EU law are characterised by some fundamental tensions, relating to both the scope of EU competence and the nature of decision-making in such cases, many of which are not easily resolved and significantly limit the transformative potential of EU action. However, as the book shows, Europeanisation of cross-border child relocation law might depend on it less than initially expected. While conditioned and constrained by EU law in varying ways, the interactions of national law with EU law are already – and will likely continue to be – driven predominantly by national actors. As of now, national laws occasionally share some (but not all) European vocabularies and reach for certain paradigms of EU law. However, EU law does not (yet) seem to fundamentally challenge the established child relocation doctrines and consistently reorient them towards the EU. In that, while convergence is, of course, a matter of perspective and degree, Europeanisation does not currently bring convergence of child relocation law, but its investigation certainly provides enough interesting insights to warrant further research on cross-border child relocation in the EU. This final chapter briefly summarises the discussion and problematises the book's findings, emphasises its main contributions and their limitations and identifies open research avenues that emanate from these observations.

8.2. THE EUROPEAN INFLUENCE AND THE SCOPE OF NATIONAL AUTONOMY

Child relocation is currently characterised by the lack of specific legislation or jurisprudence on the EU level. No EU legislative proposals are in sight. In that, there has been no substantive standard-setting on the EU level. However, questions about the nature of legal obligations that are or could be imposed by EU law, and their consequences, have been raised and require clarification. Additionally, as seen, there are reasons to believe that EU law can influence national laws despite the lack of an explicit EU action on child relocation. This section discusses, therefore, the book's findings on the nature and limits of various types of EU influences. It addresses the first three key objectives of the book: the question of EU competence in the field and prospects of legislative harmonisation; the scope and nature of obligations imposed on Member States by the existing European legal frameworks, both in reference to fundamental rights and fundamental freedoms; and the contextual influence of EU law that can go beyond the formal constraints of EU legal doctrines. These discussions trigger broader questions about the limits and nature of national autonomy, as well as the dynamics of Europeanisation under various conditions set out by European law.

8.2.1. THE EU COMPETENCE AND HARMONISATION PROSPECTS: LIMITED BUT NOT EXCLUDED?

When national legislation is scrutinised as to its compatibility with EU law, it is perhaps a short step to suggest a harmonised European solution. This is understandable, as an approximation of national child relocation laws would certainly alleviate some of the concerns regarding the unequal access to free movement across the Union. This is, in principle, the argument behind the initial calls for the EU's engagement with cross-border child relocation.[1174] However, harmonisation is always conditioned by the existence of a legislative competence in the field under discussion. The question of competence is, therefore, very pertinent, not only because it determines whether the EU can act in the field, but also because – due to the dynamics of negative integration in the EU – it determines the scope and intensity of the CJEU's scrutiny when interpreting EU legal obligations imposed on national law. In that, the extensive discussion of the EU's competence in the field of cross-border child relocation is both interesting in its own right and necessary for any further analysis of child relocation in the EU legal context.

The book argues that the EU's competence to legislate on *substantive* aspects of child relocation law should be refused. While the distinction between substance and procedure is not clear-cut, this lack of competence would broadly refer to norms determining *when* a parent is required to obtain permission to relocate or *what kind of factors* a court needs to consider when deciding a relocation case. Such a competence cannot simply be established based on the Treaty provisions. This conclusion concerns not only Article 81(3) of the TFEU, the traditional legal basis of family law measures, but also alternative bases suggested in the literature: Article 21(2) or Article 352 of the TFEU. The latter two, when seen in their systemic context, cannot be said to expand the EU competence beyond Article 81(3) of the TFEU. Regarding the *procedural*

[1174] Y.M. Bérénos, above n. 12.

dimension of child relocation – encompassing also certain judicial co-operation measures – one can expect further debates on the scope of the competence. This is so because Article 81(3) of the TFEU requires that matters subject to harmonisation have 'cross-border implications', a requirement that would need to be interpreted in a more extensive way in the child relocation context than seen so far in other family matters. Whether this broader interpretation would be accepted remains an open question.

From this – seemingly technical – discussion of the scope of competence emerges an important observation on the nature of any potential EU intervention into child relocation. The book shows that, even if the EU is said to possess competence on certain aspects of cross-border child relocation, harmonisation might be desirable in some respects but will not necessarily be a suitable answer to all the issues raised. This is not only because family law is a sensitive area, but also because the added value of any such intervention is not universally clear and yet triggers a highly complex debate on the scope of EU competence with far-reaching consequences. The child's best interests principle would necessarily have to guide any intervention in this area, and it is explicitly the implementation of the principle that generates the diversity of child relocation laws across the globe. In that, a very general intervention of the EU is unlikely to bring more uniformity and/or certainty. Some aspects of child relocation, even if not explicitly substantive in nature, are also so closely intertwined with the substantive core of family laws' normative designs that their regulation on the EU level would immediately prove difficult, severely impinging on the freedom of the Member States to organise their family law as they see fit. For example, while a general requirement to have effective procedures for seeking relocation might not be highly controversial, more specific provisions in that regard could closely intertwine with the broader substantive distribution of parental rights and obligations in national family laws. From this perspective, the full achievement of objectives driving the call for harmonisation – legal certainty, equality, and more uniformity across the EU – most likely would require more detailed measures that are as much procedural as they are substantive. While this assertion by no means excludes harmonisation altogether, it should be read against the background of past (political) struggles over the legitimate reach of the EU into family matters, with Member States consistently asserting their own competence in substantive law. Specific proposals should, therefore, be subjected to a careful subsidiarity and proportionality assessment, taking account of various tools at EU lawmakers' disposal. Given the requirement of unanimity in the Council for family law instruments to come to life, many questions raised by the possibility of harmonisation of child relocation laws will turn out to be dependent on the political will of Member States. On the other hand, some measures (e.g. involving assistance of central authorities) could relatively easily be introduced into a future recast of the Brussels II*ter* Regulation, currently in force, and are likely to be met with less resistance.

8.2.2. FUNDAMENTAL RIGHTS: A WIDE MARGIN OF APPRECIATION UNDER THE ECHR AND A CAREFUL CJEU

The EU Charter of Fundamental Rights contains provisions relevant for the analysis of child relocation, in particular Article 7 (the right to private and family life), Article 24 (rights of the child), and Article 45 (freedom of movement). However, due to the limited competence, family rights have rarely been a direct concern of EU law. It is the ECtHR, not constrained by this competence limitation, that remains the leading European court in cases touching upon family matters and is a significant source of legal inspiration for EU law. Article 52(3) of the CFR requires moreover that the meaning and scope of the Charter rights which correspond to rights guaranteed by the ECHR shall be the same as those laid down by the Convention. Therefore, the analysis of child relocation in the context of EU law necessarily presupposes a closer look at the ECHR and the jurisprudence of the ECtHR. Cross-border child relocation disputes can clearly give rise to human rights claims under Article 8 of the ECHR (the right to respect for private and family life), as discussed in Chapter 4, but these claims can both support the free movement rationale of EU law and be raised to oppose it. Considering this orientation of EU law, the book has drawn attention to the interplay of Article 8 of the ECHR with Article 2 of Protocol 4 to the Convention (freedom of movement). It has shown that this interplay, while interesting, remains largely of a theoretical relevance. The analysis of the existing jurisprudence of the ECtHR on child relocation suggests that child relocation cases are predominantly brought and analysed under Article 8 of the ECHR, conceptualised within their familial context first and foremost.

While it is recognised that the ECtHR's approach to the best interests of the child is not the same across all fields of law, the approach in child relocation cases that reached the Strasbourg Court seems consistent with the Court's broader jurisprudence on parental disputes. The ECtHR recognises the context-specificity of child relocation disputes and the need for individualised assessments of the best interests of the child, granting national authorities a wide margin of appreciation in such matters – regardless of whether they have relatively restrictive or relatively permissive approaches to child relocation. One can identify a certain ambiguity in how the ECtHR conceptualises parental claims in such cases. An individual autonomy interest of the relocating parent – certainly relevant for the conceptualisation of such disputes in EU law – can be, but not always is, explicitly recognised. However, as the cases are resolved predominantly under Article 8 of the ECHR and emphasise the best interests of the child, this ambiguity might have limited practical consequences for their outcomes. This finding in principle confirms the suggestions put forward in the literature but provides an empirical grounding for these claims. Nevertheless, the jurisprudence of the ECtHR does not necessarily bring more clarity to the highly contested field of child relocation, nor does it allow for a construction of any specific guidelines for the resolution of child relocation disputes. National authorities need to meet the general obligations imposed by the Court in parental disputes but, beyond that, adaptational pressures stemming from the ECHR system in child relocation matters are substantively limited.

The wide margin of appreciation afforded to Member States in the ECHR system has been shown to have specific consequences for the analysis of EU legal obligations. This is so due to particular dynamics of EU fundamental rights in sensitive areas, including many family-related issues involving children, characterised by three important features. The first relates to the fact that, where EU Charter rights correspond to Treaty rights (as in the case of free movement), the CJEU might choose to resolve the dispute in reference to EU Treaty provisions only. Secondly, the CJEU will often rely predominantly on EU law if it is sufficient to resolve the dispute at hand, and also where the ECtHR jurisprudence on a given matter exists. Lastly, the ECtHR remains, nevertheless, an important point of reference for fundamental rights in sensitive matters in particular, with the CJEU wary of its jurisdictional and legitimacy constraints. It needs to be pointed out that Article 24 of the CFR does not have a corresponding provision in the ECHR and in principle creates an opportunity for the CJEU to develop its own child-centred standards. However, given the sensitive nature of cross-border child relocation and the competence question, the CJEU is more likely than not to adopt the ECtHR's wide margin of appreciation in the child relocation context in its own decision-making. However, if the CJEU decides to guide Member States towards a more specific test within this broad margin of appreciation, the analysis will most likely focus on the interpretation of the EU framework of fundamental freedoms, rather than an elaboration of a standard of human rights protection departing from the jurisprudence of the ECtHR.

8.2.3. FUNDAMENTAL FREEDOMS: CHILD RELOCATION LAW AS A RESTRICTION OF FREE MOVEMENT

Despite the EU's lack of competence over (substantive) child relocation and the wide margin of appreciation granted by the ECtHR, EU law requires measures discouraging or hindering free movement to be removed as far as possible. It can certainly be seen to favour a pro-relocation approach and a narrow interpretation of permissible restrictions.[1175] As such, restrictions of child

[1175] R. Lamont, above n. 12; H. Stalford, above n. 17, pp. 225–26.

relocation could constitute unlawful restrictions of EU law, unless objectively justified and proportionate. Therefore, the CJEU – the primary interpreter of the free movement law and EU citizenship provisions – could gradually address the alleged inequality and insufficient protection of individual rights stemming from the lack of a uniform approach to cross-border child relocation if such cases made it to the Court. However, this book demonstrates that the analysis of child relocation law under the EU legal framework is not necessarily straightforward, and different constructions of national laws and specific circumstances of individual disputes might lead to different conclusions regarding the restrictive character of a given measure under EU law.

Already, the question of applicability of EU law to child relocation cases might generate varying answers. Explicit child relocation provisions can be argued to demonstrate a closer link to EU law than general provisions on parental responsibilities that apply to relocation cases in most jurisdictions. Different rules for internal and intra-EU relocations can lead to a finding of a discriminatory restriction on EU freedom of movement under Article 18 of the TFEU, constituting indirect discrimination based on nationality.[1176] At the same time, even provisions applying equally to cross-border and internal relocations could potentially be discriminatory if the situation of nationals and non-nationals is deemed to be different and the national legal framework does not account for such differences. The previous case law of the Luxembourg Court seems to confirm this assertion. However, the comparability of situations of nationals and non-nationals is rather fact-specific, and the outcome of its assessment would be highly dependent on the legal framework, circumstances, and argumentation of a specific case. Nevertheless, in principle, all non-discriminatory measures limiting intra-EU child relocation (if only not purely hypothetical) could be argued to discourage free movement and amount to a restriction under EU law. Simultaneously, there are arguments against the CJEU's intervention in this area of law. Given the nature of child relocation, restrictions on certain parental freedoms might be argued as inherent in the organisation of parenting or too indirect to discourage EU free movement, leading to a conclusion that child relocation measures should not be caught by the Treaty. This analysis reveals the complex nature of certain EU doctrines, for example the doctrine of remoteness, of which application is not entirely straightforward in a new context such as child relocation. A child relocation case could, therefore, definitely push the CJEU into new territory.

The book shows, however, that even if child relocation measures are caught by the Treaty, they will arguably be quasi-universally justified and proportionate. While any analysis of justification and proportionality necessarily depends on the exact nature of the restriction and the arguments

---

1176 R. Lamont, above n. 12, 241.

raised, most justifications will relate either to the protection of the best interests of the child or the design of familial relationships. While procedures to relocate should be available, the CJEU will, more often than not, be hardly able to meaningfully question their legal frameworks due to its institutional setup and the competence limitation. Even where measures are deemed discriminatory, the differentiation might be relatively easily justifiable in reference to the child's best interests and the objective differences between internal and cross-border relocation (as a move abroad can be legitimately argued to be qualitatively different than a move within the country). However, one can expect that when the Court will put national measures under full free movement scrutiny, it will impose certain adjustment requirements. The CJEU would likely require national courts to meaningfully engage with the assessment of the child's best interests, recognise mutual trust requirements and take account of the personal circumstances of the individuals involved that are derived from their transnational lives and free movement rights. However, the analysis of proportionality sensu stricto – the balancing of rights and interests involved – would, in most cases, be left to national courts. Here, the analysis conducted in the book can be read normatively, as normative arguments about the legitimate reach of EU law are implicit in this discussion.

This analysis outlines certain consequences for the scope of national autonomy and indicates how the Court's interventions would condition Europeanisation of child relocation. Child relocation could certainly be subject to harmonisation pressures beyond legislation, regardless of the variety of rules and procedures applied by different Member States. However, if the limits of this intervention suggested in this book are accepted, the scope of adaptational pressures would turn out to be of a predominantly procedural nature. The substantive assessments would still be left to the Member States, and therefore the Court's intervention would most likely not radically change the outcomes of cross-border child relocation cases. Even if explicitly required to be interpreted in conformity with EU law, the open-ended adjudicative standard such as the child's best interests principle both allows and requires great flexibility. Its assessments necessarily must be conducted by national courts in highly individualised circumstances and in line with national doctrines that will still be able to approach mobility as a factor of varying relevance against the broader background of the dispute. As such, EU law might lead to a certain reconceptualisation of the reasoning used but will not require a radical transformation of the methodology of national family laws. The substantive impact on national laws might be, therefore, more limited than initially expected. However, the intervention of the Court would have, in any case, an important signalling value. It would certainly reconfigure the current scope of legal uncertainty characterising child relocation in the EU context. Depending on the exact nature of the intervention, it could also have more far-reaching consequences for EU legal doctrines, as child relocation would require the Court to reinterpret them in a new context on the fringes of EU competence. It remains to be seen what the CJEU will decide if a child relocation case ever comes to the Court. The ultimate scope of autonomy left to Member States will depend on the decision to subject child relocation to the CJEU's scrutiny and its exact degree.

8.2.4. THE CONSTRUCTIVIST APPROACH AND THE CONTEXTUAL INFLUENCE OF EU LAW: BRIDGING THE GAP

The absence of an explicit EU law on child relocation does not presuppose that EU law does not exert any influence on national legal frameworks. The literature has previously recognised that many decisions on free movement, non-discrimination, or EU citizenship – while not directly concerned with family law – might nevertheless exert some influences on national law.[1177] However, they do not extend EU competences nor impose any obligations regarding substantive family law in a doctrinal sense.[1178] Therefore, the relationship between such influences and the Europeanisation of national laws have remained somehow implicit. This book suggests conceptualising EU law from a constructivist perspective, as a meaning generating practice with a normative dimension ascribed to culture, values, ideas, or belief systems.[1179] Such influences, as already noted, are often less tangible and not linear. They do not refer to norms that Member States have to comply with, but are rather co-constitutive in nature, potentially helping to frame and define the situations of legal subjects in national family law. In that, the doctrinal analysis of child relocation in the EU legal context is not the end of the story, but merely sets out constraints within which another layer of EU influence, one not dependent on these constraints, comes into play.

From this constructivist perspective, the book proposes thinking about EU law as constructing particular categories of 'contextual legal subjects'.[1180] As already recognised in the EU law literature, such constructions of EU law not only represent specific visions of social realities of EU citizens and their expectations, but also draw from such contexts to reach normative decisions about the rights that need to be granted to them.[1181] The book's contribution lies in the conceptualisation of the contextual and methodological nature of EU

1177 e.g. K. Carr, above n. 3.
1178 e.g. J.M. Scherpe, above n. 51.
1179 B. Lange, above n. 58, pp. 263–66.
1180 R. Leckey, above n. 57.
1181 L. Azoulai, S. Barbou des Places and E. Pataut, above n. 25; L. Azoulai, above n. 26.

influence on child relocation law specifically. It shows how these constructions concern both individual rights – including those of minor EU citizens – and family relationships, influencing subtly the scope of autonomy that might be granted to parents in child relocation cases and the values that might implicitly enter the contextual best interests assessments. The book divides these contextual influences into two interrelated categories: the infrastructure-oriented influences and the principle-oriented influences. The infrastructure-oriented influence is located in the space of rights – the legal infrastructure built upon a mobility paradigm and mutual trust – that is created through EU law, both in family law and beyond. It has been shown how the EU law's interventions into cross-border aspects of family law simultaneously build on the alleged social reality of mobile family life and project it into legal constructions, normalising such family mobility. This concerns, in particular, the Brussels II*ter* Regulation, the most important EU instrument in the area of cross-border parental matters. The book demonstrates also how EU law, via its mutual trust and mutual recognition doctrines, reconceptualises the welfare function of family courts as one shared across Member States. For future-oriented assessments in child relocation cases, this infrastructure creates increased certainty and stability, but such processes are normatively inflicted by the broader free movement objectives of the EU.

The principle-oriented dimension, while closely related, emerges from EU law's contextual accounts of European citizens and their entitlements. When family life is discussed, the reorientation of the point of reference towards the whole territory of the EU prompts an expectation that EU citizens may lead a normal family life in all Member States. In that, family life becomes 'portable' across the Union. However, while EU citizens can expect to be able move with their family, they might at times also be reasonably expected to move for their family if the child's interests do not oppose it. Such contextual judgments might push national courts to reconceptualise the status quo in relocation cases and indirectly invite them to consider the mobility of the non-relocating parent as well. Moreover, there are also more tangible value propositions projected by EU law via its cosmopolitan construction of the child. As EU law requires protection of children's rights to a particular version of a worthy future, one that offers them the possibility to exercise their future autonomy within this broader EU space, such projections might subtly transform how children's interests are perceived and assessed.

The contextuality applied by the CJEU or instrumentalised by the EU legislator does not have to generate effects in national child relocation law. They are, in principle, interested in different normative phenomena and from a systemic point of view, family law largely remains outside of the scope of EU law. However, as these constructions of EU law can travel beyond their doctrinal or jurisdictional boundaries – and as national judges are also judges of European law – it cannot be a priori excluded that the normatively inflicted methodology governing the latter will not interplay with the methodology governing national family law, and child relocation law more specifically. This might be the case not only where EU law applies and is taken into account in its own right, but also where it is taken as a particular context of a case, or where EU law's values are subsumed (explicitly or implicitly) under the assessment of the child's best interests principle. These methodological overlaps between EU law and child relocation law can have some beneficial effects, validating the relocating parent's autonomy claims and drawing attention to the qualitatively different contexts in which mobile EU citizens or their children might organise their lives, but they might also bear the danger of a particular generalisation of children's interests or the risk of a further form of weakening of the right to stay of the non-relocating parent. The adaptational pressure exerted by such constructions might, however, not be as radical as it immediately seems, as it will be heavily qualified and moulded by the construction of national doctrines. Perhaps paradoxically, there are several ways in which such normatively inflicted methodologies could be employed in the child's best interests, drawing attention to the broader pool of options available to national courts in relocation cases. The viability and normative desirability of such interactions between EU law and national family law remain an open question. Regardless of whether these constructions have consequences in an empirical sense, this conceptualisation allows for a more holistic investigation of Europeanisation of national laws, including where an explicit EU action is lacking.

8.3. THE EUROPEANISATION OF CROSS-BORDER CHILD RELOCATION LAW: LEGAL PRESSURES AND BEYOND

This book identifies and conceptualises various types of European influences that can have consequences for national child relocation laws, conditioning Europeanisation in different ways. Unsurprisingly, the implications for national law will differ depending on whether there is a direct EU action on child relocation, whether it is a legislative action, or a particular interpretation of EU free movement law put forward by the CJEU, and what exactly this action entails. Currently, child relocation cases are decided in a state of legal uncertainty as to the obligations imposed by EU law. If the EU takes a stance on child relocation directly, the nature and scope of this legal uncertainty will be reconfigured. Nevertheless, the book shows that the presence of an explicit EU law on child relocation is not a necessary precondition to Europeanisation. Even if national family judges might not be obliged to engage with EU law directly, they regularly face EU citizens whose life plans, expectations, rights and responsibilities might need to be evaluated in a new EU (legal) context.

The book is, therefore, built on the assumption that, in constructing this context and deciding about its legal relevance, national judges might be influenced by the contextual dimensions and the normatively inflicted methodology of EU law. The analysis of the dynamics of this engagement on the national level – the Europeanisation of cross-border child relocation law at this moment in time – was the last objective of this research project.

8.3.1. KEY FINDINGS

The qualitative analysis of case law in England and Wales, Germany, and Poland reveals interesting features of the national laws in their EU context. The findings are of value both in reference to each individual jurisdiction, due to the novel EU-focused perspective, and in a comparative light. The research material is discussed in detail in Chapter 7, but several key observations emerge from the analysis. Most importantly, the nature of national courts' engagement with the EU differs depending on the doctrinal frameworks of child relocation, including their constitutional framing, and the broader socio-political context of each given jurisdiction. This confirms the need, emphasised several times throughout the book, to investigate the real-life impacts of the European influence on child relocation cases on a national level. The engagement with EU law and the European (legal) space features most clearly where national doctrines require clarification or reformulation. This is demonstrated by the German doctrine on relocation in cases involving parents with the exclusive right to determine the child's residence and shared parental responsibilities otherwise, or the differentiation between internal and external relocations in English law. At the same time, the absence of any explicit references to EU law and its space might be hypothesised to stem either from the in-built indifference of family law towards EU law or from a broader context that makes such references particularly open to contestation, as discussed in reference to Polish law.

Perhaps surprisingly, freedom of movement – the most straightforward normative imperative of EU law – has had limited influence on national child relocation law in all three jurisdictions. Neither German nor Polish judgments discuss it in the EU legal context, and the English engagement with the EU legal framework did not lead to 'freer' movement in intra-EU child relocation cases, but rather to a reformulation of the approach towards a stronger focus on the child's best interests. This shows that the normatively inflicted methodology of EU free movement law, even where recognised, does not need to go against the intrinsic methodologies of national family law. Simultaneously, the lack of engagement with EU free movement does not necessarily mean that a broader scope of autonomy of the relocating parent goes unrecognised or is not sufficiently protected. The German example demonstrates that no EU legal pressures might be felt in that regard where the domestic legal framework recognises the constitutional relevance of free movement and, in that, already provides extensive protection. On the other hand, Polish judges seem to construct the relevant context of the cases in recognition of this EU-conditioned scope of autonomy, even if explicit references to EU free movement – perhaps due to their contestable nature against the broader social context – are absent. In that, neither does engagement with EU law imply a straightforward 'free movement imperative', nor does lack of it result necessarily in a 'free movement deficit'.

Other elements of the EU legal infrastructure appear in national judgments in various contexts, often implicitly. The Brussels II*bis* (now *ter*) Regulation, while its relevance is undisputed in the cross-border EU space, has not featured particularly often in national child relocation judgments outside of England. English judges took note of this instrument as issues of recognition and enforcement are regularly discussed in child relocation cases. Where this is not the case, as in Germany and Poland, similar references are lacking. However, this legal framework must be implicitly present in the decision-making processes, as the Regulation has been referred to in other relocation-related cases, e.g. regarding passports or short-term travels. The broader imperatives of mutual trust might also limit the scope and nature of certain considerations regarding the child's situation after relocation. This is illustrated by the German court's remark that realisation of social law claims in another EU Member State, directly linked to its rule of law, cannot in principle be questioned. In the more contextual or ideational dimension, the EU can also feature in the constructions of the child's best interests (Germany) or the parental scopes of autonomy (in all three jurisdictions). While such constructions draw from the social context of the cases, they are also explicitly intertwined with the legal layer of the supranational space offered to EU citizens. Also here, however, the exact nature of the engagement with the EU depends on the needs of the national doctrine and/or a particular case and might produce varying results. Moreover, while EU law is clearly present in this contextual layer and might lead to a different framing of disputes, it does not necessarily lead to different normative results than those observed in non-EU cases.

8.3.2. IMPLICATIONS AND LIMITATIONS OF THE FINDINGS

Despite the numerous examples of national engagement with EU law and its supranational space in child relocation cases, the analysis does not lead to the conclusion that there is a consistent reorientation of national approaches towards Europe. It cannot, therefore, be ascertained that the European influence, as discussed above, unambiguously drives a convergence among the Member States, bringing more coherence to this highly complex field of law. The EU hardly produces tangible benchmarks for the Member States to follow and it is the Member States that define the adaptational pressures, even when they can be said to emerge, and decide what kind of action they require (if any). In that, national actors both use and avoid EU law for rather pragmatic reasons and do so strategically. However, this still allows for the EU and EU law to be occasionally employed to obtain a particular normative result and, depending on circumstances, even to reconstruct a particular doctrinal question in a new light. In that, as the development of national law is an active process, the engagements with Europe might eventually lead to more convergence, but do not necessarily need to do so. Currently, EU law provides a resource for, rather than a challenge to, national conceptualisations. Simultaneously, this analysis reveals the added value of the more constructively oriented investigation, as many of the encounters discussed above could not be captured – at least not at the current stage of EU legal development – by a purely doctrinal analysis. To account for the subtle influence of identities, beliefs and ideas carried by EU law, including its normatively inflicted methodology, a closer attention needs to be paid to how national judges frame their legal subjects and reconstruct them using EU law.

These findings also confirm that the doctrinal effects of EU law – if the limits of its reach discussed in this book are accepted – might be indeed rather less transformative than originally feared or hoped. Even where national courts take account of EU law, in particular its free movement rights, their consideration is not in itself sufficient for a substantive reorientation of national doctrines. This is so, first, because the focus of the cases remains on the child's best interests, a consideration of which is required by EU law as well. Freedom of movement should never supersede the primary importance of children's interests, and it is national courts that will conduct their assessment. More broadly, however, it is exactly this doctrinal and institutional setup – arguably reinforced by the limitation of EU competence – that makes national child relocation law relatively resilient to any challenge coming from EU law. On the surface, EU law can demand national family law to consider certain EU legal entitlements in child relocation cases and, if that happens, national courts will naturally be obliged to do so. However, while such demands might put pressure on national legal actors to rethink certain aspects of their conceptualisations of cross-border child relocation cases, they will not reach far or deep enough to significantly alter the methodologies of national family law if national actors are not open to do so. This is illustrated by the varying dynamics of national engagement with EU law discussed above. Therefore, doctrinally speaking, the contribution of EU law can be rather procedural. Substantive change, if any, can be co-constituted by the normatively inflicted methodology of EU law and its broader contextual influences, but will be driven by national actors.

This leads to the discussion of the limitations of the findings discussed here. Many of these limits were already discussed, but one needs to be aware principally of two points. First, the nature of the approach adopted here is qualitative, and the account presented is a question of plausibility. Meanings, as communicative phenomena, are not simply given but are rather (re)constructed in the research process, and this remains the case even if interpreted within the material constraints of legal doctrines. Certain limitations flow also from the selection of the research material. The research relied predominantly on published court cases, with the particular consequences of such a choice discussed already in the introduction (e.g. discretionary reporting of cases, quantitative variation in data). This approach has obvious implications for the generalisability of findings. It cannot be excluded that an analysis of a differently selected sample of cases or a different jurisdiction would require a reformulation of the interpretations offered above. Here, the exploratory dimension of the research design is revealed. The methodological proposal of this book allows national laws to be looked at from a new perspective, one that provides novel insights but leaves many questions open. Hence, regarding the analysis of national encounters with Europe, one needs to be aware that this book offers *an* understanding rather than *the* understanding of such processes. Further research can, however, directly draw on this understanding to refine the analysis or pose new questions.

8.4. AN EYE ON THE FUTURE

The book shows that – while it is clear what draws child relocation actors to EU law and what might draw EU lawmakers to child relocation – the transformative potential of EU law is perhaps less far-reaching than immediately expected. However, this conclusion should not be seen as closing the discussion, but rather as a starting point for further analysis. On the level of supranational law, this book – while signalling certain issues – invites a more explicit reflection on the normative desirability of an EU action in cross-border child relocation. One can discuss wider systemic consequences of such actions in light of the conferral principle in more detail, but also scrutinise what the recently suggested changes to EU Treaties (including a revision of Article 81(3) of the TFEU)[1182] could mean for child relocation. A more critical discussion of the approach of the ECtHR to child relocation cases would also be of value for broader discussions of the transformative potential of the European human rights framework. The findings of the book might further provide a (starting) reference point for broader policy-oriented research on the European level, also beyond the EU, and an inspiration for

[1182] European Parliament resolution of 22 November 2023 on proposals of the European Parliament for the amendment of the Treaties (2023) 2022/2051(INL), Amendment 104.

reconceptualisation of national doctrines and legal frameworks. Additionally, the book invites further explorations of the intersections of family law and EU law from the constructivist perspective, for example regarding cultural constructions of childhood in EU law and its consequences for various strands of national law.

While one should probably not expect any rapid legal developments on the EU level, national courts face child relocation disputes on a daily basis. It has been shown how their engagement with EU law looks in England and Wales, Germany, and Poland. Taking these observations as a starting point, the investigation of the national engagement with EU law in child relocation cases can usefully continue. As research undertaken in this book was limited to court judgments broadly, and published judgments in particular, other types of qualitative investigations could test or complement the answers provided in this book. One could focus on how selected national courts approach child relocation cases and construct their arguments, analysing the entirety of such cases decided by a specific court in a specific time frame. Courts in border areas or in areas with particularly high emigration could provide interesting insights. This could also shed light on the role of judges as individual actors in the creation of law. Further, interviews with judges or legal professionals or detailed case studies could reveal how exactly European arguments or discourses find their way into the text of a judgment, and how relevant actors conceptualise their role in the Europeanisation processes. Similarly, one could trace the legislative history of new child relocation laws (e.g. in Austria) and investigate whether and how Europe played any role in the legislative process. Such research could also provide more insights on how the socio-political context and the national legal culture might condition engagement with the EU (legal) context. Quantitative research, for example tracing the ratio of approved relocation applications and the frequency of European references over the years, could accompany the qualitative research to establish whether such processes have implications for outcomes in relocation cases. This book could not investigate such questions in more detail, and hence signals the dynamics rather than analyses them in an exhaustive way. However, these themes and the respective findings of this book might be of interest also for those interested in questions of the socio-political nature of family law, issues of European identity, or the dynamics of integration through law in general.

Another set of questions to be asked concerns people's experience with the law, understood broadly. One could investigate on a broader scale whether the European Union indeed alters parents' expectations in child relocation cases, as suggested by previous research, and how they experience national proceedings from that perspective.[1183] It could also be investigated whether the EU changes

[1183] See, for example, S. Morano-Foadi, above n. 273.

how people behave and negotiate decisions out of court. It was argued that the indeterminacy of relocation laws makes the cases difficult, since 'people cannot bargain in the shadow of law if the law casts no shadow'.[1184] The shadow of law is indeed difficult to delineate due to the factual complexity of the cases and the diverse characteristics of family configurations. However, one cannot exclude that as people 'bargain in the shadow of law', they also bargain in the shadow of European law and the life-worlds it creates. For example, one of the German judgments makes a reference to a parental agreement stipulating that the right to determine the child's place of residence should be held exclusively by the mother, but only with reference to the territory of the European Union and Switzerland.[1185] This reference is clearly not purely geographical, as it does not encompass other European countries, but suggests a certain socio-legal spatiality (the inclusion of Switzerland, next to the EU Member States, is likely justified not only by the shared free movement framework, but also by the common language and other cultural factors). All such questions call for different research designs but can usefully draw on the findings of this book.

8.5. THE EPILOGUE

Family law and EU law are strange bedfellows. The former is a firmly established and consistently defended competence of the Member States, concerned with normative determinations of good family relationships. The latter is driven by free movement rights and the 'internal market imperative'. And yet, while they remain concerned with normatively different phenomena, it would be a mistake not to appreciate all the different ways in which family entitlements and EU citizenship rights intersect. In many cases, EU law strengthens individuals' family rights, but in certain contexts – such as child relocation – it might be equally perceived as a threat, be it to family law's own methodologies or to some groups of EU citizens more broadly. Similarly, therefore, it would be a mistake not to recognise the fact that the path of harmonisation of child relocation measures, be it legislative or judicial, raises questions about its legal and political feasibility as well as systemic and societal legitimacy. This is not to say that it should be shied away from, but rather to call for an in-depth consideration of what is to be gained and what is to be possibly lost due to such intervention. A degree of divergence in some values, and family values in particular, might be inherent

1184 P. Parkinson, above n. 210, p. 166.

1185 *OLG Karlsruhe, Beschluss vom 17.01.2018* – 18 UF 185/17, para. 2: 'Nach Einholung eines familienpsychologischen Gutachtens kamen die Eltern in einem Termin beim Amtsgericht Konstanz am 06.02.2013 überein, das Sorgerecht für … gemeinsam auszuüben, bis auf das Aufenthaltsbestimmungsrecht für die EU und die Schweiz, welches der Mutter weiter allein zustehen sollte'.

in the pluralistic society of the EU. While it is up to the EU legal actors to determine the extent to which such divergence should be accommodated when it encounters EU law, this decision should recognise the formal constraints of EU competence as well as the structural and substantive limits of its intervention, fully appreciating family law's purpose and the nature of its decision-making. In the meantime, national judges – and simultaneously EU law judges – will continue to filter and mould a consensus from within national legal doctrines, perhaps encountering Europe in more ways than meets the eye. The EU and EU law might, therefore, very well already be part of cross-border child relocation law, but whether and how child relocation should become part of the EU legal project should invite detailed considerations.

BIBLIOGRAPHY

Abrams K., 'The Legal Subject in Exile' (2001) 51 *Duke Law Journal* 27

Ackers L., *Shifting Spaces: Women, Citizenship and Migration Within the European Union*, Policy Press, London 1998

——, 'Citizenship, Migration and the Valuation of Care in the European Union' (2004) 30 *Journal of Ethnic and Migration Studies* 373

Ackers L. and Stalford H., 'Children, Migration and Citizenship in the European Union: Intra-Community Mobility and the Status of Children in EC Law' (1999) 21 *Children and Youth Services Review* 987

——, *A Community for Children? Children, Citizenship, and Internal Migration in the EU*, Ashgate Publishing, Hampshire 2004

Albertus L. and Sloth-Nielsen J., 'Relocation Decisions: Do Culture, Language and Religion Matter in the Rainbow Nation?' (2010) 2 *Journal of Family Law and Practice* 86

Alves de Faria G., 'Sexual Orientation and the ECtHR: what relevance is given to the best interests of the child? An analysis of the European Court of Human Rights' approach to the best interests of the child in LGBT parenting cases' (2015) *Family & Law*, DOI: 10.5553/FenR/.000018

Antokolskaia M., 'Family Law and National Culture. Arguing against the Cultural Constraints Argument' (2008) 4 *Utrecht Law Review* 25

Archard D., 'Children, Adults, Best Interests and Rights' (2013) 13 *Medical Law International* 55

Arnull A., 'Article 60 – Protocol (No 30) on the Application of the Charter of Fundamental Rights of the European Union to Poland and the United Kingdom' in S. Peers, T. Hervey, J. Kenner and A. Ward (eds), *The EU Charter of Fundamental Rights: A Commentary*, Hart Publishing, Oxford 2014

Ashiagbor D., 'Article 15 – Freedom to Choose an Occupation and Right to Engage in Work' in S. Peers, T. Hervey, J. Kenner and A. Ward (eds), *The EU Charter of Fundamental Rights: A Commentary*, Hart Publishing, Oxford 2014

Azoulai L., 'The Court of Justice and the Social Market Economy: The Emergence of an Ideal and the Conditions for Its Realization' (2008) 45 *Common Market Law Review* 1335

——, '"Euro-Bonds" The Ruiz Zambrano Judgment or the Real Invention of EU Citizenship' (2011) 3 *Perspectives on Federalism* 31

——, 'The European Individual as Part of Collective Entities (Market, Family, Society)' in L. Azoulai, S. Barbou des Places and E. Pataut (eds), *Constructing the Person in EU Law: Rights, Roles, Identities*, Hart Publishing, Oxford 2016

——, 'The Law of European Society' (2022) 59 *Common Market Law Review* (Special Issue) 203

Azoulai L., Barbou des Places S. and Pataut E. (eds), *Constructing the Person in EU Law: Rights, Roles, Identities*, Hart Publishing, Oxford 2016

Baarsma N.A., *The Europeanisation of International Family Law*, T.M.C. Asser Press, The Hague 2011

Bainham A., 'Taking Children Abroad: Human Rights, Welfare and the Courts' (2001) 60 *Cambridge Law Journal* 489

Baker H., Hirsch J. and Sauvage N., 'International Family Relocation from an English, French and German Perspective' (2012) *International Family Law* 97

Bala N., Wheeler A., Paetsch J. and Bertrand L., 'Canadian Relocation Cases: Heading Towards Guidelines, 2011' (2013) <https://hdl.handle.net/10864/10333>.

Barnard C., *The Substantive Law of the EU: The Four Freedoms*, 5th ed., Oxford University Press, Oxford 2016

Bartolini S., 'In The Name Of The Best Interests Of The Child: The Principle Of Mutual Trust In Child Abduction Cases' (2019) 56 *Common Market Law Review* 91

Bast J. and Wetz K., 'Chapter 3: System of Competences' in P.J. Kuijper, F. Amtenbrink, D. Curtin, B. De Witte, A. McDonnell, and S. Van den Bogaert (eds), *The Law of the European Union*, 5th ed., Kluwer Law International, The Hague 2018

Beaumont P., 'International Family Law in Europe – the Maintenance Project, the Hague Conference and the EC: A Triumph of Reverse Subsidiarity' (2009) 73 *Rabels Zeitschrift für ausländisches und internationales Privatrecht* 509

——, 'Private International Law Concerning Children in the UK after Brexit: Comparing Hague Treaty Law with EU Regulations' (2017) 29 *Child and Family Law Quarterly* 213

Bérénos Y.M., 'Time to Move On: The International State of Affairs with Respect to Child Relocation Law' (2012) 8 *Utrecht Law Review* 1

Berkemann J., 'Freie Rechtsprechung für freie Bürger ?!' *JurPC-Web-Dok* 354/2002 <https://www.jurpc.de/jurpc/show?id=20020354>

Boele-Woelki K. (ed), *Perspectives for the Unification and Harmonisation of Family Law in Europe*, Intersentia, Oxford 2003

——, 'The Principles of European Family Law: Its Aims and Prospects' (2005) 1 *Utrecht Law Review* 160

——, 'The CEFL Principles Regarding Parental Responsibilities: Predominance of the Common Core' in K. Boele-Woelki and T. Sverdrup (eds), *European Challenges in Contemporary Family Law*, Intersentia, Oxford 2008

——, 'What Comparative Family Law Should Entail' (2008) 4 *Utrecht Law Review* 1

Boele-Woelki K., Braat B., Curry-Sumner I., Jeppesen de Boer C.G., Lokin P., Vonk M., de Vries N. and Schrama W., 'Research Questions in Family Law Derived from a Comparative Synthesis of General Trends and Developments' (2008) 4 *Utrecht Law Review* 279

Boele-Woelki K. and González Beilfuss C. (eds), *Brussels II bis: Its Impact and Application in the Member States*, Intersentia, Antwerp 2007

Boele-Woelki K. and Martiny D., 'The Commission on European Family Law (CEFL) and Its Principles of European Family Law Regarding Parental Responsibilities' (2007) 8 *ERA Forum* 125

Boucon L., 'EU Law and Retained Powers of Member States' in L. Azoulai (ed), *The Question of Competence in the European Union*, Oxford University Press, Oxford 2014

Boyd S.B., 'Autonomy for Mothers? Relational Theory and Parenting Apart' (2010) 18 *Feminist Legal Studies* 137

——, 'Relocation, Indeterminacy, and Burden of Proof: Lessons from Canada' (2011) 23 *Child and Family Law Quarterly* 155

Bradley D., 'Convergence in Family Law: Mirrors, Transplants and Political Economy' (2001) *Oxford University Comparative Law Forum* 2 <https://ouclf.law.ox.ac.uk/convergence-in-family-law-mirrors-transplants-and-political-economy/>

——, 'Comparative Law, Family Law and Common Law' (2003) 23 *Oxford Journal of Legal Studies* 127

——, 'A Note on Comparative Family Law: Problems, Perspectives, Issues and Politics' (2005) *Oxford University Comparative Law Forum* 4 <https://ouclf.iuscomp.org/a-note-on-comparative-family-law-problems-perspectives-issues-and-politics/>

Brems E., 'Procedural Protection: An Examination of Procedural Safeguards Read into Substantive Convention Rights' in E. Brems and J. Gerards (eds), *Shaping Rights in the ECHR: The Role of the European Court of Human Rights in Determining the Scope of Human Rights*, Cambridge University Press, Cambridge 2014

Burbergs M., 'How the Right to Respect for Private and Family Life, Home and Correspondence Became the Nursery in Which New Rights Are Born: Article 8 ECHR' in E. Brems and J. Gerards (eds), *Shaping Rights in the ECHR: The Role of the European Court of Human Rights in Determining the Scope of Human Rights*, Cambridge University Press, Cambridge 2014

Cambien N., 'EU Citizenship and the Right to Care' in D. Kochenov (ed), *EU Citizenship and Federalism: The Role of Rights*, Cambridge University Press, Cambridge 2017

Carr K., 'Deconstructing and Reconstructing Family Law through the European Legal Order' (2014) PhD Thesis, European University Institute <http://cadmus.eui.eu/handle/1814/32811>

Castro-Martín T. and Cortina C., 'Demographic Issues of Intra-European Migration: Destinations, Family and Settlement' (2015) 31 *European Journal of Population* 109

Ceran O., 'Child Relocation, Soft Law, and the Quest for Uniformity at the European Court of Human Rights – Part One' (2020) 15 *Studia Prawa Prywatnego*

——, 'Child Relocation, Soft Law, and the Quest for Uniformity at the European Court of Human Rights – Part Two' (2021) 16 *Studia Prawa Prywatnego*

——, 'Expeditiousness of child abduction proceedings, procedural autonomy, and what it has to do with sincere cooperation: *Rzecznik Praw Dziecka and Others*' (2023) 60 *Common Market Law Review* 1787

Chalmers D., 'The Persona of EU Law' in L. Azoulai, S. Barbou des Places and E. Pataut (eds), *Constructing the Person in EU Law: Rights, Roles, Identities*, Hart Publishing, Oxford 2016

Chalmers D., Davies G. and Monti G., *European Union Law: Text and Materials*, 4th ed., Cambridge University Press, Cambridge 2019

Cherubini F., 'The Relationship Between the Court of Justice of the European Union and the European Court of Human Rights in the View of the Accession' (2015) 16 *German Law Journal* 1375

Chisholm R., 'The Paramount Consideration' (Conference Paper) (18 March 2002) *10th National Family Law Conference*, Melbourne

Choudhry S. and Herring J., *European Human Rights and Family Law*, Hart Publishing, Oxford 2010

Chzhen Y. and Bradshaw J., 'Lone Parents, Poverty and Policy in the European Union' (2012) 22 *Journal of European Social Policy* 487

Coenraad L.M., 'A European Approach to Child Relocation Issues' (2015) 4 *International Family Law* 312

Coester-Waltjen D., 'Relocation – from Theory to Practice. Kindeswohl als Richtschnur bei Familiärem Auslandsumzug' (2012) *Interdisziplinäre Zeitschrift für Familienrecht* 311

——, 'The Impact of the European Convention on Human Rights and the European Court of Human Rights on European Family Law' in J.M. Scherpe (ed), *European Family Law (Volume I): The Impact of Institutions and Organisations on European Family Law*, Edward Elgar Publishing, Cheltenham 2016

Colombi Ciacchi A., 'Non-Legislative Harmonisation of Private Law under the European Constitution: The Case of Unfair Suretyships' (2005) 13 *European Review of Private Law* 285

Commission on European Family Law, 'CEFL Principles Regarding Parental Responsibilities' (2004) <http://ceflonline.net/wp-content/uploads/Principles-PR-English.pdf>

——, 'Parental Responsibility Reports by Jurisdiction' <http://ceflonline.net/parental-responsibility-reports-by-jurisdiction/>

Condinanzi M., Lang A. and Nascimbene B., *Citizenship of the Union and Freedom of Movement of Persons*, Brill Nijhoff, Leiden 2008

Cooper I., 'The Watchdogs of Subsidiarity: National Parliaments and the Logic of Arguing in the EU' (2006) 44 *Journal of Common Market Studies* 281

——, 'Is the Subsidiarity Early Warning Mechanism a Legal or a Political Procedure? Three Questions and a Typology' (2016) RSC Working Paper, European University Institute <http://hdl.handle.net/1814/40765>

Costello C., 'Market Access All Areas – The Treatment of Non-Discriminatory Barriers to the Free Movement of Workers' (2000) 27 *Legal Issues of Economic Integration* 267

——, 'Metock: Free Movement and "Normal Family Life" in the Union' (2009) 46 *Common Market Law Review* 587

Cotta C., 'Is an International Consensus Possible with Regard to Child Relocation?' (2011) LLM Thesis, University of Dundee (UK)

Coutts S., *Citizenship, Crime and Community in the European Union*, Hart Publishing, Oxford 2019

Creutzfeldt N., Kubal A. and Pirie F., 'Introduction: Exploring the Comparative in Socio-Legal Studies' (2016) 12 *International Journal of Law in Context* 377

Cullen H., 'Children's Rights' in S. Peers and A. Ward (eds), *The EU Charter of Fundamental Rights: Politics, Law and Policy*, Hart Publishing, Oxford 2004

Cvejić Jančić O., 'Rights of the Child in a Changing World' in O. Cvejić Jančić (ed), *The Rights of the Child in a Changing World*, Springer, Cham 2016

Daly A., 'The Right of Children to Be Heard in Civil Proceedings and the Emerging Law of the European Court of Human Rights' (2011) 15 *International Journal of Human Rights* 441

Davies G.T., 'The Right to Stay at Home: A Basis for Expanding European Family Rights' in D. Kochenov (ed), *EU Citizenship and Federalism: The Role of Rights*, Cambridge University, Cambridge Press 2017

De Búrca G., 'After the EU Charter of Fundamental Rights: The Court of Justice as a Human Rights Adjudicator?' (2013) 20 *Maastricht Journal of European and Comparative Law* 168

de Cecco F., 'Fundamental Freedoms, Fundamental Rights, and the Scope of Free Movement Law' (2014) 15 *German Law Journal* 383

de Schutter O. and Tulkens F., 'Rights in Conflict: The European Court of Human Rights as a Pragmatic Institution' in E. Brems (ed), *Conflicts Between Fundamental Rights*, Intersentia, Oxford 2008 <https://ssrn.com/abstract=2446909>

de Vries S.A., 'Balancing Fundamental Rights with Economic Freedoms According to the European Court of Justice' (2013) 9 *Utrecht Law Review* 169

De Witte B., 'The Place of the OMC in the System of EU Competences and Sources of Law' (2018) 3 *European Papers – A Journal on Law and Integration* 207

De Witte B. and Smulders B., 'Chapter 6: Sources of European Union Law' in P.J. Kuijper, F. Amtenbrink, D. Curtin, B. De Witte, A. McDonnell, and S. Van den Bogaert (eds), *The Law of the European Union*, 5th ed., Kluwer Law International, The Hague 2018

de Witte F., 'Kick off contribution: Freedom of Movement Under Attack: Is It Worth Defending as the Core of EU Citizenship?' in F. de Witte, R. Bauböck and J. Shaw (eds), 'Freedom of Movement Under Attack: Is It Worth Defending as the Core of EU Citizenship?' (2016) RSC Working Paper, European University Institute <https://cadmus.eui.eu//handle/1814/44567>

——, 'EU Citizenship, Free Movement and Emancipation: A Rejoinder' in F. de Witte, R. Baubock and J. Shaw (eds), 'Freedom of Movement Under Attack: Is It Worth Defending as the Core of EU Citizenship?' (2016) RSC Working Paper, European University Institute <https://cadmus.eui.eu//handle/1814/44567>

Diduck A., 'The Unmodified Family: The Child Support Act and the Construction of Legal Subjects' (1995) 22 *Journal of Law and Society* 527

——, 'Public Norms and Private Lives: Rights, Fairness and Family Law' in J. Wallbank, S. Choudhry and J. Herring (eds), *Rights, Gender and Family Law*, Routledge-Cavendish, Abingdon 2009

——, 'What Is Family Law For?' (2011) 64 *Current Legal Problems* 287

Doughty J., 'Identity Crisis in the Family Courts? Different Approaches in England and Wales and Australia' (2009) 31 *Journal of Social Welfare and Family Law* 231

Douglas-Scott S., 'A Tale of Two Courts: Luxembourg, Strasbourg and the Growing European Human Rights Acquis' (2006) 43 *Common Market Law Review* 629

Dubout E., 'The Protection of Fundamental Rights and the Allocation of Competences in the EU: A Clash of Constitutional Logics' in L. Azoulai (ed), *The Question of Competence in the European Union*, Oxford University Press, Oxford 2014

Duggan W.D., 'Rock-Paper-Scissors: Playing the Odds with the Law of Child Relocation' (2007) 45 *Family Court Review* 193

Editorial Comment, 'EU Law as a Way of Life' (2017) 54 *Common Market Law Review* 357

Editorial Comment, 'Freedoms Unlimited? Reflections on Mary Carpenter v. Secretary of State' (2003) 40 *Common Market Law Review* 537

Eekelaar J., 'The Importance of Thinking That Children Have Rights' (1992) 6 *International Journal of Law, Policy and the Family* 221

——, 'Children Between Cultures' (2004) *18 International Journal of Law, Policy and the Family* 178
——, 'The Role of the Best Interests Principle in Decisions Affecting Children and Decisions about Children' (2015) 23 *International Journal of Children's Rights* 3
——, 'Two Dimensions of the Best Interests Principle: Decisions About Children and Decisions Affecting Children' in E.E. Sutherland and L.A. Barnes Macfarlane (eds), *Implementing Article 3 of the United Nations Convention on the Rights of the Child: Best Interests, Welfare and Well-being*, Cambridge University Press, Cambridge 2016
——, 'Family Law and Legal Theory' in E. Brake and L. Ferguson (eds), *Philosophical Foundations of Children's and Family Law*, Oxford University Press, Oxford 2018
Ellman I.M., 'Why Making Family Law Is Hard' (2003) 35 *Arizona State Law Journal* 699
Elrod L.D., 'National and International Momentum Builds for More Child Focus in Relocation Disputes' (2010) 44 *Family Law Quarterly* 341
Elster J., 'Solomonic Judgments: Against the Best Interest of the Child' (1987) 54 *University of Chicago Law Review* 1
Ervo L., 'The Hidden Meanings in the Case Law of the European Court for Human Rights' (2016) *Semiotica* 209
Eschelbach D. and Rölke U., 'Internationale Relocation – Umzug eines Elternteils mit dem Kind ins Ausland' (2012) 6 *Das Jugendamt* 290
Eßer D., 'Die Veröffentlichungspflicht der Gerichte und das Internet' *JurPC-Web-Dok* 119/2001 <https://www.jurpc.de/jurpc/show?id=20010119>
Estin A.L., 'Families Across Borders: The Hague Children's Conventions and the Case for International Family Law in the United States' (2010) 62 *Florida Law Review* 47
——, 'Nationality and Migration Status in International Children's Law' in G. Douglas, M. Murch and V. Stephens (eds), *International and National Perspectives on Child and Family Law: Essays in Honour of Nigel Lowe*, Intersentia, Cambridge 2018
European Commission Press Release, 'Building Trust in Justice Systems in Europe: "Assises de La Justice" Forum to Shape the Future of EU Justice Policy' (Brussels, 21 November 2013) <http://europa.eu/rapid/press-release_IP-13-1117_en.htm>
European Commission, 'Europeans' Opinions on the European Union's Priorities' (2018) *Standard Eurobarometer Report* 90 (2215/STD90) <https://europa.eu/eurobarometer/surveys/detail/2215
European Commission, 'Promoting our European way of life' <https://commission.europa.eu/strategy-and-policy/priorities-2019-2024/promoting-our-european-way-life_en>
European Commission, 'Annual Report on Intra-EU Labour Mobility 2022' (2023) https://data.europa.eu/doi/10.2767/560178
European Court of Human Rights, 'Guide on Article 8 of the European Convention on Human Rights' (2022) <https://www.echr.coe.int/Documents/Guide_Art_8_ENG.pdf>
European Court of Human Rights, 'Guide on Article 14 of the European Convention on Human Rights and on Article 1 of Protocol No. 12 to the Convention' (2022) <https://www.echr.coe.int/documents/d/echr/Guide_Art_14_Art_1_Protocol_12_ENG>
European Court of Human Rights, 'Guide on Article 2 of Protocol No. 4 to the European Convention on Human Rights (Freedom of Movement)' (2022) <https://www.echr.coe.int/documents/d/echr/Guide_Art_2_Protocol_4_ENG>

Eurostat: Statistics Explained, 'Migration and Migrant Population Statistics' <http://ec.europa.eu/eurostat/statistics-explained/index.php/Migration_and_migrant_population_statistics>

Everson M., 'A Very Cosmopolitan Citizenship: But Who Pays the Price?' in M. Dougan, N.N. Shuibhne and E. Spaventa (eds), *Empowerment and Disempowerment of the European Citizen*, Hart Publishing, Oxford 2012

Faber E., 'Sorge- und Umgangsrecht bei Umzug oder geplanter Auswanderung des betreuenden Elternteils' (2012) *Familie und Recht* 464

Fenton-Glynn C., *Children and the European Court of Human Rights*, Oxford University Press, Oxford 2020

Ferrer-Riba J., 'Parental Responsibility in a European Perspective' in J.M. Scherpe (ed), *European Family Law (Volume III): Family Law in a European Perspective*, Edward Elgar Publishing 2016

Fichera M., 'Sketches of a Theory of Europe as an Area of Freedom, Security and Justice' in M. Fletcher, E. Herlin-Karnell and C. Matera (eds), *The European Union as an Area of Freedom, Security and Justice*, Routledge, Abingdon 2017

Fineman M., 'Dominant Discourse, Professional Language, and Legal Change in Child Custody Decisionmaking' (1988) 101 *Harvard Law Review* 727

Finger P., 'Umzug mit dem Kind – Zustimmung des anderen Elternteils' (2009) *Familienrecht und Familienverfahrensrecht* 134

Fiorini A., 'Rome III – Choice of Law in Divorce: Is the Europeanization of Family Law Going Too Far?' (2008) 22 *International Journal of Law, Policy and the Family* 178

——, 'Which Legal Basis for Family Law?: The Way Forward' (2012) European Parliament Publications Office <https://data.europa.eu/doi/10.2861/42262>

Forastiero R., 'The Charter of Fundamental Rights and the Protection of Vulnerable Groups: Children, Elderly People and Persons with Disabilities' in G. Palmisano (ed), *Making the Charter of Fundamental Rights a Living Instrument*, Brill Nijhoff, Leiden 2014

Freeman M., *Article 3: The Best Interests of the Child (A Commentary on the United Nations Convention on the Rights of the Child)*, Martinus Nijhoff, Leiden 2007

——, 'Relocation. The Reunite Research' (2009) *Reunite* <https://web.archive.org/web/20111216014043/http://www.reunite.org/edit/files/Library%20-%20reunite%20Publications/Relocation%20Report.pdf>

——, 'Abduction and Relocation – Links and Messages' (2013) 38 *Children Australia* 143

Geiger R., 'Article 352 TFEU' in R. Geiger, D.-E. Khan and M. Kotzur (eds), *European Union Treaties: A Commentary: Treaty on European Union, Treaty on the Functioning of the European Union, Charter of Fundamental Rights of the European Union*, C.H. Beck/Hart Publishing, Munich/Oxford 2015

George R., 'The International Relocation Debate' (2012) 34 *Journal of Social Welfare and Family Law* 141

——, 'Relocation Disputes in England and Wales: First Findings from the 2012 Study' Oxford Legal Studies Research Paper No 91/2013 (2013) <https://papers.ssrn.com/sol3/papers.cfm?abstract_id=2306097>

——, *Relocation Disputes: Law and Practice in England and New Zealand*, Hart Publishing, Oxford 2014

——, 'Payne v Payne – The Long Goodbye Continues' (2015) <https://www.familylaw.co.uk/news_and_comment/payne-v-payne-the-long-goodbye-continues>

——, 'How Do Judges Decide International Relocation Cases' (2015) 27 *Child and Family Law Quarterly* 377

——, 'The Child's Welfare in a European Perspective' in J.M. Scherpe (ed), *European Family Law (Volume III): Family Law in a European Perspective*, Edward Elgar Publishing, Cheltenham 2016

George R. and Gallwey A., 'How Do Parents Experience Relocation Disputes in the Family Courts?' (2016) 38 *Journal of Social Welfare and Family Law* 394

Gerards J., 'Judicial Deliberations in the European Court of Human Rights' (2008) *Social Science Research Network*, SSRN Scholarly Paper ID 1114906 <https://papers.ssrn.com/abstract=1114906>

——, 'Freedom of movement' in P. van Dijk, F. van Hoof, A. van Rijn and L. Zwaak (eds), *Theory and Practice of the European Convention on Human Rights*, 5th ed., Intersentia, Cambridge 2018

Glendon M.A., 'Fixed Rules and Discretion in Contemporary Family Law and Succession' (1986) 60 *Tulane Law Review* 1165

Glennon T., 'Divided Parents, Shared Children: Conflicting Approaches to Relocation Disputes in the USA' (2008) 4 *Utrecht Law Review* 55

Gluza P., Kołakowska-Halbersztadt Z. and Tański M. (ed.), *Dziecko w rozstaniu rodziców*, Wydawnictwo Prawnicze LexisNexis, Warszawa 2013 <https://sip.lex.pl/#/monograph/369312586/8>

González Beilfuss C., Carpaneto L., Kruger T., Pretelli I., and Župan M., *Jurisdiction, Recognition and Enforcement in Matrimonial and Parental Responsibility Matters: A Commentary on Regulation 2019/1111 (Brussels IIb)*, Edward Elgar Publishing, Cheltenham 2023

Granet F., 'Alternating Residence and Relocation. A View from France' (2008) 4 *Utrecht Law Review* 48

Guild E., *Immigration Law in the European Community*, Kluwer Law International, The Hague 2001

Guild E., Peers S. and Tomkin J., *The EU Citizenship Directive: A Commentary*, Oxford University Press, Oxford 2014

Hailbronner K. and Thym D., 'Case C-34/09, Gerardo Ruiz Zambrano v. Office National de'emploi (ONEm), Judgment of the Court of Justice (Grand Chamber) of 8 March 2011' (2011) 48 *Common Market Law Review* 1253

Hanson K. and Lundy L., 'Does Exactly What It Says on the Tin? A Critical Analysis and Alternative Conceptualisation of the So-Called "General Principles" of the Convention on the Rights of the Child' (2017) 25 *International Journal of Children's Rights* 285

Harding R., 'Legal Constructions of Dementia: Discourses of Autonomy at the Margins of Capacity' (2012) 34 *Journal of Social Welfare and Family Law* 425

Hayes M., 'Relocation Cases: Is the Court of Appeal Applying the Correct Principles?' (2006) 18 *Child and Family Law Quarterly* 351

Henrich S. and Khan D.-E., 'Article 21 TFEU' in R. Geiger, D.-E. Khan, and M. Kotzur (eds), *European Union Treaties: A Commentary: Treaty on European Union, Treaty on the Functioning of the European Union, Charter of Fundamental Rights of the European Union*, C.H. Beck/Hart Publishing, Munich/Oxford 2015

Herring J., 'The welfare principle and the rights of parents' in S. Gilmore (ed), *Parental Rights and Responsibilities*, Routledge, Abingdon 2017

Herring J. and Taylor R., 'Relocating Relocation' (2006) 18 *Child and Family Law Quarterly* 517

Hirth J.A., *Internationale Relocation: Eine rechtsvergleichende Untersuchung über den grenzüberschreitenden Wohnortwechsel eines Elternteils mit dem Kind gegen den Willen des anderen Elternteils*, Peter Lang, Berlin 2018

Hodson D., 'David Hodson on International Family Law: The London Conclusions and Resolutions' (2010) <http://www.familylaw.co.uk/news_and_comment/DavidHodson160810#.WQcHtMakI2w>

Hyltén-Cavallius K., 'Who Cares? Caregivers' Derived Residence Rights from Children in EU Free Movement Law' (2020) 57 *Common Market Law Review* 399

Iglesias Sánchez S., 'The Court and the Charter: The Impact of the Entry into Force of the Lisbon Treaty on the ECJ's Approach to Fundamental Rights' (2012) 49 *Common Market Law Review* 1565

——, 'A Citizenship Right to Stay? The Right Not to Move in a Union Based on Free Movement' in D. Kochenov (ed), *EU Citizenship and Federalism: The Role of Rights*, Cambridge University Press, Cambridge 2017

——, 'Purely Internal Situations and the Limits of EU Law: A Consolidated Case Law or a Notion to Be Abandoned?' (2018) 14 *European Constitutional Law Review* 7

Iliopoulou Penot A., 'The Transnational Character of Union Citizenship' in M. Dougan, N.N. Shuibhne and E. Spaventa (eds), *Empowerment and Disempowerment of the European Citizen*, Hart Publishing, Oxford 2012

Jagielski M. and Niedużak M., 'Publiczna Dostępność Orzeczeń Sądowych' (2010) Forum Obywatelskiego Rozwoju, Helsińska Fundacja Praw Człowieka, Akademia Leona Koźmińskiego

Jansen N., 'Comparative Law and Comparative Knowledge' in M. Reimann and R. Zimmermann (eds), *The Oxford Handbook of Comparative Law*, 2nd ed., Oxford University Press, Oxford 2019

Janssens C., *The Principle of Mutual Recognition in EU Law*, Oxford University Press, Oxford 2013

Jaremba U. and Mayoral J.A., 'The Europeanization of National Judiciaries: Definitions, Indicators and Mechanisms' (2019) 26 *Journal of European Public Policy* 386

Jeppesen de Boer C.G., 'Parental Relocation: Free Movement Rights and Joint Parenting' (2008) 4 *Utrecht Law Review* 73

Jędrejek G., 'Art. 95' in G. Jędrejek (ed), *Kodeks Rodzinny i Opiekuńczy. Pokrewieństwo i Powinowactwo. Komentarz*, System Informacji Prawnej LEX, 2014

Kalimo H., Meyer T. and Mylly T., 'Of Values and Legitimacy – Discourse Analytical Insights on the Copyright Case Law of the Court of Justice of the European Union' (2018) 81 *Modern Law Review* 282

Kamba W.J., 'Comparative Law: A Theoretical Framework' (1974) 23 *International and Comparative Law Quarterly* 485

Kelemen R.D., 'Talking about the European Court: Discourses of Judging in the European Union' (2012) 58 *Studies in Law, Politics and Society* 139

Kelly J.B., 'Children's Living Arrangements Following Separation and Divorce: Insights from Empirical and Clinical Research' (2007) 46 *Family Process* 35

Khan D.-E. and Wessendorf N., 'Article 45 TFEU' in R. Geiger, D.-E. Khan, and M. Kotzur (eds), *European Union Treaties: A Commentary: Treaty on European Union, Treaty on the Functioning of the European Union, Charter of Fundamental Rights of the European Union*, C.H. Beck/Hart Publishing, Munich/Oxford 2015

——, 'Article 49 TFEU' in R. Geiger, D.-E. Khan, and M. Kotzur (eds), *European Union Treaties: A Commentary: Treaty on European Union, Treaty on the Functioning of the European Union, Charter of Fundamental Rights of the European Union*, C.H. Beck/Hart Publishing, Munich/Oxford 2015

Khazova O., 'International Children's Rights Law: Child and the Family' in U. Kilkelly and T. Liefaard (eds), *International Human Rights of Children*, Springer, Singapore 2020

Kilkelly U., 'The CRC in Litigation Under the ECHR' in T. Liefaard and J.E. Doek (eds), *Litigating the Rights of the Child: The UN Convention on the Rights of the Child in Domestic and International Jurisprudence*, Springer, Dordrecht 2015

——, 'Protecting Children's Rights under the ECHR: The Role of Positive Obligations' (2010) 61 *Northern Ireland Legal Quarterly* 245

——, 'Relocation: A Children's Rights Perspective' (2010) 1 *Journal of Family Law and Practice* 23

Klamert M., 'What We Talk About When We Talk About Harmonisation' (2015) 17 *Cambridge Yearbook of European Legal Studies* 360

Kochenov D., 'The Right to Have What Rights? EU Citizenship in Need of Clarification' (2013) 19 *European Law Journal* 502

——, *EU Citizenship and Federalism: The Role of Rights*, Cambridge University Press, Cambridge 2017

Kostakopoulou D., 'European Union Citizenship: Writing the Future' (2007) 13 *European Law Journal* 623

——, *Institutional Constructivism in Social Sciences and Law: Frames of Mind, Patterns of Change*, Cambridge University Press, Cambridge 2018

——, *EU Citizenship Law and Policy: Beyond Brexit*, Edward Elgar Publishing, Cheltenham 2020

Kotzur M., 'Article 81 TFEU' in R. Geiger, D.-E. Khan, and M. Kotzur (eds), *European Union Treaties: A Commentary: Treaty on European Union, Treaty on the Functioning of the European Union, Charter of Fundamental Rights of the European Union*, C.H. Beck/Hart Publishing, Munich/Oxford 2015

——, 'CFREU: Introduction' in R. Geiger, D.-E. Khan, and M. Kotzur (eds), *European Union Treaties: A Commentary: Treaty on European Union, Treaty on the Functioning of the European Union, Charter of Fundamental Rights of the European Union*, C.H. Beck/Hart Publishing, Munich/Oxford 2015

Kreiner L., 'Aufenthaltsbestimmungs- und Wohnortbestimmungsrecht nach §162 ABGB' (2014) Master's Thesis, University of Graz (Austria) <http://unipub.uni-graz.at/obvugrhs/download/pdf/252083?originalFilename=true>

Kroeze H. and Van Elsuwege P., 'Revisiting Ruiz Zambrano: A Never Ending Story?' (2021) 23 *European Journal of Migration and Law* 1

Krommendijk J., 'The Use of ECtHR Case Law by the Court of Justice after Lisbon: The View of Luxembourg Insiders' (2015) 22 *Maastricht Journal of European and Comparative Law* 812

Kruger T., 'Article 42' in C. González Beilfuss, L. Carpaneto, T. Kruger, I. Pretelli, and M. Župan, *Jurisdiction, Recognition and Enforcement in Matrimonial and Parental Responsibility Matters: A Commentary on Regulation 2019/1111 (Brussels IIb)*, Edward Elgar Publishing, Cheltenham 2023

Krzyżanowski M., 'Brexit and the Imaginary of "Crisis": A Discourse-Conceptual Analysis of European News Media' (2019) 16 *Critical Discourse Studies* 465

Kuijer M., 'The Challenging Relationship between the European Convention on Human Rights and the EU Legal Order: Consequences of a Delayed Accession' (2020) *International Journal of Human Rights* 998

Kurki-Suonio K., 'Joint Custody as an Interpretation of the Best Interests of the Child in Critical and Comparative Perspective' (2000) 14 *International Journal of Law, Policy and the Family* 183

Lacey N., 'Feminist Legal Theory and the Rights of Women' in K. Knop (ed), *Gender and Human Rights*, Oxford University Press, Oxford 2004

LaFrance A.B., 'Child Custody and Relocation: A Constitutional Perspective' (2008) 34 *University of Louisville Journal of Family Law* 1

Lamont R., 'Free Movement of Persons, Child Abduction and Relocation within the European Union' (2012) 34 *Journal of Social Welfare and Family Law* 231

——, 'Article 24 – The Rights of the Child' in in S. Peers, T. Hervey, J. Kenner and A. Ward (eds), *The EU Charter of Fundamental Rights: A Commentary*, Hart Publishing, Oxford 2014

——, 'Care Proceedings with a European Dimension under Brussels IIa: Jurisdiction, Mutual Trust and the Best Interests of the Child' (2016) 28 *Child and Family Law Quarterly* 67

——, 'Not a European Family: Implications of "Brexit" for International Family Law' (2017) *Manchester Centre for Regulation and Governance and Public Law* <https://research.manchester.ac.uk/en/publications/not-a-european-family-implications-of-brexit-for-international-fa>

Lanci M., 'In the Child's Best Interests? Rethinking Consideration of Physical Disability in Child Custody Disputes' (2018) 118 *Columbia Law Review* 875

Lange B., 'How to Conceptualise Law in European Union Integration Processes? Perspectives from the Literature and Empirical Research' in V. Gessner and D. Nelken (eds), *European Ways of Law: Towards a European Sociology of Law*, Hart Publishing, Oxford 2007

Laufer-Ukeles P., 'The Relational Rights of Children' (2016) 48 *Connecticut Law Review* 741

Lavrysen L., 'The Scope of Rights and the Scope of Obligations: Positive Obligations' in E. Brems and J. Gerards (eds), *Shaping Rights in the ECHR: The Role of the European Court of Human Rights in Determining the Scope of Human Rights*, Cambridge University Press, Cambridge 2014

Lázár N., 'Euroscepticism in Hungary and Poland: A Comparative Analysis of Jobbik and the Law and Justice Parties' (2015) 12 *Politeja* 215

Łazowski A., '"Darling You Are Not Going Anywhere": The Right to Exit and Restrictions in EU Law' (2015) 40 *European Law Review* 877

Leckey R., *Contextual Subjects: Family, State, and Relational Theory*, University of Toronto Press, Toronto 2008

Legrand P., 'Public Law, Europeanisation, and Convergence: Can Comparatists Contribute?' in P. Beaumont, C. Lyons and N. Walker (eds), *Convergence and Divergence in European Public Law*, Hart Publishing, Oxford 2002

Leloup M., 'The Principle of the Best Interests of the Child in the Expulsion Case Law of the European Court of Human Rights: Procedural Rationality as a Remedy for Inconsistency' (2019) 37 *Netherlands Quarterly of Human Rights* 50

Lemke C., 'Germany's EU Policy: The Domestic Discourse' (2010) 33 *German Studies Review* 503

Lenaerts K., 'The Court of Justice of the European Union and the Protection of Fundamental Rights' (2011) 31 *Polish Yearbook of International Law* 79, SSRN Scholarly Paper ID 2218538 <https://papers.ssrn.com/abstract=2218538>

Lenaerts K. and Gutiérrez-Fons J.A., 'The Place of the Charter in the EU Constitutional Edifice' in S. Peers, T. Hervey, J. Kenner and A. Ward (eds), *The EU Charter of Fundamental Rights: A Commentary*, Hart Publishing, Oxford 2014

Lindahl H., 'Inside and Outside the EU's "Area of Freedom, Security and Justice": Reflexive Identity and the Unity of Legal Space' (2004) 90 *ARSP: Archiv für Rechts- und Sozialphilosophie/Archives for Philosophy of Law and Social Philosophy* 478

Linton M., 'Abolition of Exequatur, All in the Name of Mutual Trust!' in B. Hess, M. Bergström and E. Storskrubb (eds), *EU Civil Justice: Current Issues and Future Outlook*, Hart Publishing, Oxford 2016

Lock T., 'Article 7 CFR' in M. Kellerbauer, M. Klamert and J. Tomkin (eds), *The EU Treaties and the Charter of Fundamental Rights: A Commentary*, Oxford University Press, Oxford 2019

——, 'Article 52 CFR' in M. Kellerbauer, M. Klamert and J. Tomkin (eds), *The EU Treaties and the Charter of Fundamental Rights: A Commentary*, Oxford University Press, Oxford 2019

Loth M., *Private Law in Context: Enriching Legal Doctrine*, Edward Elgar Publishing, Cheltenham 2022

Lowe N.V., 'The Impact of the Revised Brussels II Regulation on Cross-Border Relocation' (2010) *The Judges Newsletter (Special Edition)* 69

Magnus U. and Mankowski P., 'Introduction' in U. Magnus and P. Mankowski (eds), *European Commentaries on Private International Law: Brussels IIbis Regulation*, Otto Schmidt/De Gruyter, Berlin/Boston 2012

Maliszewska-Nienartowicz J., 'Direct and Indirect Discrimination in European Union Law – How to Draw a Dividing Line?' (2014) 3 *International Journal of Social Sciences* 41

Martin D., 'Article 21 CFR' in M. Kellerbauer, M. Klamert and J. Tomkin (eds), *The EU Treaties and the Charter of Fundamental Rights: A Commentary*, Oxford University Press, Oxford 2019

——, 'Article 23 CFR' in M. Kellerbauer, M. Klamert and J. Tomkin (eds), *The EU Treaties and the Charter of Fundamental Rights: A Commentary*, Oxford University Press, Oxford 2019

——, 'Article 45 CFR' in M. Kellerbauer, M. Klamert and J. Tomkin (eds), *The EU Treaties and the Charter of Fundamental Rights: A Commentary*, Oxford University Press, Oxford 2019

Martiny D., 'European Family Law' in J. Basedow, K.J. Hopt, R. Zimmermann and A. Stier (eds), *Max Planck Encyclopedia of European Private Law*, Oxford University Press, Oxford 2012

MasGiralt R., 'The Emotional Geographies of Migration and Brexit: Tales of Unbelonging' (2020) 9 *Central and Eastern European Migration Review* 29

McClain L., 'Love, Marriage, and the Baby Carriage: Revisiting the Channelling Function of Family Law' (2007) 28 *Cardozo Law Review* 2133

McEleavy P., 'The Brussels II Regulation: How the European Community Has Moved into Family Law' (2002) 51 *International and Comparative Law Quarterly* 883

McGlynn C., 'The Europeanisation of Family Law' (2001) 13 *Child and Family Law Quarterly* 35

——, 'Rights for Children: The Potential Impact of the European Union Charter of Fundamental Rights' (2002) 8 *European Public Law* 387

——, *Families and the European Union: Law, Politics and Pluralism*, Cambridge University Press, Cambridge 2006

——, 'Families and the European Charter of Fundamental Rights: Progressive Change or Entrenching the Status Quo?' (2001) 26 *European Law Review* 582

McGough L., 'Starting Over: The Heuristics of Family Relocation Decision Making' (2003) 77 *St. John's Law Review* 291

Mertz E., 'Conclusion: A New Social Constructionism for Sociolegal Studies' (1994) 28 *Law & Society Review* 1243

Michaels R., 'The Functional Method of Comparative Law' in M. Reimann and R. Zimmermann (eds) *The Oxford Handbook of Comparative Law*, Oxford University Press, Oxford 2006

Micklitz H.-W., 'Rethinking the Public/Private Divide' in M. Maduro, K. Tuori and S. Sankari (eds), *Transnational Law: Rethinking European Law and Legal Thinking*, Cambridge University, Cambridge Press 2014

Migration Observatory, 'Net Migration to the UK' (2023) <https://migrationobservatory.ox.ac.uk/resources/briefings/long-term-international-migration-flows-to-and-from-the-uk/>

Millum J., 'The Foundation of the Child's Right to an Open Future' (2014) 45 *Journal of Social Philosophy* 522

Mitsilegas V., 'The Limits of Mutual Trust in Europe's Area of Freedom, Security and Justice: From Automatic Inter-State Cooperation to the Slow Emergence of the Individual' (2012) 31 *Yearbook of European Law* 319

Mnookin R.H., 'Child-Custody Adjudication: Judicial Functions in the Face of Indeterminacy' (1975) 39 *Law and Contemporary Problems* 226

Moens G.A. and Trone J., 'The Principle of Subsidiarity in EU Judicial and Legislative Practice: Panacea or Placebo' (2015) 41 *Journal of Legislation* 65

Morano-Foadi S., 'Problems and Challenges in Researching Bi-National Migrant Families Within the European Union' (2007) 21 *International Journal of Law, Policy and the Family* 1

Morano-Foadi S. and Andreadakis S., 'Reflections on the Architecture of the EU after the Treaty of Lisbon: The European Judicial Approach to Fundamental Rights' (2011) 17 *European Law Journal* 595

Moraru M., '"Mutual Trust" from the Perspective of National Courts: A Test in Creative Legal Thinking' in E.R. Brouwer and D. Gerard (eds), 'Mapping Mutual Trust: Understanding and Framing the Role of Mutual Trust in EU Law', (2016) Working Paper MWP 2016/13, European University Institute

Morley J.D., 'The Impact of Foreign Law on Child Custody Determinations' (2013) 10 *Journal of Child Custody* 209

Morokvasic M., '"Settled in Mobility": Engendering Post-Wall Migration in Europe' (2004) 77 *Feminist Review* 7

'Mounting Support for a Review of Poel and Payne' (2010) <https://www.familylaw.co.uk/news_and_comment/mounting-support-for-a-review-of-poel-and-payne>

'Moving/Settling Abroad with Children: Bulgaria', *European e-Justice Portal* (2020) <https://beta.e-justice.europa.eu/289/EN/movingsettling_abroad_with_children?BULGARIA&member=1>

Muir E., 'Fundamental Rights: An Unsettling EU Competence' (2014) 15 *Human Rights Review* 25

——, 'The Essence of the Fundamental Right to Equal Treatment: Back to the Origins' (2019) 20 *German Law Journal* 817

Myslinska D.R., 'Not Quite Right: Representations of Eastern Europeans in ECJ Discourse' (2021) *International Journal of Politics, Culture, and Society* 271 <https://doi.org/10.1007/s10767-020-09368-2>

Neier C., 'New Clarifications on Ending the Union Citizen's Right of Residence: The Grand Chamber Decisions of the European Court of Justice of 22 June 2021 in C-718/19 and C-719/19' (2021) 6 *European Papers – A Journal on Law and Integration* 941

Neuvonen P.J., *Equal Citizenship and Its Limits in EU Law: We the Burden?*, Hart Publishing, Oxford 2016

Newark F.H., 'Twine V. Bean's Express, Ltd.' (1954) 17 *Modern Law Review* 102

Nielsen R., 'Is European Union Equality Law Capable of Addressing Multiple and Intersectional Discrimination Yet?: Precautions against Neglecting Intersectional Cases' in D. Schiek and V. Chege (eds), *European Union Non-Discrimination Law: Comparative Perspectives on Multidimensional Equality Law*, Routledge-Cavendish, London 2008

Niemi-Kiesiläinen J., Honkatukia P. and Ruuskanen M., 'Legal Texts as Discourses' in Å. Gunnarsson, E.-M. Svensson and M. Davies (eds), *Exploiting the Limits of Law: Swedish Feminism and the Challenge to Pessimism*, Ashgate Publishing, Hampshire 2007

Ninatti S., 'Adjusting Differences and Accommodating Competences: Family Matters in the European Union' (2001) 6 *Jean Monnet Working Papers* (06/10) <https://ideas.repec.org/p/erp/jeanmo/p0282.html>

Nissen E., 'A Children's Rights Perspective to Ruiz Zambrano and Chavez-Vilchez: An Examination in Light of Theory, Practice and Child Development Research' (2021) 23 *European Journal of Migration and Law* 68

Nußberger A., 'Hard Law or Soft Law – Does It Matter?: Distinction Between Different Sources of International Law in the Jurisprudence of the ECtHR' in A. van Aaken and I. Motoc (eds), *The European Convention on Human Rights and General International Law*, Oxford University Press, Oxford 2018

O'Donovan K., '"Real" Mothers for Abandoned Children' (2002) 36 *Law & Society Review* 347

O'Leary S., 'The Past, Present and Future of the Purely Internal Rule in EU Law' in M. Dougan, N.N. Shuibhne and E. Spaventa (eds), *Empowerment and Disempowerment of the European Citizen*, Hart Publishing, Oxford 2012

Ottosen M.H., 'In the Name of The Father, The Child and The Holy Genes: Constructions of "The Child's Best Interest" in Legal Disputes Over Contact' (2006) 49 *Acta Sociologica* 29

Parkinson P., 'Family Law and the Indissolubility of Parenthood' (2006) 40 *Family Law Quarterly* 237

——, 'Freedom of Movement in an Era of Shared Parenting: The Differences in Judicial Approaches to Relocation' (2008) *Federal Law Review*, Sydney Law School Research Paper No. 08/87, SSRN Scholarly Paper ID 1181442 <https://papers.ssrn.com/abstract=1181442>

——, *Family Law and the Indissolubility of Parenthood*, Cambridge University Press, Cambridge 2011

Parkinson P. and Cashmore J., 'Reforming Relocation Law: An Evidence-Based Approach' (2015) 53 *Family Court Review* 23

Parkinson P., Cashmore J. and Single J., 'The Need for Reality Testing in Relocation Cases' (2010) 44 *Family Law Quarterly* 1

——, 'Mothers Wishing to Relocate with Children: Actual and Perceived Reasons' (2011) 27 *Canadian Journal of Family Law* 11

Pataut E., 'A Family Status for the European Citizen?' in L. Azoulai, S. Barbou des Places and E. Pataut (eds), *Constructing the Person in EU Law: Rights, Roles, Identities*, Hart Publishing, Oxford 2016

Petrova T., 'Children and European Citizenship: Their Autonomy and Entitlement to Care under Free Movement Law' (2013) LLM Thesis, European University Institute

Pew Research Center's Global Attitudes Project, 'Views on the European Union across Europe' (14 October 2019) <https://www.pewresearch.org/global/2019/10/14/the-european-union/>

Phoa P.S. and van Eijken H., 'The Scope of Article 20 TFEU Clarified in Chavez-Vilchez: Are the Fundamental Rights of Minor EU Citizens Coming of Age?' (2018) 43 *European Law Review* 949

Pietrzykowski K. (ed.), *Kodeks rodzinny i opiekuńczy. Komentarz. Wyd. 8*, C.H. Beck (Legalis), Warszawa 2023 Pintens W., 'Europeanisation of Family Law' in K. Boele-Woelki (ed), *Perspectives for the Unification and Harmonisation of Family Law in Europe*, Intersentia, Oxford 2003

Prechal A., 'Mutual Trust Before the Court of Justice of the European Union' (2017) 2 *European Papers – A Journal on Law and Integration* 75

Prechal S. and Peers S., 'Article 52 – Scope and Interpretation of Rights and Principles' in S. Peers, T. Hervey, J. Kenner and A. Ward (eds), *The EU Charter of Fundamental Rights: A Commentary*, Hart Publishing, Oxford 2014

Quennerstedt A., 'Children's Rights Research Moving into the Future – Challenges on the Way Forward' in M. Freeman (ed), *The Future of Children's Rights*, Brill Nijhoff, Leiden 2014

Radaelli C.M., 'Europeanisation: Solution or Problem?' (2004) 8 *European Integration online Papers* <https://ssrn.com/abstract=601163>

Recchi E., *Mobile Europe: The Theory and Practice of Free Movement in the EU*, Palgrave Macmillan, Hampshire 2015

Reece H., 'The Paramountcy Principle: Consensus or Construct?' (1996) 49 *Current Legal Problems* 267

Reich N. and Harbacevica S., 'Citizenship and Family on Trial: A Fairly Optimistic Overview of Recent Court Practice with Regard to Free Movement of Persons' (2003) 40 *Common Market Law Review* 615

Reimann M., 'The Progress and Failure of Comparative Law in the Second Half of the Twentieth Century' (2002) 50 *American Journal of Comparative Law* 671

Reynaert D. and Roose R., 'Children's Rights: A Framework to Eliminate Social Exclusion? Critical Discussions and Tensions' in M.D. Ruck, M. Peterson-Badali and M. Freeman, *Handbook of Children's Rights: Global and Multidisciplinary Perspectives*, Routledge, New York 2016

Riishøj S., 'Europeanization and Euroscepticism: Experiences from Poland and the Czech Republic' (2007) 35 *Nationalities Papers* 503

Ristuccia F., 'Ties That Bind and Ties That Compel: Dependency and the Ruiz Zambrano Doctrine' (2023) 60 *Common Market Law Review* 1227

Rose N., 'Beyond the Public/Private Division: Law, Power and the Family' (1987) 14 *Journal of Law and Society* 61

Rotman S., Tompkins R., Linzer Schwartz L. and Samuels M.D., 'Reconciling Parents' and Children's Interests in Relocation: In Whose Best Interest?' (2000) 38 *Family Court Review* 341

Ryan L., 'Transnational Relations: Family Migration among Recent Polish Migrants in London' (2011) 49 *International Migration* 80

Sarmiento D., 'Who's Afraid of the Charter? The Court of Justice, National Courts and the New Framework of Fundamental Rights Protection in Europe' (2013) 50 *Common Market Law Review* 1267

Sattler M., 'The Problem of Parental Relocation: Closing the Loophole in the Law of International Child Abduction' (2010) 67 *Washington and Lee Law Review* 1709

Schabas W.A., *The European Convention on Human Rights: A Commentary*, Oxford University Press, Oxford 2015

Scharpf F.W., 'Perpetual Momentum: Directed and Unconstrained?' (2012) 19 *Journal of European Public Policy* 127

Scheiwe K., 'Parental Conflicts over the Exercise of Joint Parental Responsibility from a Comparative Perspective: From Daily Matters to Relocation' in H. Willekens, K. Scheiwe, T. Richarz and E. Schumann (eds), *Motherhood and the Law*, Göttingen University Press, Göttingen 2019

Scherpe J.M., *The Present and Future of European Family Law*, Edward Elgar Publishing, Cheltenham 2016

Schiek D. and Burri S., 'Multiple Discrimination in EU Law: Opportunities for Legal Responses to Intersectional Gender Discrimination?' (2009) European Commission, Directorate-General for Employment, Social Affairs and Equal Opportunities

Schiratzki J., 'The Best Interests of the Child: In the Light of Normality and Exceptions' (2013) 1 *International Family Law, Policy and Practice* 8

Schmidt S.K., 'Beyond Compliance: The Europeanization of Member States through Negative Integration and Legal Uncertainty' (2008) 10 *Journal of Comparative Policy Analysis: Research and Practice* 299

Schneider C., 'The Channelling Function in Family Law' (1992) 20 *Hofstra Law Review* 495

Schuster A., 'LGBTI Migration in Europe' in C. Ashford and A. Maine (eds), *Research Handbook on Gender, Sexuality and the Law*, Edward Elgar Publishing, Cheltenham 2020

Schuz R., *The Hague Child Abduction Convention: A Critical Analysis*, Hart Publishing, Oxford 2013

Schütze R., 'Subsidiarity After Lisbon: Reinforcing the Safeguards of Federalism?' (2009) 68 *Cambridge Law Journal* 525

Senden L.A.J, 'Soft Law and Its Implications for Institutional Balance in the EC' (2005) 1 *Utrecht Law Review* 79

Shuibhne N.N., 'Margins of Appreciation: National Values, Fundamental Rights and EC Free Movement Law' (2009) 34 *European Law Review* 230

——, *The Coherence of EU Free Movement Law: Constitutional Responsibility and the Court of Justice*, Oxford University Press, Oxford 2013

Shuibhne N.N. and Edward D., 'Continuity and Change in the Law Relating to Services' in A. Arnull, P. Eeckhout and T. Tridimas (eds), *Continuity and Change in EU Law: Essays in Honour of Sir Francis Jacobs*, Oxford University Press, Oxford 2008

Shúilleabháin M.N., 'Ten Years of European Family Law: Retrospective Reflections From a Common Law Perspective' (2010) 59 *International and Comparative Law Quarterly* 1021

Simmonds C., 'Paramountcy and the ECHR: A Conflict Resolved?' (2012) 71 *Cambridge Law Journal* 498

Słyk J., 'Rozstrzyganie o istotnych sprawach dziecka w przypadku braku porozumienia rodziców (art. 97 §2 k.r.o.)' (2013) 14 *Prawo w działaniu* 44

Smart C., 'The Legal and Moral Ordering of Child Custody' (1991) *18 Journal of Law and Society* 485

Smits J., 'What Is Legal Doctrine?: On The Aims and Methods of Legal-Dogmatic Research' in R. van Gestel, H.-W. Micklitz and E. Rubin (eds), *Rethinking Legal Scholarship: A Transatlantic Dialogue*, Cambridge University Press, Cambridge 2017

Snell J., 'Non-Discriminatory Tax Obstacles in Community Law' (2007) 56 *International and Comparative Law Quarterly* 339

——, 'The Notion of Market Access: A Concept or a Slogan?'; (2010) 47 *Common Market Law Review* 437

Sormunen M., 'A Comparison of Child Protection and Immigration Jurisprudence of the European Court of Human Rights: What Role for the Best Interests of the Child?' (2019) 31 *Child and Family Law Quarterly* 249

Spaventa E., 'From Gebhard to Carpenter: Towards a (Non-)Economic Constitution' (2004) 41 *Common Market Law Review* 743

——, 'The Outer Limit of the Treaty Free Movement Provisions: Some Reflections on the Significance of Keck, Remoteness and Deliège' in C. Barnard and O. Odudu (eds), *The Outer Limits of European Law*, Hart Publishing, Oxford 2009

——, 'Article 45 – Freedom of Movement and of Residence' in S. Peers, T. Hervey, J. Kenner and A. Ward (eds), *The EU Charter of Fundamental Rights: A Commentary*, Hart Publishing, Oxford 2014

Stalford H., 'The Citizenship Status of Children in the European Union' (2000) 8 *International Journal of Children's Rights* 101

——, 'Concepts of Family under EU Law – Lessons from the ECHR' (2002) 16 *International Journal of Law, Policy and the Family* 410

——, *Children and the European Union: Rights, Welfare and Accountability*, Hart Publishing, Oxford 2012

——, 'For Better, For Worse: The Relationship between EU Citizenship and the Development of Cross-Border Family Law' in M. Dougan, N.N. Shuibhne and E. Spaventa (eds), *Empowerment and Disempowerment of the European Citizen*, Hart Publishing, Oxford 2012

Stojanowska W., 'Rozstrzyganie przez sąd na podstawie art. 24 i 97 §2 k.r.o. o istotnych sprawach rodziny w braku porozumienia między małżonkami lub rodzicami' (1985) 7–8 *Nowe Prawo*

Stojanowska W. and Hordyńska E., 'Zezwolenie sądu opiekuńczego na wyjazd małoletniego dziecka za granicę z jednym z rodziców' (1982) 16 *Zeszyty Naukowe Instytutu Badania Prawa Sądowego*

Storskrubb E., 'Civil Justice: Constitutional and Regulatory Issues Revisited' in M. Fletcher, E. Herlin-Karnell and C. Matera (eds), *The European Union as an Area of Freedom, Security and Justice*, Routledge, Abingdon 2017

——, 'EU Civil Justice at the Harmonisation Crossroads?' in A. Nylund and M. Strandberg (eds), *Civil Procedure and Harmonisation of Law: The Dynamics of EU and International Treaties*, Intersentia, Cambridge 2019

Sutherland E.E. and Barnes Macfarlane L.-A. (eds), *Implementing Article 3 of the United Nations Convention on the Rights of the Child: Best Interests, Welfare and Well-Being*, Cambridge University Press, Cambridge 2016

Świętochowska E., 'Temida Wciąż Uczulona Na Jawność. Nie Wszystkie Sądy Chcą Publikować Wyroki' (2018) *Dziennik Gazeta Prawna* <https://prawo.gazetaprawna.pl/artykuly/1150353,dlaczego-sady-nie-publikuja-wyrokow.html>

Taylor R., 'Poels Apart: Fixed Principles and Shifting Values in Relocation Law' in S. Gilmore, J. Herring and R. Probert (eds), *Landmark Cases in Family Law*, Hart Publishing, Oxford 2011

Taylor R., Gollop M. and Henaghan M., 'Relocation Following Parental Separation: The Welfare & Best Interests of Children' (2010) Centre for Research on Children and Families and Faculty of Law, University of Otago, Dunedin (New Zealand) <http://www.communityresearch.org.nz/research/relocation-following-parental-separation-the-welfare-best-interests-of-children/>

Thym D., 'Towards "Real" Citizenship? The Judicial Construction of Union Citizenship and Its Limits' in M. Adams, H. de Waele, J. Meeusen and G. Straetmans (eds), *Judging Europe's Judges: The Legitimacy of the Case Law of the European Court of Justice*, Hart Publishing, Oxford 2013

Scott T., 'Leave to Remove Children from the Jurisdiction: Does English Law Comply with the Treaty of Rome?' in The Society for Advanced Legal Studies (ed), 'Report on The

Cross-Border Movement of Children' (1999) <http://sas-space.sas.ac.uk/4294/1/SALS_Report_on_Cross_Border_Movement_of_Children.pdf>

Todorova V., 'National Report: Bulgaria', *Commission on European Family Law* <http://ceflonline.net/wp-content/uploads/Bulgaria-Parental-Responsibilities.pdf>

Toner H., *Partnership Rights, Free Movement, and EU Law*, Hart Publishing, Oxford 2004

——, 'Non-Discriminatory Obstacles to the Exercise of Treaty Rights – Articles 39, 43, 49, and 18 EC' (2004) 23 *Yearbook of European Law* 275

Torres Pérez A., 'The Right to Family Life as a Bar to the Expulsion of Third Country Nationals in the European Union' in M. González Pascual and A. Torres Perez (eds), *The Right to Family Life in the European Union*, Routledge, London 2017

Trybulska-Skoczelas E., 'Art. 95' in J. Wierciński (ed), *Kodeks Rodzinny i Opiekuńczy. Komentarz*, System Informacji Prawnej LEX, 2014

Tryfonidou A., *Reverse Discrimination in EC Law*, Kluwer Law International, Alphen aan den Rijn 2009

——, 'The Notions of "Restriction" and "Discrimination" in the Context of the Free Movement of Persons Provisions: From a Relationship of Interdependence to One of (Almost Complete) Independence' (2014) 33 *Yearbook of European Law* 385

——, *The Impact of Union Citizenship on the EU's Market Freedoms*, Hart Publishing, Oxford 2016

——, 'EU Free Movement Law and the Children of Rainbow Families: Children of a Lesser God?' (2019) 38 *Yearbook of European Law* 220

Twining W., *Law in Context: Enlarging a Discipline*, Oxford University Press, Oxford 1997

Ubertazzi B., 'The Hearing of the Child in the Brussels IIa Regulation and Its Recast Proposal' (2017) 13 *Journal of Private International Law* 568

van den Brink M.J., 'EU Citizenship and EU Fundamental Rights: Taking EU Citizenship Rights Seriously?' (2012) 39 *Legal Issues of Economic Integration* 273

——, 'The Origins and the Potential Federalising Effects of the Substance of Rights Test' in D. Kochenov (ed), *EU Citizenship and Federalism: The Role of Rights*, Cambridge University Press, Cambridge 2017

——, 'Is It Time to Abolish the Substance of EU Citizenship Rights Test?' (2021) 23 *European Journal of Migration and Law* 13

van der Mei A.P., 'The Outer Limits of the Prohibition of Discrimination on Grounds of Nationality: A Look through the Lens of Union Citizenship' (2011) 18 *Maastricht Journal of European and Comparative Law* 62

van Ostaijen M., 'Between Migration and Mobility Discourses: The Performative Potential within "Intra-European Movement"' (2017) 11 *Critical Policy Studies* 166

Vauchez A., 'From Close-Ups to Long Shot: In Search of the "Political Role" of the Court of Justice of the European Union' in C. Kilpatrick and J. Scott (eds), *New Legal Approaches to Studying the Court of Justice: Revisiting Law in Context*, Oxford University Press, Oxford 2020

Wahl N. and Prete L., 'The Gatekeepers of Article 267 TFEU: On Jurisdiction and Admissibility of References for Preliminary Rulings' (2018) 55 *Common Market Law Review* 511

Walker L. and Beaumont P., 'Shifting the Balance Achieved by the Abduction Convention: The Contrasting Approaches of the European Court of Human Rights and the European Court of Justice' (2011) 7 *Journal of Private International Law* 231

Wall S., *Reluctant European: Britain and the European Union from 1945 to Brexit*, Oxford University Press, Oxford 2020

Ward A., 'Article 51 – Field of Application' in S. Peers, T. Hervey, J. Kenner and A. Ward (eds), *The EU Charter of Fundamental Rights: A Commentary*, Hart Publishing, Oxford 2014

Warshak R.A., 'In a Land Far, Far Away: Assessing Children's Best Interests in International Relocation Cases' (2013) 10 *Journal of Child Custody* 295

Weatherill S., 'The Limits of Legislative Harmonization Ten Years after Tobacco Advertising: How the Court's Case Law Has Become a "Drafting Guide"' (2011) 12 *German Law Journal* 827

——, 'The Court's Case Law on the Internal Market: "A Circumloquacious Statement of the Result, Rather than a Reason for Arriving at It"?' in M. Adams, H. de Waele, J. Meeusen and G. Straetmans (eds), *Judging Europe's Judges: The Legitimacy of the Case Law of the European Court of Justice*, Hart Publishing, Oxford 2013

——, 'The Several Internal Markets' (2017) 36 *Yearbook of European Law* 125

Webley L., 'Qualitative Approaches to Empirical Legal Research' in P. Cane and H.M. Kritzer (eds), *The Oxford Handbook of Empirical Legal Research*, Oxford University Press, Oxford 2010

Weiner M.H., 'Inertia and Inequality: Reconceptualizing Disputes Over Parental Relocation' (2007) 40 *UC Davis Law Review* 1747

Weiß W., 'The EU Human Rights Regime Post Lisbon: Turning the CJEU into a Human Rights Court?' in S. Morano-Foadi and L. Vickers (eds), *Fundamental Rights in the EU: A Matter for Two Courts*, Hart Publishing, Oxford 2015

Weller M., 'Mutual Trust: In Search of the Future of European Union Private International Law' (2015) 11 *Journal of Private International Law* 64

Wintemute R., 'In Extending Human Rights, Which European Court Is Substantively "Braver" and Procedurally "Fitter"? The Example of Sexual Orientation and Gender Identity Discrimination' in S. Morano-Foadi and L. Vickers (eds), *Fundamental Rights in the EU: A Matter for Two Courts*, Hart Publishing, Oxford 2015

Wollenschläger F., 'A New Fundamental Freedom beyond Market Integration: Union Citizenship and its Dynamics for Shifting the Economic Paradigm of European Integration' (2011) 17 *European Law Journal* 1

Worwood A., 'International Relocation of Children in the UK (England & Wales): Overview' (2019), *Practical Law* <http://uk.practicallaw.thomsonreuters.com/5-622-2479?transitionType=Default&contextData=(sc.Default)&firstPage=true>

Worwood A. and Cummin L., 'International Family Law Report: Can We Go or Must We Stay? The International Child Relocation Rankings' (2016) <http://www.familylaw.co.uk/news_and_comment/new-international-child-relocation-rankings-reveal-that-belgian-courts-are-the-least-likely-to-grant-a-relocation-order#.WOs4-y-Ywj8>

Wysocka-Bar A., 'Enhanced Cooperation in Property Matters in the EU and Non-Participating Member States' (2019) 20 *ERA Forum* 187

Zafran R., 'Children's Rights as Relational Rights: The Case of Relocation' (2010) 18 *Journal of Gender, Social Policy & the Law* 163

Zglinski J., *Europe's Passive Virtues: Deference to National Authorities in EU Free Movement Law*, Oxford University Press, Oxford 2020

Zwaak L., Haeck Y. and Burbano Herrera C., 'Procedure Before the Court' in P. van Dijk, F. van Hoof, A. van Rijn, and L. Zwaak (eds), *Theory and Practice of the European Convention on Human Rights*, 5th ed., Intersentia, Cambridge 2018

INDEX

European Family Law Series

1. *Legal Recognition of Same-Sex Couples in Europe*, K. Boele-Woelki and A. Fuchs (eds.)
2. *European Family Law in Action Volume I: Grounds for Divorce*, K. Boele-Woelki, B. Braat and I. Sumner (eds.)
3. *European Family Law in Action Volume II: Maintenance Between Former Spouses*, K. Boele-Woelki, B. Braat and I. Sumner (eds.)
4. *Perspectives for the Unification and Harmonisation of Family Law in Europe*, K. Boele-Woelki (ed.)
5. *Family Law Legislation of the Netherlands*, I. Sumner and H. Warendorf
6. *Indépendance et interdépendance patrimoniales des époux dans le régime matrimonial légal des droits néerlandais, français et suisse*, B. Braat
7. *Principles of European Family Law Regarding Divorce and Maintenance Between Former Spouses*, K. Boele-Woelki, F. Ferrand, C. González Beilfuss, M. Jänterä-Jareborg, N. Lowe, D. Martiny and W. Pintens
8. *Inheritance Law Legislation of the Netherlands*, I. Sumner and H. Warendorf
9. *European Family Law in Action Volume III: Parental Responsibilities*, K. Boele-Woelki, B. Braat and I. Curry-Sumner (eds.)
10. *Common Core and Better Law in European Family Law*, K. Boele-Woelki (ed.)
11. *All's well that ends registered?*, I. Curry-Sumner
12. *Model Family Code – From a global perspective*, I. Schwenzer and M. Dimsey
13. *Harmonisation of Family Law in Europe. A Historical Perspective*, M. Antokolskaia
14. *Brussels II bis: Its Impact and Application in the Member States*, K. Boele-Woelki and C. González Beilfuss (eds.)
15. *Tensions between Legal, Biological and Social Conceptions of Parentage*, I. Schwenzer (ed.)
16. *Principles of European Family Law Regarding Parental Responsibilities*, K. Boele-Woelki, F. Ferrand, C. González Beilfuss, M. Jänterä-Jareborg, N. Lowe, D. Martiny and W. Pintens
17. *Juxtaposing Legal Systems and the Principles of European Family Law on Divorce and Maintenance*, E. Örücü and J. Mair (eds.)
18. *Convergence and Divergence of Family Law in Europe*, M. Antokolskaia (ed.)
19. *European Challenges in Contemporary Family Law*, K. Boele-Woelki and T. Sverdrup (eds.)
20. *Children and their parents*, M. Vonk
21. *La capacité de l'enfant dans les droits français, anglais et écossais*, L. Francoz Terminal
22. *Joint Parental Authority*, C.G. Jeppesen de Boer
23. *Debates in Family Law around the Globe at the Dawn of the 21st Century*, K. Boele-Woelki (ed.)
24. *European Family Law in Action Volume IV: Property Relations between Spouses*, K. Boele-Woelki, B. Braat and I. Curry-Sumner (eds.)

25. *Foundational Facts, Relative Truths. A Comparative Law Study on Children's Right to Know Their Genetic Origins*, R. Blauwhoff
26. *Imperative Inheritance Law in a Late-Modern Society. Five Perspectives*, C. Castelein, R. Foqué and A. Verbeke (eds.)
27. *Juxtaposing Legal Systems and the Principles of European Family Law on Parental Responsibilities*, E. Örücü and J. Mair (eds.)
28. *La justice des mineurs en Europe*, Y. Favier and F. Ferrand (eds.)
29. *The Future of Family Property in Europe*, K. Boele-Woelki, J. Miles and J. M. Scherpe (eds.)
30. *The Place of Religion in Family Law: A Comparative Search*, J. Mair and E. Örücü (eds.)
31. *Reconstructing Marriage. The Legal Status of Relationships in a Changing Society*, C. Sörgjerd
32. *Legal Recognition of Same-Sex Relationships in Europe*, K. Boele-Woelki and A. Fuchs (eds.)
33. *Principles of European Family Law Regarding Property Relations Between Spouses*, K. Boele-Woelki, F. Ferrand, C. González Beilfuss, M. Jänterä-Jareborg, N. Lowe, D. Martiny and W. Pintens
34. *Der nacheheliche Unterhalt: Grundlagen und Ausgestaltung im deutschen Unterhaltsrecht und in den Prinzipien der Commission on European Family Law*, P. Beuermann
35. *Family Law and Culture in Europe: Developments, Challenges and Opportunities*, K. Boele-Woelki, N. Dethloff and W. Gephart
36. *Children's Rights in Intercountry Adoption. A European Perspective*, C. Fenton-Glynn
37. *Nordic Cohabitation Law*, J. Asland, M. Brattström, G. Lind, I. Lund-Andersen, A. Singer and T. Sverdrup
38. *European Family Law in Action Volume V: Informal Relationships*, K. Boele-Woelki, C. Mol and E. van Gelder (eds.)
39. *Divided Parents, Shared Children. Legal Aspects of Residential Co-Parenting in England, the Netherlands and Belgium*, N. Nikolina
40. *Family Forms and Parenthood. Theory and Practice of Article 8 ECHR in Europe*, A. Büchler and H. Keller (eds.)
41. *The Child's Interests in Conflict. The Intersections between Society, Family, Faith and Culture*, M. Jänterä-Jareborg (ed.)
42. *Same-Sex Relationships and Beyond. Gender Matters in the EU*, K. Boele-Woelki and A. Fuchs (eds.)
43. *Nacheheliche Verantwortung in Frankreich und Deutschland*, K. Kaesling
44. *The Future of Registered Partnerships: Family Recognition Beyond Marriage?*, J.M. Scherpe and A. Hayward
45. *Plurality and Diversity of Family Relations in Europe*, K. Boele-Woelki and D. Martiny (eds.)
46. *Principles of European Family Law Regarding Property, Maintenance and Succession Rights of Couples in* de facto *Unions*, K. Boele-Woelki, F. Ferrand, C. González Beilfuss, M. Jänterä-Jareborg, N. Lowe, D. Martiny and V. Todorova
47. *Die Familienschiedsgerichtsbarkeit in Recht und Praxis: Eine Rechtsvergleichende Untersuchung des Deutschen und Englischen Rechts*, S.C. Zellerhoff
48. *Elderly Care and Upwards Solidarity: Historical, Sociological and Legal Perspectives*, E. Alofs and W. Schrama (eds.)

49. *Party Autonomy in EU Private International Law: Choice of Court and Choice of Law in Family Matters and Succession*, J. Gray
50. *The Interaction between Family Law, Succession Law and Private International Law: Adapting to Change*, J.M. Scherpe and E. Bargelli (eds.)
51. *International Handbook on Child Participation in Family Law*, W. Schrama, M. Freeman, N. Taylor and M. Bruning (eds.)
52. *The Child's Right to Participate in Family Law Proceedings: Represented, Heard or Silenced?*, C. Mol
53. *Cross-Border Recognition of Formalized Same-Sex Relationships: The Role of* Ordre Public, L. Vaigė
54. *Between Sexuality, Gender and Reproduction: On the Pluralisation of Family Forms*, N. Dethloff and K. Kaesling (eds.)
55. *Changing Families, Changing Family Law in Europe*, K. Duden and D. Wiedemann (eds.)
56. *The Principles of European Family Law Revisited*, K. Boele-Woelki, F. Ferrand, C. González Beilfuss, M. Jänterä-Jareborg, N. Lowe, D. Martiny and V. Todorova
57. *The Right to Identity and Access to Information on Genetic Origin and Parentage*, I. Boone and M. Vonk (eds.)

www.ingramcontent.com/pod-product-compliance
Ingram Content Group UK Ltd.
Pitfield, Milton Keynes, MK11 3LW, UK
UKHW050230160926
8657IPUK00008B/185